"This book is a remarkable achievement: it organizes the best scholarship on and about neoliberalism, summarizes the material around a selected group of key concepts, and presents them clearly, comprehensively, and in beautiful prose. This solid academic work has been carefully written for a wide readership. If you want to learn more about neoliberalism, this book is for you."

Alfredo Saad-Filho, SOAS University of London, UK

"Since 2008, and the government bail-outs that followed the financial crisis, there has been a flood of interest in neoliberalism. Eagleton-Pierce has done a sterling job in identifying the core themes and concepts and putting them into an accessible and readable volume. Highly recommended."

Ray Kiely, Queen Mary University of London, UK

"In the tradition of Raymond Williams' *Keywords*, Eagleton-Pierce provides an indispensable guide to decoding the lexicon of neoliberal political-speak. Scholars will find the etymologies highly suggestive, enabling them to contextualize and nuance their analyses of the evolving dynamics of neoliberalism."

Nik Theodore, University of Illinois at Chicago, USA

D1026915

NEOLIBERALISM

Neoliberalism: The Key Concepts provides a critical guide to a vocabulary that has become globally dominant over the past forty years. The language of neoliberalism both constructs and expresses a particular vision of economics, politics and everyday life. Some find this vision to be appealing, but many others find the contents and implications of neoliberalism to be alarming. Despite the popularity of these concepts, they often remain confusing, the product of contested histories, meanings and practices. In an accessible way, this interdisciplinary resource explores and dissects key terms such as:

- Capitalism
- Choice
- Competition
- Entrepreneurship
- Finance
- Flexibility
- Freedom
- Governance
- Market
- Reform
- Stakeholder
- State

Complete with an introductory essay, cross-referencing and an extensive bibliography, this book provides a unique and insightful introduction to the study of neoliberalism in all its forms and disguises.

Matthew Eagleton-Pierce is Lecturer in International Political Economy, SOAS, University of London, UK.

ALSO AVAILABLE FROM ROUTLEDGE

British Politics: The Basics
by Bill Jones
ISBN 978-0-415-83571-8

Capitalism: The Basics
by David Coates
ISBN 978-0-415-87092-4

Politics: The Key Concepts
by Lisa Harrison, Adrian Little and Edward Lock
ISBN 978-0-0415-49740-4

NEOLIBERALISM

The Key Concepts

Matthew Eagleton-Pierce

LONDON AND NEW YORK

First published 2016
by Routledge
2 Park Square, Milton Park, Abingdon, Oxon OX14 4RN

and by Routledge
711 Third Avenue, New York, NY 10017

Routledge is an imprint of the Taylor & Francis Group, an informa business

© 2016 Matthew Eagleton-Pierce

The right of Matthew Eagleton-Pierce to be identified as author of this work has been asserted by him in accordance with sections 77 and 78 of the Copyright, Designs and Patents Act 1988.

British Library Cataloguing in Publication Data
A catalogue record for this book is available from the British Library

Library of Congress Cataloging in Publication Data
Names: Eagleton-Pierce, Matthew, author.
Title: Neoliberalism: the key concepts/Matthew Eagleton-Pierce.
Description: New York, NY: Routledge, 2016. | Series: Routledge key guides |
Includes bibliographical references and index.
Identifiers: LCCN 2015046991 | ISBN 9780415837521 (hardback) |
ISBN 9780415837545 (pbk.) | ISBN 9780203798188 (ebook)
Subjects: LCSH: Neoliberalism.
Classification: LCC HB95.E25 2016 | DDC 330.1–dc23
LC record available at http://lccn.loc.gov/2015046991

ISBN: 978-0-415-83752-1 (hbk)
ISBN: 978-0-415-83754-5 (pbk)
ISBN: 978-0-203-79818-8 (ebk)

Typeset in Bembo
by Sunrise Setting Ltd, Brixham, UK

For Ammara

CONTENTS

LIST OF KEY CONCEPTS

ACKNOWLEDGEMENTS

This book was initially conceived at the University of Oxford during my studies as a DPhil student in international relations. My doctorate explored diplomatic struggles between countries at the World Trade Organization (WTO) and how one could better understand such contests through a sharper focus on power (Eagleton-Pierce 2013). Similar to other areas in the world of commerce, the social environment of international trade policy – from the negotiating rooms of the WTO's home in Geneva to the 'real world' of buying and selling goods and, onwards, to the academic study of such processes – features a labyrinthine set of debates. For those who are not privy to these discussions, the stakes of the trade policy game can often appear bewildering and confusing. There are many reasons for this common reaction (or non-reaction), but one possibility I dwelt on concerned how the vocabulary of trade policy is often dry and technocratic, as if its history and political economy had been ironed out. At a broader level, this observation encouraged me to consider the ways in which capitalism acquires its justifications, not only through theoretical debates and policy deliberations but also at the level of everyday discourse. *Neoliberalism: The Key Concepts* emerged out of these initial reflections.

In the course of designing, researching and writing this book, there have been many individuals who have helped me. For primary influences, I could not have completed the book without the intellectual sparkle and emotional support of my wife, Ammara Maqsood. For many entries, her astute anthropological eye caught insights that I missed, in the process broadening my field of vision and enriching the analysis. She also provided a reassuring voice throughout the entire journey, particularly when I encountered the inevitable doubts, frustrations and setbacks. I also need to thank both my parents, Mary Eagleton and David Pierce, for their diligent reading, not only in terms of correcting grammar and proposing ideas, but also for helping to shape the overall style of the book. Beyond this core trio, scholarly stimuli and support have come from many friends and colleagues. Special mention needs to be made of the enduring and wise counsel of Kalypso Nicolaïdis, the inspiring work and encouragement of Loïc Wacquant, the sharp observations of Andrew Lang and the generous praise of Matthew Watson. My understanding of the arguments contained within this book has been informed by many thinkers, but particular attention must be paid to exchanges with Luc Boltanski and David Harvey. The great work of both Jamie Peck and William Davies has also kept me motivated. At a number of venues, I have benefited from exchanges triggered by presentations on the themes of this book, including at the International Studies Association, the British International Studies Association, the University of Oxford, the University of Cambridge, the London School of Economics, the University of Warwick, the University of Exeter and at my new intellectually stimulating home, SOAS, part of the University of London.

I am grateful for the wonderful team at Routledge, who have been so patient in waiting for the final manuscript and shepherding the project to publication. In terms of initial enthusiasm and support, I would like to thank both Andy Humphries and Siobhan Poole. Iram Satti, Charlotte Endersby and Sophie Iddamalgoda were very helpful in nudging me along towards completion. I also want to thank each of the five peer reviewers for offering extremely valuable suggestions and remarks. Some of the arguments contained within the entry for 'governance' appeared in an earlier special issue of *Critical Policy Studies* under the title 'The Concept of Governance in the Spirit of Capitalism' (Eagleton-Pierce 2014). These debts notwithstanding, I remain responsible for the content of this book and for any mistakes I may have made.

Matthew Eagleton-Pierce
London
March 2016

INTRODUCTION

'Neoliberalism' has become a popular but problematic term to characterise our age. Since the 1980s, within many fields of the social sciences
and humanities, but also extending into public debates, this term has
been called upon to symbolise, clarify or, through normative inflec-
tions, denounce a whole host of things. When surveying this vast and
expanding literature, it can sometimes appear as if neoliberalism is a
kind of conceptual Swiss Army knife which can unpick and cut
through almost any argument concerning the modern world. One
finds this term deployed for explaining the behaviour of Wall Street
banks in light of the financial crisis (Duménil and Lévy 2011); the
everyday experience of life in China (Zhang and Ong 2008); the transformation of Dubai's skyline (Davis 2007); the weakening of democracy (Brown 2015); the growth of inequality, insecurity and austerity
(Schrecker and Bambra 2015); and even the making of reality-based
television shows such as *The Apprentice* (Couldry and Littler 2011). It is
the same with some of the more popular extensions of 'neoliberal',
which is found attached to states, markets, projects, discourses, techniques, technologies, rationalities, restructurings, values and cultures
(Clarke 2008). If there is a connecting thread between these debates
then it concerns the question of how to think about capitalism or, as it
is more commonly referenced, 'the market economy'. In this regard,
writers who invoke neoliberalism are often focused on the impacts of
business power, ideological expressions such as 'free trade' or related
social trends that inform society and individual comportment.

Let me say at the outset that the purpose of this book is not to engage
in defining 'neoliberalism'; there is no way of neatly encapsulating what
has now become a kind of catch-all expression or 'explanatory catholi-
con' (Goldstein 2012: 304). Rather, my aim is to explore and interrogate
a range of histories, meanings and practices that have clustered around

this pervasive label. *Neoliberalism: The Key Concepts* is designed to shed light on a group of words that are rarely out of the news.

In most cases, the words themselves are in common use and have a long and often contested history, as with 'markets', 'freedom' and 'development'. Some have specialist senses which reflect particular debates in academic disciplines, as is the case with 'competition', 'growth' and 'risk'. Other terms, such as 'welfare', 'stakeholder' and 'diversity', have been strongly shaped by actors within political and business circles. Underlying all these words is a deeper and at times troubling conceptual framework, which this book seeks to analyse and make sense of. How is it that such terms, the language of the tribe, used across a variety of places and spaces, sometimes defensively, sometimes aggressively, can at once unite and divide us? How is it that at times their political baggage remains unnoticed or, perhaps, deliberately obscured? And how do all these expressions come together under the historical umbrella of what we might call 'neoliberalism'? These are the kinds of question this book seeks to address, a book aimed at students and researchers working in many different areas including, but not restricted to, politics, economics, sociology, geography, anthropology, development studies, management and cultural studies.

What makes a thought or practice 'neoliberal' is often unclear. From the 1930s to the 1960s, 'neoliberalism' had an earlier life when it was used in a positive sense by a group of intellectuals, including the economists Ludwig von Mises, Friedrich von Hayek and Wilhelm Röpke. These thinkers had different ideas on why liberalism could or should be given the prefix 'neo'. In one sense, they drew inspiration from Victorian liberalism but, at the same time, they saw a need to manage so-called 'collectivist threats', notably state socialism, which impeded their vision of economic and political 'freedom' (Mirowski and Plehwe 2009; Jackson 2010; Peck 2010; Burgin 2012; Jones 2012). From the 1980s, in the hands of scholars and social activists who took a different view of capitalism, the term 'neoliberalism' came to mean something else. In this now dominant meaning, it denotes a set of policy tendencies that were first crafted and tested in Western countries, notably the UK and the US (but also elsewhere), before spreading to other regions. According to the geographer David Harvey (2005), neoliberalism should be read as an agenda led by, and for, powerful elites, one which emerged in reaction to the perceived failures of Keynesianism and the strength of postwar social movements. From this perspective, although 'neoliberal policy' is often a moving and ill-defined target, it is commonly associated with the expansion of commercial markets and the privileging of corporations; the re-engineering of government as an 'entrepreneurial' actor; and the imposition of 'fiscal discipline', particularly in welfare spending (Gill 1995, 1998; Saad-Filho and Johnston 2005; Boas and Gans-Morse 2009; Dardot and Laval 2013; Davies 2014).

In this book, I build upon these valuable contributions to the study of neoliberalism, but approach the subject with two initial qualifications. First, in the core sense deployed here, studying neoliberalism means uncovering the reoccurring struggles over capital accumulation, but always with an eye on how such processes are shaped by a range of conditions. These contexts – such as the legacy of older political agendas which sometimes survive in reconfigured forms; nationally specific rules, institutions and cultures; and the often unpredictable impacts of disruptions, crises and acts of resistance – offer warnings against any effort to chisel a precise definition of neoliberalism (Peck and Tickell 2002; Brenner *et al.* 2010; Peck 2010). As other writers have suggested, the term has in some ways become a victim of its success. Neoliberalism increasingly appears as an omnipresent and often omnipotent phenomenon, a presumed 'force', or *zeitgeist*, which potentially envelops everything (Barnett 2005; Clarke 2008; Eriksen *et al.* 2015; Venugopal 2015). This effect of conceptual stretching – including the many oblique, casual and ironic uses of the word – gives neoliberalism a 'troubled' analytical status (Peck 2010: 15). At times, efforts at clarification are made more difficult when scholars slip into clichés and tropes. For instance, some writers claim that neoliberals seek 'the retreat of the state', rather than probing how 'actually existing neoliberalism' involves authorities who are often 'fiercely interventionist, bossy, and pricey' (Wacquant 2009: 308; see also Brenner and Theodore 2002; Gane 2012; Wacquant 2012). It is for this reason that the entries in *Neoliberalism: The Key Concepts* are careful to avoid essentialising neoliberalism as a single 'project' which is necessarily designed in advance. Instead, I prefer to use the notion as a broad label or a 'descriptive shell' (Venugopal 2015: 182) to denote changes that have occurred within capitalism since the 1970s, all the time conscious that such changes also require conceptual resources beyond the term 'neoliberalism'.

Second, given the focus on conceptual analysis, this book takes seriously the difficult task of explaining how ideas associated with neoliberalism are stabilised or destabilised. This objective could be viewed as falling within a longer tradition of scholarship which explores how justificatory schemas reflect and constitute capitalist relations (Marx and Engels 1970[1932]; Gramsci 1971). Alongside many scholars who debate the role of ideas in economic life, my argument also dovetails with studies that explicitly address the relationship between ideology, discourse and neoliberalism (Bourdieu and Wacquant 2001; Fairclough 2006;

Boltanski and Chiapello 2007; Turner 2008; Cornwall and Eade 2010; Springer 2012; Massey 2013; Holborow 2015). Such writers have been keen to explore how the rhetoric associated with neoliberalism has become a sort of 'planetary vulgate', one that appears to serve all, yet in reality tends to benefit particular interests (Bourdieu and Wacquant 2001: 2). In one respect, I aim to strengthen this literature through a sharper engagement with political economy in all its forms, including the history of economic ideas, the material struggle over policy agendas, the organisation of power through institutions and the consequences of often uneven distributional patterns. In another respect, *Neoliberalism: The Key Concepts* argues for a more nuanced reflection on the eclectic source material for neoliberal ideas. For sure, this includes the appropriation of themes within the history of Western-derived liberalism and, in particular, strands of neoclassical economics. But my examination also goes beyond these references to incorporate a focus on management theory, consumerism and other legacies (including those opposed to, or distant from, capitalism) that have shaped such words. In sum, the creation, testing, defending and critiquing of the evolving neoliberal lexicon encompasses many voices and all of them deserve our attention.

Beyond mere buzzwords

In 1976, the literary and cultural theorist Raymond Williams published a highly acclaimed work called *Keywords: A Vocabulary of Culture and Society*. Through a series of interconnected short essays, the aim of the book was to explore 'a shared body of words and meanings in our most general discussion', including terms that were often 'strong, difficult and persuasive' (Williams 1983: 15, 14). The label 'vocabulary' was a deliberate choice by Williams. In one sense, it implied how many of the terms he investigated, such as 'culture', 'tradition' and 'violence', are deployed in similar ways by different users and thus constitute a general pattern of thought or experience. In another, it pointed to how the selected words are often more complex than they might initially appear, with a range of explicit and implicit connotations. Thus, through a method that was attentive to close semantic analysis and social history, *Keywords* offered a guide for exploring the varied meanings of such terms. Inevitably, however, given that Williams last updated the book in 1983, it does not capture important changes in the evolution of international politics and capitalism, including the mainstreaming of neoliberalism. This point has been recognised by Bennett et al. (2005) and Durant (2006), among others, and has inspired an effort to study how socially prominent terms of public discourse can be viewed afresh

('The Keywords Project': http://keywords.pitt.edu/). *Neoliberalism:The Key Concepts* has been partly designed in the spirit of *Keywords*, with each entry offering an exploration of the multifaceted and mutually constitutive relationship between language and social change, but, paradoxically, it seeks to broaden this terrain by single-mindedly focusing on neoliberalism and how this has defined our current view of the world.

When asked to describe this book, I sometimes cite *Keywords* as a source of inspiration behind the research. More commonly, however, often for the purpose of quicker communication, I suggest that *Neoliberalism:The Key Concepts* could be viewed as a critical guide to modern 'buzzwords' or, specifically in several instances, 'management speak', or 'corporate jargon'. As the *Oxford English Dictionary* defines it, a buzzword is 'a term used more to impress than to inform'. The words discussed in this book are clearly in vogue, or of the moment, and often foreground the role of business in shaping the collective imagination of many fields beyond itself. Moreover, from a normative perspective, such buzzwords or labels tap into a well of popular frustration regarding how business discourse can be marked by circumlocution (Kellaway 2000; Poole 2014), an argument that echoes George Orwell's famous critique of political language and its tendency for 'euphemism, question-begging and sheer cloudy vagueness' (Orwell 2009[1950]: 370). At the same time, however, it is important not to treat the entries in this book as *mere* buzzwords, in a pejorative way, even to the point of flippant or humorous dismissal (in this guise, on the language of finance, see Lanchester 2014). What I seek to accomplish in *Neoliberalism:The Key Concepts* is something different: to maintain a critical and wary disposition – to reconsider, or, as Marx would put it, to 'doubt everything' – but to be open to the difficult process of understanding why such terms take their objectified forms. Even buzzwords are not empty of meaning.

To this end, my argument offers three distinct contributions. First, the book provides a resource for students and researchers in the social sciences who are puzzled by the common words associated with neoliberalism. Each entry features an etymological sketch, an unpacking of meanings surrounding the term, the degree to which such meanings have changed and the critiques engendered. To aid understanding and to illustrate the wide scope of debates linked to neoliberalism, theoretical and empirical insights are drawn from many scholarly fields. Second, *Neoliberalism:The Key Concepts* engages in an exercise of decoding. All the featured terms display forms of ambiguity and imprecision. On one level, there is nothing unusual about such characteristics in language. What matters is to uncover how the particular interests of actors – be they commercial, national or otherwise – are tied to the use of such terms. In this regard, the uncertainty of language may facilitate space for manoeuvring, contestation or even obfuscation. For instance, when concepts such as 'reform', 'responsibility' or 'stability' are deployed in policy debates, they frequently carry an appearance of neutrality, yet a closer reading reveals how certain meanings and material outcomes tend to overshadow others. Third, the study of neoliberal vocabulary matters for explaining associated patterns of group-making and social struggle. To borrow a line from the anthropologist Bronisław Malinowski (1923: 315), 'ties of union are created by the mere exchange of words'. We might say that these effects stem from the easy circulation of neoliberal concepts. Such relations do not need to entail deep institutional bonds or zealous forms of loyalty, although patterns of that kind do exist, but could also include a kind of unthinking gravitation to whatever are the 'received ideas' of the moment (Flaubert 1968). The neoliberal lexicon is a kind of social glue, the function of which is as much about the mobilisation of populations as it is about the legitimation of things such as 'free markets'. Thus, it is perhaps not surprising that concepts such as 'community', 'consensus' and 'partnership' are frequently used in ways that attempt to minimise offence and encourage the widest possible acceptance.

Most of the terms addressed in *Neoliberalism: The Key Concepts* could therefore be called 'dominant': they are words which have been in use for centuries, and are recycled in a variety of institutional environments, as well as in everyday talk. At first glance, to focus on terms such as 'choice', 'global' or 'investment' may appear slightly odd for such words are surely unremarkable objects of analysis. The neoliberal perspective given to each term lies alongside many other meanings, some of which will be comparatively neutral. Yet it is through such processes that the neoliberal vocabulary cultivates a form of power, which, capillary-like, flows into the narrowest of socio-political spaces (Foucault 1980). By proposing a grammar which transcends itself – by appropriating terms that are also used for non-capitalist activity – the neoliberal spirit of capitalism is able to increase its attractiveness and complicate the strategies of critics (Boltanski and Chiapello 2007). With this in mind, this book aims to contribute to our understanding of how neoliberal practices will always be hybridized (rather than 'pure') creations and how, paradoxically, despite failures, doubts and cynicism, the vocabulary often refreshes itself or, at the very least, becomes so normalised that users struggle to imagine what an alternative discourse could look like (Crouch 2011; Peck *et al.* 2012; Mirowski 2013; Peck 2013; Schmidt and Thatcher 2013). The strength of these 'plastic words' (Poerksen 1995) is also the result of many being linked into chains of signification that feature scientific and specialist fields. For instance, a term such as 'project' was used in engineering and military contexts to denote planning and control, before spreading more widely within the business world. The concept of 'risk' reveals an even more complicated history, including influences that range from developments in actuarial science and probability theory to the growth of litigious cultures.

This brings me to the question of how the terms were selected. Following many years of absorbing relevant academic literature, policy documents and business media, I drew up a longlist of potential inclusions. There are some linchpin concepts in the neoliberal vocabulary that are more important than others, such as 'market', 'freedom', 'growth', 'competition' and 'class'. These inevitably made the shortlist. Beyond this immediate core, my main concern was centred on other established expressions that often display a deceptively taken-for-granted quality rather than every technical term which has entered into debates tied to neoliberalism. On this note, there are specialist dictionaries and handbooks, such as *The New Palgrave Dictionary of Economics* (Durlauf and Blume 2008) and *The Development Dictionary* (Sachs 1992), which offer insights into the neoliberal milieu, but such works have a different disciplinary remit than is on offer here. Elsewhere, there are many other expressions which could be considered secondary to my main listing, and are often discussed within the chosen entries, but because of the pressures of space do not merit their own entry. Since some of these more peripheral notions have a new or 'emergent' status (Williams 1977: 123), it is difficult, as yet, to determine their significance. For instance, 'resilience', noted under the entry for 'individual', is a term which is rising in popularity across many policy domains, but whether it has staying power for the future is an open question (Joseph 2013; Chandler and Reid 2016). The number of entries – 44 in total – is also reflective of a desire to facilitate a rich exploration of each term, but in a manageable way. Although *Neoliberalism: The Key Concepts* has the definite article in its title, it makes no claim to have captured every potential neoliberal concept, nor to have traced the galaxy of interpretations, translations and revisions across the world. Rather, the book is aimed at further sensitising readers to this complicated lexicon, while opening space for fresh dialogues on the meaning of neoliberalism.

How to use this book

I assume that readers will turn to this guide to explore particular concepts when needed. Although it is structured as a list of discrete entries, the book could be read as a single narrative, one which points to the difficulty but not the impossibility of mapping neoliberalism. Above all, I wish to highlight the importance of relational thinking for grasping this vocabulary. Each concept stands on its own, but as indicated by the cross-referencing at the end of each entry, it can only be fully or adequately understood with respect to other terms. These webs of meaning have a tendency to cluster, such as when 'consensus' is often invoked at the same time as 'community', 'participation' or 'stakeholder'. Every term also has its antonyms, or a dichotomous pairing, which often reinforces a particular dominant sense, such as 'state' versus 'market', 'individual' versus 'collective' and 'network' versus 'hierarchy'. Relational thinking also needs to attend to how words began and how they have changed in meaning over the centuries. I make no apology for devoting so much space to this aspect. In this sense, words – though never self-consciously – are also in dialogue with their own history and at the same time reveal so much about ourselves and the world we inhabit. In his *Outlines of the Philosophy of Right* (2008[1821]: 14), Hegel proposed that '[w]hat is rational is real and what is real is rational'. Marx and the Young Hegelians in the 1840s thought otherwise. Today, we are more inclined to believe that in the discourses and practices of neoliberalism, as elsewhere in the social world, 'the real is the relational' (Bourdieu and Wacquant 1992: 97). Only through disentangling and reconsidering what is real and what is relational can we begin to see how the tapestry of neoliberalism was formed and how it continues to function.

NEOLIBERALISM
The Key Concepts

ADJUSTMENT

There is more guile in 'adjustment' than first appears. In the context of neoliberalism, the word often passes unnoticed, and this partly accounts for its appeal to certain actors. Derived from the Old French *ajouter*, meaning to join, adjustment also carries a semantic association with justice (*juste*), hence the sense of 'correcting' a form of (in)justice. In English, from the seventeenth century, the word began to acquire other sets of meaning, including the idea of a collective agreement or settlement. With the emergence of capitalism, financial interpretations followed, especially evident in the balancing or auditing of an account. By the middle of the nineteenth century, the concept broadened further to represent a general sense of adaptation, particularly evident in the fields of biology and psychology (Spencer 1855). The idea of adjustment often takes on a modifying inflection, implying that the form or object in question is not inherently disputed but, simply, requires limited adaptation to reach a more perfect state. Because of its ambiguity, it is perhaps not surprising that the term has become allied with other notions in neoliberal vocabulary, notably reform but also, more widely, change and development. In this regard, the prefix *ad* (Latin for the preposition 'to') is a reminder that adjustment is always on the way to somewhere else.

Within economics, the notion of adjustment carries a stylistic appeal as a kind of mechanistic or Newtonian metaphor. It is also deployed in particular theoretical debates. Thus, the phrase 'self-adjusting market', an idea associated with the presumed impersonal and automatic workings of the capitalist system, with the implication that beneficial ends can be achieved without excessive government intervention, has become popular shorthand for neoliberalism as such. Although this expression has been linked to the classical liberal thought of Adam Smith (1993[1776]) and his many disciples, the first time the phrase was actually used in a significant way was by John Maynard Keynes in his critique of utilitarian economic theory. Its use is particularly evident in the idea that the economy has a tendency to return to a 'normal' equilibrium. In his key work, *The General Theory of Employment, Interest and Money* (1936), Keynes argued that the economy should not be understood as having any 'natural', self-adjusting propensity towards full employment. Rather, the economy contained many potential equilibria, one no more 'natural' than another. Along similar ideological lines, and published just eight years later, Karl Polanyi articulated his own critique of liberal thought, one that has become an influential touchstone for many scholars: '[O]ur thesis is that the idea of a self-adjusting market implied a stark utopia' (Polanyi 2001[1944]: 3; for secondary literature, see Dale 2010; Block and Somers 2014).

Two illustrations from the neoliberal period can help to reveal how the notion of adjustment may initially appear innocent but, upon closer inspection, often carries a political message. In 1979, against the backdrop of various economic crises, Robert McNamara, the President of the World Bank, made the first public reference to 'structural adjustment' in a speech which urged developing countries to reform their export industries in order to increase trade with developed countries. The following year, after internal deliberations involving Ernest Stern, the Bank's Vice President for Operations, structural adjustment loans (SALs) were approved as a new Bank instrument (Kapur *et al.* 1997; Babb 2009). Ostensibly justified for countries experiencing balance-of-payments problems and to enhance economic growth – concerns that, by 1982, were acute, following the Latin American debt crisis – SALs always had long-term reform objectives in mind. But what precisely did the Bank want to adjust? As the 1980s and 1990s unfolded, the policy content on 'adjustment' adapted to various conditions, but the general template remained relatively consistent, focused around 'fiscal adjustment, getting the prices right, trade liberalization, and, in general, a movement towards free markets and away from state intervention' (Easterly 2005: 3). For critics, however, agendas under the name of adjustment did not mean the minor, fine-tuning of policy machinery, but often entailed radical changes, such as removing state subsidies that supported the poor (Walton and Seddon 1994; Brown *et al.*, 2000; Structural Adjustment Participatory Review Inter Network (SAPRIN) 2004). As Dani Rodrik has suggested, 'structural adjustment' was partly a 'marketing' concept at the Bank to persuade recipient nations that such packages of microeconomic and macroeconomic reforms were legitimate, even when more objective analysis, both at the time and subsequently, would cast doubt on the wisdom of such strategies (Rodrik 1994: 82).

While SALs would later become politically tainted at the World Bank, the appeal to the looser sense of policy adjustment lives on in countless issues associated with neoliberalism. For instance, from 2010, in the context of the Eurozone crisis, the European Commission, the European Central Bank (ECB) and the International Monetary Fund (IMF) (collectively known at the time as 'the Troika') designed a series of bailout programmes for Greece, Ireland and Portugal, in which the term 'adjustment' featured prominently, including in the legal headings of such schemes. Like SALs, 'economic adjustment', when invoked as the solution to the Eurozone crisis, took on an aura of technocratic managerialism, an image that was reinforced by the presence of bureaucrats who had no direct line of democratic legitimacy to national populations. In the minds of many observers, not least those who were protesting on the streets, the term 'adjustment' became a euphemism for austerity. The adjustment was always towards more, rather than less, with working people experiencing the major burden. Since the option of a currency devaluation for the peripheral states was impossible and an exit from the Euro was either non-negotiable or fraught with unknowns, the Troika demanded policies of 'internal devaluation' as a way to manage the debt and increase competitiveness (Pisani-Ferry 2014). Yet since the notion of adjustment was a commonplace expression, it was also appropriated by Greek officials in their negotiations with the European institutions. In one of the most memorable accounts of the crisis in 2015, Yanis Varoufakis, the Minister of Finance, made the following remarks:

> That Greece needs to adjust there is no doubt. The question, however, is *not* how much adjustment Greece needs to make. It is, rather, what kind of adjustment. If by 'adjustment' we mean fiscal consolidation, wage and pension cuts, and tax rate increases, it is clear we have done more of that than any other country in peacetime.
>
> (Varoufakis 2015, italics in original)

In this sense, adjustment can seem not only full of guile but often far from just.

See also: **change, consensus, development, flexibility, reform, stability**.

Further reading: Polanyi 1944; Brown *et al.* 2000; Pisani-Ferry 2014.

BUSINESS

The term 'business' was originally identified with the quality or state of being busy (from the Old English *bisignes*). Although now differentiated as 'busyness', this earlier sense of the word still echoes today in the behaviour of business individuals, not only through the appeal to diligent labour and commitment, but also in how such work can be marked by anxiety and doubt. The dominant meaning of business as the collective expression of the world of trade and commerce emerges in the late fifteenth century, although it took until the early eighteenth century before it could refer to a specific company, firm or enterprise. A wide range of expressions and modifiers have been linked to this enduring concept, from 'man of business' (1640) and 'business is business'

(1797) to 'business before pleasure' (1816) and 'get down to business' (1868). In the nineteenth century, reflecting the development of industrial society in Britain and elsewhere, a host of compound phrases entered the language, such as 'business centre' (1824), 'business model' (1832), 'business travel' (1833), 'business morality' (1836), 'business associate' (1842), 'business leader' (1848), 'business English' (1855) and 'business magnate' (1867). There is little evidence that this trend of conceptual extension is in decline, not least because countless 'business gurus' (1969), who teach at proliferating 'business schools' (1862), compete to coin new phrases that are attached to this master signifier.

Business entities can take a variety of forms depending upon the country in question and its legal tradition, including cooperatives, partnerships and sole-trading outfits. However, the dominant type of business organisation, one which is increasingly pursued in different regions of the world within the neoliberal period, is the corporation. This form of organisation can be traced back to mercantile trading groups, such as The Hudson's Bay Company, before reaching commercial maturity in the nineteenth and twentieth centuries (Wilkins 2005). In the most basic definition, the modern business corporation is a state-sanctioned association which possesses a 'separate legal personality' distinct from its members. Other common characteristics include limited liability (a restriction against creditors seizing more than the assets owned by the company), transferable shares, a delegated management structure and investor ownership (Armour et al. 2009). In general, although not always, a business corporation is driven by a core profit motivation and the need to reinvest surplus capital. There are millions of small- and medium-sized enterprises within the capitalist system, but the large-scale business corporation is a special phenomenon that was created to address a particular problem: how to manage productive industries, particularly those which involve contracts that often cross national borders. Such corporate expansion has generated not only astonishing wealth, development and new consumer goods but also other notable tendencies, including concentrations in economic power, oligopolistic market structures, close relations with political rule-making processes, claims about environmental destruction and, as a consequence, renewed questions about whom business ultimately serves (Galbraith 1972; Strange 1996; Gamble and Kelly 2000; Fuchs 2007; Wilks 2013). In other words, scepticism about the business corporation is central to wider debates about the definition of freedom and responsibility in a capitalist society.

The power of global corporations is one of the most commonly invoked themes in debates about neoliberalism. The visual spectacle of such power can be seen in the construction of office skyscrapers in major cities, part of a competitive struggle among urban and national jurisdictions to host leading firms (Sklair 2005). Although there are methodological difficulties in assessing corporate power, such as in defining the extent to which businesses are transnational, how business lobbying actually operates or the ways in which firms can dictate political rule-making, significant illustrations and trends can be observed (Fuchs 2007). From 1980 to 2013, total corporate earnings before interest and taxes more than tripled and now represent almost 10 per cent of world GDP (McKinsey Global Institute 2015a). In the 2014 *Fortune* 'Global 500' list, a major index ranking, the top 500 corporations earned US$31.3 trillion in combined revenue, including the leader, Wal-Mart, which earned US$8.6 trillion. Energy-related firms have a strong hold over the top 20, taking 11 spots on the list. Elsewhere, if one examines a snapshot view of market capitalisation – that is, the total value of publicly listed shares – Apple appears as the world's largest corporation, with a market value of over US$500 billion in early 2016. These standard measures of corporate power have also been complemented by other assessments, one of the most eye-catching being comparisons between corporations and other 'economies' or 'economic units', such as cities and countries. For example, according to one analysis, the total sales of the top 20 corporations were equivalent to the combined national expenditures of the bottom 163 states. On the basis of GDP, many of these corporations are as large as middle-income countries, such as Chile or the Philippines (Mikler 2013).

Is big business, therefore, the big winner in the neoliberal era? The evidence suggests that major corporations, including a cadre of extremely wealthy executives, have tended to benefit from a favourable, if still volatile, political and economic environment. Three significant trends can be noticed. First, the location of corporate power is not fixed but always changing in response to various push and pull factors. Most multinationals still have a strong attachment to a 'home' country, as reflected in major sites of production or the constitution of board members. Notwithstanding this influence of 'national business systems' (Whitley 1999), the aspiration to be seen, and to act as, a 'global business' is characteristic of neoliberal corporate branding. This degree of 'transnationality' can be analysed in different ways (United Nations Conference on Trade and Development (UNCTAD) 2008). One major shift has involved the spreading of Western business practices to non-Western regions of the world, including those areas that were previously under Communist rule. Thus, in 2005, China had

16 corporations on the *Fortune* 'Global 500' list, but, by 2014, that figure had increased to 95 firms, second only to the US with 128 entries. The rise of Chinese-based businesses does not necessarily mean, however, that the US model of corporate power is on the wane, as the attraction of American management ideas and gurus in China testifies (Dickson 2008). Another way in which the location of corporate activity can be problematised concerns the development of flexible production chains that make up intra-industry trading. For instance, although most of the assembling of Apple's iPhone is carried out in China, the California business also outsources production to five other firms, in South Korea, Japan and Germany (Xing and Detert 2010). In this sense, the label 'made in', when attached to consumer goods, often tells only a small part of the story of where products are assembled (Elms and Low 2013).

Second, a major focus regarding big business in the neoliberal period concerns the shaping of politics in their favour. In one sense, this is not a new phenomena: close ties or 'revolving doors' between commerce and politics have a long history, from mercantilist owners in the seventeenth century to the 'robber baron' industrialists of the nineteenth century. However, in modern policymaking, the scope, intensity and sophistication of business activity are noteworthy. According to one study on lobbying in Brussels, the *de facto* capital of the European Union (EU), around two thirds of all actors campaigning to shape EU rules are business players. Each year, up to €60 billion is spent on funding an estimated 20,000 business lobbyists (Coen and Richardson 2009). Some sectors, such as finance, feature stark imbalances in lobbying efforts, with business outnumbering civil society and union groups by a factor of more than seven (Corporate Europe Observatory 2014; Lipton and Hakim 2013). Spending significant sums of money does not guarantee that business interests will be able to control EU agendas, but large firms do see considerable benefits from such activism. To take an example, in the aftermath of the global financial crisis, major banks lobbied hard to shape new laws on capital–adequacy ratios (money that has to be ring-fenced to serve as a safety buffer). The key capital ratio now stands at 7 per cent (Bank for International Settlements (BIS) 2013a). But this figure is considerably less ambitious than the target championed by some regulators and industry observers. For example, Mervyn King, former Governor of the Bank of England, argued for 'much higher levels of capital' in order to help reduce risky behaviour by banks (Guerrera and Pimlott 2010; see also Admati and Hellwig 2013).

The relationship between business power and the making of national and international rules can be traced not only through direct lobbying. At a deeper level, it could be legitimately argued that a managerial ethos, anchored around the norm of market competitiveness, is now the dominant rationality operating within many organisations in the neoliberal period (Davies 2014). This managerial rationality adopts slightly different forms depending upon the context. It is thus not easy to pin down. For instance, intellectual economists, such as Joseph Schumpeter (1983[1934]), provided theoretical justification for ideas on entrepreneurship, while contemporary management gurus, such as Michael Porter (1985, 1990), have helped to imagine countries, cities and regions in quasi-business terms through the discourse of 'competitive advantage'. In this respect, the growth in business education, with the coveted MBA becoming a 'global degree', has been important in consolidating the authority of business thinking, particularly beyond the West (Amdam 2008). At the same time, media networks, such as CNBC and Bloomberg, often glorify the world of business and, in particular, depict CEOs as modern heroes or seers. The Hollywood tradition of depicting business elites as morally bankrupt could be seen as a counter to these forces, yet, disturbingly, characters such as Gordon Gekko in *Wall Street* (1987) are hailed as behavioural models by some contemporary financiers (Lewis 2010). Through such mechanisms, a particular normative perspective, belonging chiefly to managers of enterprises, comes to be seen as desirable and applicable to many institutions. Indeed, this operates to such an extent that firms, states and even civil society groups are represented as 'ontologically equivalent and symbiotically related' (Davies 2014: 128). However, by adopting this view, one risks missing how the definition of, and material resources dedicated to, 'the public' may come under threat from promoting the vision of an elite social faction, as seen in types of 'corporate welfare' (tax incentives, subsidies) provided by governments to already rich companies.

This attention to the position of business in society brings us to the third trend, one that carries a particular neoliberal impression: corporate social responsibility (CSR). It would be wrong to claim that justifications for business are devoid of references to a sense of the 'common good'. Before the 1980s, however, CSR was often 'derided as a joke, an oxymoron and a contradiction in terms by the investment and business community' (Lee 2008: 53). For instance, Milton Friedman famously argued against the notion by claiming that the 'one and only social responsibility of business' is to maximise stockholder value (Friedman 2002[1962]: 133). The rise of CSR to the status of a strategic business priority was, in the first instance, a defensive reaction to different criticisms, including accusations that business was implicated in ecological decay, as well as to demands that firms should speak to more stakeholders, such as unions and NGOs (Carroll 2008). In this sense, efforts to address CSR can be interpreted as a form of public relations, the results of which may provoke cynicism and a belief that large firms are not as socially and environmentally committed as they claim. For instance, BP once rebranded itself as 'beyond petroleum' to highlight its green credentials, yet investments in alternative energy have always been small; in 2008, BP spent $20 billion on fossil fuel projects, but only $1.5 billion on renewables (Greenpeace 2009). But while some CSR initiatives may, indeed, be 'greenwash', this does not characterise all business activity in this area. In the last two decades, the major trend in 'corporate citizenship' has been the increasing rationalisation of such practices, not least because of the commercial benefits companies can accrue through good reputation and the preemption of legal rules. Businesses are now busy. Through such strategies, one can see how, in the neoliberal period, the large business entity has become not only very powerful but adaptable in the face of challenges to its legitimacy.

See also: **capitalism, competition, diversity, enterprise, entrepreneurship, experience, flexibility, global, investment, management, market, performance, private, responsibility, stakeholder, state, vision**.

Further reading: Fuchs 2007; Gamble and Kelly 2000; Wilks 2013.

CAPITALISM

Capitalism as a concept entered the language in the early nineteenth century to denote a particular socio-economic system in which private wealth is used in the production and distribution of goods. 'Capitalist', used to define a person who possesses and invests in capital assets, is a slightly older expression found in late-seventeenth-century Dutch, before its journey through German and French to its English application in the late eighteenth century. The financial sense of the term 'capital' has a deeper history, from the first references in English in the mid sixteenth century to more mature theorising in the context of Adam Smith's (1993[1776]) arguments and, onwards, to the coining of many compound phrases from the nineteenth century (such as capital account (1813), capital expenditure (1834), capital accumulation (1863), capital control (1914) and capital flight (1921)). As Raymond Williams (1983[1976]) notes, this specialised meaning of capital derived from its general sense of 'head' or 'chief' (from the Latin *caput*). Given this etymology, it is not surprising that questions of ownership and power are frequently implicated in the practices of being a capitalist and in the system that is said to serve such individuals. In the twentieth century, the expression enjoyed two periods of popularity: until the Second World War, in the context of debates about socialism; and from the late 1950s until the late 1970s, in the shadow of the Cold War and the renewal of social, and socialist, critiques against capitalist activities. The decline in the use of the concept parallels the mainstreaming of neoliberalism. This makes 'capitalism' an interesting word, for while it has struggled to enter neoliberal vocabulary it can still be critically deployed to better understand such particular discourses.

As is widely known, the critique of capitalism is strongly associated with Karl Marx and his efforts to dissect scientifically the workings of the system. For Marx, capitalist-like practices did exist in the ages of feudalism and antiquity, but the 'capitalist era', as he expressed it, dates from the sixteenth century (Marx 1990[1867]): 929). However, along with his colleague Friedrich Engels, Marx rarely used the word 'capitalism' in the systemic sense (the popularity of the term only accelerated in the early twentieth century through Sombart (1902) and Weber (2002[1905]; see also Chiapello (2007)). In strict Marxist use, 'capitalist' is a description of a mode of production (a method of producing things necessary for existence, such as food and housing), whereas *bourgeois* is a description of a type of society. Marx's preferred term for capitalism was '*bourgeois* society', suggesting a world that is socially divided between a ruling class (the *bourgeoisie*), who own the means of production (money, factories, land, etc.) and a *proletariat*, who have nothing to sell but their labour (Marx and Engels 1998[1848]). The analysis of commodities constitutes the bedrock of Marx's critique. Within the pages of *Capital* (1990[1867]), he seeks to explore the characteristics of a commodity, including how humans give such objects a value, why people buy them and what social effects are generated by this seemingly insatiable process. Capitalist forces, for Marx, are also laced with reoccurring tensions, crises and contradictions, to the extent that he believed the entire order would eventually collapse and be replaced by communism. Since the late nineteenth century, there have been multiple contributions to Marxism, both intellectually and politically. Indeed, the entire secondary literature on Marxism is one of the biggest in the academic canon (for initial introductions, see Harvey 2010; Fine and Saad-Filho 2010).

Because the notion of capitalism has long been tied to the Marxist legacy and other voices on the political left, for opponents of such views, the term has been handled delicately or, most of the time, scorned and avoided. We see this in the work of early neoliberal intellectuals, such as Ludwig von Mises, who argued that the concept was 'invented by socialists, not to extend knowledge, but to carp, to criticize, to condemn' (Mises 2009[1922]: 122). From the 1940s, Friedrich von Hayek followed Mises' lead, suggesting that both 'socialism' and 'capitalism' were terms that did not adequately elucidate the world (Hayek 2008[1944]). Nevertheless, a complete rejection of the word was not always advanced by this class of intellectuals. As noted, because of the Cold War context and the need to respond to roiling social movements, defenders of capitalism continued to appropriate and revise the meanings attached to the term, as seen in Milton Friedman's widely read *Capitalism and Freedom* (2002[1962]). However, the major pattern of discourse around 'capitalism', which continues today in the neoliberal period, is to deploy other phrases to denote 'the system'. For most mainstream economists, policymakers and observers, capitalism goes by the name of 'the free market', 'the market system', 'the enterprise system', 'globalisation' or, more abstractly, 'the economy' or 'business'. In the media, it is very rare to find business owners defined, or self-identified as, capitalists. In short, if one enters 'capitalism' into Google's Ngram Viewer, a dataset that charts the annual count of words in published books, one finds that the term peaked in 1979, before commencing a gradual decline to the present.

Such a decline in the application of the concept requires explanation, not least because this change has passed by many without acknowledgment. Two sets of reasons can be suggested. First, from the 1970s, led by conservative governments and business lobbies, many ideals and rights associated with collective forms of socio-economic organisation came under renewed attack. For instance, the drop in trade-union participation rates in the US and Western Europe tended to weaken union bargaining positions with management and eroded socialist-inspired goals (Rigby *et al.* 2005; Gall *et al.* 2011; Gumbrell-McCormick and Hyman 2013). Although unions remained powerful and often popular in many countries, such as Germany, it can be suggested that the attractiveness of socialism, particularly 'actually existing socialism', was fading long before the collapse of the Berlin Wall (Lebowitz 2012). For instance, from the 1960s in East Germany there was a rising demand for Westernised consumer goods (Major 2009; Rosenberg 2010). With the downfall of the Soviet Union, this tendency to assume that capitalism was the answer for all of humanity acquired a new cultural and political potency. The narrative was crystallised in Francis Fukuyama's (1992) widely debated argument that the triumph of Western capitalist democracy represented not just the end of the Cold War but 'the end of history'. Subsequently, when the major oppositional category to capitalism was seen as a political and economic failure, the practical relevance of the dichotomy began to diminish. One might imagine that this could have led to a refreshing of the popular legitimacy of the term 'capitalism', yet because the notion was so bruised through Cold War struggles – a perceived 'sour history' as expressed by Galbraith (2004: 3) – it began to be discarded. Thus, capitalism had 'won', yet its name was rarely spoken.

Second, there have been parallel developments occurring in the academic world that have contributed to the neglect of the concept. The intellectual decline of Marxism and, in turn, the rise of other agendas in the social sciences and humanities, particularly around identity politics (gender, race, ethnicity, sexuality, etc.), formed the backdrop to this shift. For example, with respect to sociology, Boltanski and Chiapello have argued:

> Dethroned from its status of key concept of the 1970s, 'capitalism' has been reduced to an inferior status – a somewhat indecent swearword – because it implied a Marxist terminology that many sociologists wished to forget, but also because it referred to something too 'large', too 'bulky' to be immediately observable and describable via the observation of specific situations.
>
> (Boltanski and Chiapello 2007: xi)

It is important to underline this latter remark on methods because it dovetails with the general (capitalist-mimicked) propensity for scholars to specialise within narrower intellectual spaces. In such moves, big-picture theorising begins to suffer and, thus, the value of a big-picture concept, such as capitalism, tends to be underappreciated. Other relevant trends have been specific to the field of economics. Although for some time history formed a sub-field of economics, the resistance of many contemporary economists to engage in historicising their objects and tools of analysis has become more pronounced in recent decades. Through the standard neoclassical lens, capitalism is read not as an historically specific and politically maintained regime, one with an unclear future trajectory, but as an apparently timeless and universal system whose formal properties can be quantifiably modelled (Heilbroner 2008). Moreover, in keeping with the legacy already noted, many economists (although by no means all) tend to disassociate themselves from language on the political left, within which capitalism would be a core concept.

In his early 'unarmed' years, Leon Trotsky suggested that the history of capitalism involved 'the subordination of the country to the town'

(Trotsky 2010[1906]: 81). Trotsky plotted his own path towards revolution and the overthrow of capitalism, but for those who consider capitalism a notion that is perhaps too unwieldy on its own, the examination of different forms of capitalism, across time and space, represents an attempt to find fresh analytical meaning. The comparative study of models of capitalism has a long pedigree, but received a new spotlight with the 'varieties of capitalism' (VoC) research agenda (Hall and Soskice 2001; Hancké 2009). The VoC approach argues that there are now two ideal-type models of capitalism in developed countries: (1) liberal market economies (LMEs), epitomised by the US, which are organised around competitive markets, limitations on collective bargaining and radical breakthroughs in innovation; and (2) coordinated market economies (CMEs), such as Germany, which tend to stress collaborative firm–government relations, higher unionisation levels and incremental steps in innovation. According to Hall and Soskice (2001), corporate organisation should be foregrounded in the comparative analysis of LME and CME forms of capitalism, rather than stressing society as a general explanation. Elsewhere, one can point to other writers who have explored similar themes, notably studies on the rapid growth of East and Southeast Asian countries since the 1960s, such as Japan, South Korea and China (sometimes referred to as 'state development capitalism' or the 'developmental state' model) (Johnson 1982; Woo-Cumings 1999; Wade 2004; Walter and Zhang 2012). Within these debates, as well as in popular discussion, one reoccurring question has been whether an Anglo-American model of capitalism – read 'neoliberalism' for many authors – is more powerful and authoritative than other models. The enlarged role for finance is one major point for analysis here. Evidence can be mobilised in support of both convergence towards, and divergence away from, a single type of capitalism. Thus, caution is needed over pronouncing any definitive answer (Boyer 2005).

In sum, reflecting upon the social struggles involved in implementing the system that goes under its name, the term 'capitalism' carries a complex history. As the greatest critic of capitalism, Marx was always impressed at the remarkable capacity of the system to produce unprecedented wealth in the form of commodities and to reinvent itself in the face of problems. In one sense, the neoliberal appeal for business managers to engage in 'constant change' – in ideas, labour, products, production systems, etc. – is merely the latest revision of Marx and Engels' famous argument that, in capitalism, 'all that is solid melts into air' (1998[1848]: 38). In contemporary use, perhaps the marginalisation of the term in recent decades is actually of benefit for the critical analysis of neoliberal phenomena. The concept of capitalism does have its problems, particularly when it appears to suffocate human agency and difference. Yet since the expression is analytically rooted in debates about capital–labour relations, exploitation, alienation and forms of resistance to orthodox orders, it arguably still offers a valuable conceptual toolkit to draw upon. From 2008, in the aftermath of the global financial crisis, the term underwent a temporary increase in use by public commentators, signaling again how it can be recovered and put to work. For instance, as President Bush (2008) argued, 'Like any other system designed by man, capitalism is not perfect. It can be subject to excesses and abuse. But it is by far the most efficient and just way of structuring an economy'. Or as the *Washington Post* asked in a lead article: 'The End of American Capitalism?' (Faiola 2008). In a crisis, therefore, it often appears as if the boundaries of the ideological universe become fractured, allowing space for other terms and ideas to enter. Interestingly, viewed in this light, neoliberalism can be seen as the conceptual slave to the master notion of capitalism.

See also: **business, choice, class, competition, development, emerge, enterprise, entrepreneurship, environment, finance, global, growth, investment, management, market, private, stability, state, welfare**.

Further reading: Boltanski and Chiapello 2007; Hall and Soskice 2001; Heilbroner 2008; Marx and Engels 1998 [1848].

CHALLENGE

The earliest use of 'challenge' carried an accusatory meaning, derived from the Latin *calumniari*, which implied not simply a rebuke but a false or slanderous one. The conflictual sense of the word, as in summoning someone for a fight, dates from the mid fifteenth century. Around the same time, challenge took on its legal meaning of objection or exception to a person or matter of debate. While these uses still exist today, challenge in the neoliberal context tends to be dominated by the popular sense that only emerged in the 1950s: that is, a difficult or demanding task, especially one that tests the ability or character of a person. The subsequent attaching of 'challenge' to a galaxy of objects and categories – such as economic challenges, political challenges, social challenges, national challenges and institutional challenges – is now pervasive. Within this conceptual spreading, some particular uses of the term are, however, very recent in origin. For instance, in the *Financial Times*, phrases such as 'business challenges' or 'management challenges' were rarely used in articles prior to the late 1980s. Likewise, in a British Library search of book titles, 'global challenges' featured in just

11 publications prior to 1988, but in the subsequent period 632 works have included the expression.

The appeal of 'challenge' as a keyword is omnipresent in the vocabulary of countless political figures, business leaders, media commentators, experts and academics. When delivering his first State of the Union Address, President Obama (2009) peppered his speech with the word, including the final paragraph where he encouraged his fellow Americans to 'confront without fear the challenges of our time'. In the aftermath of the global financial crisis, Christine Lagarde (2013), Managing Director of the IMF, was particularly fond of using the term in relation to a host of problems, from 'economic instability' and 'insufficient equity' to 'environmental damage'. When browsing through books on management, one discovers how corporate executives are told to shoulder multiple challenges, from leadership and strategy to sustainability and ethics (for instance, see Drucker 1999). Indeed, in publicity material, every major transnational company now seems keen to illustrate how their activities relate to global challenges. At Coca-Cola, one marketing representative invokes the term with these words: 'we view challenges such as water scarcity, climate change, economic disparity and obesity as interdependent – an improvement in one may positively affect outcomes in another'. Or as DuPont's website expresses it: 'we believe that the answers to the greatest challenges facing humanity can be found through inclusive innovation'. Elsewhere, on university campuses across the world the notion of challenge frames academic degree programmes, courses and research projects. One can study for a masters in Global Challenges and Leadership in Jordan, attend a conference on European Challenges in the Netherlands and visit the Centre for Global Challenges in Canada.

Understanding why challenge has become so pervasive in the lexicon of such speakers and institutions is difficult to pinpoint. It would be wrong to claim that some 'force' called neoliberalism has 'captured' the word and that all uses somehow serve a capitalist goal. The attractiveness of the term, however, does seem to coalesce around how it provides a non-offensive way of highlighting a problem. There is also the implication that the problem remains controllable and potentially resolvable. Often this sense of managing the declared challenge comes through systems of measurement: for example, if we can calculate the carbon emissions involved in manufacturing consumer goods then the challenge of climate change is at least partly met. The fuzzy glow surrounding the word is even more appealing when one sees how 'challenge' is often paired with 'opportunity'. A challenge may be taxing and tiresome but, in the old liberal spirit of onward progress, it could also bring positive changes and outcomes (Gray 1995). If we consider alternative terms that might be analytically more potent or political but are not as commonly deployed, we discover yet again its efficacy. For instance, to pose the problem of climate change as a *dilemma* or *contradiction* between nature and capitalism, rather than a challenge of coordination between worlds that are seen as compatible, offers a radically different framing. Herein lies part of any explanation for the mainstreaming of challenge: through its very ubiquity, vagueness and optimistic veneer, the term projects a message that everyone can contribute to dealing with the problem and, in turn, find rewards.

See also: **change, management, performance, reform, vision**.

Further reading: Drucker 1999.

CHANGE

Within contemporary business management as well as other organisa-tional fields, including professional politics, the appeal to the notion of 'change' has become commonplace. We can isolate four themes in how the concept tends to be imagined. First, there exists a propensity to think of change in spectacular or transformative terms, marked by rapid, frenetic and, at times, inevitable movements. For instance, tech-nological innovations, such as the internet, are cast as 'forces of change' that seemingly possess no boundaries and can propel economic growth (Sharma 2007). Second, there is often a presumption that every organ-isation, from big businesses to local community centres, and every indi-vidual, from elite politicians to casual workers, feels the effects of change. In other words, change, whether in the abstract or the partic-ular, remains omnipresent. Third, despite the not uncommon accom-panying disturbances generated by such processes, change is often painted in normatively appealing colours. Business analysts implore leaders to 'thrive on' and 'adapt to' change. Those who manage through chaotic environments, steering such entrepreneurial dynamics to their advantage, are claimed to seize new opportunities (Peters 1987, 1994; Kotter 1996). By contrast, those who cling to older, so-called 'bureau-cratic models' are depicted as inflexible, complacent or even threaten-ing. As one textbook puts it, '[a]ny organisation that ignores change does so at its peril' (Paton and McCalman 2008: 7). Fourth, related to such desires for change, is the issue of control. For many theorists and practitioners, change may be difficult, beset with episodes of failure and confrontation but, nevertheless, can be plotted and strategised, with seemingly endless new schemas, tools and step plans promising to crack the change conundrum (Sturdy and Grey 2003; *Harvard Business Review* 2011).

Through a longer historical lens, there is nothing exclusively neo-liberal about how modern enterprises promote the concept of change. The term has always carried the potential to rouse exciting emotions by tapping into the desire for newness and, in particular, self-renewal. Thus, Dale Carnegie's famous self-help guide, *How to Win Friends and Influence People* (2006[1936]), written partly for an American business audience, featured a section on 'how to change people without giving offence or arousing resentment'. Later bodies of management theory also adopted the notion. For instance, Kurt Lewin, an early-twentieth-century German-American psychologist, devised a three-stage model of organisational development for use in business and government. In Lewin's framework, the importance of resistance was built into the model: a subject is called upon to 'unfreeze' their existing (problematic) 'mind set', before initiating the desired change process and, finally, 'freezing' the newly conditioned state of mind (Lewin 1947; see Beckhard 1969 and French and Bell 1972 for how a wider literature was spawned by Lewin). Elsewhere, through the 1970s and 1980s, the model of the five stages of grief as outlined by Elisabeth Kübler-Ross (1970) was influential in management circles as an applied frame-work for understanding behavioural change under conditions of stress.

Talk of 'change management' is, however, something that parallels the mainstreaming of neoliberalism. In the 1980s, this phrase remained rather obscure, but, from the 1990s, it took off as dramatically as the phenomena it was claimed to be explaining. For instance, in a British Library title search, 'change management' was found in 69 items prior to 1995, followed by 398 recordings from 1995 to 2000, a further 654 cases from 2001 to 2007 and an additional 824 publications since 2007. Amid all this debate, the object of success has often involved different targets, including leadership issues, employee satisfaction, efficiency savings and demands for greater competitiveness and flexibility. The theory of change management seems to embrace these, and many other, aspirations. Context, explanation and performance are here closely entwined. One reading of this trend would look to particular 'forces' that are claimed to provoke calls for change. In the 1980s, in the epicentre of this discourse, the US, business observers feared that America was declining in the face of energy crises, foreign competi-tion and inflation spikes. In order to usher in 'an American corporate renaissance', as one author put it, there was a need for new 'change masters', defined as those 'people and organizations adept at the art of anticipating the need for, and of leading, productive change' (Kanter 1983: 13). Although much of this literature was written for executives looking for success stories, it is also apparent that agendas surrounding change management place considerable emphasis on 'people': that is, entrusting workers to change, yet in a manner which 'drives' them 'out of their comfort zones' (Kotter 1996: 5; see also Drucker 2011[1995]). It is not surprising, therefore, that the field of human resources has risen in importance during the neoliberal period, because such departments play a central role in disseminating ideas on change management.

The narrative of 'constant change', an elaboration often invoked by management theorists (Zook and Allen 2012; Pennington 2013), has now spilled over into many other institutional environments beyond the domain of business. In the vocabulary of modern politics, particularly within electoral democracies, 'change' has always been a keyword, as the campaigning of President Obama demonstrated (Alexander 2010). What is more distinctly neoliberal, however, is the valorisation of ideas and agendas associated with 'entrepreneurial government' over 'bureaucratic government', a dramatic dichotomy penned by David Osborne and Ted Gaebler in their highly influential study, *Reinventing Government* (1992). The significance of Osborne and Gaebler's activism lies in how they caught the ear of President Bill Clinton and, subsequently, shaped a major report into government reform (Executive Office of the President 1993). Given that Osborne was invited to help draft this report, it is not surprising that there are remarkable similarities between the two texts (Moe 1994; du Gay 2003). Like *Reinventing Government* (1992), the US government report enthusiastically advocates 'entrepreneurial management' as a new paradigm to 'cast aside red tape' and ensure reformed systems of accountability. As a government vision, it is intensely focused on the 'customer', encourages the 'empowering' of state employees through 'decentralizing authority' and aims to conduct all federal activity in the most cost efficient manner (Executive Office of the President 1993: 6–7). Through such terminology, one can see how the appeal to the latest management rhetoric, combined with the well-worn political tactic of denouncing 'big government', helped to justify a reconfiguration of expectations of how US agencies were defined and run. The call for 'change' was thus a rallying cry in such mobilisation efforts.

It is worth noting in conclusion some criticisms and concerns regarding the 'change' discourse in the neoliberal period. Most visibly, in many of the uses discussed, there exists a pattern of 'epoch-making' narratives as the justificatory premise for reform. Organisations are depicted as being incapable of confronting an unruly world, which, in turn, necessitates 'transformative change' as the only solution (du Gay 2003). However, such pictures are often sensational, with highly simplistic descriptions of failure and reward, all delivered in a sermonising, even menacing, tone beloved by business gurus. Very different types of phenomena – from 'globalisation' to terrorism to questions of diversity – can become yoked together under the master rubric of change and, in the process, confuse, rather than clarify, multifaceted and potentially contradictory trends. To declare that one is living in a rapidly changing world is, therefore, a bland truism. What one often misses in such conceptual treatments of 'change' is any real understanding of history, since the new is often glorified as an endpoint; any sense of humility, particularly with respect to forms of conflict, randomness and variability that are uncontrollable; and any subtle awareness of the wider social and political consequences of prescribing models of change, such as in respect to psychological stresses. In sum, if there is a deeper intentionality connecting the many meanings of 'change' within neoliberal contexts – and such generalisations need to be treated with great care – it seems to gravitate around the perennial problem in the history of management: how to create more supple bodies that can be controlled and motivated for whatever purpose is required.

See also: **adjustment, emerge, experience, flexibility, innovation, management, market, performance, power, reform, vision**.

Further reading: du Gay 2003; *Harvard Business Review* 2011; Moe 1994.

CHOICE

It is difficult to be neutral about the word 'choice'. The term stems from the Old French word *chois* and can be distinguished from 'option', the slightly weaker Latinate word for choice, which is closer to a wish or desire. Choice refers to the action of selecting between different proposals. In philosophy and theology, the idea of choice has historically played an important role in debates on free will and determinism (for instance, Watson 2003; Kane 2011). In this sense, choice has been a term to be fought over. Not surprisingly, the concept has a long association with liberal thinking and policymaking in the West, as seen in the struggles for political suffrage in Europe from the nineteenth century. Today, its proximity to a consumerist vocabulary has dented some of its sharper edge. However, in the context of debates surrounding neoliberalism, its seemingly unproblematic meaning can be questioned when the notion is more closely framed in relation to power. The very capacity to exercise choice, to select and discern objects of worth, will not be equally distributed in any given social system. In other circumstances, there may be disputes over not only the ability or right to choose but whether the choices are valuable in the first place. The choice may be partial or illusionary to some degree; it may be presented as a false dilemma when in reality other options remain; or the decision may be little more than a 'take it or leave it' offer (known as Hobson's choice). Such potential inequalities in the making and enacting of choices suggests that we have to tread carefully and not adopt uncritical or narrow meanings of the term.

In the discipline of economics, the concept of choice plays a central analytical role, to the extent that the entire field has been defined by some as a 'science of choice' (Robbins 1932). According to most economists, individuals make choices in a calculating, rational manner or, perhaps more precisely in many contexts, are defined as acting *as if* they were fully rational. But choices are not made in a vacuum. Rather, the choice of an individual is a product of their personal tastes or preferences under conditions of resource scarcity, such as with respect to income or time. Within this conceptualisation of human action, 'explanations of individual choices also often *justify* those choices. The factors that *cause* choices also function as *reasons* for choices' (Hausman and McPherson 2008: 235, italics in original). What are these preferences that justify the actions of individuals? The most important generalisation that economists offer is that people are materially motivated and will tend to seek out more commodities rather than fewer. Wealth generation is not the only way to satisfy preferences and not all forms of behaviour are strictly rational or self-interested, but economists argue that such conditions tend to prevail and can be used as a basis for explaining market phenomena in a capitalist system. At the same time, the preferences that structure choices always have constraints attached, beyond which a certain option may not be possible. Thus, 'freedom' to choose operates within boundaries and the extent to which constraints can shift represents a core question of political economy.

As capitalist values have spread across many societies, the meaning of choice has become conditioned by consumerism. This trend has deep roots and manifests itself in a different ways (Trentmann 2004, 2012, 2016; Fine 2002). While the neoclassical economic theory of consumer choice dates back to the late nineteenth century, the seeds of the contemporary neoliberal sense of the expression can be found in the design of product marketing in the twentieth century, particularly during the postwar period (Kassarjian and Goodstein 2010). With the rise of mass production and mass distribution, notably via the international spread of the department store and the supermarket, the problem of understanding consumer behaviour became paramount (Crossick and Jaumain 1999). What do consumers like and dislike? How do they use products? What new desires could be cultivated? When product markets became increasingly competitive, with items that were broadly similar in terms of quality and price, the development of branded goods offered a way in which choice could be more clearly defined. In this sense, as marketing professionals have closely studied, a successful brand, such as Colgate toothpaste, did not advertise itself as only performing a single function identical to other toothpastes. Rather, Colgate advertisers connected the brand to a cluster of pervasive, commonly held meanings, including subjective desires for beauty and hygiene, in order both to socially construct and, importantly, *simplify* the choice for the customer (Jones 2010; more generally, on motivational techniques used in postwar advertising, see Packard 1957; and for contemporary developments in 'neuromarketing' see Lindstrom 2008).

There are two other post-Second World War developments that have informed the contemporary meaning of choice. The first concerns how the normative appeal of consumer choice took on a political inflection during the Cold War. One of the major Western critiques of the Communist system, which arguably contributed towards the collapse of the Soviet Union, centred on how consumer choice was severely limited in Eastern European countries under the Soviet influence. It was a sentiment that was shared by many in the Communist bloc who, by the 1980s, began to draw a relationship between consumer choice and the need for social change (Rosenberg 2010). The second force derives from a range of social movements in the 1960s and 1970s, notably feminism, that contested conventional structures of power, including the organisation of the family and employment rights. Out of such struggles, the politics of abortion – a woman's right to choose, or pro-choice – was one of the most visible, if contentious, legacies. This particular feminist strategy redefines the meaning of choice to expose forms of exploitation. In a narrower and less radical manner, 'choice feminism' tends to analyse and valorise the individualised decision-making of women as a solution to inequality. For instance, Sheryl Sandberg's *Lean In* (2013), a popular bestseller, urges women to accept full responsibility for their career and livelihood, producing in the process what one writer has referred to as a 'neoliberal feminism' (Rottenberg 2014). As other feminist critics have noted, the problem with this perspective is not only how it ignores wider structures of authority that are implicated in such inequality but, alarmingly, how its discourse on personal empowerment accords with the advertising rhetoric adopted by many companies to sell their wares (Cohen 2006; Fraser 2013).

In short, there is something seductive about the word 'choice'. In many contexts, the term is invoked in a positive and morally righteous tone, impressing upon the listener that 'all choice is good' and that the act of choice-making is a pleasurable one (as in the buzz of 'grabbing a good deal'). But is choice always as liberating as the advertisers claim? In contrast to the stylised model of economic theory, the reality of choosing in a neoliberal capitalist society is often a profoundly anxious and uncertain experience. As some authors have argued, people worry not only about making the 'perfect choice' but, of equal significance, how their choice will be interpreted by others and, in turn, what separate choices others are making (Salecl 2010; Iyengar 2010). The worry caused by such dizzying and often inane possibilities, from selecting fashion styles and Facebook updates to deciding who to date and where to live, has led some behavioural economists, sociologists and social psychologists to question the limits of choice. As Barry Schwartz (2004: 3, italics in original) has commented, 'the fact that *some* choice is good doesn't necessarily mean that *more* choice is better'. Too much choice can thus lead to regressive outcomes, not just emotions of apprehensiveness or guilt, but to a kind of dazed and lethargic state as the brain strains to disentangle the knots of competing messages (Salecl 2010). Moreover, the analysis of these conditions, if such reflection occurs, tends to direct individuals to regulate themselves more intensively, evident in the explosion in self-help guides, rather than critically evaluate how systems of consumerism have reproduced particular architectures of choice. The right to choose has become an obligation to choose. Those who 'fail' to regulate themselves appropriately are then accused of making 'bad life choices'. One can also note that for those without significant disposable income, the inability to reach a certain level of consumption can result in a different form of alienation and revolt, as illustrated in an extreme case by the London riots in 2011 (Žižek 2011).

At other times, however, it appears as if arguments about the differences between valued objects can betray or camouflage important similarities. In the neoliberal period, this is particularly noticeable within some party political systems, such as the US, UK, Germany and France, which have experienced a decline in the old political left and a rise of conservatism that has reshaped the political centre (Prasad 2006). A long-established tactic of politicians looking for votes is to claim that they are offering a 'clear choice' (on ideas, policies, leadership, etc.) between themselves and their opponents. For instance, in the 2012 US election, former President Bill Clinton, acting as a surrogate campaigner for President Obama, argued in a heavily played television advertisement that the Democratic Party was markedly different from the Republican Party. In his 30-second pitch, Clinton told the audience that they have 'a clear choice', before deriding the Republican plan 'to cut more taxes on upper income people and go back to deregulation' (Landler 2012). While there are, indeed, contrasts between the two main parties, such as on tax policy for the rich, this should not detract from a deeper analysis of how the Democrats, particularly under Clinton's stewardship in the 1990s, became captive to interests emanating from Wall Street. For some analysts, therefore, the public crisis in confidence in political parties stems from a blurring of conventional ideological boundaries. Claims about 'clear choices' are in reality difficult to discern, and they often serve to increase a sense of apathy, or conversely, frustration and anger in the electorate. As for Obamanomics, this was a very elusive agenda, and appeared to be 'a series of adaptations of the mutating neoliberal order, rather than any kind of significant break with that order' (Peck 2010: 262).

See also: **capitalism, competition, enterprise, entrepreneurship, freedom, flexibility, individual, market, participation**.

Further reading: Hausman and McPherson 2008; Salecl 2010; Trentmann 2012, 2016.

CLASS

In the context of neoliberalism, class plays a waiting game. This is partly because there is an issue of how it can be invoked to (un)mask socioeconomic divisions operating within societies and transnationally, and partly because its appeal as an explanatory concept has tended to be neglected in popular discourse. Derived from the Latin *classis*, meaning the summoning of a collection of persons (from the root *caleo*, 'to call', 'to invite'), the notion was used in classical antiquity to refer to rankings and groupings, particularly according to property ownership among Romans. By the early seventeenth century, class had entered English, with an initial use as a taxonomic category for the study of living organisms. From the eighteenth century, social applications of the notion became more common, along with metaphorical extensions, such as 'classify' and 'classification'. As Raymond Williams (1983[1976]: 61) suggests, '[t]he essential history of the introduction of class, as a word that would supersede older names for social divisions, relates to the increasing consciousness that social position is made rather than merely inherited'. Thus, between 1770 and 1840, in the context of the industrial revolution, different class groupings were constructed, including 'lower class', 'middle class', 'upper class' and 'working class'. What is more difficult to trace then, as now, is how precisely such classes emerge and subsequently reconfigure in relation to various social, economic and political conditions. E. P. Thompson's magisterial study *The Making of the English Working Class* (1963) did much to shed light on the emergence of the working class in Britain in the 1830s, but we need to constantly remind ourselves of a continuing struggle in how a population can be 'forged into a collective, a "class on paper" turned (or not) into a real class, endowed with the capacity to move its (putative) members, voice demands, and act as such on the historical stage' (Wacquant 2013: 276).

The notion of class is multifaceted and contested within scholarly debates and in wider discussions. With some risk of oversimplification, different general meanings can be noted (Crompton 2008). In one sense, class can be understood as a structured pattern of inequality which tends to reproduce across generations. Identifying a social 'class system' (1877, *OED*) involves studying how certain groups possess and wield power, often to the disadvantage of other groups. Such power may include material resources (money, land, businesses, etc.), social distinctions (education, skills, networks of contacts, etc.) and ties to different institutions, particularly political, legal and media – for example, political parties, lobbying firms, rule-makers and broadcasters. Linked to this idea, classes can therefore be theorised as actual or potential 'motors of history' which can change the make-up of a society, possibly in a profound way. For instance, as Marx and Engels suggested in *The Communist Manifesto* (1998[1848]), the bourgeoisie of France and Britain were a revolutionary class in the eighteenth century who fought against the aristocracy, yet, by the nineteenth century, only the proletariat could lay claim to being 'a really revolutionary class' (for only they can abolish class as such) (Marx and Engels (1998[1848]: 47; see also Davidson 2012). Thus, under the Marxist reading of capitalism, 'class struggles' (1839, *OED*) result when the means and products of labour are treated as private property, which, in turn, makes it possible for one class to benefit from the expropriation of another (for contemporary neo-Marxist debates, see Wright 1997, 2009). At the same time, class can also be understood in more cultural terms, such as in reference to prestige, status, manners or, of particular note under neoliberal extensions of consumerism, 'lifestyle'. In popular debates, as well as in sociology, this latter meaning has received considerable attention in recent decades, sometimes in reaction to Marxism or overly economistic treatments of the notion (for foundational studies, see Veblen (2007[1899]); Weber (2013[1922]; Bourdieu (1984, 1987)).

At the juncture of class and neoliberalism, four key points can be noted. First, since the late 1970s, the term 'class' has encountered a decline in use. One can see a visual representation of this by entering 'social class' into Google Books Ngram Viewer, a dataset that charts the count of words in published books. The reasons for this trend are complex, and the extent to which something called 'neoliberalism' is involved can be debated. Within academic scholarship, as well as social activism, many have argued that other dimensions of stratification, such as those concerning gender and race, have come to the fore. Thus, a concept of class based only on material wellbeing (particularly occupational data) needs to be redefined or considered in relation to these other forms of identity or domination (Crompton 2008). Major changes in the world economy have also contributed to the argument that class is no longer as potent a social and political signifier. For instance, in the UK, the relative deindustrialisation of particular regions, combined with a weakening of trade unions, has fractured a spirit of camaraderie that was associated with being 'working class' (Charlesworth 1999). At the same time, the relationship between political parties and class-specific voting is not as pronounced as in previous generations. The traditional left–right opposition still holds in many electoral systems, but has been complicated by, among other factors, voters who are driven less by collective ideologies and more by 'issue orientated' decisions (Clark and Lipset 1991; Clark et al. 1993; Evans 1999). Others have argued that political parties have become disinterested in, or even hostile to, policies associated with the working class. Such tendencies have resulted in notable tensions within parties that grew out of working-class organisations. 'Betrayal' as a term has often been heard about Tony Blair and how he distanced the Labour Party in the UK from its trade-union roots.

Second, the general decline in the use of the term 'class' does not mean that all scholars have abandoned the concept, nor that agendas traditionally associated with 'class politics' do not resurface under different guises. As suggested, class plays a waiting game. For some prominent Marxist writers, neoliberalism can be best defined, *in toto*, as 'a class project', whereby an elite social fraction seeks to reproduce itself, both economically and politically (Harvey 2005; Duménil and Lévy 2011). However, although money and privileges are often reproduced through hereditary chains, the precise social constitution of this elite class should not be viewed as fixed. For instance, in the UK from the 1980s, Prime Minister Margaret Thatcher, with the weight of her lower-middle-class background behind her, attacked the 'aristocracy' that dominated the financial centre of the City of London and, instead, 'sided with the brash entrepreneurs and the nouveau riches' (Harvey 2005: 31).

From the late 1980s, reflecting the increasing authority and geographical reach of large businesses, the concept of a transnational capitalist
class (TCC), or ideas that approximate the notion, began to emerge
(Cox 1987; Gill 1991; van der Pijl 1998). According to Leslie Sklair
(2001), the modern TCC can be analytically divided into four main
fractions: (1) owners of major transnational corporations and their
local affiliates (the corporate fraction); (2) globalising bureaucrats and
politicians (the state fraction); (3) globalising professionals (the technical fraction); and (4) merchants and the media (the consumerist fraction). Although other authors have criticised the value of the TCC,
arguing that the concept can conceal spatial variation in the relative
cohesion of elites, there is no doubt that the question of inequality has
become more contentious in public discourse, particularly following
the financial crisis of 2007–9 (Tabb 2009).

A number of studies, including Thomas Piketty's widely debated
Capital in the Twenty-First Century (2014), have empirically demonstrated that wealth inequality has increased in many countries over the
neoliberal period. The trend is particularly pronounced in Anglophone
countries, although similar patterns can also be observed elsewhere,
including in China, India and Indonesia (Atkinson and Piketty 2010).
In the US, the share of total national wealth owned by the top 0.1 per cent
of the richest families rose from 7 per cent in 1978 to 22 per cent by
2012 (Saez 2014). For the top 10 per cent, their share of total income is
now over 50 per cent, a record high. By contrast, the bottom 90 per cent
have experienced no substantial growth in their wealth in the current
period. There are different factors behind this concentration of economic power, some of which are historically specific to particular
countries, but among them we might notice favourable tax rates for
the wealthy, and lucrative compensation packages (particularly in
financial, technology and energy firms) (Alvaredo *et al.* 2013). For
Piketty (2014), the trend line is worrying because of the tendency for
the return on capital to rise faster than the rate of economic growth.
In other words, in a world where economic growth is low and fragile,
the rich will continue to pull away from the rest by living off more
favourable returns from their existing assets (profits, rents, interest, etc.).
Such dynamics matter not only because the 'wretched of the earth', in
Fanon's (2001[1961]) telling phrase, deserve a better fate, but also
because more unequal societies tend to be worse off in many other
areas, even in terms of life expectancy (Wilkinson and Pickett 2010).
As Piketty (2014: 554) concludes, with respect to the US, 'the risk of
a drift toward oligarchy is real', a situation that some believe has already
arrived (Winters and Page 2009).

Third, in the context of such debates on inequality, the category of 'the middle class(es)' has become an important notion for many agents to mobilise around. In most countries, the term carries culturally favourable meanings, associated with the aspiration to achieve social and economic distinction (Bourdieu 1984). But defining who belongs, or should be allocated, to the middle class has long been a difficult sociological question, objectively and subjectively (on the contested and often confusing history of the category, including its relationship to 'bourgeoisie', see Moretti 2013). One common starting point is to find the median household income in a national distribution; yet working out how far the middle stretches above and below this figure is often disputed. In light of tendencies towards low wage growth and rising costs – conditions that some argue can be tied to neoliberal trends – the idea of a 'squeezed' middle class has become a major political question. For example, in the US, productivity and wages have decoupled since the 1970s, meaning that many Americans today are working harder to maintain a standard of living which is believed to be middle class (Erickson 2014). In opinion polls, when compared to other countries, Americans have historically expressed greater tolerance for societal inequality, including underestimating poverty. Since the financial crisis, however, social perceptions are drawing closer to the material reality of the class system described by some sociologists (Gilbert 2014). In this sense, Americans, who in the past typically saw class as a synonym for opportunity, are becoming Europeans. In 2008, 53 per cent of Americans self-identified themselves as being middle class, with another 25 per cent associating themselves with 'blue collar workers'. But by 2014, the former figure had dropped to 44 per cent, while the latter had risen to 40 per cent (Pew Research Center 2014). Nonetheless, the desire to be seen as middle class (even if one may not have the means) still remains highly attractive and, as a result, is consistently invoked (or exploited) by policymakers seeking votes and wider legitimacy.

A final theme of relevance in the relationship between neoliberalism and class concerns those at the poorest end of the class structure. The term 'underclass' is one focus for debate here. First coined in the early 1960s within the US, the expression exploded in use from the late 1970s, driven by conservative journalists, think-tank analysts and policymakers (Myrdal 1963; Russell 1977; Mead 1993). In common parlance, the term often has a pejorative tone, used to categorise a segment of the poor who are viewed as particularly desperate, even dangerous, and beyond meaningful improvement. Although seemingly on the decline in the US, the concept has since spread to many others parts of the world, including European and Asian countries (Theodore 2010).

As critiqued by Wacquant (2008: 89), the notion is problematic on many levels, including its 'heavily negative moral connotations which reactivate the century-old opposition between the "deserving" and the "undeserving" poor', as well as 'its falsely deracialized ring, allowing those who use it to speak about race without appearing to do so'. Rather than examining how the links between government policy and a constrained labour market can marginalise, demonise and even criminalise the urban poor, the rhetoric of the underclass tends to redirect attention to the presumed individualised, behavioural failings of such groups. Use of the term 'culture' is also frequently invoked by underclass theorists, as in 'welfare culture', 'ghetto culture' and 'work ethic culture'. Again, while giving a veneer of social-scientific credibility, such labels further contribute to the symbolic denigration of the poor, ascribing to them an apparently 'natural' and unchanging quality which is, once more, removed from a deeper analysis of the broader class structure.

See also: **capitalism, community, consensus, freedom, market, power, private, welfare**.

Further reading: Crompton 2008; Piketty 2014; Wacquant 2008; Wright 1997, 2009.

COMMUNITY

Since the fourteenth century, the term community, from the Latin joining of *com* (with, or together) with *unus* (the number one), has taken on a wide range of meanings and applications. One definition points to community as a body of people or things viewed collectively, as in the common people (to be distinguished from a privileged group) or the communal life (historically used in religious contexts, but later extended to other groups on the basis of shared characteristics, such as politics, class, race or sexuality). While these senses refer to actual social groups, a second meaning highlights a particular type of relationship. For instance, in legal discourse, one can speak of a community of property to indicate shared ownership or liability. Across all these uses, the concept is frequently invoked to define an attractive social condition, one marked by cohesion, support or a sense of belonging. When critically examining how the term has been appropriated during the neoliberal period, it is helpful to keep this particular point in mind. As Raymond Williams (1983[1976]: 76) notes, 'community' is a 'warmly persuasive word' which, importantly, 'unlike all other terms of social organisation (state, nation, society, etc.) it seems never to be used unfavourably, and never to be given any positive opposing or distinguishing term'. This does not mean, however, that the notion of community cannot also be used to exclude particular ideas or social interests. The very openness and 'fuzziness' of such a contested concept allows for multiple forms of politics, including practices of division and exploitation under its name (Hoggett 1997; Crow and Maclean 2006).

The theme of loss and recovery has been a long-standing concern in debates about community. From the nineteenth century, within Europe, the industrial revolution transformed the meaning and practice of community through a variety of complex forces, including the break-up of the medieval guild system, the commercialisation of agriculture, urbanisation and the growth of a working class. In the context of these trends, one can identify two discourses of community as a form of normative aspiration (Delanty 2010). One discourse, shaped by strains of conservative thinking, among other sources, sees community as a set of traditions that remain vulnerable to modernity and, thus, in need of protection and revival. For instance, in *Democracy in America* (2003[1835, 1840]), Alexis de Tocqueville depicts the post-revolutionary US as the place where European civilisation was redeemed and where the state does not exist outside of the civic community. A second discourse expresses community more explicitly as something to be accomplished, rather than simply recovered from the past. Here, Marxism, and its political deployment in the mould of socialism, can be highlighted as a classic illustration. As Marx argued, because capitalism encourages competition and antagonistic behaviour, the individual becomes 'withdrawn behind his [sic] private interests and whims and separated from the community' (Marx ([2000]1844: 61). Moreover, the state, upheld by writers like Tönnies ([2001]1887) as offering a space for preserving autonomy within industrial life, is, from the Marxist reading, only 'one more illusory community within capitalist society' (Plant 1978: 91). In short, many calls for an 'authentic community' are as much about the desire to fulfil an imagined ideal as they are about defining some concrete lived experience. Indeed, the struggle to bring into realisation a certain community can often appear as an elusive, utopian project.

When we turn our attention to the neoliberal period, how has the meaning of community shifted? Three uses or experiences of community can help shed light on some of the political struggles beneath this deceptively innocent expression. First, the complex ties between, on the one hand, a sense of community, urban space and social class, and, on the other, trends within capitalism have long preoccupied geographers and sociologists. For instance, from the 1970s, in the US 'rustbelt' region, deindustrialisation resulted in declining living standards for working-class populations (Bluestone and Harrison 1982; Cowie and Heathcott 2003; High and Lewis 2007). As Loïc Wacquant has argued, the 'communal ghettos' of the early postwar period, such as in Chicago, depicted as places of African-American pride, have now been transformed into 'hyper-ghettos' where 'spatial alienation and the dissolution of place' take hold (Wacquant 2008: 241). The flight of many manufacturing jobs, either internally to cheaper factory sites in the US southwest, or abroad, notably to East Asia, is only one reason for this claimed diminution or loss of community. Other trends include the expansion of a flexible services economy, with many replacement jobs featuring fewer benefits; generalised attacks on trade unions, led by conservative politicians, business elites and some journalists; and the corresponding gentrification of central urban areas as 'productive' only for richer professionals. In turn, many efforts to redevelop cities often favour a middle-class definition of community as the most worthy of investment. While it would be wrong to say that this is a novel invention under neoliberalism (think of Haussmann's radical transformation of Paris in the nineteenth century, for instance), widening wealth disparities since the 1980s have certainly crystallised such patterns.

A second way to explore the nexus between community and neoliberalism is to trace how the expression has been used as an apparent solution (or foil) to the problems of modern government. From the 1990s, in the UK, different uses of the term community were tested and politically refined by Tony Blair as part of his rebranding of the Labour Party (Hale 2006). On the one hand, Blair frequently used 'community' as a palliative vision for how society could be organised – a 'third way', as it was expressed, between the presumed individualism of the Margaret Thatcher era and the so-called 'Big Brother' tendencies of the 'old' political left. Although rooted in a different political context, similar patterns of argument were also seen in the US when Bill Clinton repositioned the Democrats. To draw on Williams (1983[1976]) again, it is perhaps not surprising that 'community', as a vague expression associated with belonging, was tapped by these two politically astute leaders. However, according to Nikolas Rose (2004: 171), references to community by Blair and Clinton during this period had a particular emphasis, tending to be 'infused with notions of voluntarism, of charitable works, of self-organized care, [and] of unpaid service to one's fellows'. Such policy initiatives had a distinct moral overtone. Importantly, this discourse on 'the local community', which continues to be reproduced in a climate of financial austerity, implies that citizens can and should engage more in the work of political governance. At the same time, this activity tends to reconfigure expectations on the role of state responsibility. Such appeals to community, or 'stakeholderism', as it is sometimes expressed, often appear to be radically democratic. Yet, for critics, it can also open the political space for the erosion of social welfare functions that helped to protect poorer members of society (welfare ideals are, arguably, best organised through the infrastructure of a modern state).

A third notable use of 'community' is to attach the notion to 'international' or 'global'. Although the phrase 'international community' can be found referenced from the early twentieth century, the expression has undergone a new surge in popularity in the neoliberal period. Similarly, the phrase 'global community' was rarely invoked prior to the early 1990s, but had become a stock phrase by the turn of the century. For instance, in a search of titles in the British Library catalogue, only 42 books featured the expression 'global community' prior to 1993. Both notions are common within the professional world of diplomacy, offering a sense of personal and moral identity (Neumann 2012). Yet the shift towards imagining humanity as a single community also took on a neoliberal inflection through the collapse of the Soviet Union, resulting in the ambition to cement 'a community of market democracies', as one senior US government advisor expressed it (Lake 1993). On the surface, given the proliferation of cross-border phenomena – from climate change to financial flows – it can make intuitive sense to appeal to 'the global community', particularly when political cooperation among nations is required. On the other hand, such uses of the phrase may also obscure complex sources of power and responsibility. In other words, the population or interests under the heading of 'global community' may not in practice be multiple or universal. Rather, the definition of 'global' could be strongly informed by particular actors. The turn to 'community speak' sometimes looks like a strategy of attracting or, more precisely, coercing recalcitrant actors into a larger agenda, to the extent that it takes on a doublespeak inflection. This was the case with Tony Blair's use of 'international community' before the invasion of Iraq in 2003 (Fairclough 2005). Such rhetorical moves can also be seen in the struggles over the limits of the European Community, a project which, in contrast to Williams' (1983[1976]) remark, has never been very successful at constructing a 'warm' feeling of solidarity among its citizens.

See also: **class, consensus, diversity, freedom, global, individual, openness, participation, stakeholder, state, welfare**.

Further reading: Delanty 2010; Hale 2006; Plant 1978.

COMPETITION

'Competition' is one of the most important words in the neoliberal lexicon. Along with the popularisation of its derivative, 'competitiveness', the concept is now commonly invoked not only as a generic solution to multiple problems in the management of capitalism but, more profoundly, as a kind of governing ethic for all individuals and organisations. Within the tradition of political economy, debates surrounding the meaning of commercial competition and how it should be organised have a long history. For a classical political economist such as Adam Smith, competition arose organically from the dynamic rivalry between buyers or sellers in markets, resulting in price definition, patterns of resource allocation, divisions of labour and consequences for wider development (Vickers 1995). In Smith's view, monopolies and bounties were the 'great enemy of good management' because such instruments interfered in the 'natural price, or the price of free competition' (Smith 1993[1776]: 148, 60). By the nineteenth century, competition had been reimagined in light of the mathematical revolution in economics, resulting in the influential model of 'perfect competition' (Cournot 1897[1838]; Edgeworth 1881; Jevons 1882). This latter meaning, unlike Smith's appeal to behavioural traits, was framed as an idealised conception whereby processes of competition had exhausted their limits (McNulty 1967). In other words, 'perfect competition' rarely, if at all, exists in the real world, but the model has historically been justified as offering a comparative analytical function. At the same time, by the twentieth century, this appeal to mathematical formalism helped to bolster the legitimation of the discipline, in the process fulfilling John Stuart Mill's call that 'only through the principle of competition has political economy any pretension to the character of a science' (Mill 2008[1864]: 50).

Starting in the 1930s, within a group of intellectuals who came to be associated with the early 'neoliberal thought collective' (Mirowski and Plehwe 2009), the concept of competition was re-examined, largely in opposition to the theory of perfect competition. For Friedrich von Hayek and Ludwig von Mises, two of the most significant voices in these debates, competition, theorised from the viewpoint of equilibrium, included false or unrealistic assumptions, such as the idea that all markets featured zero barriers to entry. In contrast, Hayek, in an echo of Smith, pioneered the argument that competition should be understood as a combative process of 'discovery', with a particular emphasis on entrepreneurship in producing such competition (Hayek 1948, 2002; see also Mises 1949). Even if other economists resisted the marginalisation of the perfect competition model, Hayek's depiction of competition was much closer to how business actors actually experienced the world of commerce (Kirzner 2000). The ability of Hayek and his contemporaries to provide a more practical conceptualisation of competition, valorised as a way of enhancing market freedoms, would eventually find a receptive audience in management theory and mainstream economics. But in the immediate postwar context, when it came to translating such ideas into political action, Hayek's meaning of competition 'offered a policy alternative to *both* planning (whether of the socialist, National Socialist or Keynesian variety) *and* traditional liberalism [in the Victorian sense]' (Davies (2014: 40, italics in original). In other words, Hayek did not renounce the state but, rather, wanted to use the authority of the state to define a particular vision of political economy, one in which the calculating spirit of competition was not restricted to the business sphere but extended into other social worlds.

As Davies (2014) suggests, competition is a difficult concept to understand within neoliberalism because the promotion of the idea generates notable paradoxes. First, it appears to offer a role for government that is both active and passive. For instance, the development of competition law from the late nineteenth century, encouraged by the need to break up massive conglomerates and cartels, such as Standard Oil, signalled to early neoliberal thinkers that government should always have a place in policing competition for the greater good. In this sense, antitrust law is 'a strange case of the state acting to *prevent* the outbreak of economic peace' (Davies 2014: 41–2, italics in original). However, the subsequent balancing act, visible today in countless concerns over policy regulation, repeats the primary question: how far should such state interventions go in the name of competition (Gerber 2005, 2010)? Second, this recognition that market competition has to be legislated and planned leads to another paradox, this time focused on (in)equality. According to one common ideological feature in capitalism, all market participants should be treated as formally equal at the start of competitive contests: that is, in a fundamental sense, they are free individuals within a mutually recognised price system. Yet competition can only exist if participants avoid collusion. Thus, even when monitored by a third party to instil a degree of formal fairness, the actual outcome of market competition often results in inequalities. Indeed, the pursuit of inequality – the triumph of one consumer product over another, one standard over another, one firm over another, etc. – is often celebrated in commercial life. In sum, within the neoliberal period, 'inequality *is* "legitimate" because it is publicly and enthusiastically legitimated' (Davies 2014: 37, italics in original).

Such core and seemingly intrinsic tensions surrounding how competition should be represented and orchestrated have the potential to alter our view of 'competitiveness'. Until the middle of the twentieth century, 'competitiveness' was an uncommon expression (for instance, in the *Financial Times*, prior to 1962, there were no references to the word). From the 1960s, however, the word began to attract users in the US, mainly among corporate officials, management experts and popular commentators, but also within political elites sensitive to America's relative position in the capitalist order (notably in relation to Japan and Germany, followed by South Korea and Taiwan). The emergence of a related literature on 'business strategy' was important in augmenting the commonsensical appeal of competitiveness. 'Strategy' has always carried a potent ring for many listeners; its historical use, strongly tied to military and state bureaucracies, seemed to reflect a sense of rational calculation and potential control (Freedman 2013). It is perhaps not surprising that management authors would appropriate and deploy such a notion in the service of agendas linked to competitiveness. Thus, writers such as Alfred Chandler (1962) and Igor Ansoff (1965) helped to popularise the idea that managers should take a long-term vision in co-ordinating their enterprises. According to these experts, acquiring a competitive edge in markets was won not only through examining supply and demand forces in the wider economy, but also through observing rival corporations and other societal actors who could enable or disable competition (Davies 2014). Through such thinking, a related cultural effect was also spawned, one that continues to flourish today: the glorification of the CEO and management guru as a military-like leader or media-savvy celebrity.

This cultural tendency can be illustrated by noting perhaps the best-known authority on business strategy, a figure who has strongly promoted the theme of competitiveness across different institutional spaces: Michael Porter of Harvard Business School. Beginning with his 'five forces' model inspired by industrial economics (1979), Porter's major breakthrough came with the publication of *Competitive Strategy* (1980), followed by the equally influential *Competitive Advantage* (1985). Although not coined by Porter himself, the phrase 'competitive advantage' has now become ubiquitous in business speak, generating a considerable 'Porter industry' of secondary literature (Matthews 2013). In Porter's view, a successful, firm-level competitive strategy was founded upon performing activities different from rivals or performing similar activities in different ways. Such strategies were engineered either through cost-related advantages or product-related differences. By the end of the 1980s, in a period when US business and political elites felt under renewed threat from Japan, Porter's ability to offer digestible and concrete illustrations of success, accompanied as it was by a nationalistic rallying cry of 'competitiveness', found a highly receptive audience. The validation of his approach was further cemented when he was appointed by President Reagan to the Commission on Industrial Competitiveness. In essence, Porter's pivotal contribution, in terms of wider influence, centred on how he offered 'a template through which policymakers and politicians could develop quasi-business strategies for entire nations, as well as cities, regions and neighbourhoods' (Davies 2014: 124; see also Porter 1990). Competitiveness was no mere buzzword at this point but was being normatively endorsed as 'the watchword for a systematic national effort to establish a new competitive culture' (Herzstein and Esty 1987).

But when the managerial logic of competitiveness is introduced into the sphere of territorial government, it brings into focus the analytical problem of what precisely is to be compared and, in turn, ultimately prized. Here, the proliferation of studies on competitiveness under the auspices of the World Economic Forum (WEF) provides a pertinent illustration of wider trends in neoliberal governmentality (Fougner 2006, 2008). Launched in 1979, under the WEF's forerunner, the European Management Forum, the production of such knowledge does not simply explain how the logic of competitiveness is reflected in different institutional settings around the world. Rather, with its ever expanding network of 'competitiveness experts' (which has always included a central place for Porter), the WEF is actively creating a new reality, one with methodologies, norms and expectations of what makes for 'correct' government behaviour. Over the past four decades, this research labour has been accumulated through reports, conferences and consultations. Such outputs tend to carry an apparent seal of authenticity, partly through involving other academics, such as the economist Xavier Sala-i-Martín, a major growth theorist, but also through mimicking neoliberal appeals to statistical rankings and benchmarks. In the *Global Competitiveness Report 2014–2015*, the WEF's flagship publication, competitiveness is defined as 'the set of institutions, policies, and factors that determine the level of productivity of a country' (WEF 2014: 4). This definition sits on top of twelve 'pillars of competitiveness', areas of concern that conceptualise the entire nation – its government agencies, businesses, civil society, education and health, infrastructure, etc. – as all orientated towards the same goal: economic productivity through a league table. Thus, from 2009 to 2015, Switzerland has ranked as the most competitive country on the planet, praised for its 'excellent infrastructure', 'strong cooperation between the academic and business worlds' and a labour market which 'balances employee protection with flexibility and the country's business needs' (WEF 2014: 12).

Three critical points can be offered by way of conclusion. First, similar to the trajectories taken by other neoliberal concepts, competition and, in particular, the embracing narrative of competitiveness, is now embedded in numerous organisations beyond business. In this way, the managerial calculus of control – rooted in a capitalist desire of unending, rivalrous struggle for profit – becomes a general template for individual and organisational comportment. Translating this sense of competitiveness into milieus that have historically kept a distance from capitalist processes, such as social agencies of the state and universities, has not been effected without resistance (Collini 2012). Yet the fear of falling down the latest ranking, under the watchful gaze of customers, authorities and opponents, often serves as a powerful mechanism of surveillance. Second, as noted, the promotion of competition ensures, by definition, winners and losers. But because such jockeying for competitive positions is partly mediated by the state, international institutions and other expert 'disinterested' bodies, the economic and social inequality that is produced tends to be accepted and validated as 'normal', rather than a problem with complex roots to be interrogated. Third, the competitiveness ethic has also been responsible for negative social and psychological conditions. For instance, in the hyper-competitive banking industry, where recruits seek status and fortune, churn rates are very high, along with patterns of addiction (alcohol, drugs) and feelings of control loss (Roose 2014). As in football, deriving one's identity from league-table position seems, in some contexts, to bring little joy for any supporter. If one's team is near the bottom, fear of relegation grows. In mid table, only mediocrity lies. But even if one is at the top, questions quickly surface over how considerable the lead is and how long it will last. The competitive player, in football or otherwise, never seems to be at rest – precisely what a capitalist system demands.

See also: **business, capitalism, choice, enterprise, entrepreneurship, flexibility, management, market, performance, responsibility, state, trade**.

Further reading: Davies 2014; Fougner 2006; Hayek 2002; Porter 1990.

CONSENSUS

For such an apparently mild word, one that is etymologically rooted in the Latin joining of *con* (together) with *sentire* (to feel), 'consensus' can invite strong reactions. As with other neoliberal keywords, it is worth distinguishing between two major uses: consensus as a concept in popular debates, and consensus as an analytical tool when used by academics to define some framework or common sense. Since the mid twentieth century, in the shadow of postwar reconstruction, consensus has become an important term within the world of professional politics. For instance, in the UK context, the phrase 'consensus politics' has been used to capture the idea that '[f]rom the mid-1940s to the mid-1970s, most of [Britain's] political class shared a tacit governing philosophy' (Marquand 1988: 2–3), regardless of whether it was the Conservative Party or the Labour Party in power (see also Heffernan 2002; Toye 2013). In a general sense, therefore, consensus carries a favourable, often aspirational, meaning of inclusivity and shared ground. It can also infer, and in many political uses has more often meant, a strategy of maneuvering around, or away from, differences of opinion in an effort to 'secure the centre' or 'occupy the middle ground'. While such performances often carry the appearance of rational deliberation, and are given normative credence by some writers in democratic theory (Lijphart 1977; Habermas 1996; Dryzek and Niemeyer 2006), one should also be alert to how much under the name of consensus not only glosses over differences between the 'consensus-builders', but also potentially excludes and marginalises others who lie outside the boundaries of the consensus (Mouffe 2005).

Within academic debates on larger themes within neoliberalism, the concept of consensus has come to play a prominent role. In particular, the term has been deployed by authors who explore the relationship between ideology and power in capitalism. The work of the political philosopher Antonio Gramsci (1971) and, specifically, his notions of common sense and cultural hegemony, has been key here. Stuart Hall, a prime mover in the development of cultural studies in the UK, used a Gramscian approach to explore a range of questions related to neoliberalism, including how Thatcherism managed to sustain itself through 'authoritarian populist' appeals (Hall et al. 1978; Hall 1988; Hall and O'Shea 2013). For Hall, the common sense of Thatcherism was pervasive in the UK in the 1980s but also open-ended: as an ideology, it strove to be hegemonic, but required not only legitimation from 'the people', in terms of election votes, but also the capacity to mobilise 'the fears, the anxieties, the lost identities, *of a people*' (Hall 1988: 167, italics mine). Such a common sense was, therefore, never a 'national consensus' incorporating all, but often worked through the demonisation of 'problematic populations', such as miners and trade unions. In a similar manner, other writers have examined how 'New Labour' under Tony Blair often invoked the language of consensus, including through the personification of Blair as a 'consensus politician' and, more fundamentally, via the narrowing of ideological differences with the Conservative Party (for example, both parties now broadly defend privatisation and competitiveness) (Fairclough 2000). Ironically, such a coming together has meant that UK politics risks losing the 'centre ground' to the power of focus groups.

Since the rhetoric of consensus is so popular in the politics of many domestic systems, it is no surprise that the term is a maxim within global diplomacy. In this respect, the conduct of negotiations through the World Trade Organization (WTO) – viewed by some critics as synonymous with neoliberal policies – can afford a pertinent illustration. As a legal principle for conducting trade talks, consensus is enshrined in WTO law (GATT 1994: Article IX). In essence, this rule states that if no delegation has a fundamental objection to an issue in the presence of the full membership, it can be said that consensus has been achieved. Most developing countries consider the retention of this principle as non-negotiable. Such opinions arise from different fears, but the experience of the Executive Board model at the IMF – where, until very recently, such countries had no seat at the table – provides a reminder of how the WTO offers, theoretically at least, more space for expression. However, the reality of WTO diplomacy presents a more problematic picture. For example, the process of 'engineering' consensus at the launch of trade talks, such as in Doha in 2001, featured a wide range of power tactics directed by developed countries against developing states. Such approaches began with the US and the EU presenting their agenda as a *fait accompli* that others should tacitly accept. Behind the scenes, those who did protest were threatened with legal action, denied political sympathy in other issue areas or bought off with financial aid. Thus, the promotion of the Doha Declaration by the US and the EU as a success for WTO consensus was, in practice, partly founded upon an unjust contest where anti-democratic practices prevailed (Jawara and Kwa 2004; Eagleton-Pierce 2013).

But perhaps the major use of the term consensus in relation to neoliberalism – one deployed across popular, political and academic settings – is the phrase 'Washington Consensus'. For many, this is interchangeable with neoliberalism. Coined in 1989 by John Williamson, an economist at the Peterson Institute think tank, it offered a shorthand for developing-country-reform prescriptions designed by three major Washington D.C. institutions: the World Bank, the IMF and the US Treasury Department. For Williamson, this consensus could be summarised in a list of ten reforms, including the declared need for such countries to undertake fiscal discipline, privatisation and the policing of property rights (Williamson 1990, 2000). In its wake, the term 'Washington Consensus' has taken on a life of its own, with frequent uses by those on the political left to imply an organised set of intentions founded upon, and for,

American hegemony (Chomsky 1998; Klein 2008). With the popularisation of the notion, along with critical investigation into World Bank and IMF agendas, Williamson was at pains to distance his understanding of the concept from 'all those unreconstructed opponents of reform who yearned for socialism' (Williamson 2003: 325). By the turn of the century, through a series of ideological contests, within which related terms such as governance played a key role, a post-Washington Consensus emerged (Kuczynski and Williamson 2003; Rodrik 2006; Serra and Stiglitz 2008). Whether or not there is a consensus over the policy content of the post-Washington Consensus remains a matter of dispute, but, at the very least, there now exists a recognition – heard from the World Bank to Ouagadougou – that 'excessive market fundamentalism' has gone too far and that, at least on paper, any development plan must pay attention to factors such as poverty reduction and domestic institutions (Stiglitz 2008; for a deeper critique, see Fine and Jomo, 2006).

In sum, claims about 'consensus' are not merely about the gentle mobilising of actors around a focal point, or the dry, bureaucratic making of policy, but, rather, often signal a struggle over the power of certain groups to define the very boundaries of 'the political', a restricted space where ideas about stability and change are judged. Part of the problem involved in analysing such claims centres on how the associated references to freedom, community and, in particular, partnership – all present in neoliberal vocabulary – often create the impression that power can be managed, mitigated or even avoided in the pursuit of the greater good. The reality of consensus-building, however, may involve very different outcomes, including the subtle marginalising of the least resourceful agents. Another risk, which often tends to be reproduced in academic debates, concerns the reification of neoliberalism as some coherent project, for which the term 'consensus' is invoked. Yet, in many explanations of neoliberalism, 'consensus' may not be the best analytical term. As Jamie Peck has rightly expressed it, 'the practice of neoliberal statecraft is inescapably, and profoundly, marked by compromise, calculation, and contradiction. There is no blueprint. There is not even a map' (Peck 2010: 210).

See also: **adjustment, class, community, freedom, network, openness, participation, stakeholder, vision**.

Further reading: Hall and O'Shea 2013; Toye 2013; Williamson 1990, 2000.

DEVELOPMENT

Along with market, development is a linchpin concept within neoliberal vocabulary, one that informs and organises a cluster of other ideas, including growth, freedom, participation, governance and reform. Derived from the Old French verb *desvoleper*, it took until the mid eighteenth century before development, as a noun, entered English. Initially, the term meant the opposite of 'envelop': that is, to unwrap or unfold. Or as Samuel Johnson (1755) has it: 'To disengage from something that enfolds and conceals'. From the late eighteenth century, within debates in the natural sciences, the concept was used interchangeably with evolution to describe how an organism moved from an 'immature' to a 'mature' form, or, in other words, from a 'lower' to a 'higher' status (Williams 1983[1976]: 121). The decisive metaphorical extension of development – from a biological term to one that could be generalised to social and political life – appeared around the mid nineteenth century (Esteva 1992; Cowen and Shenton 1996). For instance, Karl Marx's (1990 [1867]) writings are suffused with references to development, while E. B. Tylor, an important early anthropologist, referred to his arguments on social evolution as simply 'the development theory' (Tylor 1871). This core meaning of individuals and nations moving *in toto* through stages of evolution, on a similar trajectory, and towards a 'more perfect' condition, has served to 'frame a formidable and durable vision of human history' (Ferguson 1997: 154). However, despite the taken-for-grantedness of the concept, the neoliberal inflection of development needs to be carefully studied, particularly around the question of what subjects become politicised or depoliticised under its name.

The malleability of 'development' as a political term – a vessel into which actors could empty their own desires and aspirations – was already appreciated by the early twentieth century. In the interwar period, the notion was harnessed by UK and French colonial bureaucrats to relegitimise their African empires. Significantly, this meant that '[d]evelopment was something to be done *to* and *for* Africa, not with it' (Cooper 1997: 65). But such strategies were only partially effective because the concept was equally appropriated by trade unionists and political leaders in different African countries, around labour policy and economic planning (Cooper 1997). These struggles, in the sunset of colonialism, act as an important preface to some major themes in the postwar problematisation of development, including the incorporation of neoliberalism. First, the 'project' of development was conceived in universal terms. For the newly crowned superpower, the US, the ending of the European empires, with their trade preferences and privileges, was a non-negotiable item. Therefore, the rhetoric surrounding development would have to grapple with the reality of new political sovereigns and the Universal Declaration of Human Rights. Second, once the non-Western world was defined by what it lacked – 'underdevelopment', as President Truman made clear in 1949 – the problem of how to crack the development conundrum began in earnest (Rist 2008; Escobar 1995). What this meant in practice was the professionalisation of the 'new science' of development: this involved institutions such as the United Nations (UN) and the World Bank, the forming of development studies as an academic field and the rise of a plethora of civil society groups. In short, 'the development industry' was born.

Within this social world, language has always been carefully crafted, with a tendency for the use of euphemisms that, intentionally or not, often seem aimed at minimising political offence and encouraging forms of consensus. The very naming of the non-Western 'Other' is emblematic of these practices, a point long recognised by postcolonial authors (Said 1978). By the 1960s, 'underdevelopment' (synonymous with 'backward', 'primitive' or 'traditional') was beginning to decline as the dominant term to define such countries. These changes were partly encouraged by writers associated with the so-called 'dependency school', who contested not only the presumed 'natural state' of the modernisation thesis à la Walt Rostow (1960), but also how Western countries, as the 'core' of the capitalist system, actively undermined development in the 'periphery' via their control over global markets and sources of capital (Baran 1957; Dos Santos 1970; Cardoso and Faletto 1979). As Andre Gunder Frank (1967) forcefully argued, if systems of class and power between the core and the periphery did not change, programs under the name of 'development' could actually create 'underdevelopment'. The subsequent rise of the more optimistically sounding 'developing country' category, with its implied intrinsic movement and advancement, has to be read in the light of such criticism. At the same time, the larger 'developing world' notion was used synonymously with 'Third World' by many, but, as the Cold War ended, the former gradually overtook the three-worlds theory as the major orthodox collective category. This effort to bracket such a wide variety of countries under a single label has, however, faced reoccuring criticism. For instance, by 1971, a new term – 'least developed countries' – was coined to account for those nations who exhibit the lowest indicators of socio-economic development.

How have ideas and political forces associated with neoliberalism shaped the meaning and practice of development? Across a very complex terrain, different debates can be indicated. In the late 1970s and 1980s, a group of prominent economists were influential in shaping policy ideas in Western governments, international organisations and the wider media. Arguing against Keynesian-inspired approaches that were popular in the 1950s and 1960s, writers such as Deepak Lal (1983), Peter Bauer (1981) and Anne Krueger (1974, 1990) helped to usher in 'a counter-revolution in development theory and practice' (Toye 1987: vii). According to these experts, poorer countries in the Global South were not radically distinct from those found in the richer North. Rather, the basic insights of neoclassical economics – notably, conceiving of all agents, both producers and consumers, as rational calculating individuals who respond to price signals – could be applied to all sorts of postcolonial nations across Latin America, Africa and Asia. In this sense, history and geography were deemed less important; difference, in short, was overstated. At the level of policymaking, such countries were criticised for 'over-extending' the public sector and channelling resources into grandiose projects that appeared designed by, and for, elites. It was argued that all forms of government controls on the economy worked against trade and financial openness, resulting in negative effects on private enterprise and economic growth. According to this logic, if poor development performance was found, it was the fault of developing-country governments for implementing the wrong policies (Toye 1987). In turn, these ideas progressively found a home at the World Bank and the IMF, an important consequence since such institutions could offer emergency conditionality loans, as well as shape the 'global commonsense' on development policy advice (Chwieroth 2010; Harrison 2004; Woods 2006).

The development orthodoxy of the 1980s and early 1990s, as propagated by these international organisations, along with tacit and explicit support from Western governments and powerful corporations, had serious implications for many countries. In return for loans, the World Bank and the IMF introduced structural adjustment policies (SAPs) that were ostensibly designed to address balance-of-payments crises and fund development projects. The total loan book grew considerably during this period. For instance, from 1980 to 1991, the World Bank committed US$41 billion under such schemes (World Bank 1992). A common SAP formula of so-called 'reforms', deployed as a template that would seemingly fit any country, included general cuts to state expenditure, the devaluation of the currency, increased trade liberalisation at the border and the privatisation of state agencies (Brown *et al.* 2000; SAPRIN 2004). Yet, as even a cursory glance of the results of these programmes illustrated, few economic agendas associated with SAPs – conceptually bracketed as 'divorced' from politics – were successful. On the contrary, as argued by Joseph Stiglitz, former Chief Economist at the World Bank, far from promoting economic stability, SAPs appeared to do precisely the opposite, leading to:

hunger and riots in many countries; and even when results were not so dire, even when they managed to eke out some growth for a while, often the benefits went disproportionately to the better-off, with those at the bottom sometimes facing even greater poverty.

(Stiglitz 2002: xiv)

Although generalisations and causal ties are difficult to draw, the social consequences of SAPs were often severe, with increases in both unemployment and the cost of living in many countries, effects that fell disproportionately on women (Watkins 1995; Zack-Williams 2000).

In short, the critics of the neoliberal reading of development began arguing that the state had been unnecessarily 'hollowed out' in key areas, resulting in austerity conditions. According to these writers, 'trickle-down' economics, whereby wealth effects were claimed to eventually reach the poor, did not work. Rather, the economy was embedded in society, not the other way around. This critique existed in three forms, from its milder versions that called for 'adjustment with a human face' (Cornia *et al.* 1987), through the comparative benefits of the East Asian model of capitalism, where governments played a larger role in the market (Wade 2004) and, onwards, to the stronger attacks issued by civil society groups (Watkins 1995). By the mid 1990s, a new take on development had been forged. For Dani Rodrik (2007), the new orthodoxy on development policy is a kind of 'augmented Washington Consensus', one which still contains the core 'Victorian virtue' of 'free markets and sound money' (Krugman 1995: 29), but now incorporates a range of 'second generation reforms' (Serra and Stiglitz 2008). These reforms have stretched the meaning and application of development to embrace questions about the institutional design of governments and societies. The rise of the 'governance' agenda at the World Bank is representative of this shift in thinking. By 1996, under the leadership of James Wolfensohn, governance came to be associated with the rule of law, state effectiveness and, in particular, controlling corruption. By the turn of the century, another three dimensions were added to the mix: voice and accountability, political stability and regulatory quality (Kaufmann *et al.* 2007). Moreover, through the design of all these new development initiatives, a new vision for diplomacy emerged under the name of partnership. According to this line of argument, the days of top-down dictation by World Bank officials are over: ownership for development now lies primarily with representative governments (Harrison 2004).

In the context of this general widening of the notion of development, two significant extensions require noting. One concerns the idea of human development, a term that was popularised from 1990 by

Mahbub-ul-Haq, the founder of the annual UN-produced *Human Development Report*. Inspired by the work of Amartya Sen (1999), Haq argued that human development 'is a process of enlarging people's choices', not only in respect to economic wellbeing, but also 'political freedom, guaranteed human rights and personal self-respect' (United Nations Development Programme 1990: 1). In other words, for Haq and Sen, it was important to understand why economic growth, while necessary, did not always translate into wider human development. One can read this agenda, now fully quantified into indexes and rankings, as 'a partially successful UN counteroffensive to the priorities of the Washington Consensus' (Jolly *et al.* 2009: 26). However, over time, the distinctiveness of the human-development paradigm has faded, often through subtle ways, such as the involvement of the World Bank in the wider UN Millennium Development Goals. Elsewhere, a second major extension of development centres on connections to environmental sustainability. Like human development, the term 'sustainable development' was a product of UN thinking, first coined by the Brundtland Commission report, *Our Common Future* (World Commission on Environment and Development 1987). Now a commonly invoked objective of other international bureaucracies, states and businesses, sustainable development remains a liberal vision which aspires to reconcile capitalism with planetary survival, even if the historical data suggests a collision course would be a more apt metaphor.

   In sum, 'development' is a paradoxical term in the lexicon of neoliberalism. On the one hand, it remains an incredibly powerful notion, guiding how countless actors imagine and practise their lives, from government executives and city planners to community organisers and the person in the street. In keeping with the historical tradition of liberal ideology, development often carries a melioristic overtone, inspiring others with the idea that upward progress in the human condition is possible. This particular thread of meaning – associated with a sense of hope and freedom that can be adapted to any context – undoubtedly helps to explain why the concept is continually refreshed by its primary users, despite failures or setbacks that might cast doubt on such a master frame. At the same time, when state bureaucracies and academic professions associated with 'development' convert the lives of billions into discrete projects or programmable targets, the concept often appears as a 'fragile', even 'feeble', expression for giving 'substance and meaning to thought and behaviour' (Esteva 1992: 8). Despite the conceptual stretching of development from a so-called 'pure' economic sense to a range of other dimensions, one should not miss how continuities remain with postwar modernisation theory. Above all, this is evident in the belief that the spreading of capitalist ideology is a good thing. It is this inherent tension between recognising human diversity yet advocating global prescriptions that lies at the heart of many struggles over the idea. And perhaps we can discern in this echoes of the eighteenth century and how an original meaning shifted from concealment to opening out – but not quite.

See also: **capitalism, emerge, environment, freedom, governance, growth, market, participation, power, reform, state**.

Further reading: Cowen and Shenton 1996; Esteva 1992; Rist 2008.

DIVERSITY

Since its entry into English in the fourteenth century, diversity has carried a core meaning associated with difference and variety. The term's rise to prominence among professionals in the late twentieth century is a product of several factors, not all of which can be easily classified as neoliberal in their genesis and form. In the early postwar period, in the shadow of the UN Declaration of Human Rights and the push towards decolonisation, protest movements within many countries galvanised around redistributive justice demands – in particular, the principle that all individuals should be equal before the law. Within the US, the historical legacy of social inequalities and injuries – which informed the politics of race, gender, class and power – provided the impulse for new thinking on equal opportunities. The landmark passage of the Civil Rights Act in 1964, which made it illegal to discriminate against workers on the basis of race, colour, religion, sex or national origin, was the culmination of a vigorous and organised series of protests. In the late 1960s and 1970s, as a result of this legislation and, in particular, the founding of the Equal Employment Opportunity Commission, a federal agency empowered to investigate cases of discrimination, many organisations began training their employees in the new legal requirements. In other words, the institutional focus during this period can be understood through the prism of compliance, whereby companies instructed workers – both senior executives and rank-and-file – in an effort 'to avoid costly and embarrassing lawsuits and negative publicity' (Anand and Winters 2008: 357).

In Google's Ngram book search, a tool for mapping language patterns, we learn that the term 'equal opportunity' peaked in popularity in the late 1970s. Despite a brief subsequent rise during the late 1980s and early 1990s, the phrase now seems to be in decline. This is not to say that struggles around rights and powers associated with 'equal opportunity' were (and are) not ongoing within many countries. Rather, from the late 1980s, within the field of American business in particular, phrases such as 'diversity management', 'diverse workforce' and, for a period,'the multicultural organisation' began to appear as new umbrella expressions (Copeland 1988;Thomas 1990, 1991; Cox 1991). In part, this shift in terminology was due to a perceived failure of affirmative-action policies and training methods, which remained focused on assimilating less privileged groups into corporate cultures. Three concerns stood out. First, large numbers of women and minorities were still not represented and retained, particularly in higher-level positions, which tended to be occupied by white males. In 1987, this particular problem was thrown into sharper relief when an influential report, *Workforce 2000*, forecast that, due to demographic changes, 85 per cent of new entrants into the employment market would be white women or persons of colour (Johnston and Packer 1987). Second, some firms reported that members of dominant groups felt excluded from such training and were, therefore, critical of preferential treatment received by targeted groups.Third, when considering commercial implications, some experts began to argue that issues linked to equal opportunity were not simply significant from a defensive posture of legal obligation. Instead, in a so-called 'globalising' world,'sensitivity to culture', with an emphasis on 'inclusion', could generate 'better decision making, greater creativity and innovation, and more successful marketing' (Cox 1991: 34).

By the turn of the millennium, within North America and extending elsewhere, a cottage industry of consultants and in-house officers had emerged under the 'less threatening discourse of "managing diversity"' (Kirton and Greene 2005: 4). Depending upon the social histories, legal regimes and working practices within each country, such trends have moved at different paces and taken alternative forms (Klarsfeld 2010; Mor Barak 2014). But, for our purposes, what is neoliberal about this turn to diversity management? One important feature of such agendas concerns how the analytical gaze has widened, away from an overt spotlight on 'problematic' social groups, to embrace all employees in the organisation. In part, this helps to counter two of the major criticisms outlined: that corporations were failing to address the ideal of (national or global) demographic representation and, of equal importance, the latent anxieties of dominant (white, male) groups within the organisation.The neoliberal shaping of diversity management is, therefore, particularly pronounced in appeals to both individualism and universalism. Thus, some corporate policies now entice the worker to 'bring their entire life' into the office, not only through joining identity groups based on national heritage, race, religion or family role, but also through a raft of other pursuits, such as 'ethnic food days' or, particularly popular, outreach community programmes in schools. As one firm put it, '[d]iversity is about what makes each of us unique and includes our backgrounds, personality, life experiences and beliefs' (Deloitte 2011: 5). Through emphasising these aspects, the corporation begins to appear as a microcosm of what is prized in modern culture: the so-called 'cosmopolitan' community. Diversity management argues, therefore, that enforced assimilationism should be avoided: the 'difference' attached to the individual is not a problem, but part of the solution (Gordon 1995).

While such activities within the firm have increased, the justification for diversity management now extends to claims that a more 'culturally competent' workforce is a more profitable one. Prior to the mainstreaming of neoliberalism, this type of argument was rarely invoked. Today, diversity is conceptualised as a strategic priority in the competitive 'war for talent', a popular corporate phrase originally coined by a McKinsey consultant (see, for example, Hewlett and Rashid 2013). Such thinking has advanced a number of arguments, including claims that heterogeneous organisations nurture more flexible problem-solvers who are not hampered by groupthink. Many authors place a particular emphasis on the need to understand local markets and customers, which is best accomplished through the internal knowledge of a more diverse workplace (Cox and Blake 1991; Fernandez 1993). More recent studies have tried to measure such assumptions statistically, including arguments that diversity is positively correlated with higher sales revenues, more customers and greater market share (Herring 2009; Catalyst 2011; McKinsey & Company 2011). With a sharper focus on what diversity *does* to business performance, other writers and consultants have subsequently emphasised context-specific factors and risks involved in operationalising the diversity agenda (see a literature review in the UK's Department for Business, Innovation and Skills (BIS) 2013). As one author argued when comparing workers who flip burgers with those who design marketing campaigns, claims 'that diversity improves outcomes may be inaccurate if the task involves no problem-solving or prediction' (Page 2007: 319). Thus, diversity management has fully arrived on the corporate agenda worldwide, with appeals to the 'business case' positioned alongside, integrated within or, at times, superseding the 'ethical case'.

It might appear from reading the diversity visions of major public and private institutions, complete with smiling faces of different colours, that such policies are creating a fairer (and more productive) society. In its own terms, 'best practices' linked to diversity initiatives can certainly be identified and so can the benefits from new legislation in this area. But there is something profoundly unsettling about talk of diversity, for it is also apparent that countless examples of sexist, racist, ageist and homophobic discrimination are alive within organisations that laud their diversity schemes. Moreover, such forms of prejudice are often historically and institutionally embedded, seemingly resistant to major change, with government policy sometimes acting to hinder, rather than help, the cause of social reform. As Kirton and Greene (2005: 289) have concluded, on the basis of examining a considerable body of evidence from North America and Europe, there exists in many organisations a dominant privileging of the 'white, male, non-disabled, heterosexual, 25–40 years norm'. Moreover, the further one moves up the corporate hierarchy, the greater the likelihood of seeing this pattern consolidate. Consider, for example, the gender and racial composition of boards for the top 100 US-based firms (and this is not confined to the US). In 2004, 71 per cent of the total population of board members were white men. Almost ten years later, according to 2012 figures, this figure was 68 per cent, a negligible 'gain for diversity'. When one looks at the top 500 US-based companies and focuses on the powerful position of board chair, the trend is even more pronounced. On this count, in 2012, 93 per cent of individuals who occupied this role were white men (Alliance for Board Diversity 2013).

Such criticism reveals how gaps (sometimes large) exist between rhetoric and reality in the field of diversity management. But critique can also go beyond these more obvious points. Through a Foucauldian reading, Ahonen et al. (2014: 272) argue that corporate diversity agendas tend to convert humans into governable categories for the purpose of finding 'an optimal mix of talent'. When diversity becomes defined as anything based on individualised difference, not only does it 'become everything and nothing', but the historical ties to conditions of social (in)justice can 'weaken or break altogether' (Ahonen et al. 2014: 272; see also Swan 2010). In this sense, the term diversity 'invokes the existence of difference and variety without any necessary commitment to action or redistributive social justice' (Deem and Ozga 1997: 31; see also Ahmed 2012). Perhaps more profoundly, at times the circulation of the concept of diversity in the context of neoliberalism may further conceal, rather than reveal, the forms of power moving through institutions. A person impacted by racism may, for example, be reticent to speak out if the organisation, supported by its latest diversity statistics and branding profile, publically declares that 'racism is not a problem here'. It is also telling how masculinity is not explored in any detail in the mainstream diversity literature. But explaining the male bias at the top of major organisations would involve exploring the cultural construction of (hyper-)masculine codes and norms, such as men who avoid the appearance of any 'feminine' behaviour, the cult of the competitive winner who sacrifices everything for their career and the concealing of any emotions that may be read as vulnerable or weak. Finally, another major silence in the diversity management debates is class, for its absence no doubt affords a benefit to senior managers on high salaries. Thus, unmasking and confronting these forms of power requires more than, or something other than, a standard diversity plan.

See also: **business, community, freedom, management, market, participation, power, stakeholder**.

Further reading: Ahmed 2012; Gordon 1995; Kirton and Greene 2005.

EMERGE

'Emerge', from the Latin *emergere*, refers to an object that rises out of, or up from, a prior state of immersion, particularly in water. Figurative meanings accompanied the word almost from the outset. Hence, emerge evokes a visual sense of something that comes into view from obscurity or marginality, possibly in a sudden or unexpected way. One historical meaning of the word from the nineteenth century, which still carries relevance today, concerns how emergence is often used to define a positive or progressive evolution away from 'subjection', 'suffering' or 'embarrassment'. In this sense, the definition of an emergent culture or politics can only be adequately understood in relation to a discussion of dominant perspectives held within a given social system (Williams 1977). Within capitalism, all processes that generate new sources of wealth are sought after and keenly studied, particularly during periods of economic contraction. Emergence, as a process term, can therefore be paired with older liberal ideas such as innovation, growth and development. Thus, the notion of emerging technologies points to those scientific advances that may find potential commercial applications if successfully commodified. But for every new technology that becomes a business proposition, there are many others that never truly emerge. Corporate and political leaders often face acute and reoccurring problems trying to identify and judge which technologies could emerge, how such trends may shape competitiveness and what social and environmental consequences may be generated as a result. The condition of emergence – of 'permanent change', to invoke a conventional business phrase – may therefore be at one and the same time both exhilarating and unnerving.

From the 1950s, the phrase 'emerging territories' was sometimes invoked to define those countries in the process of gaining independence from colonial rule. But in the neoliberal context, the most visible appeal to 'emerging' comes when the word is linked to markets. The notion of emerging markets comes directly out of a particular capitalist ethos of expansion and commodification. The concept was coined in 1981 by a World Bank economist, Antoine van Agtmael. His aim was to entice private businesses, notably Wall Street banks and their allies, to invest in developing countries. Van Agtmael argued that such territories, while often perceived as lacking stability for economic and political reasons, were still growing at fast rates and thus offered possibilities to make money. Initially, however, van Agtmael stumbled in what one might call his sales pitch, calling his proposed investment vehicle the 'Third World Equity Fund'. The bankers were intrigued, but suggested that the phrase 'Third World' was not a good branding strategy. Van Agtmael agreed that the name had an image problem, 'rife with negative associations of flimsy polyester, cheap toys, rampant corruption, Soviet-style tractors, and flooded rice paddies' (van Agtmael 2007: 5). In point of fact, although this was not noted by van Agtmael, the 'Three Worlds' theory was also a common framing device used by many critics of capitalism during the 1960s and 1970s (the term 'third world' dates from 1952 – see Wolf-Phillips 1987; see also Solarz 2014 for a review and Rao 2010 for a perceptive critique). According to writers associated with the so-called 'dependency theory', the Third World would always tend to occupy a subservient position in the world economy due to exploitative practices conducted by First World governments and firms (Baran 1957; Frank 1966; Ghosh 2001).

In an effort to distance himself conceptually and, importantly, politically from such depictions, van Agtmael proposed a more 'positive and invigorating' phrase: 'emerging markets'. Whereas Third World implied 'stagnation', emerging markets 'suggested progress, uplift, and dynamism', as he expressed it (van Agtmael 2007: 5). His investment product was thus re-christened the 'Emerging Markets Growth Fund'. As the 1980s unfolded, the phrase began to acquire resonance within the social world of international finance, each new iteration helping to make the concept appear legitimate (for early discussions, see Errunza 1983; Errunza and Padmanabhan 1988). By 1985, the Emerging Markets Growth Fund was launched, and received enthusiastic backing from the Reagan Administration, which was keen to further internationalise 'market-orientated policies' (Farnsworth 1985). In 1988, the investment bank Morgan Stanley established the MSCI Emerging Markets Index, an equity grouping that contained 10 countries (Argentina, Brazil, Chile,

Greece, Jordan, Malaysia, Mexico, Philippines, Portugal and Thailand). Every five years since then, the index has undergone a reclassification to reflect whom the bankers consider worthy of the emerging-market appellation. In a major update in 1997, China, India and Russia were added to the index. Moves can be made in other directions as well: Israel 'graduated' to developed market status, while countries who impose capital restrictions on investors, such as Argentina and Pakistan in the past, have been removed from the index as a penalty (Bambaci *et al.* 2012). In short, by the 2000s, the notion of emerging markets had become so common in business, political and media writings that it almost appeared to unseat or, at the very least, rival the previous dominant group category: developing country.

Recounting the creation of the emerging-markets concept is not to deny, in any kind of crude manner, that significant economic changes are taking place in such locations. Rather, the point is to reveal the larger political economy expressed by such categories. However, with popularity comes the risk of extending the concept too far and, thus, potential devaluation of the original value of the term. By 2008, *The Economist* asked a question many businesses were thinking: 'is it time to retire the phrase "emerging markets"?'. Part of the worry has centred on inconsistent methodologies and statistics used by organisations with an interest in such matters. For instance, the IMF now deems Taiwan and South Korea to be 'developed', yet stocks listed in these countries account for a considerable portion of major funds, such as the Vanguard FTSE Emerging Markets ETF. In a desire for greater definitional precision, as well as to drum up new business, a series of country classifications have arisen, most notably the BRICs (Brazil, Russia, India and China) acronym and the Next 11 group, both coined by former Goldman Sachs Chief Economist Jim O'Neill (2001, 2011). In the struggle to define and profit from the BRICs, O'Neill has even proposed that the term 'emerging' now lacks meaning: 'It's just pathetic to call these four emerging markets'. Rather, he sees them as simply 'growth markets' that have arrived on the 'global stage' (quoted in Hughes 2011). Indeed, the distinction between 'advanced' and 'emerging' economies has only become more confusing in light of the global financial crisis, which led, at least initially, to significantly weaker prospects for the former compared to the latter, leading one major thinker to argue that 'the shock to public finances is undermining the analytical relevance of conventional classifications' (El-Erian 2010; for further critique, see Sidaway 2012; Kynge and Wheatley 2015).

Elsewhere, in a related conceptual link, it is worth noting how the term 'transition economy' also reveals the same normative sense of progress to (Western-derived) capitalism. Within political science and law, the notion of transition carries the imprint (or stain, for some) of modernisation theory: the argument that all countries, including the poorest, are on the path to economic 'takeoff' if Western ideas and institutions are adopted (Rostow 1960). The field of 'transitology' has thus been concerned with processes of political regime change but particularly the movement from authoritarianism to democracy (for foundational texts, see Rustow 1970; O'Donnell and Schmitter 1986; for a review, see Gans-Morse 2004). With the end of the Cold War, the 'reform' of post-Communist societies towards market-inspired norms and rules became a significant preoccupation of Western policymakers, institutions such as the IMF and businesses seeking new export markets. From the early 1990s, Russia and Eastern European countries experienced these strategies of transition – sometimes referred to as 'shock therapy' – which included demands for the massive privatisation of state assets and the closure of unproductive factories. The economist Jeffrey Sachs was particularly important in advising many Eastern European governments on the presumed benefits of such policies (Wilson 2014). The consolidation of practices associated with neoliberalism was further enhanced through European Union enlargement, a story which is subtly told in the case of Poland by Shields (2012). In short, similar to emerging, the notion of transition remains bound to a teleological core: the presumption that all societies are converging on a single endpoint of liberal capitalism.

See also: **capitalism, change, development, global, growth, innovation, investment, market**.

Further reading: O'Neill 2011; Sidaway 2012; Solarz 2014.

ENTERPRISE

Since the late fifteenth century, 'enterprise' has carried an abstract sense of a person or a process undertaking a challenge, particularly marked by an arduous or daring spirit. The use of the expression in situations of war has a long legacy; for instance, since 1775, the US Navy has christened many of its most prestigious ships with the word. Enterprise as denoting individual effort or something that can be conflated with commerce – now commonplace in the period of neoliberalism – was found in early-eighteenth-century discourse, but the most notable consolidation of this meaning took place during the nineteenth century in the context of the industrial revolution. In the twentieth century, from the interwar period into the early Cold War, when socialism was potent as an idea and a political project, 'private enterprise' or 'free enterprise' were very popular expressions in Western media and intellectual circles. As Raymond Williams (1983[1976]) perceptively noted, within this particular period, when the larger concept of capitalism came under renewed scrutiny and appeared to suffer from a legitimacy deficit, the notion of enterprise often took its place. For some writers, championing the 'enterprise system' appeared to carry the same intent as defending the 'capitalist system'. For instance, in 1938 in Paris, at the Colloque Walter Lippmann gathering of notable economists, neoliberalism, cast as a political project for the future, was partly defined in reference to 'free enterprise' (Mirowski and Plehwe 2009; Peck 2010).

This depiction of enterprise as synonymous with business has continued into the present, although the conceptual diffusion of the term has been nurtured by many different sources. One important political testing and deployment of the expression emerged in the UK from the 1970s under the influence of groups associated with the Conservative Party. In 1974, prompted by Keith Joseph, an influential Tory politician, the Conservative Party approved the establishment of the Centre for Policy Studies, a think tank for the declared promotion of 'free market economics'. Margaret Thatcher, at the time five years from assuming the position of prime minister, was appointed as vice-chair. In its foundational document, the Centre proudly declared that it would 'think the unthinkable' and, importantly, foster a 'culture of enterprise' (Morris 1991: 23). According to Joseph, UK postwar policy had been 'semi-socialist', resulting in a private sector that had been forced to work with 'one hand tied behind its back' (Joseph 1974b). How to unleash what one Tory memorandum termed a 'new crusade for private enterprise' (Harris 1974) was, in reality, still unclear, not least because, as noted by Joseph in a draft prospectus for the Centre, 'denationalisation' (an early term for privatisation) was at the time 'not politically feasible' (Joseph 1974a).

But by 1979, as Thatcher entered 10 Downing Street and her brand of conservative ideas began to spread, the appeal to an 'enterprise culture' took off and acquired a degree of social acceptance. In 1984, Nigel Lawson, the Chancellor of the Exchequer, called not simply for a shift at the level of policy to 'rediscover' an enterprise culture (depicting a UK that had 'lost its way') but, more profoundly, for the need to fight and change 'the psychology of two generations' (Lawson 1984). In one sense, therefore, the phrase 'enterprise culture' tends to applaud policy agendas where business and, in particular, the category of the consumer are treated as desirable models for changes in society as a whole. Thus, in the UK, from Thatcher through Blair and on to Cameron, the full and partial privatisation of former state assets – such as the railways and telecommunications and, later, health and education – were advocated as promoting efficiency savings via the diversification of consumer choice. Beyond the UK, the common appeal to an enterprise culture has also found itself attached to multiple policy goals, including the abolition of controls on wages, prices and dividends; the reduction in the burden of taxation (especially corporate and high-income); efforts to promote employment; and the larger drive to develop industries that compete in a 'global marketplace'.

Yet the term 'enterprise' would not have acquired such mainstream popularity – or, at least, within the minds of certain policymakers, corporate leaders and media commentators – if the debate was focused only on the technical details of business in public policy. Lawson's ambition to change the 'psychology' of the UK speaks to how enterprise – as a malleable and ambiguous conceptual frame – has been used to endorse a set of particular dispositions or mentalities as desirable for all. It should be no surprise that these core behavioural attributes are borrowed from the corporate world and, in particular, the model of the entrepreneur (a term closely allied to enterprise). Entrepreneurs are often described as living exciting lives, moving at a fast pace, boldly taking on new risks and winning high rewards (implicitly tapping into the deeper sense of enterprise as involving courageous activity). Thus, the desire to bring about an enterprise culture is also promoted through appeals to 'techniques of the self', whereby individuals are encouraged to self-care and self-manage their affairs (Rose 1992: 147). By contrast, those who appear disinterested or hostile to enterprise culture are often cast in a negative light, such as being overly dependent on state welfare. This distinction is particularly sharp in the case of so-called 'enterprise zones' set up in US cities as a way to counter deprivation and the presumed absence of a business ethic (see an early justification in Ferrara 1982). Elsewhere, beyond Anglo-American heartlands, similar ideas have spread widely, yet are often given nationally specific adaptations. For instance, in India, according to the inflated opinions of some elites, enterprising instincts are projected as not simply the reason for the country's recent economic growth but as a 'natural attribute of "all" Indians', present, but often unexploited, since precolonial times (Gooptu 2013: 11).

A very important extension of 'enterprise' has been to preface the word with 'social'. This apparently innocent elaboration is much more complex than might initially appear. While the precise origins are unclear, the phrase 'social enterprise' tends to denote, as a baseline definition, an organisation that places social and/or environmental goals at the core of its mission, rather than the maximisation of profits for shareholders, the common motivation of a commercial firm. The difficulty with the term comes when one set of advocates of social enterprise, who apply it to their activities, may contest the legitimacy of other groups who do the same (Ridley-Duff and Bull 2011). These distinctions are, at root, often reflective of competing views regarding the purpose of capitalism (or even if it should exist), the role of the state and relations between other societal institutions. The first users of the phrase were charities, voluntary groups and cooperatives. These organisations wanted to generate extra income for social endeavours or embrace a 'contracting culture' by tendering their resources to third parties. Thus, Oxfam's Enterprise Development Programme provides loans and grants to businesses in the developing world, promoted with the tagline, 'We invest where others don't go and where the potential for social impact is highest'. Later users of the expression have been businesses, including powerful firms which, in the era of corporate social responsibility, are keen to invest their surpluses in 'public interest' or 'fair trade' enterprises. However, such efforts have met with criticism, especially around charges that corporations seize upon the legitimacy of 'doing social good' in order to burnish their reputation, which, in turn, may consolidate a 'charity-based' approach to the problems of the market economy, rather than a more fundamental analysis of rights and responsibilities.

See also: **business, capitalism, choice, competition, entrepreneurship, flexibility, freedom, individual, innovation, market, private, responsibility, stakeholder**.

Further reading: Gooptu 2013; Morris 1991; Rose, 1992.

ENTREPRENEURSHIP

In the fifteenth century, the term 'entrepreneur', derived from the French *entreprenour*, referred to someone who undertakes or manages an activity. Richard Cantillon made the first scholarly reference in 1730, but it was not until the nineteenth century that it began to be debated by other writers. Jean-Baptiste Say, the French economist, was one of the first to introduce the term to a wider English-speaking audience, when the translation of his *A Treatise on Political Economy* (1971[1821]) noted how the word was difficult to render and, as a consequence, may be better expressed as 'adventurer'. According to Say, the entrepreneur was a business figure who could be found in many fields, but tended to be 'a person who takes upon himself the immediate responsibility, risk, and conduct of a concern of industry' (Say 1971[1821]: 78), a widespread meaning still found today. However, it would wrong to say that entrepreneur was in common currency, a point bemoaned by John Stuart Mill: 'French political economists enjoy a great advantage in being able to speak currently of *les profits de l'entrepreneur*' (Mill 1976[1848], footnote 406). The infrequent use of the concept was partly a reflection of disciplinary biases in economics, particularly the simplifying assumption of perfect information in markets. This, when carried to its theoretical extreme, leaves the notion of the entrepreneur, a person of subjective judgement, of marginal analytical concern (Casson 2003). Only in the twentieth century, when such assumptions were relaxed and examined in relation to the theory of the firm (Coase 1937), coupled with a rising demand for knowledge about innovation and growth (particularly in periods of economic weakness), did the appeal of entrepreneurship assume a dominant status.

The heroic vision of the entrepreneur – one that is now valorised by business gurus in the context of neoliberalism – derives its major theoretical impetus from two economists: Joseph Schumpeter and Israel Kirzner. The former stressed the role of the entrepreneur as a revolutionary innovator who provides the energy for the 'gale of creative destruction', the famous Schumpeterian metaphor for the incessant, competitive forces in capitalism (Schumpeter 2003[1942]: 84). Schumpeter was keen to explore the personality attributes and motivations of such players, including the merchants who inherit the duty of running a family firm, or the captains of industry who display the willpower to 'found a private kingdom' (Schumpeter 1983[1934]: 93). In this sense, not everyone has the capacity to become an entrepreneur. In subsequent thinking, Schumpeter went on to explore the relationship between entrepreneurship and large corporations, arguing that the latter have matured to such a size that they usurp the entrepreneurial role which was originally the preserve of extraordinary individuals. It is important to note, however, that Schumpeter 'had nothing of the militant neo-liberal about him' (Dardot and Laval 2013: 118), even though he would later be romanced by management writers such as Peter Drucker (1985). Rather, he was pessimistic about how 'the entrepreneurial function' would survive in a capitalist system struggling against socialism, arguing that bureaucratically minded managers would destroy such dynamics of innovation (Schumpeter 2003[1942]; see also Becker and Knudsen 2009).

If Schumpeter's entrepreneur is the *ne plus ultra* of capitalist society, charting new commercial territory with bold strokes, Kirzner's entrepreneur can potentially be found in *any* individual and advances made are as much evolutionary as revolutionary (Kirzner 1973). Through adopting a more expansive definition, Kirzner, building upon the intellectual legacy of his teacher, Ludwig von Mises (1949), as well as Friedrich von Hayek (1948), argued that entrepreneurship was a process of discovery and a state of alertness to opportunity, extending not simply to 'economizing activity' in the market but, more fundamentally, embracing the meaning of human nature itself (Kirzner 1973, 2000). Entrepreneurs, from this perspective, may start out '*without any means whatsoever*' (Kirzner 1973: 40, italics in original): that is, without substantial capital, specialist knowledge or familial pedigree. To be called such a name, all the entrepreneur needs is to alight on unexploited opportunities and, in turn, to organise the transactions that will capture them. Thus, one of the lasting contributions of the 'Austrian' view of entrepreneurship, as advanced by Mises and Kirzner, centres on this normative argument that entrepreneurs can be cut from many different types of cloth and, as a consequence, the conceptual division between capitalist activity and non-capitalist activity begins to blur. Since the appeal to attentiveness and exploration is constitutive of human nature, by the same logic all facets of human relations could, or should, be shaped by the entrepreneurial spirit (Dardot and Laval 2013).

From the 1970s, this particular appeal to entrepreneurship as a generalised ethic for governing both the self and different organisations became reflective of, and helped to constitute, the mainstreaming of neoliberalism. One can see the normalisation of the concept in a search of titles in the British Library. Prior to 1978, only 133 publications featured 'entrepreneurship' in the main heading, but in the subsequent period, until 1989, 542 items included the term. Such usage was still limited, however, when compared to what was to come: from 1990 to 2002, 6735 publications deployed the concept, while in the current period, since 2002, the list has rocketed to include 17,878 more titles, a 165 per cent increase in the production of knowledge on the subject. Elsewhere, since the launch of the *Journal of Small Business and Entrepreneurship* in 1983, a further 26 journals have been established in the burgeoning field of entrepreneurship studies (Armstrong 2005). Not surprisingly, the popularity of the expression also increased in the pages of the *Financial Times*. Before the 1970s, the newspaper made few references to the notion of the entrepreneur, but in the context of reporting on emerging industries and the often malign state of Western economies, it began to see value in it, both descriptively and normatively. Within these business media accounts and management guides, the growth of Silicon Valley in California, with its advances in software services and rich supplies of venture capital funding, came to be idolised for entrepreneurial success, a legacy that continues today with Google, Facebook and Twitter. As one reporter at the beginning of this period expressed it, following a tour of Stanford University and the offices of Hewlett Packard, 'Young scientists were taken out of their laboratories and made into entrepreneurs' (Irvine 1974: 20).

Beyond the world of capitalist enterprises, we might also note how the concept of entrepreneurship has been increasingly deployed as an answer to the problems of government. For instance, by 1992, in the US, David Osborne and Ted Gaebler were documenting and advocating new principles of 'entrepreneurial government', which, they argued, should be contrasted with the so-called 'old bureaucratic model'. Inspired by the management theory of Peters and Waterman (1982), Osborne and Gaebler suggested that what works for Walt Disney and Wal-Mart could work for Uncle Sam, whether in the White House or the schoolhouse. While noting that the entrepreneur could be read as a 'surprising' choice of focus for a book on political reform, they nevertheless argued for the validity and applicability of such a concept to public affairs (Osborne and Gaebler 1992: xix). Similar to the domain of the private market, Osborne and Gaebler (1992) contended that the entrepreneur in government was an actor who tried to find the greatest efficiency and productivity, a logic that has its antecedent in the work of Jean-Baptiste Say. In one of the most politically influential features of their argument, the authors proposed that public entrepreneurial organisations should 'steer' rather than 'row': that is, such institutions should aspire to be flexible bodies that place competitiveness as the central principle in all their activity. Rather than trying to accomplish everything, the entrepreneurial government style is 'results-driven', with attention to 'missions', 'customers' and the potential to make money, rather than always spend it (Osborne and Gaebler, 1992). In short, the emergence of a larger literature on new public management sought not simply new techniques of governing but new values, with those of the private sector tending to be privileged.

Three critical points, in conclusion, can help to shed further light on the concept of entrepreneurship in the neoliberal period. First, the figure of the business entrepreneur is often depicted in the media as glamorous and exciting. Such constructions are, in one sense, 'premade' due to the already mentioned historical ties of meaning between, on the one hand, entrepreneurship and, on the other, themes of individualism, freedom and the wealth and power derived from the creation of new economic value. At the same time, the images of corporate 'heroes', such as the late Steve Jobs at Apple and Richard Branson at Virgin, are the product of an exhausting and carefully built social process, involving the self and a small army of personal advisors. One could argue that the desire to become the next Jobs or the next Branson may indeed be inspiring, particularly for business-school graduates, but such appeals come with, or mask, potentially negative effects. Thus, the frenetic pursuit of exploiting some entrepreneurial advantage – which in highly competitive markets may disappear very quickly – tends to dovetail with a broader 'cult of the winner', a cultural development which some argue has been heightened by neoliberalism (Bourdieu 1998a). It should be recalled that the lived experience of being an entrepreneur, particularly for those trying to cultivate such an identity for the first time, is beset with multiple risks, which, for some, feel more 'like a mental illness than a state of nirvana' (Park 2014; see also, on the dissolution of the 'work/life balance', Dempsey and Sanders 2010). Nor should it be forgotten that 'inspiring leaders', such as Jobs, were alleged to possess problematic personality traits, including reports of narcissism and the use of intimidatory language with employees (Maccoby 2003, 2007; Isaacson 2011). The best success stories invariably have a darker side.

Second, while there exists evidence of a strong relationship between entrepreneurship, innovation and economic growth (Lerner 2010), one should be careful about depicting all entrepreneurial activity as economically beneficial. For instance, during the 1990s and 2000s, when financial innovation was widely applauded by industry players, regulators and politicians, few predicted how such forms of entrepreneurship would be a major cause of the crisis (Tett 2009; Engelen *et al.* 2010). In short, when describing the typical entrepreneur as either a hapless victim of structural forces or, on the other hand, the saviour of the economy, one misses how such behaviour may, under certain conditions, be implicated in encouraging excessive risk-taking and in the process jeopardising wider economic stability (Jones and Murtola 2011). The bankers who risked all and who were largely responsible for the global financial crash of 2008 are now some of the most despised people on the planet.

Third, similar to the neoliberal conceptual pairing of enterprise with 'the social', entrepreneurship now has an entire sub-field dedicated to the pursuit of social value, including activities that may or may not be contrasted with a profit motivation. On the face of it, this turn may viewed by some as normatively appealing, with business models and metrics advanced as the answer to a range of problems, from managing youth unemployment to global ecological decay. Again, other authors urge caution; social entrepreneurship runs a danger of 'addressing the symptoms of the capitalist system rather than its root causes' (Dey and Steyaert 2012: 91). In the near future, the concept of entrepreneurship might well embrace a wider meaning of interest beyond the bottom line, but the term will still carry, perhaps inevitably, the historical imprint of capitalism and, thus, will implicitly relegitimise a capitalistic ethic.

See also: **business, capitalism, choice, competition, enterprise, growth, individual, innovation, market, private, risk, vision**.

Further reading: Dardot and Laval 2013; Drucker 1985; Kirzner 1973, 2000.

ENVIRONMENT

The rise of the environment as a central socio-political problem has coincided with the mainstreaming of ideas and practices associated with neoliberalism. With the planet facing multiple ecological stresses, from rising animal extinction rates to global climate change, debate on the relationship between humans and their natural surroundings has become increasingly animated and contested, even assuming an apocalyptic tone. Derived from the old French *environ*, meaning to form a circle around, the term 'environment' first passed into English in the early seventeenth century. It took until the mid nineteenth century before the notion of environment emerged as a common phrase to denote the area surrounding a place or thing, although other related notions, such as 'the natural world' or 'external conditions', as Charles Darwin (2008[1859]) expressed it, gained in popularity. By the late nineteenth century, the adjective 'environmental' had been coined and begun to be used within various compound phrases, such as 'environmental impact' (1911) and 'environmental services' (1926). In 1917, 'environmentalism' entered the language, first as a general theory positing that the environment had the primary influence on development, before expanding to embrace the contemporary sense of preservation, particularly in the face of damage caused by humans.

Following the Second World War, in the context of increasing awareness of anthropogenic influences on natural ecosystems, a decisive semantic shift took place when the expression '*the* environment' began to be used: that is, with a preceding definite article. In this immediately recognisable sense, the concept refers to the entire ecological world, not a geographically bounded setting. As a major social movement and political question, modern environmentalism grew out of the 1960s and 1970s, with the US, Germany and Belgium being notable centres of activism (Wapner 1996; Carter 2007). An environmental consciousness was nurtured by different anxieties, including the effects of nuclear proliferation, air and water pollution, the destruction of tropical rainforests and other problems of resource depletion. During this period, landmark publications helped to draw wider attention to such concerns, including

Rachel Carson's *Silent Spring* (2000[1962]), which examined the dangers of chemical pesticides; the Club of Rome's *The Limits to Growth* (Meadows *et al.* 1972), which argued that capitalism was on a collision course with natural systems; and Herman Daly's *Steady-State Economics* (1977), which helped to develop the new field of ecological economics. By the mid 1970s, the verb 'green' and the word 'greening' began to be invoked as synonyms for a sensitivity to environmental issues. With this metaphorical extension, and reflecting stronger forms of organisational activism, the first green-party political groups were established. In this regard, the German Green Party, dating from 1979, has become particularly successful, both domestically and at the European level (Uekötter 2014). The growth of civil society groups, including Greenpeace, Friends of the Earth International and the Worldwatch Institute, further consolidated the mainstreaming of environmental problems.

By the 1980s, debates on environmental matters began to feature a new phrase: 'sustainable development'. Its conceptual genesis is found in the UN, although there were earlier deployments (International Union for Conservation of Nature 1980; Biswas and Biswas 1982). In 1983, the UN established the World Commission on Environment and Development (WCED) (also known as the Brundtland Commission) to explore how the desire for economic prosperity could be married with ecological survival. In 1987, the Commission published a major report, *Our Common Future*, where the notion of sustainable development played a central role. The concept was rooted in the principle of intergenerational equity: 'development that meets the needs of the present without compromising the ability of future generations to meet their own needs' (WCED 1987: 8). In the years since, as the term was appropriated by other international bodies, governments, businesses, civil society actors and academics, it has 'arguably become the dominant global discourse of ecological concern' (Dryzek 2012: 148). For instance, in a search of book titles in the British Library, 'sustainable development' is found in only 32 items before 1988, before increasing exponentially to 1663 books from 1988 to 2001. From 2002 to 2015, the frequency of use has broadly maintained the same rate, with a further 1729 works that included the phrase. In one sense, the turn to sustainable development could be read as evidence of the strength of environmentalism. On the other hand, the term might be popular because it remains inoffensive and does not threaten anyone. Moreover, for some critics, what is rejuvenated with sustainable development is, at root, 'a strategy for sustaining "development"', or, in other words, a particular project of capitalist modernisation. Inevitably, rival visions that could undermine such a project tend to be marginalised in the process (Sachs 2008[1992]: 28).

It should not be surprising, therefore, that the concept of sustainable development has comfortably found a home in many agendas associated with neoliberalism. Three other aspects are also worth noting (inspired by Himley 2008). First, a range of authors have argued that privatisation policies, whereby business actors earn property rights over certain environmental resources, can sometimes result in damaging consequences, both socially and ecologically (Lovei and Gentry 2002; Heynen *et al.* 2007). Such outcomes have been particularly controversial when a resource under exploitation has historically been treated as part of 'the commons', or public domain. Thus, in heavy polluting industries, such as oil and coal, there exists a history of divisive episodes, including the appropriation of territory, corruption and high-profile disasters, along with 'normal' pollution (leaking pipes, emissions from flaring, etc.) (on the case of ExxonMobil, see Coll 2012). The ongoing conflict in the Niger Delta, which arose in the early 1990s when foreign oil companies (notably Royal Dutch Shell) were accused by minority ethnic groups of exploiting the region, is one prominent case of the destabilising effects from the search for oil wealth (Obi and Rustad 2011). Other commodities that have been subjected to privatisation agendas have also received scrutiny. For example, the experiment in water privatisation in Bolivia from the mid 1990s became one of most widely recognised failures in the sector. Led by the US-based firm Bechtel, the French giant Suez and pressure from the World Bank, the shift from public ownership resulted in higher tariff rates for consumers and poorly maintained infrastructure. By 2000, following a series of protests and effective uprisings against the water companies and the government, a process of renationalisation was instigated (Assies 2003; Olivera with Lewis 2004; Bakker 2010).

Second, the impact of neoliberalism is not only to be observed in private sector strategies of enclosure but also in how 'the market model' becomes a generalised inspiration for dealing with various environmental problems. During the 1960s and 1970s, a suspicion of industrial growth and the use of command-and-control policies by governments were widespread. By contrast, since the 1980s, a 'compromise of liberal environmentalism' has become the main normative basis for how governments, businesses and other interested parties have addressed ecological concerns (Bernstein 2001). For instance, the creation of private markets for trading emissions (sulphur, carbon), the allocation of property rights for land, sea and air pollution and the business preference for voluntary self-regulation are representative of the shift towards the 'marketisation of environmental governance' (Newell 2008). This predilection for viewing 'market-based' thinking as both the cause of, yet also the answer to, ecological peril is clearly seen in climate-change policymaking, notably through the UN system but also through schemes at the regional and urban level. At the same time, the historical legacy of injustices tied to climate change, including allocating responsibility to particular nations and industries, is central to understanding the larger political economy. China, for example, may now be the biggest carbon dioxide polluter, but this is partly the result of a larger trend over the past half century of Western-based businesses moving their production to East and South east Asia. In short, the atmosphere has no concern for where the carbon is emitted, yet in a political world of sovereign states who are, in turn, intertwined within a capitalist system, measuring who bears responsibility has often proved contentious (Okereke 2008; Bulkeley and Newell 2010).

A third aspect concerning the relationship between the environment and neoliberalism would address activities under the heading of 'green consumerism'. The emergence of consumption patterns that are claimed to promote an environmental good now takes a variety of forms, including products that are made from natural rather than synthetic materials, more efficient uses of energy, the promotion of recycling and the investment of profits into environmental projects, such as reforestation (Mansvelt 2011). Such activities are in part due to the success of the environmental movement. But the trend also reflects the normalisation of corporate social responsibility in business. Although some of these practices may be misleading forms of 'greenwashing' (1987, *OED*) that have little, if any, tangible impact on improving 'sustainability', being environmentally cognisant – in word and deed – now makes financial sense for many businesses (Falkner 2007). This is because – as BP found out after the Deepwater Horizon oil spill in 2010 and Exxon discovered following the *Valdez* disaster in 1989 – reputation matters more in the neoliberal period and, therefore, any potential damage to corporate branding via the misuse of the environment could, or at any rate should, undermine business performance. Another related development is the creation of what some have called 'eco-chic consumerism': 'a combination of lifestyle politics, environmentalism, spirituality, beauty, and health, combined with a call to return to simple living' (Barendregt and Jaffe 2014: 1). Again, the popularity of such pursuits could be understood under the banner of trying to 'save the world', but a more sophisticated reading would locate eco-chic as the latest cultural practice for earning social recognition within particular groups and classes. For critics such as Slavoj Žižek (2009), this is what makes neoliberal forms of consumerism paradoxical and, at the same time, effective at blunting more radical criticism. The implicit 'guilt' or 'complicity' in environmental damage – thoughts shared by many individuals – becomes packaged into a commodity and, thus, consumerism becomes 'safe' again.

See also: **capitalism, development, global, growth, market, responsibility, risk**.

Further reading: Bernstein 2001; Dryzek 2012; Heynen *et al*. 2007; Himley 2008.

EXPERIENCE

Experience was originally synonymous with experiment (from the Latin *experiri*, to try out, to test). Today, experience, defined as a kind of immediate awareness, is clearly different from experience as depicted by lessons learnt. According to Raymond Williams (1983[1976]: 116), the term broadened in meaning from the sixteenth century, 'with more deliberate inclusion of the past (the tried and tested), to indicate knowledge derived from real events as well as from particular observation'. An important later extension of the word concerns how experience became associated with Anglocentric religious practices that stressed a state of mind or feeling. For instance, in early Methodism, in the eighteenth century, so-called 'experience meetings' provided an occasion for recounting one's personal revelation in a social setting and, thus, discovering not just the truth, but a presumed *authentic* kind of truth (Williams 1983[1976]; Wierzbicka 2010). In a wider context, relevant to how it has been deployed by users in the neoliberal era, experience often denotes an appeal to consciousness, subjectively sensed by an individual who may, in turn, perform actions that reshape how that experience is understood by others.

As an academic concept, the notion of experience has vexed many philosophers, anthropologists and sociologists. In Edmund Husserl's (1973[1939]) view, philosophy needed to break away from high-level, metaphysical analysis and, instead, describe phenomena in terms of human consciousness: that is, from the perspective of the one who experiences. Rather than presuming in advance the 'essence' of social practices – such as the idea that the only valid knowledge is scientific knowledge – the founder of modern phenomenology challenged philosophers to explain experience in all its complexity, including the role of perception and intuition. The problem with experience lies not in its importance as a concept but in working out how to study it. If we can only experience our own life, how can we go beyond a partial and circumscribed understanding of the experiences of others? Since there is no easy answer to this question, it is perhaps better to consider all experiences as cultural constructs that are in a state of flux, particularly in terms of the difficult and often confusing relationship between the actual lived experience and the representation of it depicted in writing, images or speech (Turner and Bruner 1986).

How can one approach the neoliberal colouring of experience? As a general rule, each period of capitalism tends to generate working practices and forms of consumerism that excite sensation in people (or hold out the hope of sensation). Some authors argue that this drive to stimulate certain emotions – which, like an addictive drug, are often transitory and therefore encourage frequent use to reproduce a 'high' – is a key means by which capitalism is rendered more attractive and its less appealing aspects, such as inequality, tolerated (Boltanski and Chiapello 2007). It could be suggested that one of the distinguishing qualities of the neoliberal period, at least with respect to advances in consumption, is how major resources are now dedicated to tapping and nurturing emotionally stimulating activities. This pattern, to be clear, did not start with the contemporary neoliberal period, as the displaying of 'conspicuous consumption' in late-nineteenth-century society attests (Veblen 2007[1899]), or in respect to the relationship between cultural taste and class in the postwar period, as documented by Bourdieu (1984). The difference today comes with the growth in the services economy, a development that has expanded the range of pleasure-pursuing leisure opportunities. Such changes have, in turn, had repercussions on how consumer relations are both conceptualised and acted out under the banner of neoliberalism.

This is where the concept of experience enters the picture. Similar to other key concepts in neoliberal discourse, the role of marketing theory as a fount for corporate strategies is important. In a pioneering article published in 1982, Morris Holbrook and Elizabeth Hirschman argued that existing approaches to consumer behaviour were too narrow in what they claimed to explain. Instead of always imagining the consumer to be a logical and rational individual, Holbrook and Hirschman (1982: 132) argued that consumption involves 'a steady flow of fantasies, feelings, and fun'. Thinking in the spirit of Husserl, they called attention to 'playful leisure activities, sensory pleasures, daydreams, esthetic enjoyment, and emotional responses', the 'experiential' aspects of consumption (Holbrook and Hirschman, 1982: 132). As the 1980s and 1990s unfolded, this definition of experience picked up supporters among those who taught and practised marketing. The consumption experience, according to these analysts, cannot be reduced to a single, point-of-sale, transaction encounter. Instead, the best brands nurture the consumer through four stages: (1) the pre-consumption experience, involving searching and fantasising about the product; (2) the purchase experience, which includes issues about choice and payment; (3) the core consumption experience, which attends to how satisfied the user becomes; and (4) the remembered consumption experience, which involves nostalgia about one's prior life through the brand (Arnould *et al.*, 2002). By the turn of the century, the concept had been elevated to such status that some writers even argued that an experience-based economy was the model for the future (Pine and Gilmore, 1999).

What do these experiences actually look like in the neoliberal period? For marketers, a consumption experience could take a variety of forms. Department stores and malls have historically been at the vanguard of efforts to entice customers with particular shopping experiences, including attention to store atmospherics, the positioning of goods, the availability and helpfulness of staff and the removal of distractions, such as clocks and windows (Arnold *et al.* 2005). But within the neoliberal era, this notion of experience has been stretched and redefined. There is the 'spectacular consumption' of large flagship stores, where the customer enters a kind of playful, Disneyfied shrine to the brand, such as in Nike Town or M&M's World (Peñaloza 1998; Kozinets *et al.* 2002). In addition, 'bodyshopping' experiences (Paterson 2005: 87) call attention to how bodily sensations are commodified, from extreme sports tourism to shampoos that claim to have bottled the smell of the Amazon rainforest. Within these examples, as well as many others, the dramatisation of the brand through a 'storytelling' technique has become a popular marketing device, one that obviously predates neoliberalism but is now supported by a more elaborate set of theoretical insights (Woodside *et al.* 2008). The ability of some companies, notably Apple, to cultivate a faithful army of devotees through theatrical demonstrations of new products has been much commented upon. To borrow from the stage model of the consumption experience, Apple has developed a particular experience throughout its entire 'ecosystem', one that tends to imply contemporary style, functionality and success. As this conception of experience becomes widely known, all Apple consumers are led to believe, or willingly commit to the belief, that they are part of the latest technological fashion.

There are, therefore, different motivations at work when the notion of experience is invoked. Nonetheless, within the business world, an obvious point needs stating, not least because it rarely surfaces in any advertising rhetoric: the construction of so-called 'experiences' is predicated upon retaining customer loyalty and, thus, protecting and increasing profit margins. From a Marxist reading, many of these experiences are interesting for how human labour has been used to create the very commodities sold within the experience. Thus, for instance, a pair of Nike trainers may be produced under exploitative or stressful conditions, but in the symbolically saturated Nike Town the appeal to self-realisation – winning and achieving – pushes such potential negative thoughts to the margins. The financial impulse tends to get lost when advertisers, particularly within influential North American debates, promote ideal consumer experiences as being 'extraordinary' and 'memorable' high points (Arnould and Price 1993). This desire for hedonistic consumption, whereby the user is called upon to 'immerse' themselves into the brand is, in turn, contrasted with everyday life, which is presumed to be monotonous and lacking in intensity. But as critics have noted, such arguments have a kind of ideological quality: the consumer is being prescribed to act in a certain way through experiences designed by businesses (Carù and Cova 2003) yet, often, will be encouraged to believe that the experience has been 'co-created' (Prahalad and Ramaswamy 2004). Again, it is worth recalling not only that disconnections may exist between the represented experience and how consumers actually feel it, but also that some people choose not to engage in the 'search for perpetual euphoria' (Bruckner 2000: 17) and, for many reasons, find alternative experiences beyond those that have a commercial dimension. Ironically, the closer 'experience' gets to 'experiment' the less persuasive it feels.

See also: **business, change, choice, freedom, individual, participation.**

Further reading: Holbrook and Hirschman 1982; Turner and Bruner 1986; Peñaloza 1998; Pine and Gilmore 1999.

FINANCE

Although financial relations have been part of human societies throughout history, one of the most distinctive and controversial features of the neoliberal period has been the increasing power of financial institutions. Following the turmoil of the financial crisis of 2007–9, the activity and impact of the financial industry has come under renewed scrutiny. The word has come down to us from the late Latin *finis*, or settled payment, and the Old French *finer*. From its earliest uses, the word carried both the sense of an end to something, or *fin* as the French has it, and the settlement of a debt. From the early seventeenth century, the job title of 'financier' began to emerge, mainly with respect to the government problem of managing monetary affairs. In the eighteenth century, the first international capital markets took root in Amsterdam and London, offering foreign bills of exchange to ease access to credit

(Neal 1990). The application of the term 'financier' to private professionals became more common in the early nineteenth century, as reflected in the phrase 'man of finance' (1816, *OED*). At the same time, with the rise of the US and Germany as important banking centres, related expressions also appeared, including 'financial year' (1800, *OED*) and 'finance company' (1837, *OED*). However, the major growth in finance capital occurred from the last quarter of the nineteenth century to the interwar years (Michie 2006, 2014). During this period, large financial houses, such as J. P. Morgan, consolidated immense economic and political power, a development that was critiqued by Marxists in particular (Hilferding 2007 [1919]). Recent events have slightly altered our view of the past for it is now apparent that the history of finance reveals that, left unchecked, financiers can distort economies and societies toward their interests, sometimes with unpredictable and damaging social consequences. In this sense, although we no longer hear *fin* in 'financial', perhaps we should.

Several justifications have been advanced for the prominence of finance in a modern capitalist system (summarised in Dixon 2014; see also Tobin 2008). First, finance provides a payments system to facilitate the wider exchange of goods and services. The primary medium of exchange – money – serves as the key measure, means of payment and store of value. With the introduction of money, the problem of how to enlarge the system of transactions and, furthermore, exchange different currencies across national boundaries became paramount. When effectively designed, capital accumulation tends to rise because of increased opportunities for trade and economic diversification. Second, the financial system plays a major role in mobilising savings, such as those found in households, pension funds and other assets. Exploring new markets and increasing the scale of production – particularly for large projects, such as transportation infrastructure or factory construction – requires financial resources that few individuals or companies can obtain on their own. Thus, financial mediators enable the transferring of capital across space and time, further expanding the potential for capital accumulation. Third, the financial system purports to 'manage risk' in different ways. For instance, according to portfolio theory – a mathematical model that tries to enhance the expected monetary return for a given amount of risk – actors should diversify their investments to improve financial security (Markowitz 1952; Sharpe 1963). Financial institutions also offer services that aim to reduce liquidity risk, such as offering to convert assets such as land into cash.

If finance has long been part of the DNA of capitalism, the appeal to the notion of financialisation marks an attempt by scholars to explain what makes the neoliberal period distinctive (for an overview, see Van der Zwan 2014; see also Kotz 2011). Such analysis requires some reference to postwar financial history. From the end of the Second World War until the early 1970s, the international monetary order was strongly controlled by governments, anchored to the power of the US dollar, in a regime called the Bretton Woods system. During this period, the volume of financial transactions across national borders was limited, partly due to the need to rebuild domestic war-torn economies in the shadow of the Cold War, but also to guard against a repeat of the inter-war years, when currency and banking crises were more common. During the 1960s and 1970s, Wall Street banks were much smaller, with most employing only a few hundred people (Ferguson 2014). The collapse of Bretton Woods in 1973 – a result of complex factors but, at root, the political reluctance of the US and Germany to sustain the system – provided an opening for the growth of private financial mar-kets (Walter 1993; Helleiner 1994; Eichengreen 2008). In the 1970s, as the neoliberal period dawned, the financial world began to switch to the current system of 'floating' exchange rates, whereby important currencies are largely traded on private exchanges. Trading in foreign exchange is now a huge market, worth US$5.3 trillion per day in 2013, a volume that has increased by more than eight-fold since 1989 (Bank for International Settlements (BIS) 1996, 2013). However, governments still confront dilemmas similar to those faced in the Bretton Woods period. Indeed, the choice between currency stability and national fiscal autonomy remains a core problem.

The rise of 'global finance' to its present status was, nonetheless, a development that few foresaw (Krippner 2011; Streeck 2014). Accord-ing to one interpretation, a finance-led agenda emerged in the 1970s in response to declining growth and productivity levels in Western countries (Arrighi 1994; Boyer 2005; Foster 2007; Krippner 2011). In the face of lower profits from manufacturing firms and stagnating wages, the finance industry stepped in to provide credit to fuel new patterns of consumption. By the 1980s and 1990s, encouraged by 'competitive deregulation' trends and technological advances (Helleiner 1994: 12), large banks transformed their business model to engage in new profit-generating pursuits. Although the financial crisis of 2007–9 has shaken some of these assumptions, the main sources of income still include: (1) trading of stocks, bonds, currencies and commodities; (2) under-writing and advisory services for mergers and acquisitions among companies; (3) investment management (such as looking after the money of rich individuals and other institutions); and (4) traditional corporate lending (Noonan 2015). These activities have been enhanced by the use of leverage (a technique of deploying borrowed money to generate outsized returns) and the extension of so-called securitisation 'food chains' (the bundling together of different assets to make more attractive financial products). As a consequence, in the US, the contribution of financial profits as a share of total corporate profits rose from 10 per cent in 1985 to over 30 per cent in 2002 (the share collapsed in 2009, but by 2014 had recovered to around 25 per cent). Even these figures probably underestimate the true scale of financialisation. For instance, many non-financial firms now have significant financial units. During the early 2000s, Ford derived more money by selling loans than by selling cars, while GE Capital once generated half of GE's total earnings (Mukunda 2014; see also Krippner 2005; Froud et al. 2006; Lapavitsas 2013).

Another interpretation of neoliberal financialisation focuses less on corporations and elite policy actors and more on how finance has become embedded in ordinary life (Seabrooke 2006; Hobson and Seabrooke 2007; Watson 2007). Easier access to credit – including mortgages, credit cards, student loans and car loans – is a defining feature of the neoliberal period. Such trends have led to elevated levels of household debt. In the US, household debt as a percentage of disposable income rose from 72 per cent in 1980 to 140 per cent by 2006 (Barba and Pivetti 2009). One major effect of this trend has been to integrate lower classes and historically marginalised groups into a larger web of credit relations, often through appeals to 'financial inclusion' (a phrase which has spread since the early 2000s). Some of this activity may be beneficial to such actors, but it also carries risks of exposure to predatory lending tactics. Scholars in this field have also adopted a cultural perspective attuned to 'the intersection between changes in the capital markets, on the one hand, and transformations in everyday spaces, practices and identities, on the other' (Langley 2008: 7). Langley (2008) has examined how the category of the 'everyday investor', a subject who is geographically removed from Wall Street or the City of London but still engaged with its risks and rewards, has emerged as a culturally specific creation of the neoliberal period. Drawing on a Foucauldian reading of neoliberalism, he notes how the social world of finance is now populated by many trainers and educators (both private and government) who seek, at least on the surface, to decode and 'democratise' such practices (Aitken 2007). Thus, from the late 1990s, propelled by the internet, there was an increase in independent 'day traders' (speculators who trade financial instruments on a short-term basis), a development that was accompanied by a raft of 'how-to' guides (Turner 2000).

Manias, panics and crashes – seen by some as part of some endgame – have long coursed through the financial veins of the capitalist system (Kindleberger and Aliber 2011[1978]; see also Minsky 2008[1986]). However, many scholars and policymakers have been preoccupied with the extent to which financial crises – which could take banking, currency or credit forms – have become more common in the neoliberal era. In the Bretton Woods period, across the world, banking crises were very rare, but as restrictions on the movement of capital were loosened from the 1970s (particularly short-term flows), the incidence of such events rose sharply. According to Reinhart and Rogoff (2009: 155), '[p]eriods of high international capital mobility have repeatedly produced international banking crises, not only famously, as they did in the 1990s, but historically'. One can cite many illustrations of financial dislocations that chequer the neoliberal period, including the Latin American debt crisis during the 1980s, the US savings and loan crisis from the late 1980s, the Mexican currency crisis in the mid 1990s, the Asian financial crisis in the late 1990s, the Argentina crisis in the early 2000s, the Enron scandal of the early 2000s and the Eurozone crisis from 2009. The social effects of these events were often profound. For instance, in the case of the Asian financial crisis, unemployment in most of the affected countries rose, but for some critics the aftermath was made worse by the implementation of austerity policies by the IMF (Stiglitz 2002). Despite the frequency of such crises, the push to expand the financial industry has continued, led by banks and their lobbies (such as the Institute of International Finance), particular governments (for instance, the US, the UK, Switzerland, the UAE, Japan and China), international institutions (including the IMF, the World Bank and the European Commission) and notable economists, who often had a role in policymaking (such as Martin Feldstein, Glenn Hubbard and Lawrence Summers).

Given such trends, the global financial crisis which emerged in 2007 was, in one sense, overdetermined. Initially triggered by rising delinquencies in the US subprime-mortgage market, by September 2008 the crisis had entered an acute phase as an interbank liquidity crunch caused a wave of economic contractions, including the collapse of the investment bank Lehman Brothers (Sorkin 2009; Wolf 2014). Disentangling the reasons for the crisis – including where to begin tracing the story, how to assess the importance of specific factors and, in particular, how to grasp the interconnections between causes – is by no means self-evident. However, four key elements which constitute a self-reinforcing cycle can be noted. First, at the fulcrum of the crisis lay risky and unscrupulous lending practices. On the eve of the crisis, at almost all the major banks, debt-to-equity ratios exceeded 30 to 1, with around 50 to 1 for both UBS and Deutsche Bank (Kalemli-Özcan *et al.* 2012). This meant that only a very small decline in assets held by these banks – less than 5 per cent, say – would render them technically insolvent. With reference to the US mortgage market, lenders such as Washington Mutual and Countrywide required little or no evidence of borrower income, requested small or zero down payments and offered introductory 'teaser' rates that would later rocket after a specified period (United States Senate Permanent Subcommittee on Investigations 2011; Aalbers 2012; Grind 2012). Higher-risk loans required borrowers to pay higher fees and, thus, generated larger profits for the lenders. These (mal)practices became more common within lending firms because rewards were linked to high loan volumes and high-commission mortgages, rather than the performance of the loan or the suitability of the customer. Elsewhere, a wider culture of mis-selling was seemingly intrinsic to other consumer markets, including insurance and credit cards (on the UK case, see Ashton 2015).

Second, new trends in securitisation deepened the financial crisis, particularly in terms of its geographical impact, and, in the process, made the entire system more volatile. This effect ran contrary to the dominant narrative – repeatedly preached by financiers and regulators from the 1990s – that risk was reduced through innovation (for instance, see Greenspan 2005). It is now clear that securitisation is a form of financial engineering whereby credit-risky assets are packaged with higher-quality assets in order to enable the sale of the former to a wider market. Although not necessarily a 'bad thing' in principle, securitisation becomes dangerous when the complexity and opacity of such financial alchemy leads to misaligned interests or the phenomena of 'moral hazard'. This can occur when investment bankers (or, more commonly, actors within the 'shadow banking system' – see Lysandrou and Nesvetailova 2014; Nesvetailova 2015) design new securities but have little interest in how the underlying loans were written (Keys *et al.* 2010). All that matters for the banker is that a profit can be booked by offloading the security on to a new buyer, further extending the securitisation chain. In 'benign' conditions, or what could be classed as the growth stage of asset bubbles in the 1990s and early 2000s, knowledge about the location of toxic assets did not appear as a major problem (Tett 2009). But when the bubbles began to burst, the task of isolating and, of equal importance, ascertaining the value of such toxic assets, became urgent. When a series of cascading defaults were experienced in the crisis, panic ensued about how to assess value. In sum, as one former director of the US National Economic Council expressed it, securitisation did not reduce risk: 'You as an individual can diversify your risk. The system as a whole, though, cannot reduce the risk. And that's where the confusion lies' (Lindsey, quoted in Financial Crisis Inquiry Commission 2011: 45).

Third, within these new dynamics, a sharp spotlight has been thrown on the credit rating agencies (CRAs), the two largest of which are Standard & Poor's and Moody's. The ratings of these organisations were claimed to represent an independent and accurate judgement on the risks of different assets, such as credit derivatives and government bonds (on the rise of the industry, see Sinclair 2005). The selling of mortgage-related securities could not have proceeded without the authenticating seal of legitimacy granted by CRAs. The dependence of investors on CRAs was partly due to legal obligations (for instance, many pension funds can only buy top-rated assets), but it was also because trust was placed in CRAs to decipher the value within mathematically complicated security structures. However, many conflicts of interest have surfaced between CRAs and their clients or issuers. In the search for new business, CRAs often softened their rating criteria, even to the point of revealing their models in return for payment (a gaming of the process known as 'ratings arbitrage'). When the crisis unravelled, many of these ratings proved worthless guides. For instance, from 2000 to 2007, Moody's judged almost 45,000 mortgage-related securities as AAA, its highest award. In 2006, as house prices dived, 83 per cent of such securities were downgraded. In the case of Lehman Brothers, on the morning of its collapse the CRAs still had investment-grade ratings on the bank's debt. Elsewhere, in the decade before the Eurozone crisis was upon us, the same firms upgraded almost all member states of the common currency to AAA status (White 2013; Gaillard 2014). As one US government-sponsored commission concluded on the basis of such evidence, 'credit rating agencies were essential cogs in the wheel of financial destruction' (Financial Crisis Inquiry Commission 2011: xxv).

Fourth, the wider monetary and regulatory policy environment also established conditions which contributed to the crisis. Accommodative interest-rate decisions by major central banks, including the US Federal Reserve, the ECB, the Bank of Japan and the Bank of England, injected an enormous amount of liquidity into the global financial system. In the US, from 2000 to 2004, following the internet-stock-bubble crash, short-term rates were cut from around 6.5 per cent to 1 per cent, before historically low levels of less than 0.5 per cent were reached in the aftermath of the crisis. Low rates drove down the cost of funding and worked to increase the credit supply. In turn, this tempted large financial institutions to increase the leverage ratios held on their balance sheets or, in many cases, off their balance sheets via special vehicles and other accounting fixes. At the same time, from the late 1990s, structural shifts in the capitalist system, notably the rise of China and other Asian economies, generated massive inflows of capital into US government debt. Due to this demand for US Treasuries, long-term interest rates were also pushed lower, further fuelling the supply of cheaper credit (Ramskogler 2014). All these trends played out on the watch of policymakers who tended to adopt 'light touch regulation', to borrow a phrase used in the UK during the Blair and Brown years (Brown 2005). Not surprisingly, the financial industry found itself obtaining tax breaks and broader political sympathy. In turn, criticism of finance was muted because politicians had to rely upon banks to fund election campaigning. In short, by the turn of the century, the relations between finance and many rule-making authorities had become so intertwined and incestuous – at structural, institutional and personal levels – that the idea of a wider democratic interest receded into the background (Connaughton 2012).

The financial crisis has produced devastating consequences. We have witnessed the biggest economic dislocation since the Great Depression of the 1930s. Since disputes exist over what to measure and many of the impacts are intangible (such as psychological effects), the precise human cost remains unclear. From late 2008, many indicators turned negative, including steep declines in output, investment and consumption. In 2009, most countries were in recession (IMF 2009a). Over 30 million people lost their jobs, not only in the US and Europe but across all regions. The crisis has disproportionately affected young people (aged 15–24), with the unemployment rate on average three times higher for this group compared to the rest of the adult population (International Labour Organization (ILO) 2015). In the US, one government study judged that the crisis had potentially produced losses of over US$10 trillion (United States Government Accountability Office 2013). Another analysis, one which featured a hypothetical estimate of activity that could have occurred without the crisis, concluded that the cost of lost income was potentially up to US$30 trillion. Moreover, this figure does not include impacts related to 'national trauma' and the extraordinary government support that was channelled into the financial sector. Even if one makes conservative assumptions, the authors conclude that the total cost is the equivalent of more than one year of national output (Atkinson *et al.* 2013). In response to the crisis, governments issued guarantees (implicit and explicit) for much of the financial system. Initial gross commitments averaged around 20 to 30 per cent of GDP in key countries. The UK was forced to adopt even more extraordinary measures, where, due to enormous losses at Royal Bank of Scotland and Lloyds, taxpayers experienced a burden of 60 per cent of GDP. Such measures were only the start of a range of strategies introduced by authorities, including maintaining ultra-low or even negative interest rates, deploying fiscal stimulus packages of various sizes and printing electronic money via 'quantitative easing'.

In the aftermath of the crisis, a number of commentators and policymakers suggested that the Great Recession signalled a watershed moment for neoliberalism, or even its 'endpoint' (Stiglitz 2008; Hobsbawm 2009). As French President Nicolas Sarkozy boldly declared, '*laissez-faire* is finished' (quoted in Erlanger 2008). However, these initial judgements now appear overcooked. Two major outcomes can be noted. First, the financial sector remains as large, complex and, notwithstanding some new rules and indictments, almost as powerful as it was pre-crisis (see the data in McKinsey Global Institute 2013). With reference to banking, corporate concentration has arguably exacerbated the problem of 'too big to fail': that is, the expectation that states will, most likely, bail out institutions that get into trouble in order to protect creditors (or their managers) (Strahan 2013; for the broader argument that the US has consolidated its financial authority, see Helleiner 2014). Equally worrying is evidence of illegal and egregious activity that continued *after* the crisis broke, such as the fixing of interest rates (the Libor scandal) or the manipulation of the foreign-exchange market. Second, due to the financial sector receiving such government largesse, debt responsibility has largely shifted onto the shoulders of the public sector, sparking considerable popular resistance at perceived injustices. Since 2007, worldwide government debt has risen by US$25 trillion (McKinsey Global Institute 2015b). In many countries, the sense of unfairness has been compounded by the parallel pursuit of austerity policies that have cut welfare budgets, in the process disproportionately hitting the poor. Such consequences have fed a generalised sense of concern regarding how the neoliberal financial genie can be put back in the bottle. Without confronting the web of power relations that are enmeshed within the financial system, future crises are inevitable. At times, you wonder how much those early French users of the language knew about the history to come when they brought together *fin* and financial.

See also: **capitalism, global, governance, growth, innovation, investment, market, power, private, responsibility, risk, stability, state**.

Further reading: Eichengreen 2008; Financial Crisis Inquiry Commission 2011; Krippner 2011; McKinsey Global Institute 2013; Reinhart and Rogoff 2009.

FLEXIBILITY

The root of 'flexibility', from the Latin *flexibilis*, refers to the capacity of an object to bend or curve. The word evokes a visual sense of something which is pliable and can withstand stress, something that will not break or change form. One interesting general meaning of flexibility, with implications for understanding applications in the neoliberal period, concerns how it has long referred to the human disposition to yield to influence or persuasion. Thus, one person may become more flexible as a result of the guidance or direction of another. The flexible individual may even become an impressionable being, one who can be managed and controlled. But such qualities only acquire a full meaning when compared to other persons or things that are said to lack flexibility, thus provoking a series of opposing terms, such as rigidity, obstinacy or resistance. It follows that flexibility has a Janus-faced quality. It often carries normatively positive overtones and may, depending upon the social context, be a highly valued attribute. In this sense, the word implies that some greater freedom of movement or choice is possible. However, as the term 'compliant' suggests, we should remain cautious about accepting definitions of flexibility uncritically and, instead, enquire into whether actions under its name may be encouraging more subtle, yet still unequal, relations of power.

As a catch-all term which normally carries positive associations, 'flexibility' has been much used in the development of, and justification for, capitalist practices. In one early manual written for business leaders, Henri Fayol wrote about how 'there is nothing rigid or absolute in management affairs' and that the principles for organising business should be 'flexible and capable of adaptation to every need' (Fayol 1949[1916]: 19). For Fayol, in order to anticipate problems and design contingencies, good managers needed to have a 'flexibility of mind' (Fayol 1949[1916]: 76). In Igor Ansoff's influential *Corporate Strategy* (1965), the notion of flexibility is conceptualised as having external and internal dimensions: the former encompasses concerns such as product diversification to guard against potential losses, while the latter includes the need to maintain the liquidity of a firm's resources. Within current management theory and today's business talk, the concept of flexibility has been stretched and applied in countless different ways, to the extent that one might question if it retains any substantive analytical value. No facet of business appears to have escaped the use of the word: from strategic flexibility and competitive flexibility to marketing flexibility and financial flexibility. In this sense, as a trend within the neoliberal period, the term has tended to extend from a more narrow focus on manager-led planning to become a generalised concern for all workers.

Why has the term 'flexibility' become commonplace? In one major sense, from the 1970s, the term was reinterpreted in the West in response to a perceived economic threat from East Asian countries. For instance, the strategies of Japanese automakers, such as Toyota's pioneering use of just-in-time (JIT) systems, which introduced parts only when the process required them, became valorised in business circles for generating efficiency and cost savings (Ohno 1988; Womack *et al.* 2007 [1990]). Indeed, such breakthroughs were so successful that by the 1980s in the US a more general narrative had developed that 'the Japanese way' was the future and, by contrast, the US was in decline (Vogel 1979). Fuelled by technological advances in logistics, more diverse sources of supply and shorter product lifecycles, 'flexibility' became an increasingly popular watchword in business. The related development of the field of 'supply-chain management', a term first coined in 1982, helped to provide further insights into how goods could be made more cost effective (Mentzer *et al.* 2001). One contemporary example of the agility of supply-chain networks can be seen in the assembling of Apple's iPhone in China. In a story told to a journalist, Apple had ordered a redesign of the iPhone screen weeks before the product was to receive its debut. Upon hearing the news, the factory foreman immediately roused his 8000 workers from their dormitories to begin refitting the new screen. Within four days, the plant was shipping 10,000 new iPhones every 24 hours. At later periods of peak demand, Chinese factories were producing around 400,000 iPhones every day. As one Apple executive commented on witnessing this episode, 'The speed and flexibility is breathtaking' (quoted in Duhigg and Bradsher 2012).

What has emerged, therefore, is a new business model, one which has been adapted across many industries in manufacturing and services, and one which promotes so-called 'lean' firms. The notion of company 'leanness', an expression that entered into corporate vocabularies in the 1990s in the US, is conceptually linked to the broader rethinking on flexibility in the neoliberal period (Holweg 2007). To draw upon the physical analogy, leanness implies thinness, without superfluous fat. The idealised slimmed-down company should, according to this model, have few grades of hierarchy between the top and bottom, subcontract many tasks that do not form part of its core operations and make investments in the form of alliances and joint ventures with other firms (Boltanski and Chiapello 2007; see also McKinsey & Company 2014). It is claimed that this grants the company a suppleness, or ambidexterity, as some authors express it, to navigate the uncertain challenges and opportunities in the marketplace. Flexibility is, thus, intuitively grasped by many corporate practitioners as a way to express a capability for managing change and risk in business environments. In other words, the term has proliferated not only because it carries positive connotations but because it appears to say something important, even vital, about the survivability of firms (Fellenz 2008).

Perhaps the most contested debates surrounding the term 'flexibility' in mainstream policy are those associated with the question of labour. Many neoclassical economists, notably those tied to institutions such as the Organisation for Economic Cooperation and Development (OECD), tend to favour 'labour-market flexibility' and, by contrast, claim that too much regulation or 'rigidities' (such as employment-protection schemes or union participation in wage setting) represent something negative. The core message from such writers has remained largely consistent since the 1970s, including particularly confident declarations in the 1990s with additional caveats since the 2000s. More flexible wages and employment laws, it is argued, help to enable a more rapid clearing of excess supply or demand, a policy environment that is useful when external shocks, like bouts of recession, hit the economy (OECD 1996; McBride *et al.* 2008). Thus, a core meaning of flexibility here may indeed be the ease with which an employer can hire and fire. These arguments need not always be specific, but are often couched in the discourse of 'enterprise' and 'competitiveness' in a 'global economy'. In addition to these debates, a more worker-centred impulse behind working-time flexibility has come from other sources, including feminist campaigners and labour unionists who have fought for women's access to the workplace and better childcare support from employers. The related notion of 'flexitime' (first conceived in the 1970s in West Germany with the term *gleitzeit*, literally 'sliding time'), where the employee has some control over their start and finish times, has now become commonplace in many professional organisations. The expansion of flexitime initiatives has been enabled by different factors, but technological developments, such as mobile computing and the growth of the internet, have nurtured alternative working patterns that previously could not have existed.

Despite these potential advantages, a number of criticisms and cautions can be made. One major worry is that the meaning of labour flexibility is sometimes narrowly conceived, with a bias towards the interests of owners and managers over workers. Across OECD countries, since the mid 1990s, more than half of job creation has come in the form of non-standard work (temporary, part-time or self-employed)

(OECD 2015a). For instance, in the US, temporary jobs have grown substantially since the 1980s, peaking at almost three million workers in 2000 (Luo *et al.* 2010). Such workers tend to earn less than full-time employees in the same position, receive fewer or no benefits (such as healthcare), have fewer chances for upward mobility, remain most at risk of being dismissed and most vulnerable to associated psychological stresses (Kalleberg *et al.* 2000; Hatton 2011). In the UK, controversy was sparked in 2013 over the use of so-called 'zero-hours' contracts by companies such as McDonald's and even Buckingham Palace. Similar to the idea of day labourers in other parts of the world, a zero-hours employee is on call with no set minimum hours or definite schedule. As critics have pointed out, this can lead to a precarious existence for such workers, including difficulties managing household budgets, family commitments and access to tax credits and other benefits (Pennycook *et al.* 2013; see also the Getting By Project (2015) for a revealing case study of thirty low-income working families in Liverpool). As one commentator bluntly put it, 'many people on zero-hours contracts do not want flexibility. They want a proper job, with training and progression' (McDermott 2013).

Flexible work programmes look less attractive when one moves from the rhetoric to the actual practice. For instance, one US study found that only 11 per cent of the full-time labour force had an official agreement with their employer to vary their hours (Weeden 2005). Joan C. Williams has coined the phase 'flexibility stigma' to account for this apparent discrepancy. The evidence tends to show that US workers fear (with good reason) that their use of flexibility policies will result in wage penalties, lower performance evaluations and fewer promotions. If accurate, 'flexibility programs appear to be merely "shelf paper," offered for public relations reasons but accompanied with the tacit message that employees use workplace flexibility at their peril' (Williams *et al.* 2013: 210). When combined with professional workplace norms of long hours, including an increase in people accepting 'extreme jobs' of more than 70 hours per week, such patterns reveal how the idealised 'work–life balance' may never be realised (Hewlett and Luce 2006). Similar patterns have been witnessed elsewhere. For example, South Koreans work some of the longest hours in the world, averaging over 2100 hours per year (OECD 2015b). Since the early 2000s, the government and large companies have tried to reduce working hours, stung by different criticisms, including high suicide rates, lower levels of productivity compared to other OECD countries and efforts to boost the overall employment rate. However, workaholic cultures are resistant to change, and the adoption of flexible working hours is still low, particularly in the manufacturing sector (Bae and Kim 2014). As one South Korean software developer commented to a journalist on annual leave entitlements, 'I can't imagine missing two weeks in a row because I don't want to upset my boss' (quoted in Jung-a 2015). We can see that there are certain tensions, even paradoxes, surrounding the term 'flexibility'. Its popularity appears to derive from its conceptual looseness and the tendency for it to carry positive overtones. On the one hand, the expression allows users to appeal to ideas associated with change, competition and innovation. On the other hand, it does not imply radical transformation and, thus, the capacity to be flexible could also refer to the robustness or stability of an object. Users of the concept appear to oscillate – consciously or unconsciously – between these various meanings. It is perhaps not surprising, therefore, that flexibility finds a comfortable home within the vocabulary of neoliberal capitalism. The word signals that all players, from CEOs to shop-floor workers, should be (perpetually) ready to act and move in response to 'the needs of the market'. The extension of the term into debates on work–life balance has only further naturalised its neoliberal applications. In this sense, the expression both reflects and constructs a general ethic of fitness that socialises agents into particular capitalist dispositions. Yet this capacity to adjust, across many social spaces, is often unequally distributed, thus prompting the perennial question: flexibility for whom and under what conditions?

See also: **adjustment, business, change, choice, competition, enterprise, experience, freedom, network, project, reform**.

Further reading: Fellenz 2008; Williams *et al.* 2013; Womack *et al.* 2007[1990].

FREEDOM

'Freedom' is one of the most slippery and controversial terms in neoliberal vocabulary, and we might well say that it even delights in displaying a kaleidoscopic-like complexity. Any evaluation of the word has to be approached with care, not least because freedom is burdened with significant historical meaning, along with criticism and suspicion. In ordinary parlance, the word implies the absence of constraint or inhibition and is commonly paired with liberty (English contains both 'freedom' and 'liberty' as separate but related terms, but French only *liberté* and German only *freiheit*). As a scholarly term, particularly within philosophy and politics, 'freedom' is often used to descriptively or normatively define the problem spaces of socio-political life, with an emphasis on questions of power, responsibility and the distribution of resources (for classic studies, see Mill 2008[1859]; Berlin 1969; MacCallum 1967; for overviews, see Connolly 1993; Carter 2003; Pereboom 2009). Interests associated with the term can range from conservative to radical and sometimes both at once. Thus, freedom can be invoked to defend an existing orthodoxy – including societies with highly oppressive features such as dictatorships – as well as to frame or underpin the articulation of a future utopia. As Wendy Brown (1995: 6) argues, 'Freedom is neither a philosophical absolute nor a tangible entity but a relational and contextual practice that takes shape in opposition to whatever is locally and ideologically conceived as unfreedom'. In short, the determination of what freedom is, what it should be, who shapes its definition and how actors experience life under its name are open and often difficult questions.

For those associated with defending neoliberalism, the appeal to freedom has served as a theoretical backbone for countless arguments. From the 1930s, within an influential network of thinkers that later formed the Mont Pèlerin Society, 'economic freedom' was promoted as 'essential not merely for the sake of freedom itself, but for efficiency in production' (quoted in Plehwe 2009: 23). Above all, this freedom was expressed in terms of the individual: the consumer to choose what they wished to purchase, the producer to decide what they wanted to make and the worker to select their place of employment. Following the experience of Nazism and the rise of so-called 'collectivist threats' that were framed in opposition to this sense of freedom (including not only state socialism and trade unions, but monopolistic corporations), writers such as Karl Popper 2002[1945], Ludwig von Mises (2007) and Friedrich von Hayek (2008[1944], 1960) sought to reimagine how liberalism could be advanced. Many of these writers drew inspiration from Victorian notions of human progress through capitalism but, at the same time, they also sought to criticise the more radical ideal of *laissez-faire* as a 'grotesque' (Lippmann 2009[1937]: 186) basis for policymaking. Although there were often disputes within this 'neoliberal thought collective' (Mirowski and Plehwe 2009), many were keen to advocate a strong state, backed by the rule of law, as the best arbitrator for a flourishing market economy (Jackson 2010; Jones 2012). In this sense, although national planning was not rejected *tout court*, in the mind of thinkers such as Hayek (2008[1944), a communist economy would always generate greater unfreedom for all.

The relationship between the idea of freedom and neoliberalism has been debated in various ways. Three illustrations can be given here. First, the concept has a seemingly endless capacity to be recycled in arguments that seek to defend capitalism. As Boltanski and Chiapello

(2007) suggest, the desire for emancipation and the cultivation of the self is one of the most durable justifications in the history of capitalism. This dichotomy between a positive freedom and a negative other reappears in many arguments, such as wage-earning power versus serfdom, urban opportunities versus rural limitations and the liberating workplace versus the restricted home. Freedom is also associated with more intangible spaces, forms of organisation or subjectivities that are claimed to result in favourable outcomes. For instance, free trade, which is often contrasted with protectionism or autarky, is sometimes considered to epitomise neoliberalism at large (Harvey 2005), although the phrase is found as far back as the late sixteenth century (Irwin 1996). The genealogy of 'free markets' (along with the associated 'free market economics', a largely pejorative phrase) is, however, something that is more distinctly neoliberal. Although this term is found in the eighteenth century, it only grew in popularity from the 1930s, with a notable conceptual take-off from the late 1970s. The opinion of popular economists (Friedman 2002[1962]; Friedman and Friedman 1979), as well as libertarian think tanks, such as the Cato Institute, helped to spread the phrase. In the pages of the *New York Times*, 'free markets' is found in 167 stories in the 1970s, 405 in the 1980s and 835 in the 1990s. By contrast, the phrase 'free enterprise' has actually experienced a decline in use over the neoliberal period, probably because it was strongly tied to certain debates in the Cold War period. However, 'enterprise', without the preface of 'free', remains an adaptable neoliberal term.

But what precisely is free within free markets? It is easy to appreciate how activities under the name of the free market may feature degrees of liberation and, equally, degrees of social suffering. Actors can encounter different experiences on the basis of geography, education, class, gender or race. In other words, relations of inequality – taking structural, institutional or personal forms – are often historically embedded within capitalist societies. The coffee farmer who earns less than US$1 per hour in Guatemala, the Starbucks barista who works for US$10 per hour and the cappuccino-sipping corporate lawyer who takes home US$1000 per hour are clearly experiencing different kinds of freedom (on contemporary questions of income inequality, see Piketty 2014; Oxfam International 2014; Milanovic 2011). At the same time, in contrast to simplified depictions of the free market as a defence against government 'meddling', the reality of statecraft, neoliberal or otherwise, has always been characterised by complex ties of dependence between 'state' and 'market', to the extent that the distinction between the two categories may dissolve in practice. For instance, state financing of infant industries or policies of 'corporate welfare' (subsidies, tax breaks, limitations on union organising, etc.), show how the definition of freedom in commercial life is always a political construction with uneven outcomes. As Karl Polanyi (2001[1944]: 146) observed, 'The road to a free market was opened and kept open by an enormous increase in continuous, centrally organized and controlled interventionism'. In recent years, in light of growing criticism, it is interesting to note that the expression 'free markets' is perhaps not uttered as enthusiastically as in the late twentieth century (for instance, the frequency of the term has declined in both *The Economist* and the *New York Times*).

A second illustration of the vexed relationship between neoliberalism and freedom surrounds the issue of democracy. For writers and policy elites associated with neoliberal ideas, political freedoms are often claimed to be best nurtured and protected through a market system. As Friedman (2002[1962]: 8) encapsulated it, 'economic freedom is also an indispensable means towards the achievement of political freedom'. For example, since the 1970s, the work of Freedom House, a non-profit group which receives US government funding, has been influential in efforts to rank freedom among nations in statistical terms (Freedom House 2014). According to some analysts, the neoliberal character of such research can be seen in the tendency of Freedom House to stress civil rights to the detriment of other socio-economic rights, as well as promoting 'the market' as an inevitably liberating force (Giannone 2010). Freedom House would have us believe that the model is applicable for all, but it clearly carries an imprint of American cultural values. By the 1990s, following the fall of the Berlin Wall and claims that the 'end of history' had arrived (Fukuyama 1992), the phrase 'free and fair elections' dramatically increased in use, having entered the UN system in the late 1950s (see also Huntington 1991; Whitehead 2002). Although this expression can be heard on the lips of policymakers, journalists and political scientists alike, the concrete realisation of free and fair elections is often a work in progress and open to interpretation or, indeed, manipulation (Elklit and Svensson 1997; Goodwin-Gill 2006). One may have an election whereby voters face few constraints on reaching the ballot box, yet the outcome could still be distorted by subsequent abuses, such as miscounting. The appeal to free and fair elections is also linked with other neoliberal concepts that help to normalise further such agendas, such as good governance, reform, voice and accountability.

If one undertakes a closer examination of the relationship between neoliberalism and democracy, more profound paradoxes and contradictions often appear. One issue concerns how practices and rules associated with neoliberalism seem to be highly adaptable across political systems, including dictatorships, monarchies and so-called 'weak democracies'. For instance, in Chile in the 1970s, under the military dictatorship of Augusto Pinochet and the influence of a group of Chicago-trained economists, radical projects in privatisation and trade liberalisation were conducted, often to the detriment of the poor (Winn 2004; Peck 2010; Van Horn *et al.* 2013). In the Middle East, countries such as Egypt and the United Arab Emirates have historically received support from Western powers to advance neoliberal reforms, despite (or perhaps because of) oppressive and paternalistic governing (Soliman 2011; Roccu 2013a; Davis 2007). Elsewhere, in the case of China, notwithstanding some local experiments at the village level, formal democratic practices have been highly circumscribed by the Communist Party (Tsai 2007; Dickson 2008). Another major controversy at the nexus between neoliberalism and the ideals of democracy concerns the increase in technocratic rule-making via experts, non-elected bureaucrats and corporations. At the systemic level, as capitalism has intensified, this problem has become more pronounced, with the entry requirements of certain professions (such as finance) featuring exacting demands for knowledge. With respect to the EU, there are longstanding debates on the democratic deficit between, on the one hand, EU institutions and, on the other, member governments and citizens (Follesdal and Hix 2006; Nicolaïdis 2013). Such concerns received a fresh spotlight in the Eurozone crisis when indebted countries, including Greece, Spain and Ireland, were forced to implement austerity measures authorised by the European Commission and the IMF, bodies that are perceived by many to have no (or a disputed) chain of delegated legitimacy to 'the public'.

A third and related area where freedom becomes a conceptual and political object of struggle relates to the question of law – in particular, the expression 'rule of law'. As argued by Raymond Plant (2012: 5), the 'idea of the rule of law lies at the heart of the neo-liberal view of the nature and role of the state'. According to Plant (2012), intellectuals such as Hayek and Mises understood the rule of law not as a panacea, but as a moral ideal bound up with their vision of a free society and the so-called 'spontaneous' market order. In the twentieth century, the phrase 'rule of law' has undergone two waves of popularity, both of which have been driven by experts and policymakers in the US, Europe and international institutions. The first period, from the late 1950s to the early 1970s, involved the promotion of the concept as a way to 'modernise' developing countries, such as through efforts to form independent judiciaries removed from professional politics (Dezalay and Garth 2002a, 2002b; Trubek 2006). The second phase, from the mid 1980s to the present, is where the neoliberal influence becomes more visible. At the World Bank, along with many organisations that follow its lead, rule of law is often imagined as an instrument to enable private transactions, a move which, in turn, is justified as a path to economic growth. The state acts as the guardian for enforcing private property rights, with a particular emphasis on protecting the interests of foreign investors, but it is not supposed to descend into local rent seeking. Former Communist countries and other societies deemed to have 'fragile states' have become key audiences for such discourse (Santos 2006). By the late 1990s, as the neoliberal period matured, 'anti-corruption' became an important ancillary concern at the World Bank, an agenda that was promoted with particular zeal under James Wolfensohn's leadership (1995–2005).

Within the larger vocabulary of neoliberalism, the term 'rule of law' is now ubiquitous and circulates with remarkable ease, in part because it offers a kind of 'easy universalism' (Humphreys 2010: 220) or 'standard menu' (Carothers 1999: 168). But the relationship between law and freedom, however precisely defined, is often ambiguous with uneven distributional effects. In one sense, rule-of-law promotion, with its roots in Anglo-Saxon (in particular, English) culture, often ignores how many countries have very different historical systems of legal understanding, such as religious-based customs. In other contexts, in the hands of some political elites, rule-of-law rhetoric appears to be little more than 'obey the law', a charge made by Hong Kong pro-democracy protesters in their struggle against the Chinese government (Pilling and Zhu 2015). One should also keep in mind that, despite all the talk about anti-corruption initiatives, various abuses are seemingly embedded within many industries, such as financial traders who have been caught fixing market prices or energy companies who use slush funds to bribe government officials. Finally, within a broader trend towards the legalisation of the world economy, one could also address how law is used as a weapon to enhance the freedoms of already powerful corporations. Such tendencies have been strengthened through many domestic and international forums, including the WTO and an expanding architecture of investment arbitration rules. When combined with scandalous levels of executive pay and displays of conspicuous consumption, one can understand why many express scepticism or even disillusion concerning what the word 'freedom' actually means. At the same time, and it is a good note to end on, without its utopian undertow we would lack so much of the negative critique 'freedom' affords.

See also: **choice, class, community, consensus, development, diversity, enterprise, experience, flexibility, governance, individual, market, network, openness, participation, power, private, project, stakeholder, state, trade, welfare**.

Further reading: Brown 1995; Connolly 1993; Friedman 2002[1962]; Hayek 1960.

GLOBAL

Despite its current popularity, the term 'global' remains curiously understudied. Sabine Selchow argues that the notion has 'triggered very little interest, investigation or critical engagement. It has been widely naturalised, which means that it is taken for granted and treated as an "innocent" or descriptive attribute – both in political practice and in the contemporary political studies discourse' (Selchow 2008: 224). Dating from the seventeenth century, and originally spelt 'globular', it acquired the unproblematic meaning of something that has a spherical form. By the nineteenth century, 'global' took on an extended meaning of anything that appeared to display comprehensiveness, universality or totality and, through these senses, became synonymous with 'world' or 'worldwide'. Nevertheless, from the late nineteenth century until the First World War, in a period that some authors have dubbed the 'first era of globalization' because of increased commercial exchange, 'global' was not a word in frequent use (Friedman 1999: xvii). Thus, during this period, *The Economist* makes only two references to the word, and even through the 1920s, a decade marked by the rising power of a transnational financial elite, it is still largely invisible. Only in the 1940s, in the shadow of war and the making of the United Nations, does 'global' begin to become a word of political note. Indeed, by 1950, *The Economist* was casually referring to 'the age of global politics' (*The Economist* 1950: 18).

In the postwar period, prior to the mainstreaming of neoliberal ideas, a number of complex forces – some combining, others disparate and even contradictory – gave rise to the notion of humanity existing as one world. Among these trends, the defeat of Nazism and the creation of the UN Charter promoted the idea that the histories of all nations – or at least in the West – were hopefully on a path to universal peace founded on human rights. The collapse of the European empires, a process that was uneven and accompanied by advances and retreats, was nonetheless driven by the related idea of self-determination, now a cardinal principle of international law. The meaning of global also took on a new twist with the desire, particularly on the part of the US, to reconstruct and advance the capitalist system in the face of communism, although the precise phrase 'global capitalism' tended only to be used by academics. However, the association between global and development was more common in political discourse, perhaps because the term 'development' remained more politically neutral. For instance, in 1968, the UN's core agency for economic policy called its main report *Towards a Global Strategy of Development* (UNCTAD 1968). At the same time, the lowering of transportation and communication costs created the conditions for Marshall McLuhan to coin his famous phrase 'global village', a prophetic vision of cross-border cultures defined by 'electronic interdependence' (McLuhan 1962: 31). Finally, one could also point to ecological fears, provoked by different social movements from the 1960s, which heightened awareness of the earth's finite natural resources and the need to protect the environment. By 1968, the sense of planetary fragility and oneness was given an acute new perspective by the publication of the first NASA images of the globe.

While 'global' peppered debates in these different contexts, the most dramatic development of the term occurred when neoliberal ideas began to test the political waters. By the 1980s, the power of major business interests had become more transnational, with networks of competition that connected three main continental centres of activity: North America, Europe and East Asia (Ohmae 1985). However, this appeal to a unified and ever expanding economic system, which, by the 1990s, was embracing so-called 'emerging markets' such as China, India and Brazil, only acquired a taken-for-granted feel with the ending of the Cold War. For instance, in the *Financial Times* prior to 1990, the phrase 'global economy' was used 18 times, but during the 1990s, it is found in 175 stories, and by the first decade of this century 809 uses are recorded. With the collapse of Communism, the notion of building a global business or, perhaps more precisely in many cases, *aspiring to be seen as* global, became a possibility for countless corporate entities. Every leading company now has global operations, global strategies and new job titles prefaced with the word. The discursive shift was quickly reflected by *Fortune* magazine, which, in 1990, perceptively changed the title of their ranking of the world's largest corporations from 'international' to 'global', commenting that

> the global village is truly upon us, it looks more like a global industrial park. We live in an expansive new world of economic interconnections where business roars through borders and time zones. To keep up with it, *Fortune* on these pages introduces the Global 500.
>
> (quoted in Pak and Solo 1990)

By the turn of the century, in the minds of many popular opinion makers, politicians and academics, globalisation was the *zeitgeist*, a dominant perspective through which to grasp seemingly inevitable commercial and technological processes. As one spokesperson for President George W. Bush expressed it in 2001, 'Globalization is a reality, not a choice or a policy' (Haass 2001). However, what the term 'globalisation' actually meant and what it was claimed to explain was less clear, despite (or perhaps because of) frequent attempts to ground the concept (Ohmae 1990; Robertson 1992; Rosenau 1997; Castells 1996; Giddens 1999a; Held et al. 1999; Held and McGrew 2000a; Scholte 2005; for a genealogy of the concept, see James and Steger 2014). Out of this academic cottage industry, came two common themes (Rosenberg 2005). First came the claim that a force called globalisation was producing a fundamental change in how human societies understood space and time. The integration of markets, the shrinking of decision-making time horizons and the use of new technology was leading to what some geographers called 'time-space compression' (Harvey 1990: 147). As David Held and Anthony McGrew argued in their often quoted summary, globalisation was 'the expanding scale, growing magnitude, speeding up and deepening impact of interregional flows and patterns of social interaction' (Held and McGrew 2000b: 4). Linked to this was a series of other debates about whether globalisation was 'a good thing', with many prominent economists arguing in the affirmative (Collier and Dollar 2002; Bhagwati 2004; Wolf 2004). Second, it was argued that these changes were becoming so profound that the 'mantle of a new paradigm' was needed (Held and McGrew 2000b: 1). Older bodies of social theory, such as Marxism or realist power politics, were seen as insufficient to grasp these conditions. Categories of analysis that had previously occupied a central place in the social sciences – including social class, the capital–labour relationship and territorialism – appeared, from the perspective of globalisation theorists, to be less valuable or even redundant for explaining the modern world.

But almost as soon as 'globalisation' had become a pervasive term, it was met with its opposite: 'anti-globalisation'. Its origins are unclear, but academic uses begin to appear around the mid 1990s and can be considered conceptually allied with 'de-globalisation', a slightly older term (see early references in MacEwan 1994; Castells et al. 1996). This period was notable for how various protest movements coalesced in opposition to policies associated with economic globalisation, particularly corporate-led privatisation. Activists argued that such trends, promoted by Western governments and institutions such as the World Bank, were increasing inequality and perpetuating poverty in less developed countries (for instance, see Watkins and Fowler 2002). Such opinions were lent extra credence by Joseph E. Stiglitz's *Globalization and its Discontents*

(2002), a book that challenged mainstream opinion and sold over one million copies. However, the anti-globalisation movement was always a contested discursive frame, not least because many actors who were claimed to be a part of it – from Greenpeace through farming unions in South Korea to critics like Naomi Klein – rejected the label. What *was* in dispute was not all the many processes associated with globalisation, since, for example, there were innovative uses of the internet for mobilisation and many of these actors valued cosmopolitan attitudes (Eagleton-Pierce 2001). Rather, these critics argued for a redesign or transformation of certain features of globalisation or, as they expressed it in many contexts, neoliberal capitalism. This led some activists to promote the phrase 'alter-globalisation' as a way of positioning themselves against the 'anti' prefix they regarded as a mischaracterisation, an idea that derived from France with the expression *altermondialisme* (literally, alternative universalism). This tactic was viewed as all the more necessary because anti-globalisation was also tied to politically right-wing voices, or even paranoid conspiracy theorists, who were strongly nationalistic on different issues (for the US case, see Barkun 2013).

If globalisation became a contested idea – a 'great debate' – the same could not be said of 'global'. The consequence of the latter term having a 'settled' and seemingly unproblematic meaning can, still, be viewed as troubling for different reasons. One worry is that 'global' in many contexts can be a confusing word. Often, it has a normative quality to describe a practice that may not actually exist, as in activists who campaign for global justice or global health. The objective is that justice and health should be fundamental rights for all people, across the globe, but such an outcome has yet to be realised and most likely never will be. This does not preclude that global should never be associated with justice and health but, rather, that when an issue is prefaced by global, it tends to enhance the gravitas of the subject (due to the core meanings of universalism and comprehensiveness and, therefore, *not* particularism and arbitrariness). As Selchow notes, the 'term "global" seems to be strangely embracing; it is used everywhere and appears to appeal to everybody and ultimately seems to refer to everybody' (Selchow 2008: 230). Yet one should always ask if other geographical or group categories are more precise for understanding the object of enquiry, such as transnational, international, regional, country or class-specific notions. 'Global' is thus a problematic term when it smooths over, or even suppresses, the complexities and unevenness of social and political life. Users of the term also risk falling into a teleological narrative which projects the global as some end stage of humanity, to be contrasted with, or developing out of, 'tradition' or the 'local' (although the portmanteau 'glocal' (1983, *OED*), with roots in business theory, has tried to respond to this criticism). Such a condescending assumption, as captured with the adjective 'globalising', is again troubling because it tends to discount non-linearity and unpredictability in the movement of history.

Given that 'global' implies no spatial boundaries, it is often held up as a desirable or unavoidable way to organise human relations; and given that it appears to lend any subject an immediate significance, it is perhaps not surprising that the term was integrated into neoliberal vocabulary. It cannot be a coincidence that the rise of the idea of globalisation parallels the decline of the more politically potent, if bruised, concept of capitalism, a phrase that conjures up images of conflict between capital and labour. This should sensitise us to the possibility that uses of 'global' – whether intentional or not – may obfuscate or confuse how power, particularly through in its financial forms, is actually distributed and maintained across borders. Phrases such as 'global markets' and 'global investors' are not simply casual business sound bites for a Bloomberg television audience, they help to constitute and validate particular configurations of political economy and not others. In one sense, within this relatively enclosed world of elites, only those who have the right financial resources, expertise, cultural standing and political acumen can consider themselves and – no less important – be identified by others as 'global players'. In another sense, however, such is the popularity of the term, and its affinity with ideals of cosmopolitanism, that the related phrase 'global citizen' has become a suit that seemingly anyone can wear if they choose, or, indeed, advertise to others as an ideal image (for instance, on the promotion of 'global citizenship' in human–rights education in Pakistan, see Khoja-Moolji 2014).

At times, in an instinctive and unthinking manner, it is almost as if the word 'global', when uttered by those brokers, dealers and close observers of the markets, resembles a tonic which reassures each participant of both their own self-importance and commonality with other powerful individuals. This feeling of self-satisfaction among what one author has called a 'global plutocracy' (Freeland 2012) is nurtured by the very exclusivity of accessing this social environment and harks back to the mid-Victorian period and self-made men like Josiah Bounderby in Dickens's *Hard Times* (2003[1854]), individuals who, as factory owners, amassed fortunes and in the process severed their ties with a common humanity. So great is the plutocracy today that fortunes, together with self-worth, can be maintained while being dispersed in acts of charity towards the greater good. The majority of humanity – the 99 per cent – will get nowhere close to this lifestyle bubble of corporate Gulfstream jets, the most expensive hotels from Los Angeles to Tokyo and invites to only the most private of private functions. Thus, appeals to the word 'global' are, in some contexts, indirectly exalting the privileges of this transnational class. In many ways – but this would take us into another discussion – we live not in a global world but in a remarkably insular world.

See also: **business, capitalism, community, emerge, environment, finance, governance, growth, market, openness, power, state, trade**.

Further reading: Bhagwati 2004; Rosenberg 2005; Scholte 2005; Selchow 2008; James and Steger 2014.

GOVERNANCE

'Governance' was a relatively dormant term until the 1990s, when it sparked into life. It is a very flexible word, deployed across a range of social spaces and institutions, but often used by actors who have different or even contradictory aims. Derived from the French *gouvernaunce*, the expression has always carried political connotations, associated with power and the action or manner of governing. In the late fourteenth century, the term entered English and was used by Geoffrey Chaucer with reference to both political and personal affairs (Cannon 1998; see also Hanawalt 1998). Governance could indicate the rule over a territory or the command of a military force, particularly in nautical contexts to define practices of steering and directing (from the Latin *guberno*). At the same time, the word also referred to general administrative control, not confined to states but also applied to control within the household (see Johnson's *Dictionary* (1755)). The expression thus shares something of its early history with the word 'economy'. For most of the twentieth century, it was not particularly popular. Indeed, in one edition of the *Chambers Twentieth Century Dictionary* published in 1972, governance was defined as obsolete. Its revival and reinterpretation has taken place within the neoliberal period, although not all meanings associated with the word should be considered reflective of a capitalist ethic. Thus, the 'comet-like' rise of governance is interesting not simply for understanding neoliberalism, but also for how the word sheds light on larger struggles over the relationship between language and power in political life (Offe 2009: 550).

Within the academic fields of political science, public policy and international relations, there remains considerable debate over what phenomena should be classified under 'governance' and how the term enhances our understanding of the political world (Rosenau 1992; Rhodes 1997; Stoker 1998; Weiss 2000; van Kersbergen and van Waarden 2004;

Kjaer 2004; Bevir 2006, 2011; Levi-Faur 2012). For many users, governance can be compared to government, either as an alternative or complementary concept. Stemming from this initial position, authors and policymakers who invoke the notion often claim that power and decision-making today do not only reside with states but, instead, are diffused among a variety of actors, such as businesses and civil society organisations. Thus, it is claimed that the concept of governance helps to explain a 'fragmented and multidimensional order *within* the state, *by* the state, *without* the state and *beyond* the state' (Levi-Faur 2012: 1, italics in original). In particular, governance often appears as a way to denote major shifts in the location or form of politics, such as from states to markets, from politicians to experts or from the national to the global. The word can thus refer both to processes of rule (the steering of policymaking) and structures (the institutions of power) (Levi-Faur 2012). However, some critics have argued that the very ubiquity of the concept risks devaluing whatever utility it might potentially hold. As Guy Peters (2000: 35) has put it, 'the real danger is that governance becomes meaningless and a tautology; something happened and therefore governance occurred'. Others have suggested that the term can have problematic connotations around the ideas of consensus and partnership as part of a pluralist worldview, the values of which are not necessarily shared by all actors (Davies 2011).

How was the term 'governance' resuscitated in recent decades? In the first instance, from the 1970s in the US, its use began to arise in the context of legitimacy problems facing American businesses. This environment would, in turn, help to inspire certain policies associated with neoliberalism. The attachment of 'corporate' to 'governance' was a response to different forces and trends, but of chief significance were 'consumer-orientated politics', demands for increased shareholder power and open business reporting (for commentary at the time, see Jacoby 1973; see also Soederberg 2010; Cheffins 2013). The behaviour of leading managers intersected with all these concerns. It is important to recall that, during this decade, the public image of the US corporation was damaged as a result of improper executive conduct, investigated with particular enthusiasm by Ralph Nader and his contemporaries (the closest of whom were referred to as Nader's Raiders) (Nader *et al.* 1976a). One prominent example was consumer safety concerns at General Motors. Other criticisms surrounded reports of illicit payments made by US firms to foreign government officials, notably the Lockheed bribery scandal that led to political controversy and almost destroyed the company (Seligman 1982). Through the establishment of Public Citizen, his consumer-rights advocacy group, Nader secured a prominent platform to promote his vision of the federal chartering of

US companies (Nader *et al.* 1976b). In short, the wider crisis of confidence that marked the 1970s – labelled by some elite watchers as a 'problem of governability' afflicting Western democracies (Trilateral Commission 1975) – was bound up with a particular corporate legitimation problem.

According to William Ocasio and John Joseph (2005), Nader deserves primary credit for promoting an analogy between the governance of democracy and the governance of the corporation. By 1976, encouraged by Nader's corporate-accountability studies, the US Senate Committee on Commerce hosted a set of hearings on 'Corporate Rights and Responsibilities'. The term 'governance' was invoked in one session by Richard M. Cyert, then Dean of Carnegie Mellon University. He used it to comment on the relationship between chief executive officers, corporate boards and shareholders. By the end of 1976, the phrase 'corporate governance' was used for the first time in an official document, namely the US government journal the *Federal Register*. The term was noted in connection with an emerging study being conducted by the US Securities and Exchange Commission (SEC), which was to explore 'shareholder participation in corporate governance and, more generally, shareholder democracy' (Ocasio and Joseph 2005: 167). Elsewhere, by the late 1970s, in a series of symposia, the American Law Institute (ALI) and the American Bar Association began to react to what was being called 'the erosion doctrine' (Werner 1981: 1613). Out of these meetings came the ALI's decision to establish an initiative which would investigate what 'corporate governance' actually meant and how it could be legally defined (Schwartz 1979). Initially viewed as controversial by some, the ALI Corporate Governance Project was set up to address this perceived erosion of legitimacy – in particular, to control those managers who were straying too far from a perceived behavioural model. As the 1980s unfolded, corporate-governance literature flourished. Every top firm dispatched their leading counsel to the annual meetings of the ALI in order to shape the new meanings of the term. By uttering the word one could show to others – both critics and sympathisers – that one was being proactive in acknowledging the need for 'business reforms' or, just simply, 'reforms'.

Nonetheless, while the 1980s reflected an interest in the term, it was only in the 1990s that 'governance' became not just an accessible term to denote an increasingly complex world but a politically important one. Two major developments help to provide the context to explain why this change took place. First, there was a growing backlash against orthodox policies, particularly those that involved privatisation and trade liberalisation (the first wave of 'roll back' neoliberalism, as some authors express it; see Peck and Tickell 2002). For instance, as even a cursory glance of the results of 'free-market adjustment' programmes across Africa and Latin America illustrated, no economic project (conceptually bracketed as divorced from 'politics' in common justifications) was likely to be sustainable unless minimum conditions of state legitimacy, social order and institutional capacity were present. Critics began arguing that the state had been unnecessarily 'hollowed out', that this impeded the development process and that such conditions were caused by policy prescriptions emanating from institutions such as the World Bank and the IMF. The economy was embedded in society, they claimed, not the other way around (for instance, in policy literature, see Cornia *et al.* 1987; in scholarship, see Brown *et al.* 2000; Stiglitz 2002; Wade 2004). Second, with the ending of the Cold War, there emerged a dramatic weakening of an organised ideological counterweight to capitalism. But while there was celebration of this fact in many quarters, it did not mean that 'the market system' would be accepted by all people as a *fait accompli*. The need to prove, or, more precisely, to enhance the legitimacy of the prevailing orthodoxy never waned; on the contrary, the arguments devised to defend it grew ever more sophisticated (Stoker 1998; Bevir 2010).

From the 1990s, beyond business, the word 'governance' was tested within many institutional cultures that faced local problems of legitimacy. What this meant in practice was something of a paradox. On the one hand, given the way it is semantically linked to the art of governing, the term 'governance' appears to open a dialogue with the wider experience of politics or 'the political'. On the other hand, sometimes within the same moment, the word could also create effects that may actually confuse or obfuscate how forms of power are exercised (Eagleton-Pierce 2014). Again, one can cite the World Bank's work as an example of such tensions. Initially, in the early 1990s, the Bank was very tentative in defining governance (the first use came in World Bank 1989). Since its Articles of Agreement officially forbid it from 'doing politics', senior officials consulted with the Bank's general counsel to receive advice on how broadly 'governance' could be interpreted. When the legal memorandum was returned, it suggested that governance could be linked to 'good order and discipline in the management of a country's resources' (World Bank 1992: 5; see also Shihata 2000; Harrison 2004, 2010; Weaver 2008). But if the Bank was increasingly interested in the traditions and institutions of authority in every country, there was a danger that this would create the image of being too closely involved in the arena of professional politics. The word 'governance' was extremely helpful at this point in terms of managing the delicate (and supposedly dichotomous) relationship between what was defined as 'economic science' and what was considered the domain of 'politics'. Thus, the Bank argued that governance was being studied and shaped if it involved areas such as civil service and administrative 'reform', as long as such projects could be linked to 'economic development', its core remit.

Aided by its army of technicians and event planners, the Bank's definition expanded to encompass a range of other 'dimensions' or 'indicators' of governance. By 1996, governance meant the rule of law, government effectiveness and controlling corruption. By the end of the decade, another three components had been added under the same rubric: voice and accountability, political stability and the absence of violence, and regulatory quality (for a summary, see World Bank 2007). At the same time, the all encompassing notion of 'institutions' was often used as shorthand for such topics, a turn that was popularised by the field of new institutional economics and, in particular, the work of Dani Rodrik (2007). Thus, through constructing the governance agenda, the Bank cannot now be accused of ignoring the importance of the broader socio-political environment within which market relations are practised and promoted. Nevertheless, criticisms of the Bank's creation and deployment of governance can be made. One concern surrounds how the concept may open space for more intense and subtle methods for controlling national polities or, at the very least, for allowing the Bank to legitimately intervene in domestic issues (Eagleton-Pierce 2014). Some of the sharpest criticisms have focused on the ancillary notion of 'good governance', a phrase used to condemn corruption and cronyism. For James Thuo Gathii (2000: 973), 'good governance' tends to echo the modernisation theories of the postwar period or even colonial-era ideologies. As he argues with respect to African countries, such policy frameworks tend to 'share a skepticism of the African, who cannot be trusted to be self-governing', a figure who is imagined as having 'irrational impulses' in need of external discipline (see also Abrahamsen 2000).

In conclusion, it is important to note one other major derivative that has emerged during recent decades of neoliberalism: 'global governance'. Again, similar to its parent, this phrase is linked to the general restructuring of political organisation, only this time the focus is on international affairs (for introductions, see Weiss 2013; Weiss and Wilkinson 2013). The concept has roots in the 1960s in ideas about 'one world', crystallised by the NASA photographs of a finite blue planet, which could be destroyed by nuclear war. The work of Willy Brandt, who established the UN Commission on Global Governance in 1992, helped to popularise the notion. Global governance tends to express a cooperative and consensual approach to world affairs, involving multiple categories of actors. It is often claimed by political actors and policy analysts who identify with it that global governance – frequently associated with democratic principles, adherence to a market system and a belief in a common humanity and destiny – is necessary, desirable or both. Thus, global governance is considered a goal by many advocates, whereas global government is taboo. The phrase 'global governance' is often heard in discussions on globalisation, although one could speculate that since the late 1990s, when the category 'anti-globalisation' became more widely used, some speakers have carefully chosen to distance themselves from the term 'globalisation' and instead attach themselves to the equally amorphous, but less politically contentious, catch-all of 'global governance'.

See also: **development, global, finance, freedom, participation, performance, power, responsibility, risk, stability, stakeholder, state, trade, welfare**.

Further reading: Davies 2011; Eagleton-Pierce 2014; Harrison 2004; Kjaer 2004; Levi-Faur 2012.

GROWTH

It is not unreasonable to suggest that almost all political leaders within the neoliberal period have been absorbed in an obsession for economic growth (Hamilton 2003). The scrutiny afforded to economic growth – including its statistical calculation and the actions that could enable it to be produced or sustained – is fixation for many government agencies, businesses and media commentators. The difficulty of even imagining an alternative public discourse which does not feature this phrase speaks to its power. In terms of etymology, the noun 'growth' emerged in the sixteenth century, often in reference to the cultivation of vegetables, before broadening in meaning to represent a general process of advancement, improvement and quantitative increase (the verb 'grow' is much older). A strong theoretical influence on the development of the word came from the new biological sciences (Thompson 2014[1917]). In the eighteenth and nineteenth centuries, classical political economists, inspired by the natural sciences, did use the term 'growth', but it was not common. For instance, Adam Smith preferred alternative phrases, such as the 'process of opulence' or 'the continual increase of national wealth' (quoted in Brewer 1995: 610). Growth was often imagined as an inevitable mechanism in commercial society. At the same time, this period also featured early thinking on the idea of limits to capitalist expansion (Malthus 2008[1798]; Mill 1976[1848]). By the twentieth century, the influence of scientific reasoning was cemented in neoclassical economics, as explored in discussions of Alfred Marshall's scholarship by Mirowski (1989) and Niman (1991).

One cannot understand how to define economic growth and account for why it has assumed a dominant status in the neoliberal period without first pausing on the notion of 'the economy', with a preceding definite article. In Latin, *oeconomia*, from which the word 'economy' is derived, referred to private household management. The idea of economic growth, however, presupposes that a bounded object called 'the economy', imagined in national terms, can be discovered, measured and engineered. As argued by Mitchell (1998, 2008), this now accepted concept only appeared in the 1930s and did not become an official category of government concern until the 1950s (see the later popularity of Rostow 1960). The development of macroeconomics and econometrics provided the intellectual backdrop to this emergence, but the problem of mathematically measuring capitalism through new methods of accounting became politically urgent following the social upheavals of the Great Depression and the Second World War. War planning, for example, necessitated much better statistical analysis of the productive value of different industries. In the 1940s, in the US, the economist Simon Kuznets played an important role in designing a measure of national output, or what would develop into the now stan-dard Gross Domestic Product (GDP) (Kuznets 1941; see also Fogel *et al.* 2013). Such 'discussions were highly technical but the underlying issue was profound: what was the meaning of economic growth and why were statisticians measuring it?' (Coyle 2014: 15). In this respect, although economists often claim to be only describing the economy as a 'real' phenomenon, to initiate such analysis entailed the construction of the concept itself (Mitchell 2008).

As a baseline definition, economic growth usually refers to a positive expansion in the output of an economy measured by changes in per capita GDP. GDP can be calculated as either the total value of output or, equivalently, as the total income of the country, in the form of wages, rents, interest and profits. Thus, if an economy produces 10 per cent more goods and services over the course of a year then the growth rate is 10 per cent. The literature dedicated to understanding the measure-ment and causes of economic growth is one of the biggest in the canon of economics. Among the reasons given for explaining variation in economic growth, social scientists have explored factors such as popu-lation trends, investment capacity, technology, political institutions, education, geography and culture (for instance, see Easterly 2001; Rodrik

2007; Commission on Growth and Development 2008; Landefeld *et al.* 2008; Jones and Romer 2010; Weil 2013). Within a longer historical perspective, before the spread and consolidation of capitalism, economic growth tended to move at a glacial pace. From 1700 to 1820, in a period sometimes referred to as proto-industrialisation, average world growth in output per head was around 0.5 per cent. From 1820 to 1913, as the industrial revolution took hold, this figure reached 1.5 per cent. In the past century, from 1913 to 2012, average world output has been around 3 per cent (Piketty 2014; the calculations prior to the twentieth century are inevitably uncertain, see the Maddison Project Database website). Such figures may still appear low, abstract and almost imperceptible to everyday experience, but when compounded over a period of a generation (such as 30 years), an annual growth rate of even 1 per cent can result in 'deep and permanent' societal change (Piketty 2014: 96). This latter point is worth keeping in mind given certain expectations, such as those made by some financiers, that so-called 'substantial' growth only begins at around 3 per cent.

For critical scholars of neoliberalism, one major debate on growth has concerned how per capita output has tended to be lower from 1970 to the present than the initial postwar decades. In the context of a structural decline in productivity and the shift to a finance-led system, some writers have argued that the resulting lower growth proves that neoliberal policymaking is flawed (Harvey 2005; Duménil and Lévy 2011). At the global level, this statistical trend on growth is correct. For instance, in the so-called 'golden age' of economic growth from 1950 to 1970, per capita world growth output was 2.8 per cent, before declining to 1.3 per cent from 1970 to 1990 and subsequently rising to 2.1 per cent between 1990 and 2012. If one pursued the argument that 'neoliberalism has produced lower growth', one could also pick out particular pieces of evidence, such as the very high rate of 3.8 per cent in Europe from 1950 to 1970, before dropping to an average of 1.9 since 1970. Elsewhere, in Africa, the 0.3 per cent growth registered from 1970 to 1990 can be compared to a more healthy 2.1 per cent from 1950 to 1970 (Piketty 2014). However, data can also be mobilised to dispute this line of reasoning, which, in turn, reveals how there is always considerable variation in growth across time and space. In the neoliberal period, it is no surprise that institutions such as the World Bank, as well as many economists, have highlighted the locations where growth has outperformed historical expectations (Dollar and Kraay 2002; Bhagwati and Panagariya 2013; Dollar *et al.* 2013). For instance, since 1978, China has averaged around 10 per cent growth per year. Moreover, the speed of Chinese growth is without historical precedent: it took Beijing 12 years to double its per capita GDP, a pace 10 times faster than the first country to industrialise, the UK (McKinsey Global Institute 2012).

One can see how economic growth often appears as a 'grand narrative' that seems to permeate countless decisions in government policymaking and beyond (Friman 2002). In general, positive growth is associated with lower unemployment, higher income and tax revenue and lower government borrowing costs. It is often argued that growth is needed, in particular, for reducing poverty. However, along with the argument that the neoliberal period has experienced lower average levels of global growth, there are other criticisms of the entire paradigm. One concern centres on the relationship between growth and the distribution of material benefits. According to one study, between 1999 and 2008, the poorest 30 per cent of the world population obtained only 1.2 per cent of the additional income generated by global GDP growth. By contrast, 95 per cent of the new income was pocketed by the richest 40 per cent (Woodward 2015). When economic growth increases, income inequality tends to widen, since the rich pull away from the rest through accruing interest on equities, savings and property (Piketty 2014). Moreover, an increasing body of evidence suggests that rising income inequality can, in turn, result in lower levels of subsequent economic growth (Stiglitz 2012; Cingano 2014; Ostry *et al.* 2014). This latter recasting of the growth–equity relationship can be compared to earlier debates in the neoliberal period where established institutions tended to marginalise distributional concerns (for instance, see World Bank 2000). A related and animated public debate has also surrounded the extent to which economic growth, beyond a certain level, may not lead to qualitative improvements in the overall satisfaction of citizens. As one book argued, '[n]ot only have measures of wellbeing and happiness ceased to rise with economic growth but, as affluent societies have grown richer, there have been long-term rises in rates of anxiety, depression and numerous other social problems' (Wilkinson and Pickett 2010: 5–6).

Beyond the social and economic costs that may be implicated in the drive for growth, there are also prominent ecological concerns. The 1970s witnessed lively debates on the potential environmental harm caused by economic growth, stimulated by landmark publications such as the Club of Rome's *The Limits to Growth* (Meadows *et al.* 1972), which argued that capitalism was leading to the destruction of natural ecosystems, and Herman Daly's *Steady-State Economics* (1977), which helped to pioneer the field of ecological economics. In the neoliberal years, in the context of increasing consumerism and resource extraction, these critiques have been re-energised. In many political discussions, 'green growth', a phrase that emerged in the early 1990s, has become a focal point. Initially used to refer to the potential development of particular sectors concerned with environmental services, such as solar panels, the term 'green growth' has now broadened to encompass the entire economy, including systems of production and consumption (Jänicke 2012). As policymakers have struggled to grapple with both the aftermath of the financial crisis of 2007–9 and threats posed by climate change, green growth has been seized upon as a potential answer, even if its definition and the intended actions under its name remain ambiguous (Schmalensee 2012; Jacobs 2013; see also OECD 2011). Beyond these mainstream debates, in an echo of the 1970s, one also sees sharper critical analysis concerning the limits to material growth and its justifications. For instance, the term 'de-growth' has become a popular identifier among some activist movements, particularly coming out of France (*décroissance*) but also elsewhere in Europe (Demaria *et al.* 2013). In contrast to the appeal to green growth or sustainable development, de-growth expresses an alternative politics and ethics whereby the 'hegemony of growth' can be disputed and replaced by 'a democratically led redistributive downscaling of production and consumption' (Demaria *et al.* 2013: 209; see also D'Alisa *et al.* 2015).

Given all these problems surrounding economic growth in the neoliberal era, some researchers and polities have proposed alternative indicators of human wellbeing that are not (or are inadequately) captured within a single GDP number. Such ideas vary according to the degree to which the core category of economic growth is contested and have been a part of debates since the 1930s, when Kuznets warned against national calculations which did not incorporate a welfare component (Coyle 2014). In 1990, the UN launched their influential Human Development Index (HDI) as a composite statistic of life expectancy, education and per capita income indicators. As argued by its lead author, the Pakistani economist Mahbub ul Haq, economic growth, while necessary for sustaining wellbeing, does not necessarily equal higher levels of human development: 'It all depends on the policy choices that countries make. And the real world offers too many uncomfortable examples of a wide divergence between income and human development levels' (Haq 1995: 26). Dissatisfaction with the notion of GDP is now heard in many quarters and is by no means restricted to activists on the political left. For instance, in 2008, French President Nicholas Sarkozy established a commission of experts to investigate how to 'go beyond GDP' in the measurement of economic performance and social progress. Even in China, land of worship at the altar of economic growth, eyebrows were raised when the Shanghai local government became the first jurisdiction in the country to dispense with a GDP target (it merely aims to 'maintain steady growth') (*The Economist* 2015). A final alternative to growth can be found in the burgeoning field of 'happiness studies', which, in its efforts to apply insights from positive psychology to policymaking, also reveals the potential for emotions to be commodified into tradable resources (Davies 2015). In this sense, discourses in the neoliberal period may in some contexts sidestep GDP, but the competitive struggle for social distinction, from happy to unhappy, remains ongoing.

See also: **capitalism, development, emerge, entrepreneurship, environment, finance, global, innovation, market, reform, trade, welfare**.

Further reading: Coyle 2014; Piketty 2014.

INDIVIDUAL

In the Monty Python satirical film *Life of Brian* (1979), a famous scene captures something of the tension between the promotion of individuality and the often simultaneous desire of humans to be part of larger collectives. Brian, a rather jaundiced and unwilling Christ figure, finds his every movement and utterance studied by a growing number of disciples. At one point, Brian confronts the crowd to declare, 'Look, you've got it all wrong! You don't *need* to follow me. You don't need to follow *anybody*! You've got to think for yourselves! *You're all individuals!*'. To Brian's claim, the crowd responds: 'Yes! We're all individuals!'. Without sounding too philosophical, we might agree that this scene has a hint of truth. Prior to the eighteenth century, the notion of seeing oneself as 'an individual', a person with a unique set of properties and aspirations, was perhaps not common. The individual, as 'in-dividual' implies, was that which could not be divided into parts. Allegiance to family, clan, religion, empire, lord or king often superseded any claims to individual identity. In the thought of the Middle Ages, there was attention to 'the soul' (*anima*) or an 'inner core', but conceiving of 'the individual' as a *particular* self, unlike other selfs or selves, was less current than it is today (Bloch 2014[1940]; Bynum 1980). The transition to our modern sense of individuality has many origins and they are not easy to summarise, but in general we can notice that in Europe the movement against feudalism and towards capitalism provided the larger backdrop to such changes. Through the erosion of traditional social, economic and religious orders, the possibility of moving beyond an inherited position in society began to acquire greater legitimacy (Williams 1983[1976]).

From the eighteenth century, intellectual debates were a major catalyst in popularising the notion of the individual. Across a range of fields, including logic, biology and political economy, the concept steadily acquired its contemporary appearance: that is, the atomistic sense of a substantial entity (Williams 1983[1976]; Taylor 1989). Within the liberal tradition, from classical writers through to the neoliberal voices of today, the moral primacy of the individual has been consistently defended (Gray 1995). At root, this line of reasoning does not necessarily deny the significance of collectives (such as the state, society, community, etc.) but, rather, seeks to promote the abstract individual as normative, as *the* ontological starting point for analysis. Thus, Adam Smith argued that commercial society was the aggregate of individual decisions. But Smith was no defender of the radical vision of *laissez-faire*: the individual, in his view, needed forms of government for the wider good, such as for security. Smith's reading of *homo economicus* – a conceptual template of core motivations – was complex. He suggested that individuals, particularly when wealthy, could become slothful and indulgent but that human psychology also went beyond self-interest to embrace empathy for others (Smith 1993[1776]). From the late nineteenth century, in a departure from this latter appeal to subjective emotions, neoclassical economists began to redefine the concept. Their thinking continues to be very influential and, at the same time, a source of controversy in the wider social sciences. In essence, the neoclassical conceptualisation of the individual is a figure driven by private tastes (or preferences), who, significantly, acts as a 'rational' decision-maker in formulating choices. The ideal individual surfaces as a calculating agent that is, or, perhaps more precisely, a figure who *should be*, attentive to his or her material efficiency (Robbins 1932; see also Jevons 1871; for a critique, see Davis 2003).

As this theoretical framing of individual was being shaped, another significant conceptual extension emerged, one which continues to have relevance in debates over neoliberalism: the idea of individualism. Like socialism and communism, this term is a creation of the nineteenth century. One will search in vain for the term in Samuel Johnson's eighteenth-century *Dictionary* (1755). As traced by Steven Lukes (1973), individualism has a rich semantic history, with a range of meanings informed by national contexts. In the US, for instance, it became 'a symbolic catchword of immense ideological significance, expressing all that has at various times been implied in the philosophy of natural rights, the belief in free enterprise, and the American Dream' (Lukes 1973: 26). By contrast, in France, in particular, but also elsewhere, individualism has carried a pejorative tone, with the implication that to become too focused on the individual jeopardises the presumed higher interests of society. This latter connotation has, therefore, made individualism a useful concept for critics of capitalism, as illustrated by Karl Marx's argument that individuals are not born free and rational, but struggle to make their own history 'under circumstances existing already, given and transmitted from the past' (Marx 1852[2000]: 329). Thus, since the notion of individualism is mobilised in both the defence and the critique of capitalism, it is not surprising that strong users of the term believe that opponents have distorted or confused its meaning. For instance, Friedrich von Hayek (1948), often considered an early neoliberal thinker, argued for a 'true' theory of individualism, one which was against socialist approaches to society, but at the same time did not treat individuals as either isolated or infallible beings removed from larger forces.

How have the concepts of individual and individualism been recast in the neoliberal period? One noteworthy focus concerns the practices of consumerism. In advertising, the perfecting of the self, through the purchase of commodities, is frequently proffered as being both desirable and necessary. This neoliberal elaboration on 'individual' is particularly visible in two ways. First, the category of 'the consumer' has now extended into other fields, such as politics, education and health. While 'consumer' has always carried an unfavourable tone, initially meaning to destroy and to waste, one could argue that the popularisation of the term beyond purely commercial settings is helping to neutralise this criticism. At the same time, the increasing deployment of the related term 'user', notably in respect to public services, also points to the same underlying concern, namely the social sensitivities implied by labelling humans as consumers. Second, with the valorisation of choice and competitiveness as guiding principles for societal organisation, the appeal to personalisation and customisation offers further extensions of neoliberal thinking. From the late 1980s, these latter expressions became concerns for many businesses, with marketing theory helping to craft, and implement, such agendas. In one sense, the rise of 'mass customisation' systems was made financially viable by new flexible manufacturing processes, such as seen in the automotive industry (Davis 1989; Kotler 1989; Alford et al. 2000). But the digital revolution – if hypothetically abstracted from privacy concerns – offers marketing nirvana: an endless cycle of direct, tailored advertising and, in turn, feedback on the desires of each consumer. It is this potential of the internet to offer superior levels of efficiency that helps to explain why leading firms, such as Facebook and Google, receive considerable attention in financial markets.

The concept of the individual remains a complex and difficult notion to understand in the neoliberal period, not least because of gaps that often appear between the ideology of individualism and how social agents actually behave or desire to behave. Many critics have argued that neoliberalism is 'causing' a more individualistic and, by implication, privatised world. Margaret Thatcher's famous remark – that there is 'no such thing as society, only individual men and women' – is often quoted to support such claims (Harvey 2005: 23). Since the 1980s, across a number of industries, there is no question that the erosion of certain collective structures, notably trade unions, has weakened ties of solidarity that proved beneficial for worker rights (Gumbrell-McCormick and Hyman 2013). In turn, this trend has fuelled a corresponding emphasis by conservative voices on 'moral individualism' and 'responsibility', with a particular focus on the alleged personal inadequacies of poorer citizens who require state welfare (rather than exploring, for instance, class politics or other historical legacies that structure inequalities) (Wacquant 2009). The recent rise of the notion of 'individual resilience' has only served to underscore this general argument that the redistributive social state model is considered out of date (on the notion of resilience, see Joseph 2013; Chandler 2014). Such debates are important for shedding light on the power struggles that intersect between forms of capitalism, state structures and citizenship. However, as suggested by Clive Barnett, this analysis potentially risks creating a polarised opposition between individualism (as bad) and collectivism (as good). Barnett proposes that a different research agenda would uncover the 'new and innovative forms of individualized collective action' operating in the modern period (Barnett 2005: 11).

One can return again to consumer culture to explore this particular idea through three themes, each of which carries its own ironies. First, many forms of advertising promote an ambiguous tension between, on the one hand, the aspiration to fulfil personal individuality and, on the other, the social comfort of fitting into larger collectives or fashions (peer groups, social classes, nations, environmentalism, fair trade, religions, etc.). Again, these basic advertising strategies are not new, but have been tested and refined over decades or even centuries (Trentmann 2005, 2012, 2016). For instance, in Pakistan, Ammara Maqsood (2014) has shown how modern desires for consumption – often predicated on an idealised West – have become fused with Islam in the sale of items such as headscarves. One can debate the extent to which such notions of 'individualized collective action' are 'real', 'satisfying' or how they may conflict with other identities of the self, but one cannot deny that neoliberal consumerism pulls many levers at the same time. Such effects are, indeed, reminiscent of the seemingly paradoxical argument proposed by the sociologist Émile Durkheim (1973[1898]) that the ideology of individualism produces a necessary form of group solidarity within industrial society (see also Lukes 1969).

Second, it is always worth recalling that behind all advertising rhetoric lies a marketing machine that does not see a world of individuals. Rather, marketers see categories and segments of populations. Consumers are organised into boxes, by virtue of their similarities, such as by nationality, gender, age or income. The double irony here is how some consumers know this fact, yet still choose to treat the communication between the advertiser and themselves as 'personal', as if the *collective belief* in individualism has to be sustained. Third, forms of neoliberal consumerism are sometimes marked by the problem of too much choice, or 'overchoice', as Alvin Toffler (1970: 263) once put it, leading to anxiety and potential paralysis in decision-making. Many companies now treat this as a major concern and, as a consequence, try to simplify their product lines and communications to make the act of choosing easier – and therefore paying (Chernev 2003; Schwartz 2004; Gourville and Soman 2005). In an echo of *Life of Brian*, it is almost as if crowds of consumers are crying out to be led towards a particular choice, even if each prefers to be known as 'an individual': we're all together *and* 'we're all individuals'.

See also: **choice, community, enterprise, entrepreneurship, experience, freedom, network, openness, private, project, responsibility, welfare**.

Further reading: Barnett 2005; Davis 2003; Hayek 1948; Lukes 1973; Trentmann 2005, 2016.

INNOVATION

'Innovation' (from the Latin *innovatio*) refers to the action of altering established forms by introducing new elements. The word entered English in the mid sixteenth century, around the same time as the scientific revolution was emerging, and has historically carried an emphasis on originality and imagination in knowledge creation. Not surprisingly, 'innovation', and the attributing of the title of 'innovator' or 'inventor' to certain individuals, is often intended to carry a prestigious meaning. In the neoliberal period, the use of the term has become commonplace, to the extent that *The Economist* once declared innovation to be the 'industrial religion of the late 20th century' (Valéry 1999). However, when the rhetoric of innovation is applied to many practices, within business and beyond, its value can become unclear or even misleading. What constitutes the difference between a so-called 'innovative' process or object and something that is merely a modification or a reform? Are some claims about innovation simply incremental changes that mask, or distract attention from, the reproduction of more important underlying conditions? Does the innovation under scrutiny offer normatively beneficial outcomes for all actors or only a select group? Probing such questions will help to shed light on the political economy of innovation rather than accepting it as a benign force for good or, in another respect, succumbing to forms of technological determinism that abstract the declared innovation from the wider social context. In this regard, we might notice how innovation has always been close to novelty but that its distribution has now undergone a change. In the eighteenth century when Samuel Johnson (1755) compiled his *Dictionary*, he was happy to say that innovation was 'to change by introducing novelties', but today, while we might want to claim a particular innovation has had profound effects, we cannot normally say the same of a novelty.

In economics, management theory and the field of science and technology studies, the role of innovation has assumed an important analytical status, particularly for understanding economic growth, competition and historical development (for reviews, see Fagerberg 2006; Fagerberg and Verspagen 2009; Martin 2012). Indeed, in some theoretical work, economists have categorised entrepreneurship or enterprise as a distinct factor of production, to be evaluated alongside the classic themes of land, labour and capital. The process of technological change has conventionally been divided into three stages: (1) invention, referring to the initial creation of new ideas; (2) innovation, meaning the commodification of an idea into a product; and (3) diffusion, referring to the spread of innovation into commercial environments or society at large (Metcalfe 2008). This linear model may appear too static for some, but nothing precludes exploring feedback linkages and relations between the stages. For Joseph Schumpeter, considered 'the father of the study of innovation' (Salter and Alexy 2014: 29) by some researchers in this area, most innovations in capitalism are not radically new, but merely novel combinations of things that already exist. For instance, as Henry Ford once remarked of the development of the Ford Model T, the first affordable automobile: 'I invented nothing new. I simply assembled into a car the discoveries of other men behind whom were centuries of work' (quoted in Hargadon 2003: 45). In other words, few innovations are crafted in a bubble but, instead, arise out of a combination of different conditions and forces.

One of the most enduring and remarkable features of capitalism concerns how it contains destructive tendencies which, in certain contexts, create new opportunities for wealth accumulation. This point has been noted by many observers and allows us to draw a mutual or symbiotic relationship between, on the one hand, crises and potential contradictions and, on the other, innovation. In this sense, an innovation may emerge as an answer to a particular problem yet, in the same moment, could trigger other socio-economic ills. For instance, Karl Marx (1990 [1867]) wrote about how new technologies in factory organisation could help to arrest the tendency of profit rates to decline, such as by using machines to increase the productivity of workers. Yet those same machines could also lead to alienation among workers who are forced to do repetitive tasks or, over time, to face the threat that further advances in technology may render their job role redundant. Inspired by Marx, Schumpeter coined the seemingly paradoxical phrase 'creative destruction' to account for how some entrepreneurs can generate growth through fresh ideas and products, even if such work simultaneously destroys established firms and methods of commercial organisation. As he put it, '[t]his process of Creative Destruction is the essential fact about capitalism. It is what capitalism consists in and what every capitalist concern has got to live in' (Schumpeter 2003[1942]: 83). In contemporary debates, Schumpeter's expression has now been adopted by countless economists and business executives as a way to encapsulate how, despite the roiling social waves generated by technological change, the net effects tend to be positive (for a biography, see McCraw 2010; for examples of management theory interest in the term, see Drucker 2011[1985]; Christensen 1997).

However, this normatively favourable position can be put under critical scrutiny when we examine problematic justifications for innovation in the neoliberal economy. The rise of 'financial innovation' is clearly relevant here. Prior to the 1980s, this phrase was rarely used but, since the 1990s, it has become a stock phrase to debate – or, more precisely, in many contexts, to 'rationally' justify – changes in the institutions and instruments of financial markets. One dominant meaning of financial innovation has concerned securitisation, a process by which a financial actor pools together different assets – such as mortgages, credit-card debts or car loans – into a single product, which, in turn, is often subdivided into different tiers to be sold to third parties. For banks involved in securitisation, the benefits can include reduced funding costs, especially when assets that have a poor credit rating can be sandwiched between higher-rated assets, rather than being 'warehoused' as unsaleable. The global market for gross issuance of securitisation rocketed from barely any activity in the early 1990s to peak at almost US $5 trillion in 2006 (IMF 2009b), generating complex webs of relations that defy easy comprehension, including among financiers themselves (Tett 2009; Admati and Hellwig 2013). However, in 2007, when the financial crisis broke out in the US mortgage market, it exposed how this declared innovation could at the same time intensify systemic risk and instability. While securitisation was not the only cause, it did exacerbate the crisis when it became too difficult to quantify the value of a security linked to 'subprime delinquencies', the lowest grade of mortgages that came under stress. Thus, the financial crisis was

> *a crisis for financial innovation* because these events have forced media commentators, politicians, officials and regulatory organizations to revalue (the dominant technocratic) notion of innovation or at least to question the ability of banks and other institutions to manage innovation in the general interest.
>
> (Engelen *et al.* 2010: 34, italics in original)

Discourses surrounding innovation in the neoliberal era have also spawned a related focus on 'creativity'. Similar to the promotion of innovation, the emphasis on creativity, as explored by firms, consultants, management experts and media commentators, aims to furnish new ideas about how to extract financial value and improve competitive positioning in markets (for instance, see De Brabandere and Iny 2013; Peck 2005). The phrase 'creative industries' has been used within many of these debates. First coined in 1994 by an Australian consultancy, it rose in popularity under the rebranding of the British Labour Party by Tony Blair. According to one major policy definition used by the UK government, the creative industries are 'those industries which have their origin in individual creativity, skill and talent which have a potential for job and wealth creation through the generation and exploitation of intellectual property' (Department for Culture, Media & Sport 2001: 5; see also Flew 2012; Cunningham and Potts 2015). Sectors which claim to contribute to the 'creative economy' include advertising, computer software, design, film and music. Within the field of cultural studies, the creative-industries discourse has been promoted by critics who argue that it reflects a particular neoliberal reading of 'culture' as a productive value or utility for furthering a national economy. Such analysis suggests that governments and other authorities (including the European Commission) now play a more active role in steering culture and the arts towards principles of commodification and popular consumption (Garnham 2005; McGulgan 2005; Miller 2009). Cultural works that fall outside these boundaries risk being treated by funding bodies as less interesting or even threatening. By focusing only on the elite-led valorisation of cultural industries, one also misses how popular culture may be produced under conditions of 'relative artistic subordination' to corporate structures, a complex story told, for example, in the case of the Japanese animation industry by Morisawa (2015: 281).

In addition to these discussions, creativity has also been used to refer to particular architectures of professional workplaces that are claimed to cultivate so-called 'creative thinking'. For instance, technology companies in California, such as Google, have been in the vanguard of constructing environments that feature visually striking design, modern art and multiple spaces for interaction. As Google justifies it on their careers webpage:

> When you want people to think creatively and push the boundaries of what's possible, their workspace shouldn't be a drab maze of beige cubicles. Our offices have become well known for their innovative, fun and – some might say wacky – design. Like most of our decisions, data shows that these spaces have a positive impact on productivity, collaboration and inspiration.
>
> (Google n.d.; see also Stewart 2013)

For some scholars, the appeal to the creative workplace – including what makes such environments appear exciting and legitimate – can only be understood through tracing its history. The ethos that accompanies the design of a Google office is, to borrow from Boltanski and Chiapello (2007), an oblique reaction to the so-called 'artistic critique' of capitalism in the 1960s and 1970s, which accused corporations of manufacturing dull, homogenous and inauthentic workplaces. The emphasis placed on spaces for 'play' (gyms, massage facilities, libraries, etc.), where workers can relax from work but still remain at work, is a feature that has become more prominent in recent years. Some writers argue that the trend dovetails with a wider cultural imperative of promoting individual wellness (Costea *et al.* 2005). The link between happiness and worker productivity has long been appreciated in the history of business, but the effort to blur the distinction between work and play, across space and time, is more apparent in the neoliberal era.

See also: **change, emerge, enterprise, entrepreneurship, finance, growth, market, network, openness, participation, performance, project**.

Further reading: Engelen *et al.* 2010; Fagerberg 2006; McGulgan 2005; Schumpeter 2003[1942].

INVESTMENT

The etymology of 'invest' betrays an interesting early history, derived from the Latin *vestis*, meaning 'clothes'. Thus, *investire* means 'to put clothes on someone', particularly the ceremonial robing of a king, military leader or high priest. In this sense, the value of 'being invested' was initially associated with questions of power, status and display. The modern connotation of investment – as the employment of money in a commercial activity for the purpose of yielding a profit – only emerges in the early seventeenth century through mercantile international trade. According to the *Oxford English Dictionary*, the term is invoked in the correspondence of the East India Company, where one letter of 1618 reads: 'Not to defer investmentes till our shippes arriuall and the Indicoes swept away'. It is significant, therefore, that the financial sense of investment – the idea of giving one's capital a new form – arises during the early development of capitalism and, later, the period of colonialism. Indeed, according to one contemporary analyst, it is worth speculating whether the emergence of the economic meaning of investment at this time had some connection to the importance of foreign trade in textile production: 'money and Indian wares are homologous with clothing' (Forman 2004: 617).

The appearance of the title 'financial investor' is a comparatively recent innovation, dating from the mid nineteenth century. By the twentieth century, it had been given a new lease of life through different means, including the expansion of banking, limited-liability laws and pensions. But who is an investor in the neoliberal period? In common financial parlance, investors can be divided into two types: retail or institutional. The former denotes an individual who buys and sells securities (a type of financial product) on their own account and not for an organisation. Institutional investors, by contrast, are the large investment banks, insurance firms, pension funds, hedge funds and mutual funds, entities that have grown in power over recent decades. For instance, adjusted for inflation, the stock-market capitalisation of the top ten investment banks rocketed from US$1 billion in 1960 to US$194 billion in 2000 (Morrison and Wilhelm 2007). Although the financial crisis damaged the equity prices of banks, stocks subsequently rebounded. By mid 2014, the top ten financials had a total market capitalisation of more than US$1894 billion (PwC 2014). At the same time, the term 'investor', as a kind of social ID card, carries appeal in contrast to other potential synonyms. An alternative and more potent word would be 'capitalist', yet this is considerably less popular among such professionals (Arnold 2010). Also noteworthy is the disputed and often politically sensitive distinction drawn between investment and speculation. While the former tends to imply longer-term interests, such as factory purchases, the latter may involve a trader who absorbs larger-than-average risks, over shorter periods, in the hope of accruing

higher-than-average profits (for a defence of investment against speculation, see Bogle 2012; on the phenomenon of high-frequency trading,
see Lewis 2014).

Thus, for actors within the social world of finance, the label 'investor'
is not simply a legal name within contracts and job titles, but arguably
signifies a type of group solidarity. If so, can one speak of an investor
class, a community with similar preferences? In the US, the question
has intrigued some observers. For instance, since the late 1990s,
the polling group Zogby has asked a sample of the US population the
following question: 'Do you believe you are in the investor class?'
(Nadler 1999). The phrase attracted the attention of Republican Party
officials who were keen to appeal to the electorate. For example, in
2005, in a speech on social welfare reform, President Bush said:
'I believe everybody's got the capability of being in the investor class.
I believe everybody should be allowed to watch their own assets grow,
not just a few people' (Bush 2009: 400). But beneath such aspirational
rallying cries lay political calculations. For proponents of the inves-
tor-class theory, the more an individual becomes involved in the stock
market and committed to the 'ownership society', the more likely they
will vote Republican. For Bush and his political soulmates, the challenge has been to spread such an idea even if, according to some
researchers, the causal relationship between asset ownership and political allegiance can be unclear (Kaustia and Torstila 2011; Cotton-Nessler
and Davis 2012). In short, the term 'investor', when used without clear
specification, may obscure uneven patterns of material distribution.
In 2010, under half of all US households had any stock holdings, with
the majority of this total fixed within retirement accounts. But the
concentration in stock ownership remains skewed towards the very
rich: the top 1 per cent capture 40 per cent of all stock wealth, with the
top fifth of households holding around 90 per cent of stock wealth
(Mishel *et al.* 2012).

If portfolio investment is concerned with buying legal rights from a
company in the form of shares and bonds, foreign direct investment
(FDI) is commonly defined as the acquisition of physical assets by a
company or a state in another country. The appeal of making certain
spaces 'attractive' for FDI – from the local and the urban to the national
or even the continental – has become a distinctive mark of neoliberal
thinking. In economics, the theory of FDI began to mature in the
1970s, with the popularity of the notion taking off in the mid 1980s
(Blonigen 2008). Since new sources of FDI may contribute to economic growth and employment, such trends are carefully monitored
by governments, businesses and relevant international organisations.

Many countries now engage in the economic equivalent of stilted beauty pageants, with marketing strategies that are aimed at nurturing that most precious and elusive prize: 'investor confidence', another phrase that has only become popular in the neoliberal period (on branding strategies deployed by policymakers to attract FDI, see Aronczyk 2013; on the links to wider agendas around 'competitiveness', see Fougner 2006; Davies 2014). Although patterns are changing, FDI flows tend to be directed towards particular locations. For instance, in 2013, developing countries experienced record inflows totalling US$778 billion, but the majority of this investment was concentrated in China, India and parts of Latin America, with sub-Saharan Africa receiving US$57 billion (UNCTAD 2014). Attractive pull factors for FDI are multiple and context-specific but, in the struggle for competitiveness, low wages can be one major element, as seen in Vietnam's efforts to outdo China in certain areas of manufacturing (OECD 2010; Bland 2012).

Concerns about the unequal distributional effects of investment flows have made certain international investment treaties particularly controversial. In the mid 1990s, the EU, Japan and the US, among others, tried to establish a Multilateral Agreement on Investment, but the strategy failed due to criticism from civil society groups. By 2003, a renewed effort had been made through the WTO to pursue a similar agenda, but this too backfired due to fierce criticism from developing countries (Sornarajah 2010). As a result, the major policy action has now shifted to over 3000 bilateral investment treaties (BITs), many of which have been quietly signed with little public scrutiny (indeed, often without the knowledge of relevant government agencies) (Poulsen and Aisbett 2013; Poulsen 2015). Such legal frameworks are commonly justified as promoting more predictable investment flows and ensuring that companies are not unduly infringed by 'bias' (political or others) in domestic courts or from government regulations. However, there is considerable evidence for contesting these claims (for a summary, see Van Harten 2010). Supported by a tight-knit phalanx of elite law firms and arbitrators, BITs have triggered waves of investor-state cases. In 2011, there were 450 known investor-state cases, many of which were filed by corporations based in developed countries against developing-country governments over a range of issues, including core social and environmental regulations that were deemed to infringe the rights of investors. For instance, Philip Morris, the tobacco giant, has exploited BITs signed by the Uruguayan and Australian governments to sue both countries for their attempts to introduce plain packaging and labelling for cigarettes. The legal and economic punch from BITs can therefore be considerable, with many arbitration hearings featuring compensation demands of over US$100 million from states (Corporate Europe Observatory and the Transnational Institute 2012). In sum, such strategies appear to be maximising the prospect for litigation in order to enhance corporate power, beginning with the very expansive and claimant-friendly definition of investment.

See also: **business, capitalism, emerge, finance, market, risk, stakeholder**.

Further reading: Blonigen 2008; Morrison and Wilhelm 2007.

MANAGEMENT

The spread of ideas associated with management is one of the most distinctive features of the neoliberal period. For some, management thinking is now a dominant rationality, which informs not only business practices but extends into other areas of social life, from the organisation of government departments to common expectations of individual behaviour. Derived from the Latin *manus*, meaning hand, the term 'manage' developed in Italian (*maneggiare*) and French (*manège*), before entering English in the mid sixteenth century. The word was initially associated with horse riding (a legacy that continues in French), before broadening out to become a general expression of control and administration. In Shakespeare's *Richard II* (2011: 211), written around 1595, the powerful sense of civil disorder facing the King is partly carried by the word 'managed', meaning 'wielded':'Yea, distaff-women manage rusty bills/Against thy seat' (spinning-women wield rusty pikes against thy throne). Interestingly, from that same decade, the concept of management already contained its core sense of the mobilisation of resources or the action of prudent supervision. Along with extensions such as 'manageable' or, less common, 'manageableness', the term could also imply conduct that was cunning or manipulative. This sharper meaning continues to be deployed when the word is treated as a synonym for discretion or the capacity of an actor to wield power over another (such as 'this problem needs to be politically managed'). In the social sciences, the invoking of this sense is also central to critiques of contemporary management. The idea of management as a group of employees who control a business organisation, separate from the labour force, was used from the mid eighteenth century with the growth of capitalism, but did not become commonplace until the twentieth century.

Towards the end of the nineteenth century, the foundations of management theory began to be constructed. Over subsequent decades, different rationales have been offered for such knowledge, from quasi-evangelical claims of defending 'progress' and the 'free world' to more limited defences, including the expansion of particular markets and the provision of employment opportunities. One significant thread that unites many writers and practitioners of management is the search for efficiency. This objective can be found in the early studies of Henry R. Towne (1886), Frederick Winslow Taylor (1911, 1919) and Henri Fayol (1949[1916]), engineers who argued for a so-called 'science' of management. For these authors, among others, greater efficiency tends to lead to a more productive enterprise and, thus, a more profitable one. In the US, the growth of large geographically dispersed firms, many of which sought to expand overseas following the First World War, motivated research in this area (Chandler 1977). As argued by Towne, 'A vast amount of accumulated experience in the art of workshop management already exists, but there is no record of it available to the world in general, and each old enterprise is managed more or less in its own way' (Towne 1886: 429). Thus, the founding of the first US business schools, such as the Wharton School of Business at the University of Pennsylvania (1881) and Harvard Business School (1908), the latter pioneering the Master of Business Administration (MBA), helped to institutionalise and legitimise management theory (Sass 1982; Amdam 2008). Such processes were further cemented by the growth of management consultancy, a profession which was increasingly influential by the 1960s, led by firms such as Bedaux, Emerson, and McKinsey & Company (McKenna 2006).

For much of the twentieth century, Taylorism was the dominant mode of management, both in the West and in planned economies such as the Soviet Union and East Germany. The Taylorist strategy consisted of simplifying tasks in an effort to exclude unnecessary waste and, once devised, enforcing such practices through strict supervision and monetary rewards. In short, for Taylor, managers think, but workers do. Corporations are conceived as machines with workers as mere cogs (Conti 2013; Willman 2014). It is often claimed that, from the middle of the twentieth century, Taylorism was superseded by other strategies of management. However, it would be more accurate to argue that elements of Taylorism still survive through a process of revision and incorporation into new theories. Over the neoliberal decades, what is now called operations management builds upon this legacy, complete with a variety of associated frameworks which have been tested by leading companies, including total quality management (TQM), lean management and the Six Sigma model (Andersson et al. 2006). For instance, the consolidation of Japanese manufacturing power by the 1980s or, later, the rise of the Chinese factory system around the turn of the millennium illustrate how the concern for industrial efficiency remains central to management deliberations (Chan 2001; Tsutsui 2001; Ngai and Chan 2012). Elsewhere, in some areas of services, such as call centres, Taylorist principles are still adopted; these are evident in the use of standardised scripts that workers have to follow, performance monitoring through targets and limited job rotation (Bain *et al.* 2002).

If efficiency remains the watchword for studying the internal mechanisms of business organisation, then the appeal to 'customer satisfaction' represents a prized outcome. During the neoliberal period, management authors have tried to persuade their audiences – principally senior managers and consultants who will, in turn, teach subordinates and clients – that customer satisfaction should be a supreme value informing every activity in the organisation. Again, this objective is not new. For instance, in the early twentieth century, Harry Gordon Selfridge, the retail pioneer, coined the phrase 'the customer is always right', while, a few decades later, Peter Drucker (2011[1954]: 32) was arguing that there is only one business purpose: 'to create a customer'. What is different in the neoliberal period is the intense focus dedicated to promoting (and cultivating) the needs of the customer, often supported by complex marketing data, elaborate infrastructure networks, and staff-training programmes for those who are directly interacting with consumers. One can see this trend reflected in the rise of the phrase 'customer satisfaction' in a search of Google's Ngram database: from the early 1980s, the notion spreads rapidly and, by the 2000s, had become the subject of careful evaluation by management theorists (for instance, see Jackson 1985; Fornell *et al.* 2006; Oliver 2010). Agendas surrounding customer satisfaction have also been justified through other notions in the neoliberal vocabulary, such as larger appeals to choice and experience, as well as more technical marketing concepts, including customer loyalty and brand equity. The rationalisation of consumer satisfaction, or consumer confidence, also needs to be understood in relation to the history of consumer protection, the legal agendas of which predate the neoliberal period but, from the 1980s, received new attention from many national regulators.

One can see how management theory has long been associated with questions of control, although how forms of power are exercised and, in particular, represented in the workplace has always been a major conundrum for writers and executives. In the 1960s and 1970s, in the face of wider social critiques of capitalism, this problem preoccupied many elites, who doubted how business could renew its attractiveness to the children of the middle class (and not, in the most profound fear, turn such young people towards communism) (Boltanski and Chiapello 2007). For instance, in an echo of Weber's (2013[1922]) influential argument, the corporation was often depicted (even by managers) as a cold bureaucracy, complete with autocratic rule-making, all of which stifled individual liberty and autonomy (Townsend 2007[1970]). On its own, the amassing of personal riches, derived from the profits of the firm, was viewed as a limited 'carrot' for inspiring commitment. According to Boltanski and Chiapello (2007), management authors – including popular 'guru' figures such as Drucker (2007), Warren Bennis (1997) and Rosabeth Moss Kanter (1989) – began to respond to this legitimacy deficit by rethinking the professional work environment and its mechanisms of justification. By the 1990s, in the context of neoliberalism, a new normative vision emerged which rejected anything that appeared excessively hierarchical or dictatorial. In its place, such authors argued (or, in many cases, preached) for workplaces where individuals felt empowered to nurture their own employability, particularly through a stress on exploring networks, projects and flexibility. The emphasis on creating a 'fun' work culture – with trappings and activities that appear 'homely' and 'playful' – has been allied to this broader shift (Costea et al. 2005; Butler et al. 2011).

The extraordinary emphasis on management during the neoliberal period would already be significant if we focused simply on the world of business. But the power of management ideology is also seen in how its values and principles have become increasingly incorporated into modern statehood, including, by extension, international organisations. A cluster of expressions, some popular, others more academic, have tried to capture this development, including 'administrative reform' (Aucoin 1990), 'national competitiveness' (Porter 1990), 'new public management' (Hood 1991, 2007), 'entrepreneurial government' (Osborne and Gaebler 1992) and, simply, 'managerialism'. As noted by Davies (2014), there is a certain irony to this trend. For most of the twentieth century, management theory sought inspiration from political and military institutions; methods of leadership constitute one example. In the neoliberal period, however, the direction of travel of these ideas has reversed, with government rationality often (although by no means always) occupying a subservient position to business-management rationality. The concrete realisation of business-friendly government has come in a variety of forms, from the privatisation of state assets and the cutting of budgets to the imposition of 'performance' auditing systems and 'target cultures'. As Davies argues, however, the spread of such ideas 'did not necessarily involve extending the market into every reach of state and society, but of reconstructing state and society in ways that are amenable to market-based techniques of evaluation' (Davies 2014: 116). In other words, management rationality seeks to generalise the dispositions of business managers into practices that all actors can – and should – follow. This ambition does not demand that everyone needs to be an entrepreneur, but it does promote particular modes of conduct, such as the instrumentalising of resources (material or human) and, particularly under neoliberalism, the desire for competition.

To conclude, three criticisms can be offered. First, by virtue of its focus on refining and constituting methods of organising capitalism, management theory has always displayed universalising tendencies. In many popular management books, the world is often depicted as a confusing landscape, roiled by frenetic change, with presumed existential threats at every turn. Yet business is still upheld as a glorious pursuit, featuring opportunities for those who are smart enough to follow the advice of the management seers. The problem with such depictions is how they frequently ignore or minimise complex historical, political and cultural traditions. In short, the orientation of many institutions towards the logic of efficiency, growth and consumption may have the look of something forced in the way it attempts to configure society. Second, in contrast to the presumed progressive culture of the neoliberal corporation, a range of authors in the burgeoning field of critical management studies have argued that such organisations have the potential to 'incubate and normalize stress and bad health, naturalize subordination and exploitation, [...] erode morality, [and] create and reinforce ethnic and gender inequalities' (Alvesson et al. 2011: 7). Such outcomes need to be empirically documented, particularly when a definition of injustice may not be immediately clear. Third, a related criticism concerns how many people find management a frustrating form of discourse, characterised by verbiage, opacity, euphemism and emptiness. It is noteworthy, in this regard, how the coining of derogatory terms, such as 'managementese' (1977, *OED*) and 'managementspeak' (1986, *OED*), coincides with the neoliberal period. Poking fun at management jargon and buzzwords, as performed by Lucy Kellaway (2000) in her *Financial Times* column, offers some degree of light relief from a frequently exasperating use of language.

See also: **business, capitalism, challenge, change, competition, diversity, market, network, performance, project, risk, stakeholder, state, vision**.

Further reading: Boltanski and Chiapello 2007; Davies 2014; Willman 2014.

MARKET

'Market' is arguably the most significant word in the neoliberal vocabulary. It is also, ironically perhaps, a term that has attracted very little dedicated examination. Business figures regularly talk about watching the market, being in the market or taking a company to market. Politicians sometimes voice fears about the market's reaction to certain policies, while regulators have been known to curb the power of particular markets. For some critical scholars, neoliberalism is often encapsulated as 'rule', 'discipline' or 'tyranny' by markets; as a process of 'marketisation'; or as the making of a 'market society', to name but three common phrases (Bourdieu 1998, 2003; Harvey 2005; Brenner *et al.*, 2010; Peck *et al.* 2012). Even for other writers of commercial life who do not invoke the theme of neoliberalism, the word 'market' is never far from the page, from 'market mechanisms' and 'market failures' to 'market sentiments' and 'market forces'. Yet, in spite of its ubiquity, the meaning of 'market' often remains vague, poorly specified and, at times, burdened by ambiguities. Where did the concept come from? Is it possible to discern any general properties of markets? Why has this notion assumed an uninterrogated status? What effects are generated by this dominant mode of social organisation? Addressing these questions will take us some way to grasping the wider significance of this key concept, including the extent to which recent decades associated with neoliberalism have changed what is meant by market or markets.

The etymology of 'market' has been a source of debate, but probably entered English in the early twelfth century via older French and Germanic uses (in Anglo Saxon, the term was preceded by *céap*, a place for purchasing cattle) (Davis 1952). European forms of the word have their origins in the Latin *mercatus*, and its cognate form, *merx*, meaning a commodity. The earliest sense of the concept, which retains relevance today, is of a physical location where commerce is transacted (as in market gate (1344, *OED*), marketplace (1389, *OED*), or market square (1567, *OED*)). In this respect, as many anthropologists and historians have argued, entities called markets or forms of material life existed before the onset of mature capitalism (Tilly 1975, 1992; Dilley 1992; Braudel 1992a, 1992b; Lie 1993). By the fifteenth century, still with reference to the sense of a gathering but reflecting the expansion in trade, the term had become attached to classes of commodity, such as 'corn market' or 'poultry market'. From the sixteenth century, in a decisive evolution, 'market' began to be theorised in more abstract terms, as not only reflecting a particular locale but a general process or principle for buying and selling. In turn, this extension allowed market to be metaphorically reimagined and treated as a flexible notion. 'As a displaced metaphor detached from its concrete referent, the term "market" has become a "pocket" whose contents are defined in relation to the uses to which it is put' (Dilley 1992: 3). Again, particularly from the nineteenth century, this conceptual expansion can be partly explained by the growth of capitalism. Defining the trading of intangible assets as markets (stocks, foreign exchange, etc.) was coined during this time, along with the popular viewing of entire countries and, ultimately, the world, under the same label ('industry has established the world market' – Marx and Engels (1998[1848]: 36)).

One could reasonably assume that the discipline of economics – long concerned with prices and outcomes within markets – would have a firm grasp on the meaning of this core concept. However, economics arrived very late to such debates and, for most of its history, tended to treat 'market' as an unproblematic expression or simplified model. As one Nobel Laureate once remarked, 'It is a peculiar fact that the literature on economics and economic history contains so little discussion of the central institution that underlies neoclassical economics – the market' (North 1977: 710). Even by 1987, in *The New Palgrave: A Dictionary of Economics*, considered a major reference guide to the field, there was no entry for markets (the situation was rectified by the second edition) (Hodgson 2008). One answer to this paradox lies in how economics, particularly its nineteenth-century neoclassical offspring, sought to promote itself as a generalisable 'science' of human behavior, or choice (Robbins 1932; on the appeal to the notion of 'science' in economics, see McCloskey 1994). To fulfil this ambition, the subject constructed and policed the use of concepts that aimed to be as universal as possible, without substantial appeals to history or geography. In this way, economists are able to speak of the ancient Greek *agora*, the haggling over carpets at a local bazaar, the trading of modern financial derivatives or even the search for a marriage partner as instances of markets (or even the singular market). Thus, part of the popularity of the concept lies in how it is *not* inspected, but rather assumes a non-institutionalised quality to the extent that it sometimes appears constitutive of human nature itself (Carrier 1997). As one famous economist once quipped, in a line that encapsulates this logic of apparently timeless application, 'in the beginning, there were markets' (Williamson: 1983: 20).

How can one outline a general definition of markets and what problems does any definition generate? As noted, in a rudimentary sense, many would agree that the concept points to the activity of buying and selling things through a common medium and store of value: that is, most of the time, money. The idea of exchange is important here. Humans have created other forms of social exchange, notably barter and gift giving, but these are conventionally not considered market-based due to differences on property rights, among other reasons (see debates in anthropology in particular, including Mauss 2002 [1950]; Gregory 1982; Parry 1986). For Rosenbaum (2000), voluntary and specified exchange would be a more accurate depiction of stylised market forms. Markets are voluntary in allowing some possibility for entering and exiting transactional relations. In this sense, they are social arenas that exhibit some scope for freedom of movement – of capital, commodities or individuals – although how such freedom is structured and constrained is a central question (Sen 1985). Indeed, this emphasis on maintaining circulation and competitive activity is reflective of a capitalist culture in general. If movement slows or stops, as in a crisis, then markets are often questioned (Marx 1990[1867]). In addition, according to Rosenbaum (2000), the market form has a specific logic. This condition does not necessarily infer that the exchange must take place in a single temporal and spatial setting. Rather, what matters is that there is substantive detail on the content of the exchange, including a judgement on value, the determination of a price and the (implicit or explicit) enforcement of the relationship, notably through legal contracts administered by the state. By contrast, in a gift exchange, this specificity does not appear but, rather, rests on a more general expectation of reciprocity.

While such points may help to anchor any discussion about the meaning of 'market', when one turns to empirical examples, the picture becomes more uncertain. Two issues are worth noting. First, many commercial transactions do not take place in environments that are commonly imagined as competitive markets. Instead, they are conducted between established firms in a single, or perhaps multi-party, relationship. Within such networks, no actor may express any interest in the creation of a market involving additional players but, instead, would seek the renewal of existing contracts (Richardson 1972; Goldberg 1980). According to some sociologists, such contracts may be formed out of 'strong expectations of trust and abstention from opportunism' (Granovetter 1985: 490). For instance, studies on intra-firm trade – exchange between businesses that belong to the same parent but are located in different countries – show how it constitutes a significant share of total world trade. In 2009, in the US, 48 per cent of imported goods entered the country through this way (Lanz and Miroudot 2011). Second, remaining with the question of competition, markets can take monopsonistic or oligopolistic forms in many industries (sometimes referred to as the market power of one or a group of producers). For example, 90 per cent of the global trading of agricultural grains is conducted by four corporations, a situation that has, moreover, remained broadly unchanged for more than a century (Murphy et al. 2012).

This tendency does not invalidate the concept of the market, but does reveal, at the very least, a tension or inconsistency between the model of 'perfectly competitive markets' in neoclassical economic theory and the reality that often exists.

One can see how the master notion of market has long operated within a conceptual universe of related expressions that help to shape its meanings, with freedom, individualism, choice and competition being particularly significant. At the same time, the concept of market is frequently defined in opposition to other major categories that are claimed to lack the qualities of a market, including, in various degrees and qualities, state, bureaucracy, politics, society, hierarchy, plan or socialism. Another major dichotomy, one which assumed a special status in Cold War politics, involved the conflation of market with 'the modern West' and, by contrast, non-market forms of organisation with the 'pre-modern, non-Western other'. In this sense, 'the Market model is more than just an idealisation of economic activities in particular times and places. It is also an idealisation that itself idealises the modern West' (Carrier 1997: 31). In addition, between and within market economies, the market model is also used in many ways to judge and classify 'worthy' and 'unworthy' subjects. For instance, in the US under President Reagan or the UK under Prime Minister Thatcher, but also elsewhere, the appeal to 'free markets' often dovetailed with the rhetoric of nationalism (Helleiner 2002; Harmes 2012). Thus, the common vision of the market opens the space for debating not only competition between commercial enterprises but also the question of 'national competitiveness' (Fougner 2006; Davies 2014). Finally, the social practices associated with the term also shape behaviour at an individual level. Entrepreneurs who create new markets are often valorised, whereas, by contrast, the unemployed, who cannot easily enter the labour market, may be treated by the state and others with apathy or disdain. For example, in the US, the Department of Labor does not count those who are unemployed unless they are 'actively' looking for work; their citizenship is implicitly devalued.

Since many assumptions, discourses and practices associated with the concept of the market predate the mainstreaming of neoliberalism, is there anything particularly distinctive about uses of the term in the past four decades? Three aspects are worth exploring. First, one could argue that the concept has become even more pervasive and adaptable, serving as a kind of a dominant rationality, mentality or, at the very least, a fashionable phrase that people feel under pressure to invoke (if only to maintain a degree of trustworthiness with others) (Carrier 1997; Brown 2006). The collapse of Communism, and thus the erosion of the main ideological counterweight to capitalism, provided the larger backdrop for enhancing the attention granted to the 'market system'. Along with accompanying appeals to enterprise, the private sector or, simply, 'the economy', the popularity of the concept grew as a consequence. For instance, in a search of titles in the British Library catalogue, 'market' is found in 4,476 publications between 1970 and 1984. But in the subsequent period its use accelerates dramatically: from 1985 to 2000, a further 76,550 titles feature the term, followed by 115,355 in the last 14 years. Within this trend, both the attachment of 'global' and 'emerging' to market is something distinctly neoliberal, whereas the growth of particular sectors, such as finance, has resulted in daily appeals to the market metaphor. At the same time, it is important to note the related decline – seen in many fields of the social sciences, professional politics and everyday conversation – of the concept of capitalism, considered by some a *passé* category yoked to the Marxist legacy or simply too unwieldy to be of analytical use (Boltanski and Chiapello 2007). Thus, according to advocates, the market now stands alone as the optimal allocation mechanism, led by 'heroic' corporate leaders who compare themselves to rock stars (for a popular critique, see Frank 2001).

Second, although 'market' is frequently treated as an ordinary term, it is also apparent that it is often haunted by suspicion and wariness. Again, the basic tone of this criticism is not radically new (see, for instance, Polanyi 2001[1944]). However, its precise questioning is largely shaped by local and historical conditions. Within the neoliberal period, from the mid 1990s, complex changes in the social forces of capitalism resulted in a more visible resistance to the market model. For instance, activists within the so-called 'anti-globalisation' movement, who targeted agendas emanating from the WTO and the WEF, argued that privatisation policies were leading to socially regressive outcomes, such as greater corporate control over everyday life (for analysis, see Held and McGrew 2007; Smith 2008). A similar wave of public concern emerged from the global financial crisis and the exposure in many countries of widening socio-economic inequalities (Piketty 2014). For such observers, therefore, the defence of 'market ideology' – a common phrase used by many on the political left – is, as Naomi Klein has polemically argued, a kind of 'cover story for greed', one that 'rationalises extremely antisocial behaviour' (quoted in McBain 2014). After the collapse of Lehman Brothers in 2008, the beautifully rampaging bronze bull outside the New York Stock Exchange looked singularly inappropriate as an icon of market capitalism. Thus, in one sense, particularly when compared to the political climate of the 1980s, the legitimacy of the concept has become tarnished, introducing a degree of caution into how proponents deploy the word (as seen in comments such as 'the market cannot solve this problem alone' or 'market fundamentalism is not the answer'). Yet, ironically, through these very interventions, the circulation of the word increases.

Third, and closely related, is the question of where power is located in the making of social environments called markets. In academic scholarship, considerable ink has been spilt on enquiries that stem from this problem. For instance, within literature that has debated globalisation, it has become customary to draw a theoretical dichotomy between states and markets, with the claim by some that the former have lost autonomy to the latter during the neoliberal period (Strange 1988; for introductions, see Held *et al.* 1999; Walter and Sen 2009). Yet this distinction, along with its mirror dichotomy of public versus private, can often obscure, rather than clarify, the reality of power and its impacts. In many societies, relations between government and business are historically connected, both institutionally and personally. Indeed, as David Graeber makes clear in his book *Debt: the First 5000 Years* (2011: 18), the state and the market 'were born together and have always been intertwined'. For instance, in China, the top 50 wealthiest members of the National People's Congress have a combined fortune of $94.7 billion, much of it acquired through favourable corporate ties (notably from mining, property and health-related industries) (*The Economist* 2013). Thus, as Loïc Wacquant has neatly proposed, neoliberalism would be better expressed as '*an articulation of state, market and citizenship* that harnesses the first to impose the stamp of the second onto the third' (Wacquant 2012: 71, italics in original). Understanding the precise configuration between state, market and citizenship is an empirical question which cannot be assumed in advance. A related problem concerns how abstract and casual references to the markets can often cloud the identification of individual and collective responsibility within such networks, as if they function without human intervention. This concern is particularly acute in the financial field, which has a predilection for secrecy.

In sum, we can see how the notion of market is problematic on a number of counts. Through both expert and common uses, the term can sometimes essentialise or fetishise particular phenomena, in the process further obscuring how social relations are concretely manifested. For some authors, market can be a rather 'washed out' or 'bleached' concept. Tellingly, this effect often occurs because users are trying to explain activity within a capitalist system without resorting to the word 'capitalism' (Carrier 1997). Despite the many inconsistencies found between the market model and how such environments work in practice, the concept continues to have far-reaching cultural implications, serving as a kind of oxygen supply to the neoliberal body. The symbolic power of the term is partly the result of its deep association with Western-derived ideals of success, which, via the spread of management ideology following the end of the Cold War in particular, have become attractive across the world. Since 'market' is now so common within many institutions, the word takes on the appearance of any modern expression that people feel a need to invoke (often without conscious reflection on its suitability or impact). Perhaps the most profound consequence in the neoliberal period concerns how the category is used to construct a standard for comportment which is applied not only in the business world but within many other social spaces, some of which were previously insulated from such forces (such as universities and arts organisations). Thus, the conceptual expansion of market is both a reflection of and a justification for the further realisation of a capitalist ethic. We might conclude that there is precious little left outside the market.

See also: **business, capitalism, change, choice, class, competition, development, diversity, emerge, enterprise, entrepreneurship, environment, finance, freedom, global, growth, innovation, investment, management, performance, power, private, project, reform, risk, stakeholder, state, trade, welfare**.

Further reading: Carrier 1997; Dilley 1992; Hodgson 2008; Rosenbaum 2000.

NETWORK

From 'networked firms' to the purported arrival of the 'network society', the term 'network' now occupies a major place in the vocabulary of neoliberalism. Taking 'networks' seriously – that is, tracing where the concept came from, what it adds to our social and political understanding and, importantly, what the notion misses or fails to illuminate – has drawn attention, particularly of those observers interested in changes in the culture of capitalism (Boltanski and Chiapello 2007; Bourgouin 2009; Davies 2011; du Gay and Morgan 2013). However, most users of the concept, such as within academia, business, and government, do not analyse the term through this particular lens and, indeed, many invoke 'network' as an uncontested expression that requires little explanation. Since entering English in the sixteenth century, network has always carried the physical, material sense of manufacturing interwoven patterns. By the eighteenth century, the term was being deployed in biology and the natural sciences and, by the nineteenth century, network had conceptually spread to its now dominant technological applications, such as in reference to transportation, electricity or tele-communications. Its use in social contexts to define an interconnected group of persons is, however, comparatively recent, initially dating from the late nineteenth century but without wider circulation until at least the postwar period. The expression also tended to be informed by unfavourable or clandestine qualities, as in 'terrorist networks', 'spy networks' or 'old boy networks', applications that still survive today but are now positioned alongside a wider variety of more normatively positive or neutral senses of the word.

In recent decades, within many areas of the social sciences, there has been a growing interest in networks, understood as either a technique for mapping and explaining interactions between social units or, more profoundly, as a form of organisation that generates particular types of identities and interests. Early uses of this understanding of the term developed in anthropology from the 1950s, notably from a cluster of Manchester-based scholars who pioneered studies on 'social networks', a rare phrase at the time (Barnes 1954; Bott 1957). From the 1970s, social network analysis (SNA), with its charting of nodes and ties between actors, became popular in sociology (particularly institutional-focused scholars) and other fields, although there was (and remains) debate over whether SNA is a metaphor, a method, a theory or some-thing of all three (Barnes 1979; see also Granovetter 1973; Craven and Wellman 1973; Wellman 1988; Powell 1990; Smith-Doerr and Powell 2005). By the 1990s, in an influential argument that reached audiences beyond academia, Manual Castells (1996) argued that a 'network society' was on the rise, underpinned by new communication technologies, notably the mainstream commercialisation of the internet. Castells claimed that the 'network society' is still a capitalist society, but one in which advanced firms operate in a 'new economy' (a popular business phrase around the millennium) where the processing of information (or knowledge) is prized. Similar to some writings in the field of 'globalisation' studies that waxed lyrical about such developments, Castells boldly claimed that '[i]n a broader historical perspective, the network society represents a qualitative change in the human experi-ence' (Castells 1996: 508).

In the shadow of trends associated with neoliberalism, the concept of networks has also found its way into a wide variety of business-management debates. As Boltanski and Chiapello argue, there was something almost inevitable about this conceptual appropriation and redefinition within the world of commerce: 'As an existing concept [...], associated with a specific vocabulary, models of causality and mathematical models, and formed to offer an alternative to hierarchical algorithms, "network" naturally enough finds itself mobilized by capitalism' (Boltanski and Chiapello 2007: 104). No longer 'a new term', as *Harvard Business Review* once quipped (Charan 1991: 104), the most successful companies are now able to organise themselves into alliances and partnerships, taking advantage of shifting supply chains and competitive jurisdictional regimes. Such 'networked' organisation is claimed to generate significant business benefits, including efficiency savings, as well as enhanced learning and innovation (Kleindorfer and Wind, with Gunther 2009; for an overview, see Borgatti and Foster 2003; Powell and Grodal 2006). Other authors argue that companies should not produce rigidly standardised products that fail to excite but, rather, 'must build a flexible "experience network" that allows individuals to co-construct and personalize their experiences' (Prahalad and Ramaswamy 2004: 16; on marketing, see the projections by Achrol 1997). Thus, networks forge a new relationship between the corporation and its customers. Elsewhere, within firms, one also finds that the network metaphor has become attached to a range of agendas, including, most prominently, 'networked teams' that digitally unite workers who are dispersed across geographic spaces (see an early, enthusiastic articulation in Lipnack and Stamps 1994).

No analysis of the term 'network' in the neoliberal period would be complete without also dwelling on the related notion of networking. In the 1940s, this phrase was coined within radio and television broadcasting, before being applied to data exchange within computer networks. The social sense of networking as the process of intentionally pursuing contacts for personal gain is, though, something distinctly neoliberal, a meaning that was not present before the mid 1970s. Indeed, one needs to wait until the 1990s until such usage patterns became established. For instance, in a search of titles in the US Library of Congress, the phrase 'business networking', when invoked in a social sense, does not return any results before 1991. Today, the appeal to social networking is commonly considered an important, even essential, activity for building and sustaining a professional career, a practice which has been given added legitimacy by the popularity of web services such as LinkedIn. Reflecting upon such trends, there now exists a cottage industry of consultants to aid professionals on how to network in an effective manner. In one manual, the author recommends to would-be networkers that they should target specific people of value, often through online searching or local knowledge; introduce oneself to such people 'with impact'; and subsequently recategorise all contacts into whether they are an 'A, B or C-lister' for future interactions

(Townsend 2011; see also *Harvard Business Review* 2012). According to these experts, once the network begins to expand, trust is nurtured and one reaches reputational tipping points ('the network works for you' as some put it). The discourse on networking has also been given a (quasi-)scientific inflection when combined with the idea of social capital, a concept originally designed by the sociologist Pierre Bourdieu (1977), but now redefined by many others in management, politics and development studies (for one evaluation, see Fine 2010).

Within neoliberal vocabulary, the notion of network is one of the more difficult to critique. As suggested, the popularity of the concept is undoubtedly due to its association with openness, freedom, participation, flexibility and innovation, related notions that can be harnessed by actors across the ideological spectrum. Not unlike the way in which the industrial revolution from the eighteenth century encouraged the use of mechanistic metaphors for imagining social life more generally, the expansion of technological networks – of which the internet is the jewel in the crown – offers an immediate mental map for thinking about how human relations are organised or, more normatively, should be organised. This is what seems to give the term 'network', and the practice of exploring and extending things called networks, a new and exciting quality (an important emotional effect for sustaining enthusiasm for whatever agendas fall under its name). By contrast, the person who is seen as poorly connected or isolated – for instance, avoiding business networking in a particular industry – can often be socially marked with a lower status and dismissed as a dinosaur who cannot keep up with the times. In other contexts, one can also observe how network-like morphologies are a major vision in both critical scholarship and activism on the 'political left'. For instance, in the work of Foucault (1980) or Deleuze and Guattari (1987), the concept is used to better understand forms of power in modern society. Thinking of networks as forces of liberation is also very common within social movements and civil society groups, such as in some feminist activism, a fact that has become even more accepted as inevitable in light of internet-aided campaigns.

Due to such wide usage patterns, one could be led to assume, therefore, that network is an unproblematic notion. There are, however, some concerns and cautions that can be raised concerning the way it has been imagined in the neoliberal period. First, there is nothing intrinsically democratic about networks. Such forms of organisation can be spaces of exploitation as much as emancipation. For example, the ability of people to increase their social capital and position themselves within networks of value is a product of many factors, including place of birth, family upbringing, education and financial standing. In other words, many social networks, particularly those associated with institutions of power, often remain highly restrictive or closed off to those who do not possess the 'correct' attributes. In this sense, the appeal to social networks does not automatically collapse hierarchies of power, but may in fact consolidate or normalise them, particularly through the ideological stress on the responsibility of the individual to build their own social networks. Moreover, even if one cracks the entry requirements for certain networks, this does not mean that forms of discrimination have been erased. According to Boltanski and Chiapello (2007), the uncritical advocacy of networks and networking as 'natural' and 'desirable' models for behaviour ignores how power relations can be reproduced in sophisticated and telling ways. For example, in the corporate office environment, the dissolving of the 'work–life balance', a feature within many professional industries, has been enabled by the use of new technologies, notably the spread of mobile computing. On the one hand, management authors promote this trend, claiming that the employee now has added flexibility and freedom to negotiate when and where they conduct their work. On the other hand, the same technologies have the potential to lead to oppressive outcomes, including extending the working day (possibly without extra pay), and encouraging an 'always on call' culture via the mobile phone.

Second, the dominance of the network paradigm brings forward a related, but often underexplored, question: what spatial or group concepts have been neglected or ignored amid all the talk on networks? Ironically, it could be argued that the notion of networks delimits certain thinking on the nature of social life and politics. As one commentator has expressed it, '[w]hat used to be easily referred to as relations within a "culture", "community", "class", or "group", is now indiscriminately being called a network' (Bourgouin 2009: 10). In analytical terms, the concept of network helps to encourage research on the visualisation of social ties that may be hidden or obscured. One should be careful, therefore, about thinking that all enquiries are best prosecuted through the network model. For instance, the value of the category of social class derives from its historical association with wage–labour relations, solidarity and competitive struggle, ideas that retain relevance for analysing many problems linked to neoliberalism. By contrast, the term 'network', partly due to its scientific legacy and common justification as a neutral methodological tool, tends not to have the same degree of descriptive potency, particularly for addressing issues related to capitalism (although this should not be treated as a fixed rule). For example, if one compared the line 'the capitalist class met up again at

Davos' with 'various social networks gathered at Davos', the former is arguably a sharper indication of the type of person privileged at such a forum, whereas the latter clouds questions of power and responsibility. Yet, for some, this is precisely why the phrase 'social network' is so attractive: if social class is seen as carrying historical and ideological baggage, the notion of social network, in a world of 1.8 billion Facebook users and 500 million daily Tweets, appears as a relatively 'untainted' reflection of today's *zeitgeist*.

See also: **consensus, flexibility, freedom, individual, innovation, management, openness, participation, performance, project, stakeholder, vision**.

Further reading: Boltanski and Chiapello 2007; Bourgouin 2009; Castells 1996; Davies 2011.

OPENNESS

With its roots in Old English, openness acquired its main oppositional sense in the early seventeenth century: that is, something that was not closed, restricted or secret. When applied to the individual, the concept carries an implication that a person has a degree of frankness, candour or sincerity. Through the twentieth century, the notion grew in popularity, probably reflective of larger global changes in the importance of democracy, a less deferential attitude towards forms of power in many countries, and the emergence of new technologies that were viewed as being liberating. For instance, Karl Popper's *The Open Society and its Enemies* (2002[1945]), an inspiration for business magnate George Soros (2000) among others, was an influential text that defended freedom and individualism against totalitarian practices (see Jones (2012) for a discussion of Popper in the context of other mid-twentieth-century neoliberal intellectuals). But openness carries a deceptively simple appeal. In response to a range of different problems, it often appears as *the* intuitive answer that everyone can agree upon, no matter where they are located on the political spectrum. The neoliberal twist on openness plays with this ill-defined 'apolitical' sense, but also extends and links the idea to other notions. In particular, openness in the neoliberal period appears to offer a twin normative benefit. In advocating certain social processes, the term is linked with participation, accountability and, in particular, transparency. At the same time, being open, when applied to nations, is claimed to bring material rewards, notably in the form of faster economic growth and more development.

In reference to this latter application, the term openness has become synonymous with debates about the extent to which countries liberalise their trade and capital accounts: that is, the amount of goods and money they allow across their borders. The linkage between trade and openness is a comparatively recent association, dating from around the late 1970s. For instance, the phrase 'equivalent openness' entered the vocabulary of US and Japanese trade negotiators at this time (McElheny 1978). In the World Bank's *World Development Report* (1981: 29), one reference to trade openness was made, but it was written in quotation marks to indicate its exceptional status. By the twenty-first century, however, the expression had become mainstream within economics and the wider field of trade policymaking. For instance, in a British Library search of titles, prior to 1999, only 10 items returned 'trade openness', but in the subsequent period until 2015, 533 items included the phrase. One reason for this rise centres on how the question of trade liberalisation became more politically contentious from the late 1990s, both within the academic world and in terms of civil society protests, such as witnessed in 1999 at the Seattle WTO conference. As a result, trade liberalisation, as a larger normative political frame, has arguably suffered an erosion in legitimacy in the eyes of many observers, particularly given struggles at the WTO to conclude the Doha Round trade deal (Eagleton-Pierce 2013). It could be speculated, therefore, that the appeal to the looser 'trade openness' has offered a way to engage in similar debates, and often promote similar commercial agendas, but through the softer and more amorphous appeal of 'integrating' into a 'global community'.

However, the appeal of openness could also be due to wider cultural appropriations. Here, the popularity of the concept has clearly been inspired by technological advances connected to the internet. Its banner has pulled in behind a wide range of other terms, including 'source', 'collaboration', 'access', 'standards' and even 'everything'. In one sense, it could be argued that such developments run counter to certain neoliberal trends, including the commodification of knowledge. Many early pioneers of the internet revolution were strongly shaped by American libertarianism and counter-culture activism; Wikipedia is an an obvious example. While often not anti-capitalist as such, these pioneers still saw the internet as highly disruptive and that this instability was generally a good thing. Decentralised participation and peer-to-peer networking has been promoted as the ideal model for social organisation, rather than one-way dictation from established centres of power. Indeed, the coining of 'open source' – now a wider movement which promotes universal access to the blueprint of computer programs in order to enhance quality (the 'wisdom of the crowd') – was a conscious decision. In 1998, at a meeting of like-minded technology thinkers in California, 'open source' was favoured over 'free source', an earlier term also in use, because it was deemed less 'politically-focused' (Open Source Initiative). The term 'open', rather than 'free', provided a way for such experts to appeal to corporate IT departments, or, in the words of one major figure who was involved, 'to work with and co-opt the market for our own purposes, rather than remaining stuck in a marginal, adversarial position' (Raymond 1998; see also Raymond 1999; Berry 2004, 2008; Tkacz 2012). One can see, therefore, that openness can also be associated with innovation and competitiveness, modes of activity which are 'perfectly compatible with a new form of capitalist accumulation' (Tkacz 2012: 395).

In trying to separate genuine from exaggerated claims about societies moving towards openness, one should not miss the many social and economic constraints that have also been associated with neoliberalism. Indeed, because appeals to openness often envelop agendas with a warm glow of 'the common good' or 'the public', there exists a risk of not understanding how power relations are actually operating and who precisely owns or manages different spaces. Thus, in reference to many urban centres, the privatisation or part privatisation of open spaces has provoked worries that the 'right to the city' (Lefebvre 1968) can potentially be 'withdrawn, restricted, regulated and controlled' (London Assembly 2011: 17). Some authors have cautioned that the definition of 'publicness' has at times been narrowly conceived in these debates. For instance, reduced accessibility to certain public spaces does not necessarily result from the 'corporate takeover' of the city (De Magalhães 2010; Langstraat and Van Melik 2013). Nonetheless, in high-profile protests, when the image of major firms becomes tarnished, one does encounter more robust monitoring and policing. In London, during the Occupy Movement protest of 2011, the owner of Canary Wharf took out an injunction to stop camps being set up by protesters outside the financial institutions on the estate (Owen and Malik 2011). The activists later returned, however, but defined themselves as 'a walking tour' rather than a protest (Emery 2011). Such incidents showcase how privately owned public spaces are not always welcoming to all members of the public. Indeed, in places like shopping malls, the removal of 'undesirables' ('anti-social' youths, homeless people, etc.) by security guards can work through more subtle or informal rules of conduct. As one author has expressed it, such 'rules are flexibly and differentially enforced in order to sustain an illusion of openness while maximizing management's control' (Kohn 2004: 10).

See also: **community, consensus, freedom, global, individual, innovation, network, participation, private, stakeholder, trade, vision**.

Further reading: Berry 2008; Raymond 1998.

PARTICIPATION

Derived from the Latin root *participare* (to share in), the term 'participation' entered English in the late fourteenth century. By the late sixteenth century, the related notion of partnership had been coined to define the condition of being a partner or, more generally, the idea of companionship (the business and legal appropriation of the word quickly followed). Since Rousseau (2008[1762]) and Mill (1991[1861]), the modern theorisation of participation has been intertwined with questions of politics, democracy and power more broadly. Not unlike the concept of community, with which it is frequently associated, participation is often, but not always, imbued with favourable, normative connotations. Indeed, this general sense offers an immediate clue as to why participation is often invoked in many different political debates. The notion of political participation is, as Birch (2007) rightly argues, not nearly as complex as that of political representation and, in the minds of many users, both academic and popular, the former can appear as relatively uncontested. However, when trying to delineate any potential meaning of participation with respect to neoliberalism, context invariably needs to be specified. One cannot speak of participation *tout court*, without attention to issues of who takes part in what and when and how (Parry 1972; see also Almond and Verba 1963; Pateman 1970). In this way, we can better reveal the political economy of practices that are conducted under the name of participation.

Before sketching out how the term has been used in the neoliberal period, it would be helpful, following Parry (1972), to note three conceptual elements of 'political participation'. First, there is a wide variety of modes of participation. In a weak sense, it could be suggested that all citizens of a modern state, be it the US or China, are participants in a political system, but most analysts would place an emphasis on the need for some degree of active engagement in the making of political life, such as through voting, joining a political party or lobbying for a policy change. Under this analysis, trying to locate how decision-making is actually conducted, including where and under what terms, constitutes a major line of enquiry. Second, there are often questions about the intensity of participation. Who is allowed to participate and with what frequency? Mary Wollstonecraft, the early feminist writer, once argued that women should be freed 'from all restraint by allowing them to participate in the inherent rights of mankind' (Wollstonecraft 1792: 406). In this case, the freedom to participate is an aspect of full humanity. The sentiment is still relevant today when one asks how women can participate in all the social spaces where politics and power are negotiated. Third, even if participation is formally open to some degree, that does not necessarily imply that such processes are meaningful. For instance, some activities of participation may be more illusory than real, generating little, if any, substantive change in outcomes. Creating the conditions for 'pseudo participation' which is read by others as 'legitimate participation' may, indeed, be the hidden objective for some actors in carrying out political contests.

Who decides is always a vital question in the management of capitalism, from the shopfloor supervisor who tries to motivate staff to the head of the IMF who bargains over multi-billion-dollar loans. The idea of industrial democracy is a long-standing theme in socialist thought (Proudhon 1970[1840]; Webb and Webb 1897; Clegg 1960). But how to realise such ideals is often problematic, not least because, as originally argued by Marx (1990[1867]), the average worker only has their labour to sell, while, by contrast, the capitalist owner controls the means of production and enjoys the major fruits of such labour. Nonetheless, at certain historical moments and in particular locations, forces of social critique have called for, and partially won, improvements in how employees participate in the running of capitalist enterprises. In the West, labour union struggles in the 1960s and 1970s provided part of the background context for how 'workplace participation' would be tested and later reimagined within the neoliberal period, in terms of both management theory and legal rights. For instance, in 1976, in Germany, under the label of 'co-determination' rights (*Mitbestimmung*), workers won enhanced authority to occupy seats on the board of directors. Around the same time, the increased frequency of strikes in France, the UK and Italy, combined with a generalised apathy about working in large, hierarchical organisations (a particular concern voiced by middle-class youth), troubled government and corporate officials (Boltanski and Chiapello 2007). In response, a new politics of participation emerged, with a growing managerial emphasis on direct worker involvement at the micro level of companies (Ramsay 1977).

The neoliberal conception of workplace participation, one that strengthened in the 1980s and, in particular, from the 1990s, is, nonetheless, paradoxical. On the one hand, to read some management authors, it can appear as if there is nothing more important that employee participation. The successful organisation, according to this narrative, develops a welcoming atmosphere, whereby workers are 'listened to' as 'stakeholders'. Activity is organised into teams and networks, rather than rigid departments and hierarchies, with a particular emphasis on self-mobilisation of effort rather than motivational cues from a boss. Being able to work within a 'diverse' and 'global' environment is expected. In turn, it is argued that participatory management enables employees to nurture a greater sense of belonging and commitment (Boltanski and Chiapello 2007). On the other hand, however, the agenda under participation also provokes considerable scepticism from many quarters. One worry centres on how trade unions – historically the major force for reform in employment rights, but now weakened in many countries, often as a result of political attacks – might 'buy into' managerial agendas as the price for maintaining some degree of power. 'Partnership' agreements, such as those including confidentiality clauses between union leaders and management, can thus be interpreted as a 'legitimation device', one which may generate some social gains for unions, but which compromises their potential capacity to demand more fundamental changes (Martínez Lucio 2010: 10; see also Stuart and Martínez Lucio 2005). Elsewhere, according to other critics, the lived experience of some workplace 'empowerment' schemes features a major irony: such practices may be more exploitative than the so-called 'regressive' models they were supposed to replace. For instance, management efforts to create in-house 'family' cultures, or the blurring of distinctions between work and play, may be viewed as suffocating or stressful by some employees, rather than expressions of liberation (Kunda 2006; Costas 2012).

Two other major uses of the related term 'partnership' have surfaced in the neoliberal period. The first concerns the rise of public–private partnerships (PPPs). In a broad sense, it could be suggested that ventures involving both government agencies and private sector actors have been present in many countries for decades. However, the label 'PPPs', with its normative emphasis on business as the solution to state or societal problems, carries a neoliberal inflection. In the 1980s, within the US, the phrase was invoked in public policy, including by President Reagan, as well as in debates on the renewal of inner cities (Berger 1986; Holland 1984). The major political popularisation of the idea came in the 1990s, with the UK's launch of the Private Finance Initiative in 1992, seen by many countries as a test case. PPPs have subsequently appeared in many forms, but tend to feature a bias towards large infrastructure projects, such as transport systems. As a policy innovation, they have been justified by recourse to: (1) budgetary constraints faced by governments that call for new sources of capital (for instance, in the EU context, in light of strict Maastricht rules or, following the global financial crisis, austerity conditions that the public is now expected to shoulder); and (2) complexity arguments concerning project management, including the belief that businesses can bring efficiency savings and knowledge that governments cannot easily provide (Greve 2010). A related discourse now circulates around such claims, including the use of 'complementarity', 'synergy' and 'trust', words that reinforce the theme of partnership. Indeed, partnership has arguably eclipsed privatisation as the master frame for discussing such activity. Nonetheless, PPPs have remained controversial – for example, in claims that societal norms attached to 'the public' may not always dovetail with commercial interests. Equally, some projects do not offer value for money or transparent systems of accountability and risk.

The other major deployment of partnership has been in the field of international development, both in 'real world' policymaking and in academic debates. Indeed, the language on partnership and participation has become so naturalised and pervasive that, from the viewpoint of some critical observers, it represents a kind of 'tyranny' around which almost all players in the 'development industry' have rallied (Cooke and Kothari 2001; for a deeper history, see Cornwall 2006). For instance, in the period from 2002 to 2012, the World Bank allocated almost US$85 billion to projects within developing countries under the category of 'local participatory development' (World Bank 2012). This emphasis on partnerships between richer donors and poorer recipients has been justified by a common critique that previous relations were too 'top-down' (a frequently repeated phrase in such circles), without giving poor communities a 'voice' in the design and implementation of such programmes. In turn, the incorporation of 'local knowledge' into development projects, such as from rural village elders, rather than urban bureaucratic officials, is claimed to lead to more equitable and efficient outcomes. By contrast, any policymaking that displays an aura of being overly technocratic and, in particular, too attached to Western values or culture, is considered *passé*. From the mid 1990s, such ideas had, moreover, merged into broader participatory governance frameworks, which argued that individuals in the developing world needed to change from 'passive residents' into 'active citizens', who would hold states and markets accountable for activity that shaped their lives (Hickey and Mohan 2004).

Although 'participation' remains a keyword in development policy, with highly malleable properties that can be attached to different forms of politics, criticisms remain. In one of the most sophisticated critiques, based upon ethnographic research in India and work for Oxfam International, David Mosse has argued that 'the project' of participatory development, conceived as an authoritative, yet highly ambiguous and contradictory orthodoxy, is 'primarily a form of representation orientated towards concerns that are external to the location' (Mosse 2003: 65). The language of partnership is politically valuable because it is can be used to 'mediate or translate between divergent interests' (Mosse 2005: 46), including, tellingly, interests that may not want to be reformed. However, notwithstanding some material gains that may be acquired by poor groups, in Mosse's (2005) reading, top-down power relations tend to be preserved within a new managerialised game of legitimacy. For instance, he documents episodes where agendas linked to participation took on a commodity-like appearance to be bargained over, or trends in the logic of a project where donor power tended to increase. Self-interested villagers, in one case, reconfigured their attitudes and professed needs to match the agenda of the project, including deferring to the ideas of outside experts. In other words, the villagers deployed a 'gaming' strategy, even if their 'real interests' lay elsewhere. In doing so, the definition of 'partnership', as initially imagined in Washington or other Western centres, was validated and 'mirrored back to them [the external experts]' (Mosse 2003: 59). Such complex social dynamics help to reveal that the concrete practices of participation are embedded within resilient structures of political economy, which the theory of participation ignores or cannot always easily explain. In many ways we might be reminded of that other meaning of 'participation' derived from the Latin of making someone a sharer, only in this case the inequality in the relationship has a decidedly different resonance.

See also: **choice, community, consensus, development, diversity, experience, freedom, governance, innovation, network, openness, power, private, project, responsibility, stakeholder, vision**.

Further reading: Cornwall 2006; Greve 2010; Mosse 2003, 2005; Parry 1972.

PERFORMANCE

As the history of capitalism repeatedly shows, a central problem has been how to control and motivate workers through systems of measurement. While invariably used in a general sense to define the action of doing a task, the more deliberate appeal to the term 'performance' in the field of management originated in the early twentieth century. The influence of Walter Dill Scott's (1911) pioneering studies on industrial psychology and Frederick Taylor's (1919) work on 'scientific' management techniques were particularly notably. Such thinking can, in turn, be situated in relation to the wider 'Efficiency Movement' in the US and in other countries, including the Soviet Union. Around the same time, performance was also being invoked to define the extent to which an investment was profitable. By the postwar period, within the US, the notion of the performance appraisal was promoted as a method for summarising and evaluating the labour of an employee, often conducted in an annual interview.

According to the advice of one influential management theorist in the 1950s, the supervisor should not only offer feedback to the worker on their current activity but, in addition, make them 'an active agent, not a passive "object"' in improving their future performance (McGregor 1957: 90). In this sense, the social construction of performance entailed the employee in defining their own strengths and weaknesses, rather than being always told what to do, a way of thinking that was further popularised by Peter Drucker's (1954) 'management by objectives' approach.

As an organisational concept associated with rationalised monitoring and self-discipline, performance did, nonetheless, take time to spread and become accepted. Similar to other notions associated with neoliberalism, such as change and risk, a literature developed from the 1970s and 1980s linking it to the field of management. First coined by Warren (1972), performance management was imagined as something more expansive than performance appraisal. Whereas the latter was a targeted, behavioural intervention, directed within a top-down logic, the former entailed a more continuous process of evaluation going beyond classroom-based training. For instance, as one early conceptualisation put it, 'performance is best developed through practical challenges and experiences on the job with guidance and feedback from superiors' (Beer and Ruh 1976: 60). The emergence of this vision was, in one respect, a reaction to criticism of the performance-appraisal model, including claims that such interactions could be counterproductive if staff continued to have low morale (Conant 1973; Patton 1973). What was needed, according to these writers, was a larger strategic framework, founded upon mutual communication between managers and employees, which embraced 'performance planning, performance review, and performance appraisal' (Plachy and Plachy 1988: i). By the turn of the century, such ideas had become increasingly normalised, particularly when framed in the context of a 'global' struggle for 'competitiveness' and 'talent', other ideas that have also been given a neoliberal colouring (Daniels and Daniels 2004; Varma et al. 2008). For instance, in a British Library search of books, the phrase 'performance management' appeared in 995 publications prior to 1988, but in the subsequent period until 2001, this list increased to 3,838 records and, in the current period after 2001, a further 4,628 publications.

Though a keyword within the vocabulary of business, the notion of performance was, by the 1990s, beginning to make its mark in other institutional fields and domains. These processes were uneven and, thus, it would be wrong to claim that the concept has become internationally widespread. With respect to public administration, the appeal to performance is closely allied with New Public Management (NPM), an expression that tries to capture the turn from the 1980s towards public service reforms, mainly, although not exclusively, within English-speaking countries (Hood 1989; Pollitt 1993; Pollitt and Bouckaert 2011). Associated with both the politics of the 'new right' as well as labour and social-democratic parties, the core of NPM has remained rather ambiguous, but essentially it represents an amalgamation of ideas drawn from corporate management, institutional economics and public choice (Aucoin 1990). According to proponents of this line of thinking, governments are assumed to be suffering from a 'performance deficit' (Kamensky 1996: 249) by trying to maintain the quality of public services yet, at the same time, relieve the burden on taxpayers and enhance democratic accountability. The private sector was seen as an inspiration for how efficiency savings could be realised, along with importing models of customer satisfaction and choice. For instance, in the US, the appeal to performance was given added legitimacy by President Clinton's promotion of the National Performance Review, an executive-led agenda which argued that the 'bureaucratic' paradigm of government needed to end and, in turn, be replaced with so-called 'entrepreneurial government' (Executive Office of the President 1993; see also Osborne and Gaebler 1992; Carroll 1995).

In the effort to operationalise the concept of performance along such lines, a seemingly endless array of indicators, targets, league tables, projects, benchmarks and audits have appeared, inscribed within government agencies and, increasingly, monitored transnationally by institutions such as the OECD and the World Bank (OECD-PUMA 1997; on the example of 'governance indicators', see Kaufmann et al. 2011). But for some writers and practitioners, such activity has led to a 'performance paradox' (Meyer and Gupta 1994). On the one hand, the rhetoric of performance claims to be making public policy more efficient, mimicking business as the presumed high watermark of 'good practice'. Yet, on the other hand, the systems associated with recording performance tend to create a 'new bureaucratic rationality' (Dardot and Laval 2013) or, more generally, an 'audit society' (Power 1997). Within many institutional cultures that have experienced new 'performance-based' regimes, from policing and health services to schools and universities, there is evidence of perverse or unintended consequences. Three effects can be noted. First, the proliferation in regulators and auditors comes with its own financial costs to respective organisations and governments. Second, the pressure to adhere to particular performance standards sometimes generates dysfunctional outcomes, such as 'tunnel vision' or lack of creativity. Third, other evidence points to symbolic practices on paper or, in other words, performance statistics that appear to be positive but, in reality, are not matched by underlying improvements (van Thiel and Leeuw 2002). Hood (2006), for example, has found 'gaming' strategies adopted by UK public authorities in order to legitimately meet performance standards. In one instance, patients have been forced to wait in ambulances outside emergency rooms until the hospital in question was confident that the patient could be seen within a four-hour waiting target, a central government priority.

These illustrations of multiple, at times shifting, performance criteria are, for other authors, reflective of how neoliberalism can be depicted as a form of governmentality or becomes interchangeable with it. As originally argued by the philosopher Michel Foucault (2008), and expanded by many neo-Foucauldians (Rose 1999; Dean 2010; Dardot and Laval 2013), this latter approach aims to capture a more subtle reading of power, one which goes beyond the government as the only institutional site of relevance, to explore how the naturalisation of market capitalism is a product of many forces beyond the state. In particular, to take a Foucauldian reading, there is also a 'performativity' to how performance metrics are constructed and normalised. As suggested by one higher-education theorist when reflecting upon the performance agenda in the UK:

> There are new sets of skills to be acquired here – skills of presentation and of inflation, making the most of ourselves, making a spectacle of ourselves. [...] We are burdened with the responsibility to perform, and if we do not we are in danger of being seen as irresponsible. Performativity is a moral system that subverts and re-orients us to its ends. It makes us responsible for our performance and for the performance of others.
>
> (Ball 2012a: 19; see also Ball 2012b; Shore 2008;
> Collini 2012; and an interesting campaign for
> 'slow scholarship' by Mountz et al. 2015)

Mirroring an increasingly image-conscious consumer society, 'to perform well' as a university is, thus, to reconfigure teaching and scholarly activities into more calculable units for public consumption. In doing so, if the performance metrics are valorised as 'the truth' or, at the very least, cannot be criticised in an effective way, it is possible 'to replace commitment with contract' (Ball 2012a: 20): that is, to further embed capitalist norms into an environment that was relatively insulated from capitalism for most of its history. Ironically, the language of performance returns us to the history of which it is a part.

See also: **business, challenge, change, competition, governance, innovation, management, market, network, project, responsibility, risk, state, vision.**

Further reading: Ball 2012a; Meyer and Gupta 1994; Pollitt and Bouckaert 2011; Power 1997.

POWER

Central to critical investigations into neoliberalism has been the concept of power, with different aspects under the spotlight, including relations of social class, the growth of financial markets, the comparative analysis of political rule-making and the everyday practices of work and consumerism (Harvey 2005; Ong 2006; Macartney 2010; Peck 2010). From the perspective of social science, power has always been an important concept for grasping who wins conflicts and who governs (Dahl 1961; Lukes 2005[1974]; Clegg and Haugaard 2009). When applied carefully, the notion can help to improve our understanding of patterns of stability and change, including why some political practices are considered 'normal' while others struggle for attention or even fail to be seen. In short, to study power is not only to trace the contests within the world of professional politics but, more broadly, to grasp the construction of 'the political' in all its social, economic and cultural forms (for an introduction to this distinction, see Mouffe 2005). At the same time, however, there is also a risk of over-analysing the notion: that is, expecting 'power' to serve as a sort of skeleton key to unlock a complete understanding of social life. Placing too much analytical burden on the notion of power can sometimes be counterproductive. While the concept has a popular resonance, notably with respect to the formal processes of democratic elections, it can also be problematic in the context of debates surrounding neoliberalism. The term is often revealing not for its explicit deployment but, rather, for how many policymakers and business elites appear to use (softer) substitute terms that are within the larger conceptual universe of power, such as 'influence', 'capacity', 'partnership' and 'stakeholder'.

The concept of power has various meanings, but most pivot around notions of ability or relationship. Power is often seen as both a capacity and the exercise of such capacity. The Latin *potentia* is associated with *posse*, meaning a faculty to exercise might and force, particularly political. Hence, in English, 'potential' and 'power' have their origin in this troublesome elision (Eagleton-Pierce 2013). A number of scholars have argued that since power invites multiple, and at times, contradictory readings it should be treated as an essentially contested concept (Lukes 2005[1974]; Connolly 1993). If one can divide the concept into sub-types, then this contestable quality becomes more revealing. When applied to the neoliberal period, we might consider three senses of power (inspired by Barnett and Duvall 2004, 2005). First, power can be viewed in coercive terms, often through a stress on materialism, such as an employer who fires a worker and, thus, demonstrates how control has been exercised over the wage–labour relationship. Laws that give employers greater 'flexibility' to lay off workers could be considered an example of such coercive power (in the US, see Kalleberg 2011). Second, power is often mediated through complex institutional networks that work to constrain or enable certain actors over others. This dimension of power has arguably become more significant in the neoliberal period, from the expansion of government rule-making to the proliferation of international institutions, such as the WTO and the WEF. Third, power can be understood in productive terms: that is, not simply as a negative 'force that says no', but as a relation that 'induces pleasure, forms knowledge, [and] produces discourse' (Foucault 1980: 119). Indeed, for some linguists and modern Foucauldians, the entire 'discourse of neoliberalism' can be understood as a form of productive power which shapes dominant mentalities and practices (Fairclough 2006; for criticism, see Holborow 2015; for an application to business, see Fuchs 2007).

A notable conceptual extension of power in the neoliberal era is the idea of empowerment. Indeed, in some settings, 'empowerment' is now probably used more often than 'power'. The reasons for this rise in popularity are complicated and reflect struggles over contested questions of legitimacy and fairness. As a starting point, the turn to empowerment represents a desire to reveal the contours and content of unequal socio-political relations but, importantly, still give a sense of hope to the marginalised that inequalities can be narrowed or even erased. In this respect, the positive sense of renewal and progress captured in empowerment can be contrasted with the legacy of negative connotations bound up with the concept of power, such as dictation and violence. Under agendas linked to empowerment, the gaze is predominately focused on those who are believed to lack agency. In Samuel Johnson's *Dictionary* (1755), two meanings of empower are given: to authorise and to enable. As the term has become incorporated into neoliberal vocabulary, it has retained something of these original senses, but has also bent towards new uses, which include a role for ideology and the politics of concealment.

In the 1960s, in the context of waves of social activism across the world, 'empowerment' was occasionally invoked, such as in the US in relation to civil rights (see a 'black empowerment' reference in Tolbert 1968;

see also Solomon 1976). Nonetheless, it was in the 1980s and, in particular, the 1990s, when use of the expression soared. For instance, in the *New York Times*, there were 18 uses of the word in the 1970s, 208 references in the 1980s, but 1515 during the 1990s. In business management, empowerment became a new catchphrase, particularly around diversity agendas, which called for giving less privileged employees (women, minorities) more authority in decision-making. Advocates of the term drew links between empowerment projects, leadership skills and enhanced organisational performance (Kanter 1979, 1989; Block 1987; Conger and Kanungo 1988). Such thinking has also been reinforced by the frequent call from theorists and practitioners for participatory styles of management. In this context, the ideal firm should be organised through networks, rather than hierarchies, with an emphasis on individual creativity and 'play' in the workplace, rather than receiving repeated instructions from a boss (Boltanski and Chiapello 2007; although for criticism which shows how this is not uncontested in business strategy, see Argyris 1998). Paralleling such trends, it is not surprising that empowerment, often invoked as a non-offensive and non-political idea that everyone should accept, has also found a home in many other settings, from government investment in marginalised urban areas ('Empowerment Zones') to self-help books for the confused (Gershon and Straub 2011) and even, it is claimed, to the songs of Beyoncé.

Another significant application of the concept of empowerment is found in the field of international development. The initial appropriation of the phrase arose in the mid 1980s and owes much to feminist campaigning, particularly organisations from South Asia and Latin America. For instance, a Bangalore-founded network called DAWN (Development Alternatives with Women for a New Era), as well as other groups in Mexico, were important in mounting a critique of various UN agendas. Such activists were critical of the 'additive vision' inscribed in the dominant Women in Development approach, which tended to treat 'women' as an homogenous category which could be incorporated into existing models and policies. Instead, DAWN argued for a deeper examination of institutions and ideologies of power that fostered unequal gendered relations, including decision-making processes where women were excluded (Sen and Grown 1987). Theoretical inspiration was derived from, among others, Paulo Freire and Antonio Gramsci (Batliwala 2010; see also Kabeer 1994). The resulting activism, whereby empowerment was understood as a perspective and a process, gave rise to the now dominant Gender and Development approach (for an overview, see Visvanathan *et al.* 2011). In one sense, therefore, this turn to empowerment, which conveyed a sense of the active potential of the subject, was productive in mobilising civil society institutions around an agenda to transform relations between men and women. However, as soon as this discourse was established, the term was seized upon by many other actors within the larger 'development industry'. Following the UN World Conference on Women in 1995, where the word was featured in the first sentence of the mission statement, it began to be adopted by the World Bank, along with national donors, such as the US Agency for International Development. For instance, by 2005, more than 1800 projects associated with the World Bank's lending portfolio featured 'empowerment' in their documentation (Alsop *et al.* 2006).

This movement towards the mainstreaming of the idea of empowerment is not without controversy and, for some researchers, can be viewed as symptomatic of broader tendencies within the neoliberal era. One criticism surrounds how 'empowerment' has become a 'washed out' word through overuse, particularly when in the hands of international donors, with meanings and effects that are sometimes unclear (Batliwala 2010; Prügl 2015). At first glance, this point may not always seem obvious, particularly when consulting the reams of statistical measures, rankings and studies that have been produced with the declared purpose of improving empowerment. However, as Sharma (2008: xx) argues in the case of India, 'empowerment is a risky and deeply political act whose results cannot be known in advance'. When seen from the perspective of certain civil society groups and those marginalised people they claim to represent, these risks pivot around how some empowerment agendas can dovetail with a managerial ethos that seeks to produce self-governing agents, people who are focused on entrepreneurial ends in a capitalist economy and, in the process, who are less dependent on state assistance (Sharma 2008). Not unlike the related notion of participation, the open-ended discursive quality of empowerment, combined with its association with debates on rights and justice is, in one sense, a major reason for its popularity. But when stretched, the concept serves as a vessel into which different sets of actors can pour multifarious meanings, from the hegemonic to the counter-hegemonic. Although not directly linked to the field of development, a similar critique has been expressed within feminism. As Angela McRobbie (2009: 49) has argued, '[W]omen are currently being disempowered through the very discourses of empowerment they are being offered as substitutes for feminism'. Paradoxically, therefore, one of the problems with empowerment is that it does not talk sufficiently about power.

See also: **change, class, development, diversity, finance, freedom, global, governance, market, participation, private, responsibility, stability, stakeholder, state, welfare**.

Further reading: Argyris 1998; Eagleton-Pierce 2013; Lukes 2005[1974]; Sharma 2008.

PRIVATE

'Private', derived in part from the Latin *privatus*, is a complex and often controversial term. It remains fundamental to how politics, law and commercial life are imagined within the neoliberal period. In Skeat's *Concise Etymological Dictionary* (1901), prominence is given to the literal meaning of 'private' as 'sundered from the rest'. But in the translation from Latin to modern English, the term lost some of its earlier negative meaning of 'deprivation'. 'We no longer think primarily of deprivation when we use the word "privacy," and this is partly due to the enormous enrichment of the private sphere through modern individualism' (Arendt 1998[1958]: 38). In Samuel Johnson's *Dictionary* (1755), private is associated with secrecy, lack of openness or 'retirement'. Such connotations were bound up with the wider development of individual personhood and the idea of withdrawal into private spaces, both literally and metaphorically (Calhoun 2005). Thus, from the sixteenth century, special uses of 'private' began to proliferate and took on the wide range of applications that are common today: private education (1581, *OED*), private property (1642, *OED*), private bank (1663, *OED*), private collection (1692, *OED*), private law (1702, *OED*), private company (1711, *OED*), private carriage (1787, *OED*), private development (1910, *OED*), and private sector (1930, *OED*). As Raymond Williams (1983[1976]) notes, in most, but not all of these uses, 'private' implies a form of special status. The assumption is that a right or an advantage – originally in reference to law, *privilegium*, but now extended to a variety of social contexts – has been granted to one individual or group over a larger collective.

With roots in Roman law, the distinction between the categories of 'public' and 'private' constitutes one of the 'grand dichotomies' in Western thought (Bobbio 1989). As with types of land use, the boundaries between public and private can sometimes be sharply defined, stable and the subject of vigorous policing. For some, the distinction may feel 'preconceptual, almost instinctual, rooted in the orientations of the body and common speech' (Warner 2005: 23). Such practices and experiences are a response to deep trends involving the rise of the bureaucratic state and the growth of capitalism. Thus, when the public/private distinction is raised, actors are often pivoting around jurisdictional claims, particularly the line between the 'public' authority granted to governments and the voluntary associations among 'private' citizens (Vincent 1987; Weintraub, 1997). Upon closer examination, such a dichotomy can often become blurred and difficult. One may encounter certain things that appear to be both public and private at the same time, in varying degrees or in different ways. For instance, some actors may draw upon public resources or values to pursue private ends, yet downplay or deny such actions. Alternatively, other agents may donate private resources to better a public good, which, in turn, may lead to the long-term protection of their specific private interests. In such ways, the 'negotiation' – a richer term than 'confrontation' – between the private and the public can become multifaceted and indeed confusing, either intentionally or inadvertently.

In the analysis of capitalism, from the natural–rights doctrine adopted by Adam Smith to the socialist visions of Karl Marx, the definition and normative implications of private property have been intensely debated. In its idealised form, a property right entitles its holder to a form of authority or ownership over an asset, such as a piece of land, a factory or even certain ideas (and other intangibles). Private property rights are a necessary but not sufficient condition for the existence of capitalism, justified for promoting more efficient use of resources, capital accumulation and the resolution of disputes (Alchian and Demsetz 1973; Alchian 2008; Rubin and Klumpp 2012). But private property is not the only ideal type of property. Alternative systems often clash and compromise with private property, including state property and common property (sometimes referred to as 'open access' or 'group' among a wider community) (Michelman 1982; Waldron 1985). In the twentieth century, lawyers recast the notion of private property from a physical thing that was owned – still a common understanding – to the less monolithic 'bundle of rights' approach. According to the latter, the notion of 'exclusive ownership' of private property is often misleading, with interests that could be divided over time, among different people or informed by a host of other limiting factors, such as public policy rules and norms (Grey 1980; Heller 2005). Thus, private property and the material processes associated with its name are not simply matters of legal theory but part of a socio-political struggle to define and organise recognised rights of action.

For intellectuals associated with neoliberal thought, private property has a totemic status. As Ludwig von Mises expressed it, 'The programme of liberalism if condensed into a single word would have to read: *property*, that is, private ownership of the means of production' (Mises 2005[1927]: 2, italics in original). In addition to the specific reasons for defending private property, Mises, along with his student, Friedrich von Hayek, argued that private property was aligned with higher principles of freedom, particularly of the idealised individual. In Hayek's words, 'law, liberty and property are an inseparable trinity' (Hayek 2013[1973]: 102). According to this perspective, the state should uphold the rule of law and guarantee policing, but not interfere with how private property is maintained through entrepreneurial incentives. In turn, these conditions are claimed to constitute a more just and productive order. By contrast, the Marxist critique of private property, a prominent oppositional discourse during the time of Mises and Hayek, expresses scepticism about the presumed benefits of private property. For Marx, capitalist private property is a distinctive social system in two ways. First, it can operate only by concentrating power in the hands of the few and, thus, it tends to reinforce an unequal class system between owners and non-owners. One must deny private property to others in order to open up a differentiation of power. Second, the products produced by the worker remain the property of the owner, for which the owner will try to derive a profit. Wages are not a payment for the worker's labour, but their *labour power*: that is, when the labour activity is converted into a commodity form (Marx 1992 [1885]; see also Sayer 1995). In turn, Marx argues that these processes lead to a host of regressive outcomes for workers, including alienation and estrangement from the products they produce, from the activity of work itself and from each other (Marx and Engels 2007[1927]). Indeed, for Marx, if a communist society is to be realised, private property would need to be abolished.

If private property is a foundational principle within capitalism, then the movement towards the privatisation of state-owned assets or services carries a more distinctive neoliberal edge. In the early postwar period, one can find occasional examples of privatisation, or 'denationalisation', as it was commonly called. For instance, in 1961, the German government sold a stake in Volkswagen in a public share offering (Megginson and Netter 2001; see also Bel 2006). However, the major experiment with privatisation was from the 1980s in the UK under Prime Minister Margaret Thatcher's administration (see Elliott 2013 for the debut of the term). In the first Thatcher term, the Tory vision of privatisation was not well conceived and tended to proceed cautiously and haphazardly, often justified as a quick, revenue-raising mechanism to meet financial imperatives. The rationale became clearer in response to disillusionment with the performance of some nationalised industries, particularly coal and rail, which were claimed to 'lack efficiency' and 'competition' (Parker 2009). According to some, privatisation was aligned with a broader effort by certain interests – within business, the media and think tanks as much as government – to undermine public sector trade unions and, thus, to reconfigure class relations (Gamble 1994; see also Jackson and Saunders 2012). At the same time, when doubt was cast on Keynesianism, privatisation received theoretical support from rival approaches, including monetarism, Austrian economics and public choice theory. The extent to which Thatcher and other conservatives actually read Hayek or Milton Friedman (2002[1962]) has been debated, but there is no question that such reasoning provided legitimacy for privatisation debates. Between the sale of British Telecom in 1984 and the early 1990s, the UK witnessed a series of massive share-issue privatisations, including of gas, water and electricity utilities. In Thatcher's own words, privatisation was a form of 'popular capitalism', or 'a crusade to enfranchise the many in the economic life of the nation' (Thatcher 1986; see also Thatcher 1993; Parker 2012).

With the UK as a laboratory for testing privatisation, other countries soon followed. In the 1990s, this trend was particularly concentrated in Western Europe and Latin America, before spreading to all other regions by the turn of the century. The meaning of privatisation varies immensely across countries. It can include full government withdrawal from certain responsibilities, restrictions in the volume or quality of public services, the transfer of public assets into private hands or government financing of private services (Starr 1988; Hermann and Flecker 2012). In another respect, the impact of such policies often depends upon where a country is positioned within the world economy, including its degree of openness (or vulnerability, to adopt a different sense) to foreign investment. This factor is particularly telling for developing countries which have experienced privatisation as the shift of public ownership to foreign-based corporations and local elites. In Egypt, for instance, under the encouragement of the IMF, a privatisation wave from 2004 to 2008 opened up once strategic sectors, including banks, the petro-industry and steel. In the eyes of the World Bank, these changes made the country into a 'success story' for ease of doing business, yet critics have argued that privatisation strengthened a 'capitalist oligarchy' at the expense of the middle and working classes (Roccu 2013b: 437; see also Farah 2009; Joya 2011). Since 2009, partly in response to the global financial crisis, privatisation agendas have continued to spread. According to one global survey, from 2009 to 2014, governments directly or indirectly divested assets worth more than US$1.1 trillion. Reflecting its transformation over the neoliberal period, China now leads the world in privatisation projects. For example, in 1978, state-owned enterprises produced around 80 per cent of

China's GDP, but by 2013, this figure had fallen to less than 25 per cent (Privatization Barometer 2014).

Privatisation agendas have sparked some of the most heated debates associated with neoliberal policymaking. Three criticisms can be noted. First, claims that privatisation reduces the administrative and fiscal burden of the state are often misleading. While one-off sales do result in revenue gains, the retention of certain assets over the long-term may prove better value for society. At the same time, government is often still involved in monitoring newly privatised entities, particularly when failures and abuses emerge. Second, privatisation should not be automatically equated with enhanced competition and, by common inference, consumer choice, quality and value. On the contrary, many newly privatised markets have not realised such declared goals. In some instances, public monopolies have been replaced by private ones, yet without any corresponding need for firms to consider wider social inequalities (Jomo 2008). For instance, in Bolivia from the mid 1990s, water privatisation produced higher tariff rates for customers and poorly maintained infrastructure, outcomes that triggered protests and a process of renationalisation (Olivera with Lewis 2004; see also Swyngedouw 2005). Third, privatisation has brought forward far-reaching changes in labour relations. To enhance competitiveness in newly privatised organisations, labour costs are often targeted, including lowering wages, extending working hours and limiting collective bargaining (Hermann and Flecker 2012). From the mid 2000s, the privatisation debate, at least in policy and media circles, began to react to some of these criticisms. Advocates now admit that some privatisation agendas proceeded too quickly and without appropriate regulatory conditions yet, importantly, still defend privatisation as a universally desirable vision (Jomo 2008). Interestingly, due to such criticism, the word 'privatisation' seems to have peaked in popularity around the millennium. In the current neoliberal context, 'public-private partnership' has become the default phrase, along with a looser appeal to 'cooperation' and 'involvement' with business or, just simply, the private sector.

See also: **business, capitalism, class, enterprise, entrepreneurship, finance, freedom, individual, market, openness, participation, power, state**.

Further reading: Jomo 2008; Megginson and Netter 2001; Rubin and Klumpp 2012; Starr 1988; Waldron 1985; Weintraub 1997.

PROJECT

A project is not to be confused with a projectile or something jutting out, even if this is where the term began. Rather the meaning lies in something planned or designed, a *projet* in modern French. It is this transferred meaning that plays a significant role in how a variety of modern organisations conceptualise and conduct their activity. As an analytical construct, the concept has become so popular and taken-for-granted that, for some, life itself is imagined as a 'personal project' or proceeding through a series of projects. Because of its naturalised appearance and deployment by users spanning the ideological spectrum across corporations, governments, academia and civil society groups, the neoliberal politics of the notion are difficult to fully decipher. However, like other key concepts in this book, the meaning of project can be better grasped when one tracks its course in addressing business management problems. Here, we find that 'project' pivots around a cluster of related ideas, notably freedom and individualism at a deeper level, but also vision, flexibility, innovation, trust and networks. When used in commercial settings, the notion of project seems to subtly assist in renewing enthusiasm for capitalist agendas. At the same time, through applying such a common term to a variety of activities, the differences between capitalist and non-capitalist pursuits can become uncertain, to the extent that the former may be privileged over the latter (Boltanski and Chiapello 2007).

It could be suggested that projects have always existed, even if the label was not always used. However, for the purpose of understanding neoliberal vocabulary, we need to revisit the early twentieth century. Similar to our current phase of capitalism, business leaders at this time faced challenges in how to enhance economic efficiency, particularly labour productivity. Frederick Winslow Taylor's (1911, 1919) work on 'scientific management', which tried to distil insights from engineering science to business, proved particularly important. 'Taylorism', as the theory became known, emphasised rational methods of empirical logic in order to better organise the working day, including breaking down labour processes into specific tasks, targeting waste and encouraging knowledge transfer between employees. Subsequent students of Taylor refined these basic insights. Henry Gantt (1919), a mechanical engineer, created a graphic workload schedule (the Gantt Chart) that was later used to complete the Hoover Dam and the US interstate highway system (see also Wilson 2003). Henri Fayol (1949[1916]), another disciple of Taylorism, devised his own principles of business administration, which stressed not only the value of forecasting and the division of work, but management techniques centred around authority, discipline and the 'unity of command' (see also Wood and Wood 2002). Although the notion of project was not common in the writings of these authors, when seen through the eyes of modern business commentators, the thinking of Taylor, Gantt and Fayol laid the foundations for a new field of professional study: project management.

From the 1940s to the 1950s, in the US again, the concept of project management largely circulated within social worlds that in some way touched the 'military-industrial complex', the phrase coined by President Eisenhower to denote the close ties between government legislators, national defence agencies and private firms involved in military issues. The Manhattan Project, which created the first atomic bomb, is an obvious illustration, but from the 1960s, the term spread through mimetic processes to many other business organisations. As project became a more attractive concept, it was accompanied with the inevitable efforts to codify and standardise what the *problématique* of project management should be, including the desirable attributes of project managers (Gaddis 1959; Lundin and Söderholm 1998; Morris 2011, 2013; Barker and Cole 2012). This process of normalisation involved the establishment of professional associations, such as the Swiss-based International Project Management Association and the US-based Project Management Institute, as well as related publications like the *Project Management Journal* and the *International Journal of Project Management*. Cumulatively, through this activity, the 'legitimization' (Grabher 2002: 207) of the concept of the project took root.

But what precisely are the generic characteristics of a project and how have processes linked to neoliberalism informed the meaning of the notion? Three themes can be highlighted here. First, in what may appear like a trivial point, a project is a *temporary* system of organisation that will end. According to Boltanski and Chiapello (2007), it is very important to study the temporal limitation of projects because it helps to explain how neoliberal ideology, at a fundamental level, plays with, yet struggles to ultimately satisfy, human desires for freedom. In contemporary business theory, the corporation is presented not as a Weberian 'iron cage' suffocating individual freedom – a popular critique in the 1960s and 1970s era of capitalism, when transnational businesses grew in size – but, on the contrary, as an enabler of creativity and innovation. What are rejected in the neoliberal period are management methods that appear authoritarian, excessive bureaucracy and the separation between one's private and professional lives. Thus, rather than staying within one company for life, acting out the dictates of an overbearing boss, the notion of voluntarily progressing through a series of projects presents a more appealing vision of personal fulfilment and choice. Safe in the knowledge that every project, whatever the exact content, will ultimately dissolve, this intrinsic feature is held up as encouraging participation by giving individuals visible exits. Job satisfaction is therefore linked to the pursuit of near-term targets and, upon crossing the finishing line, the so-called 'deliverables' of the project.

Second, projects are frequently explained as a prime way for workers to improve their employability and, by implication, enhance their security. This theme has assumed greater importance in the neoliberal period because it can no longer be assumed that the employer will provide job security, including various benefits (wages that rise with inflation, reliable pensions, etc.). Through a project, contacts are formed, skills are nurtured and reputations are burnished. In particular, the discourse surrounding project management proposes that employability is enhanced if the individual remains flexible in the face of competitive forces of change. In many industries, networking activity is aimed at generating potential projects and, thus, more opportunities to self-promote. Higher goals may frame the overall justification for the project – such as building shareholder value or improving consumer satisfaction – but the personalised rationale to engage in project activity is never far behind. For instance, in some new media fields, where flexible labour contracts are the norm, one finds individuals listing points on their *résumé* not according to the organisations they have been hired by, but by skill sets they possess and projects they have completed (Grabher 2002; Christopherson 2002). Although this may appear as an exciting and less routine life, where the movement from project to project adds 'spice' (Barker and Cole 2012: 6), it can also be a precarious existence because income sources are not stable. By contrast, according to the new management literature, the less desirable worker is one who cannot easily engage with projects and, in particular, navigate between or juggle multiple projects. In the eyes of many project leaders, such figures do not inspire confidence and they may be interpreted as rigid or unenthusiastic (that is, the opposite of flexible) (Boltanski and Chiapello 2007).

A third theme of interest in project management centres on leadership and trust issues. The ideal project leader, according to the latest models, combines intellectual, managerial and emotional competencies (Dulewicz and Higgs 2005; Müller and Turner 2010). In particular, such figures are claimed to be people-centred and good at inspiring others with their vision as to how the project can succeed. Visionary, 'transformational' leaders, such as the late Steve Jobs of Apple (the emblematic 'corporate hero'), are sought after because of their claimed ability to 'unite leader and followers in the pursuit of a higher purpose which transcends individuals' self-interest' (Partington 2007: 749). Finding this desired project leadership is, however, something of a Holy Grail in business lore. The leadership conundrum (or even contradiction) is difficult to resolve because, to return to the idea of freedom again, project participants are told that they have autonomy to express themselves, yet the leader cannot afford unlimited forms of expression. As one writer summarised it, 'experience shows that attempts at employee empowerment can have negative outcomes, including lack of direction, alienation, over-work and stress' (Partington 2007: 741). This is where the notion of trust enters the picture as a way to potentially manage, yet often never resolve, how social discipline can be maintained in the fluid, networked world of projects. The project manager appeals to trust for many reasons, but one is to encourage the followers to discipline themselves in alignment with the vision of the project. To succeed, the project leader must inspire trust and, in turn, the followers must be trustworthy. Trust, in other words, is the 'cement of projects' (Boltanski and Chiapello 2007: 119).

See also: **flexibility, freedom, individual, innovation, management, market, network, participation, performance, vision**.

Further reading: Boltanski and Chiapello 2007; Grabher 2002; Morris 2011.

REFORM

When the verb 'reform' (from the Latin *reformare*, to form again) entered English in the fourteenth century, it had two senses: to re-establish an original form and to make something into a new form. The idea of changing something for the better was closely intertwined with the notion of restoring an earlier and perhaps 'purer' condition. What actors in different periods have viewed as the 'correct' or 'orthodox' form has often been shaped by their own sense of tradition and their reading of history. Such meanings of the word have continued into the neoliberal present where, as Raymond Williams has expressed it, the term 'can move towards *restoration* as often as towards *innovation*' (Williams 1983[1976]: 263, italics in original). Thus, reform can be used to defend or to contest systems of authority, ranging from the radical to the conservative (and sometimes both at once). For instance, in the political struggle for suffrage in nineteenth-century Britain, reform became closely attached to radical connotations, to the extent that many campaigners and public figures, from Birmingham unionists to Westminster Whigs, called themselves 'radical reformers'. In this regard, it was fitting that George Eliot chose to situate *Middlemarch* (2003[1871]), her novel about the advance of the middle class onto the political stage of history, in 1832, at the time of the Reform Bill, for that was the bill which significantly extended the franchise to the class which would dominate her century (for a good introduction to the early history of the concept, see Innes 2003). Interestingly, by the turn of the twentieth century, in the midst of debates over revolutionary socialism, this sharper sense of radical reform had given way to a less contentious mainstream sense of reform as denoting a controllable process of change (for instance, see Luxemburg 1898[2008]). As a result, a clearer conceptual dichotomy began to emerge, at least in the political rhetoric of aspiration, between reform and revolution.

In the neoliberal period, 'reform' has become a highly adaptable catch-all expression. This trend is particularly visible in the phrase 'economic reform', a well-worn expression among many policymakers, experts, business figures and commentators. For instance, in the *New York Times*, the phrase is found in 205 pieces in the 1970s, and 569 records in the 1980s, before jumping to 1,698 references in the 1990s, the peak decade for usage patterns. Although there are countless local contexts where the word has a specific resonance, reflecting a variety of ideological and social positions, one can also discern stronger threads of meaning that reappear throughout the neoliberal years. For instance, John Williamson (1999), who coined the phrase 'the Washington Consensus' (which many scholars equate with neoliberalism writ large), once summarised 'the debate on economic reform' as being concerned with 'macroeconomic stabilization, microeconomic liberalization, and opening to the outside world' (see also Williamson 1994). In other words, many policy agendas associated with neoliberalism, including low-inflation targeting, privatisation initiatives and the deeper integration of countries into an expanding capitalist system, can all be grouped under the apparently simple heading of 'economic reform'. The extent to which all actors agree with the parameters and content of such reform agendas runs to the heart of many political struggles, including questions about who shapes the dominant meanings of the word. When Joseph Stiglitz was Chief Economist at the World Bank (1997–2000), he encapsulated such sentiments in the following way: 'the term has evolved to take on "politically correct" overtones: reforms are now those changes that "we" approve of, while changes that we do not condone can be labeled with terms of censure such as "backsliding" and "antireform"' (Stiglitz 2000: 551).

An interesting illustration of how the concept of reform has become politically valuable can be seen in the case of China. In 1978, Deng Xiaoping, as the new paramount leader, introduced a series of changes which would lead to the transformation of the country, including the decollectivisation of agriculture, greater acceptance of domestic entrepreneurship and the enabling of foreign investment. The name given to

this reorientation of China towards capitalism (or in official government speak, 'socialism with Chinese characteristics') was called *gaige
kaifang*, literally 'reform and opening' (for an overview, see Naughton
2007). As suggested by Gungwu (1993: 72), the utility of the term *gaige*
can be better understood when compared to *geming* (revolution),
which 'is widely greeted with indifference and a tinge of fear' by current Chinese elites. Tellingly, the notion of *gaige* 'assumes that the *political* structure is here to stay': economic reforms are promoted as 'the
key to salvation and progress', whereas *geming*, associated with violence
and revolt, is treated by the regime as a word from the past (Gungwu
1993: 88, 87, italics in original). In this sense, given such associations,
every use of the word 'reform' by the Communist Party and their allies
appears, directly or indirectly, to exalt their actions and privileges. In
doing so, alternative definitions of reform, including political changes
which could foster greater democracy or accountability, do not receive
the same level of attention. There is little evidence that Chinese
government officials have tired of the use of the term. As Premier
Li Keqiang (2013–) expressed it in a speech which featured the word
77 times: 'Reform has brought us the greatest benefits. Reform is the
top priority for the government' (quoted in Huanxin 2014).

Another revealing general use of 'reform' in neoliberal discourse is
associating the term with the emotion of pain. From one perspective,
this application shows traces of the early religious sense of sacrifice or
punishment in the face of misfortune or misbehaviour. Indeed, due to
uneven distributional effects, many reforms involving trade or fiscal
policy are sometimes explained as being both desirable and painful, or
desirable because they are painful. Representatives from the IMF are
particularly prone to using 'pain' and 'reform' in the same sentence. For
instance, in the organisation's official history of the 1980s debt crisis in
developing countries, the authors note how the IMF's efforts 'calmed
the initial panic and defused its explosive potential. But a long road of
painful reform in the debtor countries, and additional cooperative
global measures, would be necessary to eliminate the problem' (International Monetary Fund n.d.). Similarly, with respect to the European
sovereign-debt crisis from 2009, the qualifier of pain resurfaced in
many deliberations. In return for emergency loans to Greece, Ireland
and Spain, IMF and EU officials demanded reforms to public sector
programmes in these countries. In one media article, the opinion of the
head of the ECB was summarised thus: 'Mr Draghi has also called for
more power to be handed to Brussels to force countries to undertake
painful reforms' (Jones and Wagstyl 2015). It could be suggested, therefore, that the phrase 'painful reform' refers not only to the potential

social suffering of a population (as experienced through cuts to public pensions or healthcare), but also serves as a more direct warning to politicians that social and political stability (including their own professional job security) may be at stake.

In sum, 'reform' has become so embedded in political, business, academic and everyday language that it seems to take on a natural or self-evident quality. The term is undoubtedly one of the most versatile notions in the neoliberal lexicon because it can be moulded to fit a multitude of agendas, from the orthodox to the heterodox. It often serves as an entry point into larger debates, but, at the same time, one may find that not every actor wants to see a close scrutiny of the reform in question. In this respect, some find the word appealing by virtue of what it is *not*, as in the common opposition to 'transform', 'conform' or, as noted, 'revolution'. It is no surprise that politicians and bureaucrats find the word so attractive when it seems to appear as polite and unassuming, yet still conveys an image of purposeful and authoritative planning. However the concept is invoked, one needs to try to expose the political roots and biases it may contain. This is particularly important when a speaker who is justifying an apparently new form is actually trying to conceal the reconstitution of an old form. The word can be equally deceptive when the aspirations or actions associated with the declared reform are, in reality, masking more fundamental changes than those conveyed by the term. In this sense, to recall Williams again, the dance between restoration and innovation often lies at the heart of many uses of the term.

See also: **adjustment, development, flexibility, growth, market, stability, state, trade, welfare**.

Further reading: Gungwu 1993; Stiglitz 2000.

RESPONSIBILITY

The term 'responsibility', particularly in association with 'individual', has become common in the context of neoliberalism, with frequent use by politicians and moral guardians. Following its earlier French origins, the notion of responsible entered English in the mid sixteenth century, with the noun 'responsibility' coming later in the mid seventeenth century. By the eighteenth century, responsibility developed its major meaning of the capacity to fulfil a duty or obligation, a sense informed by discourses within legal and juridical institutions. According to the philosopher Paul Ricoeur (2000), 'responsibility' is a complex term which tries to combine, or reconcile, two older concepts: imputation, referring to how an action or accusation is linked to an agent; and accountability, associated with questions of justice, punishment and praise. The phrase 'one's own responsibility', meaning at one's own risk or without reference to a higher authority, has a neoliberal resonance, but its roots lie, again, in the eighteenth century. Likewise, the expression 'responsible government', which implies the virtue of collective stewardship in the name of a population (citizens or subjects), was generalised in the nineteenth and twentieth centuries, notably in debates about the welfare state. Although certain practices of responsibility have become more codified and monitored within complex societies, the term can be elusive and disputed, particularly when actors struggle within power relations to improve their perceived rights and rewards.

Depending upon the social and spatial context, there are many grounds upon which individual responsibility may be justified as a desirable condition. 'Personal responsibility could matter for reasons of fairness, but it can also matter for reasons of utility, self-respect, autonomy, [and] human flourishing' (Brown 2009: 6). Not all these general justifications should be immediately grouped under the master heading of neoliberalism. Since the 1980s, however, there has been a revival and promotion of the ideal of individual responsibility by those associated with the political right, a loose category that not only refers to political parties of a conservative description but could also embrace social-democratic parties together with media figures and public intellectuals. As Ronald Reagan expressed it in 1979 before becoming US president, 'We will uphold the principles of self-reliance, self-discipline, morality and – above all – responsible liberty for each individual' (Reagan 1979). In 1992, President Clinton sought 'to end welfare as we know it' and, by 1996, through the Personal Responsibility and Work Opportunity Reconciliation Act, achieved his ambition of a new 'workfare' regime, whereby government benefits would be matched by an expectation that the recipient worked (on the rise of the word 'workfare', see Peck 1998; Wacquant 2009). Similarly, in the UK, the theme of individual responsibility resurfaced in the rhetoric of all prime ministers over the neoliberal period, from Margaret Thatcher's assertions that the welfare state eroded the virtues of hard work, through Tony Blair's claims that 'benefit scroungers' should not exploit other taxpayers, to David Cameron's appeal to volunteerism as the solution for a 'broken society' (Brown 2009).

Thus, within the Anglo-Saxon heartlands of neoliberalism, and increasingly within other national political discourses, one finds the trope of 'individual responsibility' serving as a kind of 'motivating discourse and cultural glue' (Wacquant 2012: 72). However, criticism of the term is not hard to find. For instance, in the US, with respect to those at the lower end of the social class structure, the discrimination, penalisation and, in some cases, criminalisation of poverty provides a wider lens through which to examine the politics of individual responsibility. The notion of responsibility cannot, therefore, be constructed and applied within a social and economic vacuum. Rather, any definition needs to address the pervasive structures of class, race, gender and geography. Equally, people may have other conceptions of responsibility, such as those involving family or religion (Trnka and Trundle 2014). Thus, in terms of racial discrimination, African-American unemployment has consistently averaged twice the level of the white population whether in periods of economic expansion or contraction. The frequent media and political depictions of the American poor as 'lacking responsibility' – not working, not working hard enough, not retraining to work in the 'right jobs', not relinquishing their state dependence, not properly rearing their children, etc. – is only one side of the story and needs the corrective of a parallel analysis of the 'devolution, retraction, and recomposition' of the welfare state (Wacquant 2009: 307). Defining individual responsibility without recourse to circumstance, such as enduring conditions of poverty, can therefore at times seem heartless or, paradoxically, lacking in responsibility.

It follows that the flipside of individual responsibility in the neoliberal context is how forms of collective responsibility have been defined, constituted and practised. One important theme under this heading would be the rise of corporate social responsibility (CSR). Although one can find evidence of an enhanced social conscience in business since the industrial revolution, the emergence of a dedicated literature around the notion of CSR is rooted in the experiences of the 1960s and 1970s, particularly in the US context (Carroll 1999, 2008). Initially invoked as simply the 'social responsibility' of business (for instance, see Bowen 1953), the adding of the term 'corporate' reflected a recognition of the increasing power of major enterprises and, accordingly, a common accusation that such power should be held accountable in relation to larger societal ends. This sense of corporate duty or care beyond the bottom line arose out multiple grievances, echoing larger social movements of the time, including demands for firms to be more philanthropic, to produce products in an environmentally sustainable manner and to create more diverse cultures of consent (Committee for Economic Development 1971; Manne and Wallich 1973). Through the 1980s and 1990s, CSR moved from being a peripheral concern to a core agenda item. Today, CSR seems to encompass almost any activity that can be associated with ethical governance and, not surprisingly, is conceptually allied to notions such as stakeholderism, performance and accountability. In a negative sense, therefore, CSR was driven by two generalised anxieties: so-called 'reputational risk' in a world where brands matter and the threat of legal liability from commercial ventures that could go astray (Power 2007).

However, CSR in the neoliberal period is not simply a defensive strategy for managing corporate intellectual property or pre-empting legal rules. Rather, through the internalisation of such 'soft norms', CSR has become interwoven into particular profit-generating initiatives, blurring the distinction between where capital accumulation ends and the pursuit of a wider 'social good' begins. This means that one needs to tread carefully when claiming that all instances of CSR are merely paying lip service to an objectified problem – for example, 'greenwash' in the case of environmental issues. Take the mainstreaming of fair trade goods or organic agriculture as one illustration, the advertising of which appears to appeal simultaneously to both individual and collective responsibilities. As argued by critics such as Slavoj Žižek (2009), the Starbucks cup of fair trade coffee is, on the surface, sold to the richer customer through the logic of helping the poorer farmer in the developing world. But from Žižek's (2009) viewpoint, this sales pitch has an unspoken emotional subtext: a play between vague feelings of guilt on the part of the consumer (towards the plight of the imaginary farmer, the relationship to 'the world's poor', 'the planet', etc.) and the offer of immediate consolation (via the purchasing of a US$4 caffè latte). 'Doing good' is thus packaged into a commodity. At the same time, Starbucks presents itself as only one cog in a global fair trade system, thus sharing in a wider aspiration for equity in trading relations but, tellingly, without providing any information on why or how such inequality arose in the first place. In sum, what results is a commercialised form of charity which, while granting some benefits to certain farmers, only partially reveals the historical lines of responsibility that constitute an uneven capitalist order.

Another example of the complex relationship between individual and collective senses of responsibility can be seen in the global financial crisis. Within many countries, the question of who was to blame for the crisis has been an ongoing source of social and political friction. One dominant explanation has focused on the incentives and working culture found within the financial sector, including risky lending practices by major banks and poor monitoring by private credit rating agencies. Another set of reasons has addressed government policymaking since the 1990s, particularly the cheap credit conditions enabled by central banks, notably the US Federal Reserve. Others still have argued that the responsibility lies not only with private lenders and political elites, but also with all those consumers who accepted easy money in an environment of low interest rates. In the aftermath of the crisis, many heated debates have circled around how financial groups have been able to privatise their gains but socialise their losses. This is particularly the case with those financial institutions that are called 'too big to fail' (Strahan 2013). We are, or were, constantly told that if such an organisation becomes very large and central to the wider financial system, such as J. P. Morgan Chase or Goldman Sachs, any potential collapse could be disastrous; hence, the government has to support the firm in case of difficulty. Yet having an implicit government safety net underneath such institutions – in other words, access to the public purse – creates a potential moral-hazard problem. If bankers know that protective state guarantees will be deployed in a crisis, they may increase their risk appetite and engage in speculative activities that magnify economic volatility. In such situations, the ethics of (ir)responsibility are central (Sorkin 2009; Admati and Hellwig 2013; Strahan 2013).

In sum, the relationship between responsibility and power is often analytically complicated, embracing struggles over causality and historical expectations concerning accountability. How 'responsibility' is defined and materially organised is inevitably, therefore, a social construction. Two concluding points can be made here. First, as noted, although the ideological rhetoric associated with neoliberalism has notable appeals to individualised responsibility – the logic of self-governance and self-care in a competitive market society – one should also observe the many 'innovative forms of individualized collective action' in contemporary capitalism (Barnett 2005: 11). This fluid distinction (or dichotomy) between individual and collective responsibility is, indeed, something that characterises many forms of 'actually existing' neoliberal policy-making. However, such reasoning – the 'we are all in this together' logic – should always be critically unpacked to reveal the particular interests that may be concealed. This brings me to my final and deliberately contentious observation: the frequent denial of responsibility by political and business elites in the neoliberal period. For such privileged actors, one of the most efficient strategies for conserving their power or relative autonomy revolves around ignoring or evading questions of responsibility that could enlarge the space for democratic protest. A retreat into technocratic, expert discourses, for example, can be seen in part as a form of betrayal and a turning away from a critical engagement with power and the long and distinguished history of responsibility.

See also: **business, community, enterprise, environment, finance, governance, individual, participation, performance, power, risk, stakeholder, state, welfare**.

Further reading: Brown 2009; Carroll 2008; Ricoeur 2000; Trnka and Trundle 2014.

RISK

The precise genesis of the term 'risk' is difficult to determine, but it probably lies in nautical contexts and the early history of shipping insurance. From the fourteenth century, before the founding of dedicated insurance companies, the Italian word *risco* was used by Genoese merchants in the drawing up of trade contracts. In Latin the word *resecum* meant 'that which cuts', which may have been associated with potential damage that ships suffer at sea and the need to account for such hazards. 'Risk' is also partly derived from *rixicare*, meaning to quarrel and dispute. By 1728, the term had passed into English via the French *risque*. Today, the notion continues to have an important role in the legal codification of commercial agreements and insurance in particular, but uses of 'risk' within neoliberalism have broadened to embrace the construction and monitoring of problems that are beyond the immediate domain of business. As a consequence, as one writer famously put it, we now live in a 'risk society', whereby the assessment and management of a variety of so-called 'risks' – from financial crises to environmental degradation and beyond – have arisen out of 'hazards and insecurities induced and introduced by modernisation' (Beck 1992: 21). In particular, such trends represent a society preoccupied with the future and concerns for safety (Giddens 1999b). In a larger sense, therefore, risk can be viewed as conceptually intertwined with a number of other notions in neoliberal vocabulary, particularly stability, governance and responsibility.

In order to gain some conceptual distance from commonplace uses of the term 'risk', which, in turn, will help to explain its neoliberal inflection, two propositions can be noted (Dean 2010). First, in a general sense, using the word 'risk' is a way of defining and ordering reality. In particular, naming something a risk often helps raise its profile and opens the prospect for developing techniques of measurement and calculation. Such activities are often justified with a view to better controlling the risk or, perhaps, as a cynic might argue, creating the *appearance* of better controlling the risk. By drawing attention to this labour, various critical scholars, particularly those who follow the philosopher Michel Foucault, try to show that risks are not natural and preordained but, rather, only have meaning within certain historical and socio-cultural contexts. As argued by François Ewald (1991: 199, italics in original): 'Nothing is a risk in itself; there is no risk in reality. But on the other hand, anything *can* be a risk; it all depends on how one analyses the danger, considers the event'. Second, it follows that the 'significance of risk lies not with risk *itself* but with what risk gets attached to' (Dean 2010: 206, italics in original). Ewald draws to our attention how bodies of knowledge that appeal to scientific or 'objective' principles, such as in accountancy and statistics, legitimise particular meanings of (non-)risky activity. In other words, designating things as risks can be understood as a form of ideology, one that now has considerable power across various institutional environments. (Along similar theoretical lines on the cultural construction of risk, but predating Foucauldian work, see Douglas and Wildavsky, 1983.)

The rise of modern forms of risk analysis to the status of a 'commonsensical' problem is a complex story. As plotted by Power (2007), there are various factors that have informed this development over the twentieth century, some aspects of which helped to later shape a larger neoliberal vision, while others took more independent paths. Among specific influences, one can highlight advances in actuarial science, particularly through computing; the application of probability theory to a range of areas (such as in agriculture and engineering); and quality-control studies in fields that require high reliability (such as in the nuclear and chemical industries). The trend towards a more litigious culture around consumer safety and health, not least in the US, also gave credence to popular meanings of risk. At the same time, through more diffuse and long-term processes, other cultural forces have helped to normalise risk analysis. Indeed, methods of quantification used in risk analysis have been seen as indicative of a deeper 'trust in numbers' as the basis for presumed rational decision-making (Porter 1996). In turn, having confidence in impersonal and cold calculations is clearly connected to bureaucratic cultures, at the level not only of states but also of international organisations and corporate enterprises. Whereas once a danger from the natural world or an undesirable twist in the course of life was understood as an act of God over which humans had no control, agendas under the name of risk now aim to control incalculable uncertainties, or at least on paper (Power 2007).

The growth of risk management as an academic and professional field is a phenomenon that carries a particular neoliberal imprint, although the origins of the subject were laid before the mainstreaming of neoliberal ideas. First coined in 1948, it took until the 1960s and 1970s before the early conceptual underpinning of risk management was fully articulated, with a particular concentration around finance. The cultivation of an expert community focused on risk management – with players that often moved back and forth between academia and business – was fostered through the founding of specific journals and societies, such as the US-based *Risk Management* (formerly known as *The National Insurance Buyer*), along with the publication of early textbooks (Mehr and Hedges 1963; Williams and Heins 1964). The development of modern portfolio theory – a mathematical model that seeks to maximise the expected monetary return for a given amount of risk – was an important breakthrough in debates about diversification within investment strategies (Markowitz 1952; Sharpe 1963). Another significant theoretical contribution came in financial derivatives with studies on how to design a formula for pricing options (a contract that allows an owner to buy or sell an asset at a fixed price until a specific date) (Black and Scholes 1973; for a critique, see MacKenzie 2006). By the 1970s, in the context of economic dislocations triggered by the collapse of fixed exchange rates and volatility in commodity markets, major banks and insurers began to make greater use of such derivatives to protect themselves from financial risks. To this end, the founding of the Chicago Board Options Exchange in 1973 was significant and helped to usher in a 'marketized, mathematicized risk-evaluation culture', one that became increasingly internationalised (MacKenzie and Millo 2003: 136).

By the 1990s, risk management had become firmly established as a concern for business and policy regulators, both within national and transnational settings. The popularity of the subject can be seen in a British Library search of all titles that feature the phrase. From 1982 to 1991, there were only 351 works that included 'risk management' in the main heading, but in the following decade, until 2002, this spikes to 9,137 publications. Since 2002, the trend has continued, with an additional 17,324 items incorporating the term or idea. The spreading and naturalisation of risk management across different organisations has been strongly encouraged by disasters and scandals that, in turn, have raised social and political alarm. Examples can be seen in many fields, notably financial services, but also energy provision, health, transportation, large-scale infrastructure and security services. In the UK, for instance, the BSE (or 'mad cow' disease) crisis 'had a catalytic effect on government, creating a pressure to manage risk more explicitly'; this included a new discourse around 'risk communication' as a way to shape public expectations on legitimate state behaviour (Power 2007: 17). In this regard, as in others, the models and blueprints used for designing government risk communication were imported from the private sector. This managerial calculus of governing so-called 'reputational risk' – which tends to treat public perceptions as sources of risk – now dovetails with the continuing need for governments to protect or enhance their legitimacy. As Power (2007: 21) puts it, 'risk governance is in part a strategy to govern unruly perceptions and to maintain the production of legitimacy in the face of these perceptions'.

Yet the promotion of risk management in the context of neoliberal trends is also riven with tensions and paradoxes, particularly in the financial industry (for an introduction, see Allen and Saunders 2012). On the one hand, as in other domains of capitalism, financiers try to judge and guard against problems which are now called risks, such as 'market risks', 'geopolitical risks', 'environmental risks' and 'regulatory risks' (all common phrases used by financial professionals and the relevant media). On the other hand, financiers cannot be overly cautious in a competitive market system, otherwise potential sources of profit may be missed or only partially exploited. This generalised anxiety has even produced its own phrase: 'risk appetite', which tries to capture the tension between precautionary and entrepreneurial forms of action. Although risk appetite might appear to be striking a balance between opposites, the most desirable attitude for many financial actors still leans towards the confident and 'rational' risk-taking sense. For instance, in 2014, the chairman of HSBC felt it necessary to publically warn of the 'growing danger of disproportionate risk aversion creeping into decision-making' at the bank (Arnold 2014). Again, such thinking not only reveals the desire to manage banking supervision rules in a post-crisis world, but also reflects a wider ethos that risk appetite can be 'unambiguously known and understood by organizations and the individuals within them' (Power 2009: 851; see also Mikes 2009). Yet this assumption has been strongly critiqued on different grounds. For example, as shown by the crisis of 2007–9, the size, complexity, opacity and interconnectedness of the global financial system defies the neat calculations of risk management schemas (Engelen et al. 2012; see also Huber and Scheytt 2013). Elsewhere, other research has argued that chronically elevated levels of testosterone in financial traders can lead to harmful forms of impulsive behaviour, including excessive risk-taking associated with what Alan Greenspan, former US Federal Reserve chairman, called 'irrational exuberance' (Coates and Herbert 2008).

In sum, the concept of risk has been popularised through neoliberal trends, building upon the symbolic power of the term within the longer liberal tradition (O'Malley 2004). Returning to Power (2007) and his Foucauldian analysis, we can suggest that risk management represents the coming together of two logics. On the one side, the appeal to the model of the commercial enterprise encourages individuals and organisations to self-police their risk evaluation in multiple social spheres. On the other side, the logic of auditability and closer policy surveillance is a reaction to political and cultural demands that systems of power should be held accountable. In the process, risk management becomes not a set of apolitical 'technical tools' within the private sector but a more pervasive form of rationality informing how individuals think and organisations represent themselves. At the deepest level, references to risk and the instutionalisation of risk management reflect a desire to guard against blame and, at the very least, to act 'as if' one could know and control such declared risks. Doubtless, the Genoese merchants who gave us the term would have understood exactly what is going on.

See also: **entrepreneurship, environment, finance, governance, investment, management, market, performance, responsibility, stability, stakeholder**.

Further reading: Allen and Saunders 2012; Dean 2010; Ewald 1991; Power 2007.

STABILITY

'Stability' (from the Latin *stabilitas*) has worn its credentials well. In an age of kings, stability was what monarchs desired or reflected in their person or state. In a religious age, monks sought stability and questioned the vagaries of personal ambition or vanity. Underlying the word is the sense of a physical object that has the power to endure, despite forces that may work to undermine it. Along with its opposite, 'instability', the word today sits within a conceptual grouping of terms which are preoccupied with questions of order, predictability and resistance. The more modern meanings that are associated with stability have been shaped by the rise in the seventeenth and eighteenth centuries of the natural sciences and, by extension of the scientific method, economics in particular. Its contemporary meaning is most in evidence when stability is linked to ideas about equilibrium and the normative pursuit of balance or harmony (for instance, see Walras 2014[1900]; Hicks 1939; for a critique, see Mirowski 1989). Such connotations have in turn merged into the vocabulary of neoliberalism. At first glance, as is the case with other entries in this book, the word 'stability' appears to be innocent and, indeed, may provoke little protest. However, not all uses of the term are so benign, particularly when it is used to benefit the security or interests of certain groups and political issues over others. Equally, it is worth recognising that not all systems that survive are inherently stable, that properties called unstable in one context may become tolerated as 'normal' in another environment and that conditions of volatility may facilitate opportunities for privileged actors to exploit others.

The desire for stable economic conditions is a paramount concern for participating actors within a capitalist system. According to intellectuals associated with neoliberalism, such as Anna Schwartz, the issue of price stability in monetary policy should be cast as a public good, a goal that promotes overall financial stability, employment and a rising standard of living (for an introduction, see Schwartz 1995; see also Bordo and Schwartz 1987; García-Herrero and del Río 2005; Cagan 2008). Thus, the pursuit of price stability, principally led by central banks, works to prevent the costs associated with excessive inflation or deflation. If prices are stable, companies and consumers should benefit through more informed decisions as to the allocation of their resources. By contrast, price instability tends to increase uncertainty if actors encounter difficulties in distinguishing between relative prices that are favourable from those that are not. In the neoliberal period, price stability has assumed a hallowed status among central-bank elites. Indeed, the transmission of authority from governments to an 'insulated technocracy' has strengthened the belief that 'noble' economic directorship is being conducted on behalf of the majority and away from political 'interference' (Hall 2008: 183). When this assumption is pierced, as seen when the strategies of the ECB were criticised in the early phase of the Eurozone crisis in 2010–11, then nerves can fray. For instance, in reaction to German critics, departing ECB President Jean-Claude Trichet was adamant that the ECB had done more to contain inflation in Germany than the country's esteemed Bundesbank: 'We have delivered price stability over the first 12 years of the euro impeccably! Impeccably!' (quoted in Atkins 2011). Note the exclamation marks.

Since Karl Marx, many supporters and critics of capitalism have argued that the system seems to have instability written into its DNA (Schumpeter 2003[1942]; Harvey 2006[1982]; Minsky 2008[1986]; Kindleberger and Aliber 2011[1978]). In boom times, it can appear as if 'prudent stability', a phrase cherished by former UK prime minister Gordon Brown, is eminently achievable and here to stay. But in light of the global financial crisis of 2007–9, considerable academic and political attention has been preoccupied with understanding the links between enhanced capital mobility, however defined or enacted, and conditions of economic and social instability. The evidence tends to show that financial crises have increased in frequency, scope and severity over the neoliberal period. Researchers have documented a high correlation between the liberalisation of national capital accounts and the incidence of banking crises in both developed and developing countries (Eichengreen 2004; Reinhart and Rogoff 2009). It is interesting to note, therefore, that the precise expression 'financial stability', which, from the early 1990s, and following the Asian Financial Crisis (1997–8) in particular, became a catchphrase within the social world of investors, regulators and governments (see Howard Davies's (2006) personal reflections on the term), is a comparatively recent innovation. For instance, a search of the British Library Catalogue reveals that only 41 publications contained 'financial stability' in titles prior to 1992, yet the growth subsequently is dramatic: the term is used 123 times in the period between 1992 and 1999, followed by 630 uses in a second phase from 2000 to 2008 and in the titles of a further 1,126 publications registered from 2009 to the present.

Yet despite such increased chatter, there remains no precise and unambiguous definition of what financial stability actually looks like. The picture is made more complicated by understanding how some investors do not run away from instability, but actively calculate volatility in the hope of realising a profit. In one sense, volatility in shares or derivatives (a contract whose price is dependent upon an underlying asset) may not necessarily be a bad thing: at root, it is only a price mechanism for conveying information on risks and rewards. However, in the context of an increasing use of automated trading by computers, there have been greater efforts to chart and predict more accurately the often wild movements of financial markets. One of the most popular and closely tracked indicators is the Chicago Board Options Exchange (CBOE) Volatility Index, known as 'the VIX', or, in colloquial finance speak, 'the fear gauge' (on the origins of the idea, see Brenner and Galai 1989; Whaley 1993). Since its inception in 1993, the VIX has become the metaphorical pulsating heartbeat of Wall Street. The value of the index is based on the *implied* volatility priced into derivatives from the Standard & Poor's (S&P) 500 stock index. In other words, it is a subjective measure: if traders believe that the S&P 500 index options will fall, the VIX tends to rise. By 2004, the financial alchemy embroiled in the VIX calculations had advanced to the point where investors could *trade in volatility* via the introduction of futures contracts. Volatility has now become commoditised and packaged like a stock. Thus, in the same moment, for large financial institutions at least, when equities are losing money, volatility is paying out, and vice versa (Whaley 2008).

Elsewhere in recent decades, the phrase 'political stability' and its opposite, 'political instability', has also been affected by processes associated with neoliberalism, although detecting this is not always easy. Through multiple tools and guises, political theorists and scientists have analysed the causes and consequences of political (in)stability, yet there are few dedicated analyses of the concept itself (for worthy exceptions, see Hurwitz 1973; Dowding and Kimber 1983; Freeden 2013). In the policy world, politicians often repeat the word 'stability' because it evokes dispositions of toughness and resolve, desirable images they believe carry weight with different audiences. Problems arise when agendas and presumptions in its name pass misrecognised and, therefore, only certain meanings of political (in)stability come to be accepted as 'normal'. In short, like other terms in the vocabulary of neoliberalism, one needs to ask whose 'political (in)stability' becomes the object of attention and how such definitions and practices are reproduced.

Two illustrations will serve for many in showing how this deceptively simple expression often lends credence to particular neoliberal worldviews. First, at a general level, within the financial industry and fields such as international development, the phrase 'political stability' often expresses an idealised policy environment, which is, among other factors, considered 'business friendly'. In the hands of the World Bank, notably its Worldwide Governance Indicators project and Ease of Doing Business index, political stability tends to be associated with a country that has an absence of violence, an independent judiciary, regular elections and a pluralistic civil society. Also considered in a favourable light is a central role for a market economy in which political rule-making is receptive to investors and not unduly 'arbitrary' or 'unpredictable' (Kaufmann *et al.* 2009). Nevertheless, there are problems in how this definition has been formulated. For instance, civil protests that are judged to pose a threat to investors can be read by the World Bank and private financial analysts as a raised indicator of political instability. Yet the same protest may be viewed by demonstrators as a necessary form of resistance, as seen in Hong Kong and Brazil in 2014. It is also worth noting that the related term 'political risk', now promoted with particular zeal by a cottage industry of consultants such as PwC and the Eurasia Group, can help to consolidate the legitimacy of foreign investors as a powerful social group (for an evaluation of the concept in light of neoliberal debates, see Campisi 2014; for a study in reference to the Arab Spring, see Sottilotta 2015).

Second, according to popular critics such as Naomi Klein (2008), the neoliberal period has featured regular crises that have served as opportunities for implementing new strategies of profit generation. One such crisis is particularly telling in this regard. The early experimentation of policies associated with neoliberalism in Chile necessitated considerable state-backed violence and repression. As documented by Klein and others, the 1973 *coup d'état* by Augusto Pinochet against the democratically elected, Marxist government of Salvador Allende was supported by the US government and business officials who were troubled by the shift towards socialism (Winn 2004; Haslam 2005). In this historical example, stability, under the watchful eyes of the Central

Intelligence Agency, meant reducing the power of labour unions and other 'leftist' organisations, privatising public assets and facilitating freer trade over the original model of import substitution. Writing in 1977, James Chace, Managing Editor of *Foreign Affairs*, the mouthpiece of the establishment Council on Foreign Relations, put it bluntly when commenting on US interests in the Chilean coup. In a quasi-Orwellian tone he noted that, 'stability, not justice, was the priority in our search for a "stable structure of peace"' (Chace 1977: 211). Bringing about stability in one form can, thus, involve radical instability in another and, by implication, neither peace nor democracy is necessarily 'just'.

See also: **adjustment, capitalism, finance, governance, power, reform, risk, state**.

Further reading: Dowding and Kimber 1983; Freeden 2013; Minsky 2008[1986]; Schwartz 1995.

STAKEHOLDER

Around the early seventeenth century, the term 'stakeholder' entered English as a way to define a person or an organisation with whom money was deposited. The use of the verb 'stake' is older, dating from the early sixteenth century. It then broadened from the action of striking or piercing to include engagement in risky wagers. 'Stakeholder' too underwent a form of stretching away from the association with gambling. Today, under the sway of rationalities that are claimed to carry a neoliberal mark, stakeholder has become conceptually interconnected with ideas that stress partnership, cooperation and governance in the management of complex problems. In business circles, where a cottage industry of experts on stakeholderism has emerged over the past three decades, the notion is now a central term of reference, either descriptively or normatively, and sometimes both at once. The commercial and political agendas underneath the stakeholder frame are, however, not all innocent. Rather, we need to reflect on the historical reasons why the term has assumed popularity, particularly in respect to relations of unequal power that intersect within, and without, the contemporary enterprise.

As a body of management literature, stakeholder theory emerged out of the 1960s in response to a nexus of social and economic forces which, collectively, questioned the legitimacy of the modern corporation. From the perspective of business executives in US-based companies, for whom much of this literature was written, there were many sources of anxiety. One set of changes were largely internal to the commercial world, including increasing shareholder activism that was contesting the power of management, rising expectations that bosses should adopt more participatory styles of governance with workers, and heightened competition with other countries (notably Japan and Germany) for consumer markets and product development. Another set of trends derived from the expansion of US government law into areas that had a bearing on business performance, such as the Consumer Bill of Rights in 1962 and the establishment of the Environmental Protection Agency in 1970. Many of these latter developments were strongly informed by social movements and the prominent campaigning of particular individuals. For instance, in 1971, Ralph Nader established Public Citizen, a Washington D.C.-based advocacy group that pressured major corporations, such as General Motors, to improve their safety and environmental practices (Friedman and Miles 2006).

In the midst of these turbulent times, the term 'stakeholder' began to appear in management debates, including early references from the Stanford Research Institute's collaboration with Lockheed in 1963, Rhenman (1964) and, of particular note, Igor Ansoff's widely read manual, *Corporate Strategy* (1965). For contemporary writers of stakeholder theory, however, the pivotal contribution came a little later, in 1984, with the publication of R. Edward Freeman's *Strategic Management: A Stakeholder Approach*. Here, we see the first substantive attempt to address the questions that have preoccupied business writers since: who is a legitimate stakeholder and what is at stake? Calling for a 'conceptual revolution' (Freeman 1984: 7) in how the corporation was perceived, Freeman argued that managers should 'take into account all of those groups and individuals that can affect, or are affected by, the accomplishment of the business enterprise' (Freeman 1984: 25). In this sense, such thinking opposed the classic Milton Friedman definition that the 'one and only social responsibility of business' was to maximise stockholder value, in terms of profits, growth or dividends (Friedman 2002[1962]: 133). Freeman (1984) saw the picture differently and issued a warning to boot: if businesses did not adopt the stakeholder framework, they could suffer reputational damage, law suits, loss of market share and, potentially, extinction. Understanding diverse stakeholder relations was no longer an ancillary option for business, it was now a core objective.

By the end of the century, the notion of stakeholder had taken off in business literature and was increasingly used in the branding strategies of global corporations. For instance, from 1990 to 1998, 43 management journal articles directly engaged with stakeholder theory, but from 1998 to 2008, this figure had jumped to 135 articles (Laplume *et al.* 2008).

With such popularity, came conceptual contestation, to the extent that some asked if the entire debate had become 'confused' (Miles 2012) with a central idea that was 'vague, slippery and shallow' (Friedman and Miles 2006: 28). In one review of 75 managerial publications, 55 different definitions of stakeholder were found (Friedman and Miles 2006). Yet some common lines of discussion can be outlined. According to one influential article, the extent to which company managers pay attention to different stakeholders is shaped by three main factors: (1) how much power they wield over the firm, (2) how the actor is deemed socially legitimate and (3) the relative urgency of the problem (Mitchell *et al*. 1997). Thus, an activist investor, such as billionaire Carl Icahn, who owns controlling positions in many leading companies, would be categorised as a high-profile stakeholder because he could exercise power over senior managers. At the same time, a community-based environmental group that is financially poor but pursues a legitimate cause may be viewed by some companies as a valuable partner with which to cooperate, rather than oppose outright. In short, at the centre of these concerns over stakeholderism rest different perceptions over what makes for legitimate partnership and corporate social responsibility.

Beyond the business field, an interesting extension of the concept of stakeholder emerged in the mid 1990s in the UK under the direction of Tony Blair. During the election campaign for New Labour, prior to taking office at 10 Downing Street, Blair tested out the phrase 'stakeholder economy'. Searching for unthreatening words that demarcated New Labour from both the Conservatives and the recent history of his own party, in one speech Blair argued that the 'stakeholder economy is the key to preparing our people and business for vast economic and technological change. It is not about giving power to corporations or unions or interest groups. It is about giving power to *you*, the individual' (Blair 1996: 291). Blair kept the notion of the stakeholder economy deliberately loose. As his press secretary put it, the phrase was 'a washing line from which to hang all the different parts of economic policy' (Campbell 2007: 99). The term does not, however, appear to be one that Blair coined. Will Hutton, a journalist at *The Guardian* newspaper, was the first to speak of the stakeholder economy in relation to debates on social welfare (Hutton 1994, 1995). On a trip to the US, the future prime minister also displayed some awareness of the deeper American origins of stakeholderism in corporate governance (Safire 1996). At the time, struggling to understand how the frame could potentially resonate, the reaction from rival Conservative politicians was mixed: some saw the stakeholder economy as a revision of Margaret Thatcher's legacy, while others painted Blair as still beholden to trade unions (Davies 1996). What was clearer, however, was that Blair, along with his shadow chancellor, Gordon Brown, consistently reassured business leaders in the UK and around the world that there would be 'no unnecessary legislative restraints' on corporations, whatever the rhetorical appeal of giving power to the people (Peston 1996, see also Melville-Ross 1996).

The notion of stakeholder has now been mainstreamed within many institutions far beyond the US and the UK. In Japan, for instance, the concept was absorbed into business discourse in the early 1990s, led by executives at Sony, Mitsubishi and other major companies who, one could suspect, were alert to new Western-derived trends in management philosophy (Steadman *et al.* 1995). Another indication is how the term has travelled through countless international networking events, of which the WEF is particularly special (originally named the European Management Forum, until 1987). The WEF Founder, Klaus Schwab, a former business studies professor, has long preached the benefits of 'multi-stakeholder partnerships' to the elite executives, political leaders, civil society actors and thinkers who gather in Davos each year. Like the US-based corporate officials who grappled with a generalised crisis of governability in the 1970s, Schwab also saw how European firms risked undermining their global competitiveness if they did not conduct outreach efforts with different constituencies, some of whom may be hostile to business interests (Pigman 2007). For instance, among the many activities of the WEF, Schwab has persistently engaged with Chinese audiences since 1979, the time when Deng Xiaoping launched the economic reforms that opened China to the wider capitalist system (Schwab 2008). It is not surprising that a thin conception of stakeholder has become one of Schwab's touchstones to frame any kind of debate on China. Politically inoffensive to Chinese elites, the expression demands little more than a vague appeal to togetherness and, thus, fits comfortably into patterns of Chinese political rhetoric in a one-party state.

It is necessary to conclude on two critical points to give our understanding of stakeholder added perspective. First, in many uses of the term, particularly public-orientated business presentations, it can seem as if all stakeholders are equal in regard to voice, credibility and influence. But this seductive appeal to democratic expression – a 'balancing of interests', as it is sometimes put – often conceals considerable inequalities in power and differences in ideological perspective. In addition, in a theme that resurfaces throughout this book, the historical struggles that gave birth to the legitimation of certain stakeholders, such as environmental movements, are often given marginal attention in the relevant literature. This convenient amnesia about historical origins is important to note because, through subtle ways, it helps socially to embed 'stakeholder' as an apparently timeless expression that nobody can contest, rather than viewing the entire corporate-inspired stakeholder theory as a strong reaction to a crisis of capitalist governance. Second, and related, a more penetrating examination of stakeholder theory would help to dissect how the 'managing' of actors under this label, via the latest models and techniques refined by business schools, is less concerned with a search for harmonious partnership and more interested in the instrumental controlling of different forces that could fundamentally disrupt capital accumulation. The incorporation of potentially recalcitrant actors into a dominant order is one classic strategy of power, even if the declared strategists do not always see a single overarching strategy. As one author summarises it, '[a]ttributes of power, legitimacy and urgency that determine stakeholder salience are ultimately a function of power discourses between institutional, state and corporate actors and the process of stakeholder integration tends to either disallow alternative practices or assimilate them' (Banerjee 2007: 32). In other words, what emerges is not a new ethics but a 'new ethicalism': the managerial commonsense of stakeholderism carries 'a soft moral spin; but this is not so moral or so binding that it overwhelms neoliberalism's economic imperatives' (Sum 2010: 68).

See also: **business, community, consensus, diversity, enterprise, freedom, governance, investment, management, market, network, openness, participation, power, responsibility, risk**.

Further reading: Banerjee 2007; Friedman and Miles 2006; Miles 2012.

STATE

When we examine 'the state' in relation to neoliberalism, we must always be on guard against making quick or easy conclusions. The state can often appear as both an omnipresent and amorphous entity. This is partly because the state has many concrete forms (such as departments, armies, courts, etc.), but also because this social creation exists, as it were, in the minds of individuals (such as through shaping values and expectations about civic life) (Weber 2004[1919]; Abrams 1988). As suggested by Pierre Bourdieu (2014: 3), '[i]f it is so easy to say easy things about this object, that is precisely because we are, in a certain sense, penetrated by the very thing we have to study'. The word 'state' is derived from the Latin *status*, meaning stature, standing or prestige. The etymology is also bound up with 'estate', particularly in French, as in the modern *état* (hence drawing an association between property, stability and rank) (Vincent 1992). The need to justify power in relation to 'the public', 'the commonwealth' or 'the universal' has a long legacy from the classical notion of *status reipublicae* to the 'mirror-for-princes' writers who advised European monarchs on how to govern with fairness (Kantorowicz 1997[1957]; for a classic illustration of the latter, see Machiavelli 2008[1532]).

The movement from the personal, dynastic state to the impersonal, bureaucratic state was a profoundly complex and ambiguous historical process, one which took shape in England and France in the seventeenth century, but would not reach full maturity until suffrage was expanded in the nineteenth and twentieth centuries (Tilly 1992; Spruyt 1994). Sovereign power gradually became associated with the state, rather than a single ruler, resulting in debate about the meaning of statehood and the powers of the state. In turn, once 'state' became 'accepted as the master noun of political argument', it 'set up a series of reverberations in the wider political vocabularies' that continue to the present, such as the contrast between subjects versus citizens (Skinner 1989: 123; see also Skinner 1979; Oakeshott 1975). The more recent exporting of the European state model to other parts of the world, particularly in the postwar period, has also prompted a wide range of reactions, from violent hostility to utopian optimism (Nandy 1992). For instance, in the context of independence struggles, Kwame Nkrumah, the first prime minister of Ghana, once argued that, 'The essence of neocolonialism is that the State which is subject to it is, in theory, independent and has all the outward trappings of international sovereignty. In reality its economic system and thus political policy is directed from outside' (Nkrumah 1965: ix).

Walking, therefore, on the conceptual battlefield of 'the state' is a potentially fraught exercise, with many metaphorical landmines likely to detonate (for an introduction, see Vincent 1987, 1992). Three common confusions or disputes over the term can be highlighted, each of which remains problematic in the neoliberal period. First, in both academic and everyday discourse, the state is often treated as synonymous with government. However, for some writers, it would be better to distinguish between these two categories. The state can refer to bureaucratic institutions of rule, but the concept can also mean a specific domain of territory and the political association of a group of people within such a space (Oakeshott 1975; see also Robinson 2013). Governments are temporary collections of named individuals who, through some capacity, represent the state. But no government official could ever, for instance, shoulder the fiscal burden of the state (Runciman 2003). Second, the state is often viewed as analytically separate from (civil) society, a particular tendency seen in conceptions of popular sovereignty. Such an idea raises yet more questions. For example, the laws and customs of the state may be deeply intertwined within a societal culture (Migdal 2001; see also Ferguson and Gupta 2002 on the spatial construction of the state as 'above' society). Despite appearing to serve the wider society, the state may also be read as benefiting some groups over others. For instance, as Marx and Engels (1998[1848]: 37) put it, '[t]he executive of the modern state is but a committee for managing the common affairs of the whole bourgeoisie'. Third, the historical relationship between the state and the nation (or nationalism) is often unclear and an enduring source of political debate. Such questions are, in turn, bound up with analysing the mechanisms of coercion (or force) and consent (or will) in social life, mechanisms which the state both reflects and constitutes.

In any evaluation of the vocabulary of neoliberalism, one needs to keep returning to the dichotomy which structures many debates: the relationship between state and market. Through a series of common oppositions which support and reinforce each other, this distinction has acquired a powerful resonance and, for some users, a feeling of unquestioned acceptance. For instance, the state is often associated with the public interest, coercive power, hierarchy and planning, whereas the market is connected to the private domain, freedom, individualism and competition (Bourdieu and Wacquant 2001). Within the longer liberal tradition, suspicion of and resistance to the powers of the state have been a reoccurring theme. Such debates have reflected the political and social controversies of the time, from Adam Smith's (1993[1776]) argument for a 'spontaneous' commercial world free from government monopolies to Herbert Spencer's (1996[1851]) polemical call for individuals to have the 'right to ignore the state'. From the 1930s to the 1960s, among a network of intellectuals who became associated with neoliberalism, the role of the state was reconsidered. On the one hand, figures such as Friedrich von Hayek, Ludwig von Mises, Karl Popper and Wilhelm Röpke viewed state institutions as being controlled by their ideological enemies, including Keynesians, Austromarxists and Nazis. On the other hand, it would be wrong to argue that these writers were fixated on some ideal of a *laissez-faire* economy which had no role for the state (Mirowski and Plehwe 2009; Peck 2010; Dardot and Laval 2013). As Ben Jackson (2010: 137–8) argues, these neoliberal proponents 'were not opposed to planning *tout court*, but to planning that involved the central direction of all economic resources according to a conscious blueprint'. Indeed, within the German 'ordoliberal' vision, which emerged in the Weimar Republic in the 1920s, the defence of a 'free economy' always presupposed the exercise of strong state authority, notably through enforcing law, anti-trust legislation and the provision of welfare services that would ulti-mately sustain capitalism (Ptak 2009; Bonefeld 2012).

Thus, stemming from this early intellectual thinking, neoliberalism has never been virulently 'anti-state' in either theory or practice. One may hear some rhetoric which condemns or demonizes the state – such as Ronald Reagan's (1981) famous line that 'government is the problem' – yet a closer inspection of actual policies and legacies in the neoliberal period reveals a more complex and nuanced picture. For instance, in the UK from the 1980s, one witnessed many conservative politicians and moral guardians championing the reduction of govern-ment welfare. Perhaps the clearest material impacts of this agenda involved cuts to unemployment benefit and social housing (Lawson 1992; see also Gamble 1994). For Margaret Thatcher and her allies, such policies formed part of the promotion of a 'family-centred, moralistic individ-ualism' (Sutcliffe-Braithwaite 2012: 497), whereby the poor were pro-vided with a limited state safety net, but one that tried to encourage thrift and commitment to an 'enterprise society'. Thatcherism was an ideology which drew on different sources. It was partly rooted in a reading of political economy that rejected Keynesianism and socialism (under the influence of Hayek and the Virginia 'public choice' school), but it also encompassed a petit bourgeois mentality and an interpreta-tion of Christian Methodism as a way to 'revive' British morality. As Thatcher (1977) once expressed it, 'where the state is too powerful, efficiency suffers and morality is threatened'. Importantly, this redraw-ing of the boundaries of the social state was also directed at the middle classes who, in the eyes of Thatcherites, received disproportionate benefits, such as free healthcare and education. In this sense, the 'aim was not to abolish the welfare state, but to make it irrelevant to those on middle and high incomes; to push them towards market-based pro-vision' (Sutcliffe-Braithwaite 2012: 516).

It is germane to note that the precise phrase 'states versus markets', and even the looser expression 'states and markets' – defining concep-tual anchors in many debates in the social sciences – only became popular within the neoliberal period and, in particular, following the end of the Cold War (see early uses in Evans *et al.* 1985; Strange 1988). The normalisation of this dichotomy was a reflection of the enhanced status acquired by business, not only in the West but also in the rest of the world. In this respect, organisations such as the World Bank were important in constructing and policing agendas that were aimed at furthering capitalism across different jurisdictions. But the World

Bank's 'theory of the state' has never been permanently fixed, either in its high-profile publications or in the minds of the apparatchiks who move within the organisation (Harrison 2004). Rather, throughout the neoliberal period, in response to political pressures, intellectual trends and criticism of its prior policy actions, the relationship between 'state' and 'market' has been repeatedly reconfigured. From the 1980s, within many donor countries, there was considerable criticism of how the World Bank often requested significant reductions in state budgets in return for emergency loans. For instance, in Côte d'Ivoire, demands were made for cuts in education spending, including slashing teachers' wages (Aribisala 1994). Despite this and other measures, the country continued to suffer economic contraction and high current-account deficits (Easterly 2005). If such tendencies represented a destructive, 'roll-back' of the state, the period since the mid 1990s represents, for some observers of neoliberalism, a more creative 'roll-out' of state agencies (Peck and Tickell 2002). For instance, the embrace of agendas under the heading of 'governance', by the World Bank and others, is partly a response to a legitimacy critique that developing country states had been 'hollowed out' and that such actions impeded, rather than enabled, development.

How can one critically examine the recomposition of states in the neoliberal period? Three lines of inquiry could be advanced. First, when one returns to examine welfare spending patterns with respect to developed counties, various literatures (both academic and popular) have argued that welfare *retrenchment* is underway in many societies and that such developments can be explained by the consolidation of neo-liberalism (for a review, see Swank 2010). In practice, however, the empirical data reveals a more complicated picture. For example, across all major types of welfare state (Anglo-Saxon, Scandinavian, Central European, Japanese, etc.), the period between 1980 and 2005 featured an increase in social spending as a share of GDP. Such growth was not merely a response to demographic pressures (such as aging populations), but included the expansion of services in many countries (Glennerster 2010). Since the 2008 financial crisis, there have been cuts (and threats of more in the future) in some countries. For instance, Greece experi-enced double-digit percentage reductions in healthcare spending in 2010 and 2012, leaving the country with an overall expenditure of 25 per cent less than the peak year of 2008 (OECD 2014). From 2009, the UK embarked on cuts in public spending per person at levels deeper than those of Portugal and Italy, countries that were adversely hit by the Eurozone crisis. Nonetheless, average OECD social spend-ing has consistently remained at historically high levels (in 2014, as a percentage of GDP, around 22 per cent across OECD countries) (OECD 2014). This discrepancy between the professed rhetoric of 'neoliberal ideology' and the reality of a reasonably resilient welfare state may appear puzzling. However, the picture becomes clearer when one considers that welfare retrenchment is politically hard to achieve, not only because it generates popular resistance in some quarters, but also because past political and legal legacies can 'lock in' current governments to spending patterns beyond their control (Pierson 1995).

Second, many debates that pivot around the 'state versus market' narrative often fail to appreciate how particular agencies of the state have acquired significant disciplinary power within the neoliberal period. As seen in the US, but also elsewhere (such as, in different forms, France, Brazil, Egypt and China), Loïc Wacquant (2009: 308) has argued that while the neoliberal state model may appear to embrace '*laissez-faire* at the top, releasing restraints on capital and expanding the life chances of the holders of economic and cultural capital', relations with poorer citizens are often radically different. Through investigating the rise in the US prison population and the related increase in resources devoted to criminal justice and security, Wacquant (2009: 308) proposes that neoliberal government is 'fiercely interventionist, bossy, and pricey'. Importantly, the construction of this 'penal state' is not directed at all citizens, but is socially and spatially concentrated on so-called 'problematic populations' (often the poor and persons of colour) who struggle to enter, and contribute to, a market economy. In the US, the call for 'tough action' on 'law and order' serves as a common impetus for the expansion of the penal state. For politicians who seek legitimacy, such appeals are seized upon, partly to replace other forms of legitimacy that have been lost (or forfeited) via attacks on the older social state model. Thus, for Wacquant (2012: 66, italics in original), neoliberalism would be better expressed not through some blunt opposition between state and market but, rather, as '*an articulation of state, market and citizenship* that harnesses the first to impose the stamp of the second onto the third'. In a similar vein, one can also point to how security agencies of the state, such as the police, are frequently deployed in the protection of capital. Coercion, in this sense, appears as 'integral to the allegedly benign and pacific liberal order' (Laffey and Weldes 2005: 78).

A final approach for rethinking statehood would critique how the nexus between state, market and citizenship is often presented as a cooperative alliance in which antagonisms can be managed or even erased. For instance, agendas around 'national competitiveness' (Porter 1990) or 'entrepreneurial government' (Osborne and Gaebler 1992) speak to a desire for imagining government, business and civil society groups as being 'ontologically equivalent and symbiotically related' (Davies 2014: 128; on the 'competition state', see also Cerny 1997). However, for some authors and observers, this is not a conceptualisation or policy practice that should be automatically accepted. Rather, underneath the appeal to 'public-private partnerships' or 'engagement with the community' lie a series of interest groups that may be in conflict with each other. At the same time, one needs to investigate the extent to which business interests, in particular, may be privileged in such arrangements, on structural, institutional or personal levels. In conclusion, the state remains a perplexing and, at times, contradictory site of struggle in the neoliberal period. On the one hand, to take certain discourses at face value, it often appears as if the state is the *bête noire* for neoliberals, something to be shrunk and condemned. On the other hand, however, the practical realisation of many outcomes associated with neoliberalism, such as the emergence of new sectors or the regulation of commercial competition, often requires state investment, an expansion of bureaucracies and the creation of supranational authorities (Mazzucato 2013). Such patterns lead one to conclude that the state may, in fact, be 'the greatest conquest' of neoliberalism (Schmidt and Woll 2013: 112).

See also: **business, capitalism, community, competition, development, finance, freedom, global, governance, management, market, performance, power, private, reform, responsibility, stability, trade, welfare**.

Further reading: Dardot and Laval 2013; Jackson 2010; Peck 2010; Runciman 2003; Schmidt and Woll 2013; Vincent 1987, 1992.

TRADE

The association between freedom and commercial exchange, either internally within a certain jurisdictional space or externally across territories, is an ancient theme in the Western liberal tradition. The origins of the phrase 'free trade', or, to be more precise, 'a free trade' or 'freedom to trade', as it was initially expressed, are difficult to locate precisely but seem to first appear in the late sixteenth century. Within this period, in the context of parliamentary debates in England, political figures and merchants debated how to reform royal grants which gave monopolistic rights to certain traders to engage in foreign commerce. The meaning of 'freedom' in these debates was not focused on the lowering of tariffs – a primary topic of attention in our contemporary period – but, rather, pivoted around who had privileged access to lucrative trade routes (Irwin 1996; Heckscher 1934). Although neoliberal forms of capitalism are radically different in many ways, the competitive or collaborative ties between state and business elites that marked such debates still echo today in how trade is both theoretically imagined and materially constructed. Indeed, the promotion of free trade is often read as one of the most emblematic features of neoliberalism. As David Harvey has argued, along with the generalisation of free markets and private property rights, the construction of institutional frameworks and rules in the name of 'free trade' defines neoliberalism (Harvey 2005).

In the discipline of economics, as well as international law, the study of global trade occupies a major place in debates about the nature of capitalism. Although Adam Smith (1993[1776]) furnished a classical liberal articulation for commercial exchange, it was David Ricardo (2004[1817]), along with James Mill (1821), who composed a mathematically founded justification for 'freer trade' through comparative advantage: the idea that mutual gains from trade can be realised when nations specialise in producing those goods in which their opportunity cost is lowest. When Paul Samuelson, a leading twentieth-century economist, was asked to name one proposition in the social sciences that was both true and non-trivial, he named 'the Ricardian theory of comparative advantage' (Samuelson 1969: 9). Thus, from the early theorists, through the Victorian valorisation of Smith as a liberal godfather and the repeal of the Corn Laws, the popular image and professionalisation of economists has become closely associated with arguments that defend free trade as a quasi-law of capitalism (Howe 1997; Magnusson 2004). Similar to our current debates, the legitimation of such arguments (or 'beliefs', to paint an alternative complexion) has always been informed by an opposition to a 'negative Other': protectionism, a category which had become crystallised in a dichotomy with free trade by the mid nineteenth century. This struggle over the meaning of trade has, however, never been the sole preserve of economists and lawyers who plot dry calculations of subsidies and the like. Rather, in the UK at least, the power of the free-trade argument has also been tied to wider visions of national identity, moral virtues and the cultivation of new consumer identities (Trentmann 2008).

With this complex intellectual and political context in mind, there are many potential stories that address how trade, both as an idea and a practice, has been reshaped under the shadow of neoliberalism. One major problem that confronts any initial evaluation is what phenomena should be included in the category of trade. This question is no mere exercise in academic clarification but is intertwined with power struggles that, in turn, shape uneven distributional outcomes. Historically, international trade meant the distribution of goods that you could tangibly feel or hold in your hand, from wine, spices and clothes to cars, computers and solar panels. But since the 1970s, the concept of trade has extended to include other meanings. For instance, the growth in businesses that produce services, such as tourism or finance, initially presented problems for trade lawyers trying to keep up to date with changes in the market. As *The Economist* (1981) once quipped, services are things that can be bought and sold, 'but not dropped on your foot'. How the category of 'trade in services' moved from being an arbitrary expression to a major agenda item of the WTO is an interesting illustration of the malleable boundaries of the trade concept (Drake and Nicolaïdis 1992; Lang 2011). What trade in services actually means is not rules at national borders, such as tariff levels, but encouraging deeper reforms in the make-up of economies, including how much foreign investment should be allowed. Similar conceptual contests over the boundaries of trade can also be seen in how tougher intellectual property rules – previously not considered a 'trade issue' – became part of the WTO's mandate at the insistence of the US, the EU and Japan (Sell 2003; May and Sell 2005).

Whether trade liberalisation is a 'good thing' is a well-rehearsed debate that, in the context of neoliberal trends, has received further scrutiny. As noted, most economists, including high-profile theorists and commentators such as Jagdish Bhagwati (2004) and Martin Wolf (2004), argue for trade openness. The experts who fall within this broad tradition claim that trade liberalisation exists in a positive relationship with economic growth. Increasing trade provides access to global resources and markets, enlarging the consumption capacities of a country and enabling economies of scale. Trade helps to reward those countries that possess a comparative advantage, whether in terms of labour efficiency (such as cheaper or more skilled workforces) or other so-called 'factor endowments' (such as land or capital). In turn, it is argued that with more growth, a country is in a better position to reduce poverty (Krueger 1998; Sachs and Warner 1995; Dollar and Kraay 2004; Winters 2004). Thus, Irwin (2009) argues that countries with more open trade policies tend to perform better than those with more restrictive regimes, citing the record of South Korea, which opened its trade account in the 1960s; Chile, which liberalised in the 1970s; and India, which liberalised in the 1990s. At the same time, in the larger postwar picture, such arguments have been reinforced by a suspicion of other trade policy models, notably import substitution industralisation (ISI). Popular in many developing countries of the

Global South during the 1950s and 1960s, ISI sought to nurture domestic infant industries through close state management, including limits on how much foreign competition could enter such markets (Bruton 1998).

However, since the 1990s, the consensus surrounding the benefits of free trade has come under careful examination, resulting in more nuanced debates. On the one hand, theorists have issued more cautious assessments regarding what precisely international trade can accomplish for countries and firms, particularly in terms of the ties between trade, growth and poverty (Love and Lattimore 2009; Wade 2004). For instance, scholars have debated the use of different measurements of openness and encountered problems with evaluating causal relationships. In one prominent analysis, Francisco Rodríguez and Dani Rodrik (2000: 266) critiqued the econometrics underpinning some major studies, arguing that the case for the relationship between trade openness and growth was not 'general' and 'unambiguous', but most likely 'contingent' and 'dependent on a host of country and external characteristics'. Other studies have revealed how the relationship between domestic trade policy and poverty reduction is highly complex and case specific, making generalisation difficult (Turner et al. 2008). Such conclusions have dovetailed with a broader concern for examining how the consequences of trade policy changes are connected to factors such as industrial organisation, the governance of domestic political institutions and the so-called 'sequencing of reforms'. In sum, as a normative baseline, while trade liberalisation continues to be treated in positive terms by many prominent voices in the field, such opinions are now marked by many different shades of grey. In Dani Rodrik's (2002) words, these additional reform proposals, together with trade liberalisation, have created an 'augmented' neoliberal orthodoxy, one that looks slightly different from harsher agendas promoted in the 1980s.

Another way in which the political economy of trade has been debated has been to focus on the gap between the theoretical justification for openness and how trade rules have been actually designed and prosecuted. Here, it is worth underscoring that the WTO's legal agreements, as well as a maze of newer bilateral and regional ties between nations, are as much about protectionism as they are about something called 'free trade' (Wilkinson 2006; Eagleton-Pierce 2013). The actual neoliberal world economy is, therefore, by no means a *laissez-faire* vision but, rather, features a labyrinthine variety of interventions by governments. For instance, agricultural trade has long been marked by many 'distortions'. In 2012, across the OECD area, governments provided more than US$258 billion in subsidies to farmers (OECD 2013).

While some of these payments are transferred to poorer farmers who would not survive without such help, a range of other powerful food companies and landowners can also claim such public funds, including, in the EU context, Nestlé and the Queen of England (farmsubsidy.org). The effects of such subsidies on developing countries have been widely debated by experts and civil society groups (Oxfam International 2002; Weis 2007; Magdoff and Tokar 2010; Clapp 2012). Among many problems, there have been claims that farmers in poor countries are squeezed out of markets (both international and domestic) by the 'dumping' of highly subsidised foreign produce. For example, Oxfam International (2004) estimates that due to EU sugar subsidies, competing countries have suffered major foreign-exchange losses, including Brazil at US$494 million and Thailand at US$151 million. In short, the WTO's agricultural rules have largely perpetuated a system where trade patterns are strongly informed not by comparative advantage in terms of competitiveness, but by access to subsidies, an area in which richer countries have a superior advantage.

A final important consideration in the conceptual analysis of trade in the period of neoliberalism concerns the mainstreaming of 'fair trade' in many countries. On the surface, fair trade has a deceptively attractive appeal. Who could not advocate fairness? As conventionally depicted, fair trade can refer to different phenomena, including a market for goods, a social movement or, more abstractly, a politicised form of consumerism. By invoking 'fair', one immediately implies that existing forms of trade – often defined under the frame of free trade – are somehow lacking in fairness. Fair trade thus invites critical debate on how capitalist relations may feature inequalities and injustices. However, through the exercise of particular ethical strategies that partner poor producers with rich consumers, the incomes and empowerment of the former are said to be improved. In terms of its genesis, fair trade emerged in the aftermath of the Second World War, largely centred around the activism of Christian organisations. By the 1960s and 1970s, so-called 'alternative trade organisations', such as Oxfam, appeared on the high streets of Western Europe and North America. But it was only from the 1980s and, in particular, around the turn of the century, that the major institutionalisation and popularisation of fair trade took off. Chief among the factors aiding this process was the development of various certification schemes, such as the creation of Fairtrade International (FLO) in 1997, which helped to codify what a fair trade product actually looked like (Raynolds and Long 2007). As a result, fair trade sales continue to increase in many countries. In 2012, more than 1.3 million farmers and workers in 70 countries participated in FLO-linked schemes, with consumer spending on such items topping €4.8 billion (Fairtrade International 2013).

At the same time, it is worth concluding on certain tensions and criticisms that have been raised with respect to fair trade. First, in seeking to maximise the perceived positive benefits from fair trade projects, the movement has engaged much more with transnational businesses, entities that historically have been considered part of the problem of free trade. Does working within conventional markets erode the mission of the movement to contest unjust forms of international trade? Is corporate fair trade an oxymoron? Can the ethical values of fair trade participants be upheld if Wal-Mart, Starbucks and McDonald's all claim to be advocates? Such questions are difficult to resolve and have been asked with greater frequency. Second, within anthropology and geography, some scholars have been alert to how fair trade can invite different interpretations of the 'transnational moral economy' (Goodman 2004: 891). According to this critique, images of fair trade help to rework the 'commodity fetish', to borrow a Marxist term. In part, fair trade 'defetishises': that is, through 'storytelling advertising', the commodity chain is explained to the consumer. By contrast, most consumer products are not accompanied by a narrative of how they were made (the product is fetishised from its labour). However, fair trade is still fetishism to the extent that the consumer is purchasing a comforting emotion or an image of themselves 'saving the world' (Lyon 2006). It is also worth considering that, while such initiatives may bring some local good, the most profound fairness that could be accomplished in global trade relations would be to correct legal rules that structure an unequal commercial world.

See also: **competition, freedom, global, governance, growth, market, openness, reform, state**.

Further reading: Bhagwati 2004; Eagleton-Pierce 2013; Irwin 1996; Lyon 2006; Winters 2004.

VISION

When they encounter the word 'vision', the cynical might only hear the famously deflating comment made by George Bush Senior in 1988 about 'the vision thing', but its history had a more auspicious start. In its earliest meaning, from the thirteenth century, vision referred to seeing something in a prophetic, mystical or supernatural way. The modern sense of vision as the ability to conceive a goal, which, in turn, is projected to an audience as potentially achievable, only emerges in the late eighteenth century. Associations with politics became increasingly pronounced through the nineteenth century, with predictable conceptual links drawn to leadership, strategy and the desirable dispositions of statesmen. As one reference expressed it, 'Bismarck, intensely practical as he was, had always the vision of a united Germany, powerful and respected' (Stearns 1899: 89). By the early twentieth century, in discourses about American business, the term 'vision' began to spread as an apparent answer to ongoing questions about the effectiveness of capitalist enterprises. For instance, in one handbook written by the general sales manager of the Chevrolet Motor Company, the author tries to inspire his fellow car dealers through optimistic parables on persistence and moral character. Taking a cue from the Bible – 'Where there is no vision, the people perish' (Proverbs 29:18) – he argues that the same logic applies to sales pitches, suggesting that 'a man who hasn't vision will soon find himself without a business' (Sills 1920: 19). While often vague and ill-defined, 'vision' was a term that conveyed a sense that company executives and, in particular, entrepreneurs establishing new businesses should always be teaching the values and aspirations of the firm.

Nevertheless, while 'vision' was used in these earlier commercial debates, it would be wrong to say that the term was commonplace. Rather, it was only from the 1980s, in the context of the mainstreaming of neoliberalism, that it picked up supporters in business studies (Bennis and Nanus 1985; Peters 1987; Kouzes and Posner 1989). With such popularity came the inevitable questions: what precisely is 'vision', why is it necessary and how should the 'visioning' process be conducted? In the literature that flourished, these issues were not easily resolved. As a baseline, according to one summary, 'vision is about the future, induces people to act towards a common goal, provides a sense of direction, and is important for strategy and planning' (Kantabutra 2008: 130). For instance, the Chevron vision, according to its website, is defined as 'to be the global energy company most admired for its people, partnership and performance'. Beyond such starting points, many management authors express frustration over how company 'vision statements' – a 1990s elaboration – often contain a bewildering range of policies, objectives and cultural tropes, with the benefit and links between each element often unclear. Yet, despite such confusion, almost all business leaders, along with a small army of 'vision experts', agree that talking about vision is crucial to successful companies. According to some writers, those corporations with a 'strong shared culture' are more likely to grow revenue, profits and their stock price. 'Performance follows vision. Without vision a firm may be profitable, but its competitive performance will suffer significantly' (Quigley 1994: 40; 1993). In turn, through the search for such rewards, studies have tried to pinpoint how different leadership styles are coupled with 'vision strength', including intangible qualities like charisma (Berson *et al.* 2001; Strange and Mumford 2002).

Despite its soft and fuzzy exterior, there are some deeper tensions at play when vision is articulated as a normative task in business management. Unpicking these tensions helps to clarify some of the neoliberal content associated with the concept. First, the move towards constructing visions is arguably part of a broader updating of the core justifications used to defend corporate-led capitalism. It is rare to find a vision statement from a major company that explicitly identifies profit as its primary mission. Although the reasoning for this omission is not often stated, it becomes more understandable when considering research that shows profit maximisation, as an argument on its own, is insufficient to ensure the commitment of many workers. The mundane and seemingly endless quest for profit does not differentiate one capitalist entity from another. But a vision articulated by an inspiring leader (a 'visionary') with references to the wider social good, such as partnership projects with diverse communities or practices that are environmentally friendly, could help ensure 'commitment without recourse to compulsion, by making everyone's work meaningful' (Boltanski and Chiapello 2007: 76). Importantly, it often appears as if the vision is trying to stimulate enthusiasm and excitement among its audience (which, by implication, cannot be easily accomplished if one relies upon the pay cheque alone).

Second, despite all these efforts, the dependence upon finding leaders to articulate persuasive visions is, in Boltanski and Chiapello's interpretation,

> the weakest link in the new mechanisms [of neoliberal ideology] for everything rests on the shoulders of an exceptional being; and it is not always clear how to train or even recruit such beings, especially in sufficient numbers, since every firm needs them.
>
> (2007: 76)

By the turn of the century, management authors were trying to grapple with this particular problem. One 'solution' has been to argue that the CEO should not assume exclusive responsibility for composing the company vision (isolated in their office, 'thinking great thoughts') but, rather, that the work should be a collective project involving many others in the organisation (Avery 2004). This rejection of a top-down approach to corporate socialisation is something that is distinctly neo-liberal, or, to be more precise, the practical ideology composed by business writers argues that the most desirable company form features networked, rather than hierarchical, relations. But whether or not such visions are concretely 'owned' and accepted by employees is always an open question. 'True believers' of the vision may sit alongside those who consider the exercise 'fluff'. Indeed, one should not assume that all CEOs accept that 'visioning' is a worthy use of resources, particularly in a crisis. As Lou Gerstner famously put it when he saved IBM from bankruptcy in the 1990s: 'the last thing IBM needs right now is a vision statement' (Gerstner 2002: 71).

See also: **business, challenge, consensus, entrepreneurship, management, network, openness, participation, performance, project**.

Further reading: Boltanski and Chiapello 2007; Quigley 1993; Kantabutra 2008.

WELFARE

Welfare was originally spelt *wel faran*, combining *well* with *fare*, that is, a journey or a passage. From the fourteenth century, welfare acquired its common meaning of happiness or prosperity. At the same time, in an interesting legacy, still extant in the neoliberal period, the term also tends to imply self-indulgence and extravagance. In the second half of the nineteenth century, in the context of the growth of industrial capitalism, the rise of labour movements and pressures exerted upon traditional social support networks (family, charity groups, feudal institutions, religious bodies, etc.), the notion of welfare was extended to represent a general object of care and provision. By the early twentieth century, a variety of compound phrases entered the language to reflect the profound socio-political changes underway, including welfare policy (1905, *OED*), welfare service (1911, *OED*) and welfare reform (1913, *OED*). For instance, early insurance systems for workers can be found in Bismarck's Germany. In Britain, the founding of the Fabian Society in 1884 laid the foundations for the birth of the Labour Party, although disputes existed with Marxists who sought revolutionary means for furthering a different kind of society beyond capitalism (Hennock 2007).

The phrase 'welfare state', as opposed to the warfare state, was first coined in 1894, but it would take until the 1940s, following the Second World War and demands for a new social compact, before it acquired currency in Western Europe and elsewhere (Williams 1983[1976]). For instance, in the UK, the Beveridge Report of 1942 led to the establishment of the National Health Service, while in the US, from the 1960s, the Johnson administration launched its Great Society programmes (building on the New Deal policies from the 1930s). Thus, the early postwar decades have been subsequently described – 'with a mixture of hindsight and nostalgia' (Castles *et al.* 2010: 8) – as a 'golden age' for the welfare state, a period in which social justice was enhanced for a larger majority. Not surprisingly, researchers have argued that a positive correlation exists between welfare state spending and declining levels of poverty (Kenworthy 1999; Moller *et al.* 2003; Brady 2005). For example, in France, prior to the introduction of welfare programmes in the twentieth century, the relative poverty rate was around four times higher (Moller *et al.* 2003).

Defining the welfare state is a difficult task. This is not only because one can find considerable cross-national variation in how such systems have been constructed, including the timing of consolidation, policy objectives, finance mechanisms and the role of the private sector, but also because the welfare state has encountered vocal criticism since its inception (King and Ross 2010; see also Esping-Andersen 1990; Arts and Gelissen 2002). Sceptics have come from across the political spectrum, including some actors that appeal to, or define themselves as, social democrats, but the most organised and trenchant critiques have been made by thinkers associated with neoliberalism. From the 1940s, in the context of attacks against socialism and Keynesianism, Friedrich von Hayek (2008[1944], 1960) and Ludwig von Mises (1944), among others, contested the general principles of the new welfare state. In Hayek's eyes, governments that try to pursue social justice through an elaborate welfare infrastructure risk compromising the defence of individual freedom, which, in his view, was best accomplished through private market transactions. Mises, 'whose abhorrence of the New Deal was unmitigated' (Jones 2012: 34), was equally (if not more) suspicious of how the welfare state fostered special interests to the detriment of the individual. As he curtly put it, the 'so-called welfare state is in fact the tyranny of the rulers' (Mises 1944: 42). By the 1960s, these ideas had begun to spread, not only in the English-speaking world but also beyond (on the Denmark case, see Larsen and Andersen 2009). In the US, Milton Friedman (2002[1962]) was particularly influential, arguing that minimum-wage laws were counterproductive. In his view, if wages rose, the employer would compensate by reducing staff and, thus, the unemployment level would rise higher.

By the 1980s, the critique of the welfare state was strengthened by a cluster of conservative thinkers, including leading politicians, think-tank researchers, academics and journalists. Such thinkers retained the classical liberal emphasis on individualism, but incorporated a heavier moral emphasis, one that at times appeared to reactivate the old distinction between the 'deserving' and 'undeserving' poor. One particular theme in these debates surrounded the promotion of so-called 'traditional values' associated with an idealised family. As Margaret Thatcher argued, with her appeal to 'Victorian virtues', individuals who worked in the interests of their family would help to produce not just a more prosperous society but a more moral one (Thatcher 2013; see also Sutcliffe-Braithwaite 2012). For Thatcherites, the welfare state was blamed for causing a presumed breakdown in the 'traditional' family unit. In the US, similar ideas were explored by two conservative political scientists who were close to policymakers: Charles Murray (1984) and, in particular, Lawrence Mead (1986, 1993). Both these writers argued that US welfare entitlement schemes made recipients too reliant on the government, of which the Aid to Families with Dependent Children programme (1935–96) was singled out as being notably egregious. Far from state benefits alleviating poverty, Murray and Mead argued that 'paternalistic' government was perpetuating a so-called 'culture of dependency' across generations, one which was bad for both the recipients and the country. Mead's solution was to promote a stronger work ethic as 'payment' for welfare and, on related moral grounds, to foster attitudes of 'personal responsibility' within the communities of welfare claimants, such as discouraging births out of wedlock.

By the 1990s, driven by conservative media voices, this depiction of welfare recipients as caught between their own implied immoral pathologies and an overly generous welfare state had produced a set of popular caricatures, which, in turn, were endlessly redeployed in social-policy debates. For instance, as critiqued by Loïc Wacquant (2009: 84), the so-called 'welfare queen' has become one potent stereotypical image, who, it is suggested by some commentators, 'shirks employment, cheats the public aid bureaucracy, and spends her assistance check high on drugs and liquor, leaving her many children in appalling neglect' (see also Hancock 2004). Indeed, a mini vocabulary of derogatory labels has been used to define welfare users, such as 'fraudster', 'scrounger', 'sponger' and 'chav'. As noted, for political parties on the right and their supporters, the mainstreaming of these myths fits into an historical pattern of representing or caricaturing segments of the poor. What is more distinctive in the neoliberal period is how parties on the left – including Clinton's Democrats in the US, Blair's New Labour in the UK, Schröder's Social Democrats in Germany and Howard's Liberals in Australia – began adopting similar rhetoric and prescriptions. Such practices were given an academic veneer of authenticity by the 'third way' argument of Anthony Giddens (2000), which suggested that older socialist agendas should give way to greater accommodation with capitalism (see also the advocacy of 'quasi-markets' in public services by Le Grand 2007). With respect to social-protection policies, these ideas translated into new systems that sought to revise or devolve state responsibility. For instance, in the US, the conversion of the right to welfare into the obligation of 'workfare' made it harder (or even impossible) to access welfare receipts until the individual had found work (Peck 1998, 2001; Wacquant 2009; on the adoption of workfare models in East Asia, see Chan and Ngok 2011).

Criticisms and qualifications of, and the paradoxes within, the neoliberal turn in welfare politics are not hard to find. Four points can be made here. First, as argued by many scholars and activists, the punitive sharpening of welfare policy has, far from lowering the poverty rate, tended to further diminish the fortunes of such targeted groups. For instance, in the US, the poverty rate has remained broadly stable over the neoliberal period at around 14 per cent. Within this category, however, there is considerable variation, most notably according to race. For example, in 2012, the African-American poverty rate was at 27 per cent, compared to 10 per cent for the white, non-Hispanic population. Moreover, in periods of economic contraction, the former figure tends to spike higher than the latter (DeNavas-Walt and Proctor 2014). In other words, although workfare agendas may on paper promote work as the tonic for welfare dependency, the creation of a market in decent, well-paid and gainful employment is often lacking or disconnected from welfare delivery. Indeed, in Wacquant's reading of the Clinton era of welfare reform, this is one of the most telling (and apparently ironic) features of the Personal Responsibility and Work Opportunity Act of 1996: '*the law had absolutely no jobs component*' (Wacquant: 2009: 85, italics in original; see also Piven 1998). At the same time, it is important to note that the practical side of the experience of welfare reform, such as monetary transfers, has a psychological component in feelings of shame and embarrassment at being 'on welfare', emotions that have arguably been fermented by the very demonisation of poor citizens in the neoliberal period (Jones 2011). Unlike their presence in state statistics, those on welfare have their own stories to tell, but these surface only intermittently in the mass media (because, among other reasons, those with fewer resources will often have no access to journalists) (but see the Voices of Welfare project at: http://blogs.elon.edu/voicesofwelfare/).

Second, these debates can lead one to question again if the recasting of welfare has other objectives or tendencies that are not officially stated. This type of enquiry is difficult to conduct but may get us closer to how welfare is situated in relation to larger systems of statecraft and capitalism. In the eyes of some researchers, there is nothing intrinsically beneficial about welfare. Indeed, as we have seen, some policies in the neoliberal period often appear to be part of a mechanism for disciplining and normalising the poor as a 'problematic population' that require ongoing monitoring. In Piven and Cloward's (1993: xvii) classic study of US policy, these mechanisms can be understood within a history of social relief programmes which 'are initiated to deal with dislocations in the work system that lead to mass disorder, and are then retained (in an altered form) to enforce work'. At the same time, the neoliberal vision of welfare partakes in a notable remasculinisation of the state, which can be understood as an oblique reaction to collectivist movements of the 1960s that threatened androcentric norms in capitalism. Opposition to feminist activism is part of this cross-country trend (Fraser and Gordon 1994; Fraser 2013). Other critiques are specific to class contexts within the politics of nationalism, such as the stigmatisation of migrants who try to access welfare but are denied by tighter rules. All these themes come together in the communications of public officials, who often strain to maintain a diminishing credit of legitimacy for their status as governors. For some leaders, the framing of poor citizens, or those who search for citizenship, into figures of abuse represents an easier strategy for acquiring credibility with certain audiences. An obsessive focus on such issues may also distract some segments of the electorate from asking other difficult political questions (such as how middle-class groups extract as much, or even more, value from the welfare state as lower-income groups).

In general, we can see how welfare reform in the neoliberal period has resulted in more disciplinary forms of government surveillance, including cuts to certain services, notably in areas where the targeted social group has a weak political voice. However, one can overstress the 'retrenchment' thesis of the welfare state, and this takes me to my third point. If one takes the metric of government social spending as a share of GDP, the evidence shows an increase in spending across almost all OECD countries during the period of neoliberalism. For instance, from 1980 to 2005, Anglo-Saxon countries increased their social spending share of GDP by around a fifth, Scandinavian countries did the same from a higher base and Japan increased its outlays by 75 per cent (Glennerster 2010). In 2013, notwithstanding some budget cuts in the aftermath of the financial crisis (particularly within southern Europe), the average OECD social spending remained at around 22 per cent (OECD 2014). Social scientists have grappled with this apparent paradox between neoliberal rhetoric and reality, inspired by the work of Claus Offe (1984), Paul Pierson (1995) and others. One major explanation has focused on interest groups, some operating with strong institutional power, which have a vested concern in the maintenance of welfare state agendas. These groups include political parties of the left (who often still need to at least appeal to socialist ethics), trade unions, certain civil society organisations and charities, military veterans and seniors. Together, working in alliances or through disparate means, from the enactment of state laws to the publishing of opinion letters in local newspapers, these supporters of the welfare state are often able to rein in the ambitions of those who seek to shrink welfare budgets. Inevitably, none of these struggles is static and the future of the welfare state, in respect to all its diversity, remains to be written (Levy 2010).

A final point involves the conceptual developing of the term 'welfare' to include debates about 'corporate welfare'. This phrase was found in the nineteenth century but had a more abstract sense of the general health of a corporate body. The modern meaning, which often carries a pejorative tone, has its roots in the 1970s in Canada (see uses by politicians on the left, such as Lewis 1972), before being popularised by Ralph Nader in his struggles against American corporate power (Nader 2000). The phrase carries strong negative connotations in the US, partly because it has become a common object of distaste not only for those on the left but also for libertarian groups on the right, such as the Cato Institute (DeHaven 2012). As a starting point, corporate welfare may be broadly defined as 'those efforts made by the state to directly or indirectly subsidise, support, or rescue corporations, or otherwise socialise the cost and risk of investment and production of private profits and capital accumulation of corporations' (Glasberg and Skidmore 1997: 2). Policy measures under this category are numerous, including direct grants, other subsidies, low-cost loans, tax breaks, government equity purchases and advisory services. Tracing how 'the public' is deprived or 'competition' is curtailed by such corporate welfare is not always clear. For instance, industries that arose in the context of the Cold War, such as aerospace and computing, were heavily supported by governments and have, in turn, produced goods and services that are widely accepted. However, as noted by Farnsworth (2012), it is telling how little is actually known about the various forms of corporate welfare in different countries. In sum, recent corporate welfare, not least the bank bailouts of Wall Street and the City of London, reveals how neoliberalism is, not, at root, marked by some blunt opposition between state and market. Rather, the compass of neoliberalism points in different directions, with the position of the needle never quite fixed for those in power to feel comfortable one way or the other.

See also: **capitalism, class, community, freedom, governance, growth, individual, market, power, reform, responsibility, state**.

Further reading: Arts and Gelissen 2002; Castles *et al.* 2010; Esping-Andersen 1990; Farnsworth 2012; Levy 2010; Mead 1986, 1993.

BIBLIOGRAPHY

Aalbers, M. (ed.), *Subprime Cities: The Political Economy of Mortgage Markets* (Oxford: John Wiley & Sons Ltd., 2012).

Abrahamsen, R., *Disciplining Democracy: Development Discourse and Good Governance in Africa* (London: Zed Books, 2000).

Abrams, P., 'Notes on the Difficulty of Studying the State', *Journal of Historical Sociology*, 1 (1988), 1, 58–89.

Achrol, R. S., 'Changes in the Theory of Inter-organizational Relations: Toward a Network Paradigm', *Journal of the Academy of Marketing Science*, 25 (1997), 1, 56–71.

Admati, A. and Hellwig, M., *The Bankers' New Clothes: What's Wrong with Banking and What to Do About It* (Princeton: Princeton University Press, 2013).

Ahmed, S., *On Being Included: Racism and Diversity in Institutional Life* (Durham, NC: Duke University Press, 2012).

Ahonen, P., Tienari, J., Meriläinen, S. and Pullen, A., 'Hidden Contexts and Invisible Power Relations: A Foucauldian Reading of Diversity Research', *Human Relations*, 67 (2014), 3, 263–86.

Aitken, R., *Performing Capital: Toward a Cultural Economy of Popular and Global Finance* (Basingstoke: Palgrave Macmillan, 2007).

Alchian, A. A., 'Property Rights', in Henderson, D. R. (ed.), *The Concise Encyclopedia of Economics* (Indianapolis, IN: Liberty Fund Inc., 2008). Available at: http://www.econlib.org/library/Enc/PropertyRights.html.

Alchian, A. A. and Demsetz, H., 'The Property Right Paradigm', *The Journal of Economic History*, 33 (1973), 1, 16–27.

Alexander, J. C., *The Performance of Politics: Obama's Victory and the Democratic Struggle for Power* (Oxford: Oxford University Press, 2010).

Alford, D., Sackett, P. and Nelder, G., 'Mass Customisation – An Automotive Perspective', *International Journal of Production Economics*, 65 (2000), 1, 99–100.

Allen, L. and Saunders, A., 'Risk Management in Banking', in Berger, A. N., Molyneux, P. and Wilson, J. O. S. (eds), *The Oxford Handbook of Banking* (Oxford: Oxford University Press, 2012).

Alliance for Board Diversity, *Missing Pieces: Women and Minorities on Fortune 500 Boards* (2013). Available at: http://theabd.org/Reports.html.

Almond, G. A. and Verba, S., *The Civic Culture: Political Attitudes and Democracy in Five Nations* (Princeton: Princeton University Press, 1963).

Alsop, R., Bertelsen, M. F. and Holland, J., *Empowerment in Practice: From Analysis to Implementation* (Washington D.C.: World Bank, 2006).

Alvaredo, F., Atkinson, A. B., Piketty, T. and Saez, E., 'The Top 1 Percent in International and Historical Perspective', *Journal of Economic Perspectives*, 27 (2013), 3, 3–20.

Alvesson, M., Willmott, H. and Bridgman, T., 'Introduction', in Alvesson, M., Bridgman, T. and Willmott, H. (eds), *The Oxford Handbook of Critical Management Studies* (Oxford: Oxford University Press, 2011).

Amdam, R. P., 'Business Education', in Jones, G. and Zeitlin, J. (eds), *The Oxford Handbook of Business History* (Oxford: Oxford University Press, 2008).

Anand, R. and Winters, M-F., 'A Retrospective View of Corporate Diversity Training From 1964 to the Present', *Academy of Management Learning & Education*, 7 (2008), 3, 356–72.

Andersson, R., Eriksson, H., Torstensson, H., 'Similarities and Differences between TQM, Six Sigma and Lean', *The TQM Magazine*, 18 (2006), 3, 282–296.

Ansoff, I., *Corporate Strategy: Business Policy for Growth and Expansion* (New York: McGraw-Hill, 1965).

Arendt, H., *The Human Condition* (Chicago: University of Chicago Press, 1998[1958]).

Argyris, C., 'Empowerment: The Emperor's New Clothes', *Harvard Business Review*, May–June 1998.

Aribisala, F., 'The Political Economy of Structural Adjustment in Côte d'Ivoire', in Olukoshi, A. O., Olaniyan, R. O. and Aribisala, F. (eds), *Structural Adjustment in West Africa* (Lagos: Pumark Nigeria for Nigerian Institute of International Affairs, 1994).

Armour, J., Hansmann, H. B. and Kraakman, R., 'What is Corporate Law?', in Kraakman, R., Armour, J., Davies, P., Enriques, L., Hansmann, H. B., Hertig, G. and Hopt, K. J. (eds), *The Anatomy of Corporate Law: A Comparative and Functional Approach* (Oxford: Oxford University Press, 2009).

Armstrong, P., *Critique of Entrepreneurship: People and Policy* (Basingstoke: Palgrave Macmillan, 2005).

Arnold, G., *The Financial Times Guide to Investing: The Definitive Companion to Investment and the Financial Markets* (Harlow: Pearson Education, 2010).

Arnold, M., 'HSBC Chairman Douglas Flint Warns of Rising Staff Risk Aversion', *Financial Times*, August 4, 2014.

Arnold, M. J., Reynolds, K. E., Ponder, N. and Lueg, J. E., 'Customer Delight in a Retail Context: Investigating Delightful and Terrible Shopping Experiences', *Journal of Business Research*, 58 (2005), 8, 1132–45.

Arnould, E. J and Price, L., 'River Magic: Extraordinary Experience and the Extended Service Encounter', *Journal of Consumer Research*, 20 (1993), 1, 24–45.

Arnould, E. J., Price, L. and Zinkhan, G. M., *Consumers* (New York: McGraw Hill, 2002).

Aronczyk, M., *Branding the Nation: The Global Business of National Identity* (Oxford: Oxford University Press, 2013).

Arrighi, G., *The Long Twentieth Century: Money, Power, and Origins of Our Times* (London: Verso, 1994).

Arts, W. and Gelissen, J., 'Three Worlds of Welfare Capitalism or More? A State-of-the-Art Report', *Journal of European Social Policy*, 12 (2002), 2, 137–58.

Ashton, J. K., 'The Scale and Scope of Financial Mis-selling', in Harrison, T. and Estelami, H. (eds), *The Routledge Companion to Financial Services Marketing* (Abingdon: Routledge, 2015).

Assies, W., 'David Versus Goliath in Cochabamba: Water Rights, Neoliberalism, and the Revival of Social Protest in Bolivia', *Latin American Perspectives*, 30 (2003), 3, 14–36.

Atkins, R., 'Trichet Defends "Impeccable" ECB Record', *Financial Times*, September 8, 2011.

Atkinson, A. B. and Piketty, T. (eds), *Top Incomes: A Global Perspective* (Oxford: Oxford University Press, 2010).

Atkinson, T., Luttrell, D. and Rosenblum, H., 'How Bad Was It? The Costs and Consequences of the 2007–09 Financial Crisis', *Dallas Fed. Staff Papers*, No. 20, July 2013.

Aucoin, P., 'Administrative Reform in Public Management: Paradigms, Principles, Paradoxes and Pendulums', *Governance*, 3 (1990), 2, 115–37.

Avery, G. C., *Understanding Leadership* (London: Sage, 2004).

Babb, S., *Behind the Development Banks: Washington Politics, World Poverty, and the Wealth of Nations* (Chicago: Chicago University Press, 2009).

Bae, K. S. and Kim, K-M, 'Long Working Hours', in Bae, K. S. (ed.), *Employment Relations in South Korea: Evidence from Workplace Panel Surveys* (Houndmills: Palgrave Macmillan, 2014).

Bain, P. M., Watson, A. C., Mulvey, G., Taylor, P. and Gall, G., 'Taylorism, Targets and the Pursuit of Quantity and Quality by Call Centre Management', *New Technology, Work and Employment*, 17 (2002), 3, 170–85.

Bakker, K., *Privatizing Water: Governance Failure and the World's Urban Water Crisis* (Ithaca: Cornell University Press, 2010).

Ball, S. J., 'Performativity, Commodification and Commitment: An I-Spy Guide to the Neoliberal University', *British Journal of Educational Studies*, 60 (2012a), 1, 17–28.

Ball, S. J., *Global Education Inc.: New Policy Networks and the Neoliberal Imaginary* (Abingdon: Routledge, 2012b)

Bambaci, J., Chia, C-P. and Ho, B., *Built to Last: Two Decades of Wisdom on Emerging Markets Allocations* (New York: MSCI Applied Research, October 2012).

Banerjee, S. B., *Corporate Social Responsibility: The Good, the Bad and the Ugly* (Cheltenham: Edward Elgar Publishing, 2007).

Bank for International Settlements (BIS), *Central Bank Survey of Foreign Exchange and Derivatives Market Activity* (Basel: Bank for International Settlements, 1996).

Bank for International Settlements (BIS), *Triennial Central Bank Survey; Foreign Exchange Turnover in April 2013: Preliminary Global Results* (Basel: Bank for International Settlements, 2013b).

Bank for International Settlements (BIS), *International Regulatory Framework for Banks (Basel III)* (Basel: Bank for International Settlements, 2013a). Available at: http://www.bis.org/bcbs/basel3.htm.

Baran, P. A., *The Political Economy of Growth* (New York: Monthly Review Press, 1957).

Barba, A. and Pivetti, M., 'Rising Household Debt: Its Causes and Macroeconomic Implications – A Long-Period Analysis', *Cambridge Journal of Economics*, 33 (2009), 1, 113–37.

Barendregt, B. and Jaffe, R., 'The Paradoxes of Eco-Chic', in Barendregt, B. and Jaffe, R. (eds), *Green Consumption: The Global Rise of Eco-Chic* (London: Bloomsbury, 2014).

Barker, S. and Cole, R., *Brilliant Project Management: What the Best Project Managers Know, Do and Say* (Harlow: Pearson Education, 2012).

Barkun, M., *A Culture of Conspiracy: Apocalyptic Visions in Contemporary America* (Oakland, CA: University of California Press, 2013).

Barnes, J. A., 'Class and Committees in a Norwegian Island Parish', *Human Relations*, 7 (1954), 1, 39–58.

Barnes, J. A., 'Network Analysis: Orienting Notion, Rigorous Technique, or Substantive Field of Study?', in Holland, P. W. and Leinhardt, S. (eds), *Perspectives on Social Network Analysis* (New York: Academic, 1979).

Barnett, C., 'The Consolations of "Neoliberalism"', *Geoforum*, 36 (2005), 1, 7–12.

Barnett, M. and Duvall, R. (eds), *Power in Global Governance* (Cambridge: Cambridge University Press, 2004).

Barnett, M. and Duvall, R., 'Power in International Politics', *International Organization*, 59 (2005), 1, 39–75.

Batliwala, S., 'Taking the Power Out of Empowerment – An Experiential Account', in Cornwall, A. and Eade, D. (eds), *Deconstructing Development Discourse: Buzzwords and Fuzzwords* (Dunsmore, Warwickshire: Practical Action Publishing Ltd., 2010).

Bauer, T., *Equality, the Third World, and Economic Delusion* (Cambridge, MA: Harvard University Press, 1981).

Beck, U., *Risk Society: Towards a New Modernity* (London: Sage, 1992).

Becker, M. C. and Knudsen, T., 'Schumpeter and the Organization of Entrepreneurship', in Adler, P. S. (ed.), *The Oxford Handbook of Sociology and Organization Studies: Classical Foundations* (Oxford: Oxford University Press, 2009).

Beckhard, R., *Organizational Development: Strategies and Models* (Reading, MA: Addison-Wesley, 1969).

Beer, M. and Ruh, R. A., 'Employee Growth Through Performance Management', *Harvard Business Review*, 54 (1976), 4, 59–66.

Bel, G., 'The Coining of "Privatization" and Germany's National Socialist Party', *Journal of Economic Perspectives*, 20 (2006), 3, 187–94.

Bennett, T., Grossberg, L. and Morris, M. (eds), *New Keywords: A Revised Vocabulary of Culture and Society* (Oxford: Blackwell, 2005).

Bennis, W., *Why Leaders Can't Lead: The Unconscious Conspiracy Continues* (Hoboken, NJ: Wiley & Sons, 1997).

Bennis, W. and Nanus, B., *Leaders: The Strategies for Taking Charge* (New York: Harper & Row, 1985).

Berger, R. A., 'Private-Sector Initiatives in the Reagan Administration', *Proceedings of the Academy of Political Science*, 36 (1986), 2, 14–30.

Berlin, I., *Four Essays on Liberty* (Oxford: Oxford University Press, 1969).

Bernstein, S., *The Compromise of Liberal Environmentalism* (New York: Columbia University Press, 2001).

Berry, D. M., 'The Contestation of Code: A Preliminary Investigation into the Discourse of the Free/Libre and Open Source Movements', *Critical Discourse Studies*, 1 (2004), 1, 65–89.

Berry, D. M., *Copy, Rip, Burn: The Politics of Copyleft and Open Source* (London: Pluto Press, 2008).

Berson, Y., Shamir, B., Avolio, B. J. and Popper, M., 'The Relationship Between Vision Strength, Leadership Style, and Content', *Leadership Quarterly*, 12 (2001), 53–74.

Bevir, M. (ed.), *The Encyclopaedia of Governance, 2 vol* (London: Sage, 2006).

Bevir, M., *Democratic Governance* (Princeton: Princeton University Press, 2010).

Bevir, M. (ed.), *The Sage Handbook of Governance* (London: Sage, 2011).

Bhagwati, J., *In Defense of Globalization* (Oxford: Oxford University Press, 2004).

Bhagwati, J. and Panagariya, A., *Why Growth Matters: How Economic Growth in India Reduced Poverty and the Lessons for Other Developing Countries* (New York: PublicAffairs, 2013).

Birch, A. H., *The Concepts and Theories of Modern Democracy* (Abingdon: Routledge, 2007).

Biswas, M. R. and Biswas, A. K., 'Environment and Sustained Development in the Third World: A Review of the Past Decade', *Third World Quarterly*, 4 (1982), 3, 479–91.

Black, F. and Scholes, M., 'The Pricing of Options and Corporate Liabilities', *Journal of Political Economy*, 81 (1973), 3, 637–54.

Blair, T., *New Britain: My Vision for a Young Country* (London: Fourth Estate, 1996).

Bland, B., 'Vietnam Offers Companies China Alternative', *Financial Times*, March 14, 2012.

Bloch, M., *Feudal Society* (Abingdon: Routledge, 2014[1940]).

Block, F. and Somers, M. R., *The Power of Market Fundamentalism: Karl Polanyi's Critique* (Cambridge, MA: Harvard University Press, 2014).

Block, P., *The Empowered Manager* (San Francisco: Jossey-Bass, 1987).

Blonigen, B. A., 'Foreign Direct Investment', in Durlauf, S. N. and Blume, L. E. (eds), *The New Palgrave Dictionary of Economics* (Houndmills: Palgrave Macmillan, 2008).

Bluestone, B. and Harrison, B., *Deindustrialization of America: Plant Closings, Community Abandonment and the Dismantling of Basic Industry* (New York: Basic Books, 1982).

Boas, T. C. and Gans-Morse, J., 'Neoliberalism: From New Liberal Philosophy to Anti-Liberal Slogan', *Studies in Comparative International Development*, 44 (2009), 2, 137–61.

Bobbio, N., *Democracy and Dictatorship: The Nature and Limits of State Power* (Minneapolis: University of Minnesota Press, 1989).

Bogle, J. C., *The Clash of the Cultures: Investment vs. Speculation* (Hoboken, NJ: John Wiley & Sons, 2012).

Boltanski, L. and Chiapello, E., *The New Spirit of Capitalism* (London: Verso, 2007).

Bonefeld, W., 'Freedom and the Strong State: On German Ordoliberalism', *New Political Economy*, 17 (2012), 5, 633–56.

Bordo, M. D. and Schwartz, A. J., 'The Importance of Stable Money: Theory and Evidence', in Schwartz, A. J., *Money in Historical Perspective* (Chicago: Chicago University Press, 1987).

Borgatti, S. P. and Foster, P. C., 'The Network Paradigm in Organizational Research: A Review and Typology', *Journal of Management*, 29 (2003), 6, 991–1013.

Bott, E., *Family and Social Network* (London: Tavistock, 1957).

Bourdieu, P., *Outline of a Theory of Practice* (Cambridge: Cambridge University Press, 1977).

Bourdieu, P., *Distinction: A Social Critique of the Judgement of Taste* (London: Routledge, 1984).

Bourdieu, P., 'What Makes a Social Class? On the Theoretical and Practical Existence of Groups', *Berkeley Journal of Sociology*, 32 (1987), 1–18.

Bourdieu, P., 'The Essence of Neoliberalism', *Le Monde Diplomatique*, December 1998a.

Bourdieu, P., *Acts of Resistance: Against the New Myths of Our Time* (Cambridge: Polity Press, 1998b).

Bourdieu, P., *Firing Back: Against the Tyranny of the Market 2* (London: Verso, 2003).

Bourdieu, P., *On the State* (Cambridge: Polity Press, 2014).

Bourdieu, P. and Wacquant, L., *An Invitation to Reflexive Sociology* (Chicago: Chicago University Press, 1992).

Bourdieu, P. and Wacquant, L., 'NewLiberalSpeak: Notes on the New Planetary Vulgate', *Radical Philosophy*, 105 (January–February 2001), 2–5.

Bourgouin, F., 'From Network to Class? Towards a More Complex Conception of Connection and Sociability', DIIS Working Paper, 2009, 31 (Copenhagen: Danish Institute for International Studies, 2009).

Bowen, H. R., *Social Responsibilities of the Businessman* (New York: Harper & Row, 1953).

Boyer, R., 'How and Why Capitalisms Differ', *Economy and Society*, 34 (2005), 4, 509–57.

Brady, D., 'The Welfare State and Relative Poverty in Rich Western Democracies, 1967–1997', *Social Forces*, 83 (2005), 4, 1329–64.

Braudel, F., *Civilization and Capitalism, 15th–18th Century, Vol. I: The Structure of Everyday Life* (Oakland, CA: University of California Press, 1992a).

Braudel, F., *Civilization and Capitalism, 15th–18th Century, Vol. II: The Wheels of Commerce* (Oakland, CA: University of California Press, 1992b).

Brenner, M. and Galai, D., 'New Financial Instruments for Hedging Changes in Volatility', *Financial Analysts Journal*, 45 (July–August 1989), 4, 61–5.

Brenner, N. and Theodore, N., 'Cities and the Geographies of "Actually Existing Neoliberalism"', *Antipode*, 34 (2002), 3, 349–79.

Brenner, N., Peck, J. and Theodore, N., 'Variegated Neoliberalization: Geographies, Modalities, Pathways', *Global Networks*, 10 (2010), 2, 182–222.

Brewer, A., 'The Concept of Growth in Eighteenth-Century Economics', *History of Political Economy*, 27 (1995), 4, 609–38.

Brown, A., *Personal Responsibility: Why It Matters* (London: Continuum, 2009).

Brown, E., Milward, B., Mohan, G., Zack-Williams, A. B. (eds), *Structural Adjustment: Theory, Practice and Impacts* (London: Routledge, 2000).

Brown, G., 'Full Text: Gordon Brown's Speech to the CBI', *Financial Times*, November 28, 2005.

Brown, W., *States of Injury: Power and Freedom in Late Modernity* (Princeton: Princeton University Press, 1995).

Brown, W., 'American Nightmare: Neoliberalism, Neoconservatism, and De-Democratization', *Political Theory*, 34 (2006), 6, 690–714.

Brown, W., *Undoing the Demos: Neoliberalism's Stealth Revolution* (New York: Zone Books, 2015).

Bruckner, P., *L'euphorie perpétuelle: essai sur le devoir de bonheur* (Paris: Grasset, 2000).

Bruton, H. J., 'A Reconsideration of Import Substitution', *Journal of Economic Literature*, 36 (1998), 2, 903–36.

Bulkeley, H. and Newell, P., *Governing Climate Change* (Abingdon: Routledge, 2010).

Burgin, A., *The Great Persuasion: Reinventing Free Markets Since the Depression* (Cambridge, MA: Harvard University Press, 2012).

Bush, G. W., 'Remarks in a Discussion on Strengthening Social Security in Louisville, Kentucky', March 10, 2005, in US Government Printing Office, *George W. Bush, Book 1: January 1 to June 30, 2005, Public Papers of the Presidents of the United States* (Washington D.C.: US Government Printing Office, 2009).

Bush, G. W., 'Speech on the Economic Crisis', *Council on Foreign Relations*, New York, November 13, 2008. Available at: http://www.cfr.org/financial-crises/bushs-speech-economic-crisis-november-2008/p17767.

Butler, N., Olaison, L., Śliwa, M., Sørensen, B. M. and Spoelstra, S., 'Work, Play and Boredom', *Ephemera: Theory and Politics in Organization*, 11 (2011), 4, 329–35.

Bynum, C. W., 'Did the Twelfth Century Discover the Individual?', *The Journal of Ecclesiastical History*, 31 (1980), 1, 1–17.

Cagan, P., 'Monetarism', in Durlauf, S. N. and Blume, L. E. (eds), *The New Palgrave Dictionary of Economics* (Houndmills: Palgrave Macmillan, 2008).

Calhoun, C., 'Private', in Bennett, T., Grossberg, L. and Morris, M. (eds), *New Keywords: A Revised Vocabulary of Culture and Society* (Oxford: Blackwell Publishing, 2005).

Campbell, A. *The Blair Years: Extracts from the Alastair Campbell Diaries* (London: Random House, 2007).

Campisi, J., 'Reconsidering the Role of Political Risk in the Neoliberal Era', Paper presented at ECPR Standing Group on Regulatory Governance Fifth Biennial Conference, Barcelona, June 25–7, 2014.

Cannon, C., *The Making of Chaucer's English: A Study of Words* (Cambridge: Cambridge University Press, 1998).

Cantillon, R., *Essay on the Nature of Trade in General* (London: Frank Cass and Co., Ltd, 1959[1730]).

Cardoso, F. H. and Faletto, E., *Dependency and Development in Latin America* (Oakland, CA: University of California Press, 1979).

Carnegie, D., *How to Win Friends and Influence People* (London: Vermilion, 2006[1936]).

Carothers, T., *Aiding Democracy Abroad: The Learning Curve* (Washington D. C.: Carnegie Endowment for International Peace, 1999).

Carrier, J. G., 'Introduction', in Carrier, J. G. (ed.), *Meanings of the Market: The Free Market in Western Culture* (Oxford: Berg, 1997).

Carroll, A., 'Corporate Social Responsibility: Evolution of a Definitional Construct', *Business and Society Review*, 38 (1999), 3, 268–95.

Carroll, A., 'A History of Corporate Social Responsibility: Concepts and Practices', in Crane, A., Matten, D., McWilliams, A., Moon, J. and Siegel, D. (eds), *The Oxford Handbook of Corporate Social Responsibility* (Oxford: Oxford University Press, 2008).

Carroll, J. D., 'The Rhetoric of Reform and Political Reality in the National Performance Review', *Public Administration Review*, 55 (1995), 3, 302–12.

Carson, R., *Silent Spring* (London: Penguin Books, 2000[1962]).

Carter, I., 'Liberty', in Bellamy, R. and Mason, A. (eds), *Political Concepts* (Manchester: Manchester University Press, 2003).

Carter, N., *The Politics of the Environment: Ideas, Activism, Policy* (Cambridge: Cambridge University Press, 2007).

Carù, A. and Cova, B., 'Revisiting Consumption Experience: A More Humble but Complete View of the Concept', *Marketing Theory*, 3 (2003), 2, 267–86.

Casson, M., *The Entrepreneur: An Economic Theory* (Cheltenham: Edward Elgar Publishing, 2003).

Castells, M., *The Rise of the Network Society; The Information Age: Economy, Society and Culture Vol. 1* (Oxford: Blackwell, 1996).

Castells, M., Yazawa, S. and Kiselyova, E., 'Insurgents Against the Global Order: A Comparative Analysis of the Zapatistas in Mexico, the American Militia and Japan's AUM Shinrikyo', *Berkeley Journal of Sociology*, 40 (1995), 21–59.

Castles, F. G., Leibfried, S., Lewis, J., Obinger, H. and Pierson, C., 'Introduction', in Castles, F. G., Leibfried, S., Lewis, J., Obinger, H. and Pierson, C. (eds), *The Oxford Handbook of the Welfare State* (Oxford: Oxford University Press, 2010).

Catalyst, *The Bottom Line: Corporate Performance and Women's Representation on Boards (2004–2008)* (2011). Available at: http://www.catalyst.org/knowledge/bottom-line-corporate-performance-and-womens-representation-boards.

Cerny, P. G., 'Paradoxes of the Competition State: The Dynamics of Political Globalization', *Government and Opposition*, 32 (1997), 2, 251–74.

Chace, J., 'How "Moral" Can We Get?', *New York Times Magazine*, May 22, 1977.

Chambers Twentieth Century Dictionary (Edinburgh: Chambers, 1972).

Chan, A., *China's Workers Under Assault: The Exploitation of Labor in a Globalizing Economy* (Armonk, NY: M.E. Sharpe, 2001).

Chan, C. K. and Ngok, K. (eds), *Welfare Reform in East Asia: Towards Workfare* (Abingdon: Routledge, 2011).

Chandler, A. D., *Strategy and Structure: Chapters in the History of the American Industrial Enterprise* (Cambridge, MA: MIT Press, 1962).

Chandler, A. D., *The Visible Hand: The Managerial Revolution in American Business* (Cambridge, MA: Belknap Press, 1977).

Chandler, D., 'Beyond Neoliberalism: Resilience, the New Art of Governing Complexity', *Resilience: International Policies, Practices and Discourses*, 2 (2014), 1, 47–63.

Chandler, D. and Reid, J., *The Neoliberal Subject: Resilience, Adaptation and Vulnerability* (Lanham, MD: Rowman & Littlefield Publishing, 2016).

Charan, R., 'How Networks Reshape Organizations – For Results', *Harvard Business Review*, 69 (1991), 104–15.

Charlesworth, S. J., *A Phenomenology of Working-Class Experience* (Cambridge: Cambridge University Press, 1999).

Cheffins, B. R., 'The History of Corporate Governance', in Wright, M., Siegel, D. S., Keasey, K. and Filatotchev, I. (eds), *The Oxford Handbook of Corporate Governance* (Oxford: Oxford University Press, 2013).

Chernev, A., 'When More Is Less and Less Is More: The Role of Ideal Point Availability and Assortment in Consumer Choice', *Journal of Consumer Research*, 30 (2003), 2, 170–83.

Chiapello, E., 'Accounting and the Birth of the Notion of Capitalism', *Critical Perspectives on Accounting*, 18 (2007), 3, 263–96.

Chomsky, N., *Profit Over People: Neoliberalism and the Global Order* (New York: Seven Stories Press, 1998).

Christensen, C. M., *The Innovator's Dilemma: When New Technologies Cause Great Firms to Fail* (Boston: Harvard Business School Press, 1997).

Christopherson, S., 'Project Work in Context: Regulatory Change and the New Geography of Media', *Environment and Planning A*, 34 (2002), 11, 2003–15.

Chwieroth, J. M., *Capital Ideas: The IMF and the Rise of Financial Liberalization* (Princeton: Princeton University Press, 2010).

Cingano, F., 'Trends in Income Inequality and Its Impact on Economic Growth', OECD SEM Working Paper No. 163 (Paris: Organisation for Economic Co-operation and Development, 2014).

Clapp, J., *Food* (Cambridge: Polity Press, 2012).

Clark, T. N. and Lipset, S. M., 'Are Social Classes Dying?', *International Sociology*, 6 (1991), 4, 397–410.

Clark, T. N., Lipset, S. M. and Rempel, M., 'The Declining Political Significance of Social Class', *International Sociology*, 8 (1993), 3, 293–316.

Clarke, J., 'Living With/In and Without Neo-Liberalism', *Focaal – European Journal of Anthropology*, 51 (2008), 135–47.

Clegg, H. A., *A New Approach to Industrial Democracy* (Oxford: Blackwell, 1960).

Clegg, S. R. and Haugaard, M. (eds), *The SAGE Handbook of Power* (London: Sage, 2009).

Coase, R., 'The Nature of the Firm', *Economica*, 4 (1937), 16, 386–405.

Coates, J. M. and Herbert, J., 'Endogenous Steroids and Financial Risk Taking on a London Trading Floor', *Proceedings of the National Academy of Sciences (PNAS)*, 105 (2008), 16, 6167–72.

Coen, D. and Richardson, J., 'Learning to Lobby the EU: 20 Years of Change', in Coen, D. and Richardson, J. (eds), *Lobbying the European Union: Institutions, Actors, and Issues* (Oxford: Oxford University Press, 2009).

Cohen, P. 'Today, Some Feminists Hate the Word "Choice"', *New York Times*, January 15, 2006.

Coll, S., *Private Empire: ExxonMobil and American Power* (London: Penguin, 2012).

Collier, P. and Dollar, D., *Globalization, Growth, and Poverty: Building an Inclusive World Economy* (Washington D.C.: World Bank, 2002).

Collini, S., *What Are Universities For?* (London: Penguin Books, 2012).

Commission on Growth and Development, *The Growth Report: Strategies for Sustained Growth and Inclusive Development* (Washington D.C.: World Bank, 2008).

Committee for Economic Development (CED), *Social Responsibilities of Business Corporations* (New York: CED, 1971).

Conant, J. C., 'The Performance Appraisal: A Critique and an Alternative', *Business Horizons*, 16 (1973), 3, 73–8.

Conger, J. A. and Kanungo, R. N., 'The Empowerment Process: Integrating Theory and Practice', *The Academy of Management Review*, 13 (1988), 3, 471–82.

Connaughton, J., *The Payoff: Why Wall Street Always Wins* (Westport, CT: Prospecta Press, 2012).

Connolly, W. E., *The Terms of Political Discourse* (Oxford: Blackwell, 1993).

Conti, R. F., 'Frederick Winslow Taylor', in Witzel, M. and Warner, M. (eds), *The Oxford Handbook of Management Theorists* (Oxford: Oxford University Press, 2013).

Cooke, B. and Kothari, U. (eds), *Participation: The New Tyranny?* (London: Zed Books, 2001).

Cooper, F., 'Modernizing Bureaucrats, Backward Africans, and the Development Concept', in Cooper, F. and Packard, R. (eds), *International Development and the Social Sciences* (Berkeley: University of California Press, 1997).

Copeland, L., 'Valuing Diversity: Making the Most of Cultural Differences at the Workplace', *Personnel*, 65 (1988), 6, 52–60.

Cornia, G. A., Jolly, R. and Stewart, F. (eds), *Adjustment with a Human Face: Volume I: Protecting the Vulnerable and Promoting Growth* (Oxford: Oxford University Press, 1987).

Cornwall, A., 'Historical Perspectives on Participation in Development', *Commonwealth & Comparative Politics*, 44 (2006), 1, 62–83.

Cornwall, A. and Eade, D. (eds), *Deconstructing Development Discourse: Buzzwords and Fuzzwords* (Dunsmore, Warwickshire, UK: Practical Action Publishing, 2010).

Corporate Europe Observatory (CEO) and the Transnational Institute (TNI), *Profiting from Injustice: How Law Firms, Arbitrators and Financiers are Fuelling an Investment Arbitration Boom* (Brussels: CEO and Amsterdam: TNI, 2012).

Corporate Europe Observatory (CEO), *The Fire Power of the Financial Lobby: A Survey of the Size of the Financial Lobby at the EU Level* (Brussels: Corporate Europe Observatory, 2014).

Costas, J., '"We Are All Friends Here": Reinforcing Paradoxes of Normative Control in a Culture of Friendship', *Journal of Management Inquiry*, 21 (2012), 4, 377–95.

Costea, B., Crump, N. and Holm, J., 'Dionysus at Work? The Ethos of Play and the Ethos of Management', *Culture and Organization*, 11 (2005), 2, 139–51.

Cotton-Nessler, N. C. and Davis, G. F., 'Stock Ownership, Political Beliefs, and Party Identification from the "Ownership Society" to the Financial Meltdown', *Accounting, Economics, and Law – A Convivium*, 2 (2012), 2, 1–30.

Couldry, N. and Littler, J., 'Work, Power and Performance: Analysing the "Reality" Game of *The Apprentice*', *Cultural Sociology*, 5 (2011), 2, 263–79.

Cournot, A. A., *Researches into the Mathematical Principles of the Theory of Wealth* (London: Macmillan, 1897[1838]).

Cowen, M. P. and Shenton, R. W., *Doctrines of Development* (London: Routledge, 1996).

Cowie, J. and Heathcott, J. (eds), *Beyond the Ruins: The Meanings of Deindustrialization* (Ithaca: ILR Press Books, 2003).

Cox, R. W., *Production, Power, and World Order: Social Forces in the Making of History* (New York: Columbia University Press, 1987).

Cox, T. H., 'The Multicultural Organization', *Academy of Management Executive*, 5 (1991), 2, 34–47.

Cox, T. H. and Blake, S., 'Managing Cultural Diversity: Implications for Organizational Competitiveness', *Academy of Management Executive*, 5 (1991), 3, 45–56.

Coyle, D., *GDP: A Brief But Affectionate History* (Princeton: Princeton University Press, 2014).

Craven, P. and Wellman, B., 'The Network City', *Sociological Inquiry*, 43 (1973), 3–4, 57–88.

Crompton, R., *Class and Stratification* (Cambridge: Polity Press, 2008).

Crossick, G. and Jaumain, S. (eds), *Cathedrals of Consumption: The European Department Store, 1850–1939* (Farnham: Ashgate, 1999).

Crouch, C., *The Strange Non-Death of Neoliberalism* (Cambridge: Polity Press, 2011).

Crow, G. and Maclean, C., 'Community', in Payne, G. (ed.), *Social Divisions* (Basingstoke: Palgrave Macmillan, 2006).

Cunningham, S. and Potts, J., 'Creative Industries and the Wider Economy', in Jones, C., Lorenzen, M., and Sapsed, J. (eds), *The Oxford Handbook of Creative Industries* (Oxford: Oxford University Press, 2015).

Dale, G., *Karl Polanyi: The Limits of the Market* (Cambridge: Polity, 2010).

D'Alisa, G., Demaria, F. and Kallis, G. (eds), *Degrowth: A Vocabulary for a New Era* (Abingdon: Routledge, 2015).

Dahl, R., *Who Governs? Democracy and Power in the American City* (New Haven: Yale University Press, 1961).

Daly, H., *Steady-State Economics: The Economics of Biophysical Equilibrium and Moral Growth* (San Francisco: W.H. Freeman, 1977).

Daniels, A. C. and Daniels, J. E., *Performance Management: Changing Behavior that Drives Organizational Effectiveness* (Atlanta, GA: Peformance Management Publications, 2004).

Dardot, P. and Laval, C., *The New Way of the World: On Neoliberal Society* (London: Verso, 2013).

Darwin, C., *On the Origin of Species* (Oxford: Oxford University Press, 2008[1859]).

Davidson, N., *How Revolutionary Were the Bourgeois Revolutions?* (Chicago, IL: Haymarket Books, 2012).

Davies, G., 'Tony Blair Puts Meat on the Stakeholder Bones', *The Independent*, January 15, 1996.

Davies, H., 'Two Cheers for Financial Stability', *The Ninth William Taylor Memorial Lecture* (Washington D.C.: Group of Thirty, 2006).

Davies, J., *Challenging Governance Theory: From Networks to Hegemony* (Bristol: The Policy Press, 2011).

Davies, W., *The Happiness Industry: How the Government and Big Business Sold Us Well-Being* (London: Verso, 2015).

Davies, W., *The Limits of Neoliberalism: Authority, Sovereignty and the Logic of Competition* (London: Sage, 2014).

Davis, J. B., *The Theory of the Individual in Economics* (London: Routledge, 2003).

Davis, M., 'Sand, Fear, and Money in Dubai', in Davis, M. and Monk, D. B. (eds), *Evil Paradises: Dreamworlds of Neoliberalism* (New York: The New Press, 2007).

Davis, N., 'The Proximate Etymology of "Market"', *Modern Language Review*, 47 (1952), 2, 152–5.

Davis, S., 'From Future Perfect: Mass Customizing', *Planning Review*, 17 (1989), 2, 16–21.

De Brabandere, L. and Iny, A., *Thinking in New Boxes: A New Paradigm for Business Creativity* (New York: Random House, 2013).

De Magalhães, C., 'Public Space and the Contracting-out of Publicness: A Framework for Analysis', *Journal of Urban Design*, 15 (2010), 4, 559–74.

Dean, M., *Governmentality: Power and Rule in Modern Society* (London: Sage, 2010).

Deem, R. and Ozga, J., 'Women Managing Diversity in a Postmodern World', in Marshall, C. (ed.), *Feminist Critical Policy Analysis II: A Perspective from Post-Secondary Education* (London: The Falmer Press, 1997).

DeHaven, T., 'Corporate Welfare in the Federal Budget', *Policy Analysis*, 703, July 25, 2012 (Washington D.C.: Cato Institute, 2012).

Delanty, D., *Community* (Abingdon: Routledge, 2010).

Deleuze, G. and Guattari, F., *A Thousand Plateaus: Capitalism and Schizophrenia* (Minneapolis: University of Minnesota Press, 1987).

Deloitte, *Only Skin Deep? Re-examining the Business Case for Diversity*, September 2011. Available at: https://www.ced.org/pdf/Deloitte_-_Only_Skin_Deep.pdf

Demaria, F., Schneider, F., Sekulova, F. and Martinez-Alier, J., 'What is Degrowth? From an Activist Slogan to a Social Movement', *Environmental Values*, 22 (2013), 2, 191–215.

Dempsey, S. E. and Sanders, M. L., 'Meaningful Work? Nonprofit Marketization and Work/Life Imbalance in Popular Autobiographies of Social Entrepreneurship', *Organization*, 17 (2010), 4, 437–59.

DeNavas-Walt, C. and Proctor, B. D., *Current Population Reports, P60–249, Income and Poverty in the United States: 2013*, US Census Bureau (Washington D.C.: US Government Printing Office, 2014).

Department for Business, Innovation and Skills (BIS), 'The Business Case for Equality and Diversity: A Survey of the Academic Literature', *BIS Occasional Paper No. 4*, January 2013.

Department for Culture, Media and Sport (DCMS), Creative Industries Mapping Document 2001 (London: Department of Culture, Media and Sport, 2001).

Dey, P. and Steyaert, C., 'Social Entrepreneurship: Critique and the Radical Enactment of the Social', *Social Enterprise Journal*, 8 (2012), 2, 90–107.

Dezalay, Y. and Garth, B. G. (eds), *Global Prescriptions: The Production, Exportation, and Importation of a New Orthodoxy* (Ann Arbor, MI: University of Michigan Press, 2002a).

Dezalay, Y. and Garth, B. G., *The Internationalization of Palace Wars: Lawyers, Economists, and the Contest to Transform Latin American States* (Chicago: University of Chicago Press, 2002b).

Dickens, C., *Hard Times* (London: Penguin Books, 2003[1854]).

Dickson, B. J., *Wealth into Power: The Communist Party's Embrace of China's Private Sector* (Cambridge: Cambridge University Press, 2008).

Dilley, R., 'Contesting Markets: A General Introduction to Market Ideology, Imagery and Discourse', in Dilley, R. (ed.), *Contesting Markets: Analyses of Ideology, Discourse and Practice* (Edinburgh: Edinburgh University Press, 1992).

Dixon, A. D., *The New Geography of Capitalism: Firms, Finance, and Society* (Oxford: Oxford University Press, 2014).

Dollar, D. and Kraay, A., 'Growth is Good for the Poor', *Journal of Economic Growth*, 7 (2002), 3, 195–225.

Dollar, D. and Kraay, A., 'Trade, Growth, and Poverty', *The Economic Journal*, 114 (2004), 493, F22–F49.

Dollar, D., Kleineberg, T. and Kraay, A., 'Growth Still Is Good for the Poor', World Bank Policy Research Working Paper 6568 (Washington D.C.: World Bank, August 2013).

Dos Santos, T., 'The Structure of Dependence', *The American Economic Review*, 60 (1970), 2, 231–6.

Douglas, M. and Wildavsky, A., *Risk and Culture: An Essay on the Selection of Technological and Environmental Dangers* (Berkeley: University of California Press, 1983).

Dowding, K. M. and Kimber, R., 'The Meaning and Use of "Political Stability"', *European Journal of Political Research*, 11 (1983), 3, 229–43.

Drake, W. and Nicolaïdis, K., 'Ideas, Interests, and Institutionalization: "Trade in Services" and the Uruguay Round', *International Organization*, 46 (1992), 1, 37–100.

Drucker, P., *The Practice of Management: A Study of the Most Important Function in American Society* (New York: Harper & Brothers, 1954).

Drucker, P., *Innovation and Entrepreneurship* (Oxford: Elsevier, 1985).

Drucker, P., *Management Challenges for the 21st Century* (New York: HarperCollins, 1999).

Drucker, P., *The Essential Drucker* (Oxford : Elsevier, 2007).

Drucker, P., *The Practice of Management* (Abingdon: Routledge, 2011[1954]).

Drucker, P., *Innovation and Entrepreneurship* (Abingdon: Routledge, 2011[1985]).

Drucker, P., *Managing in a Time of Great Change* (Abingdon: Routledge, 2011[1995]).

Dryzek, J. S. and Niemeyer, S., 'Reconciling Pluralism and Consensus as Political Ideals', *American Journal of Political Science*, 50 (2006), 3, 634–49.

Dryzek, J. S., *The Politics of the Earth: Environmental Discourses* (Oxford: Oxford University Press, 2012).

du Gay, P., 'The Tyranny of the Epochal: Change, Epochalism and Organizational Reform', *Organization*, 10 (2003), 4, 663–84.

du Gay, P. and Morgan, G. (eds), *New Spirits of Capitalism?: Crises, Justifications, and Dynamics* (Oxford: Oxford University Press, 2013).

Duhigg, C. and Bradsher, K., 'How the U.S. Lost Out on iPhone Work', *New York Times*, January 21, 2012.

Dulewicz, V. and Higgs, M. J., 'Assessing Leadership Styles and Organizational Context', *Journal of Managerial Psychology*, 20 (2005), 2, 105–23.

Duménil, G. and Lévy, D., *The Crisis of Neoliberalism* (Cambridge, MA: Harvard University Press, 2011).

Durant, A., 'Raymond Williams's *Keywords*: Investigating Meanings "Offered, Felt For, Tested, Confirmed, Asserted, Qualified, Changed"', *Critical Quarterly*, 48 (2006), 4, 1–26.

Durkheim, É., 'Individualism and the Intellectuals' [1898], in Bellah, R. N. (ed.), *Émile Durkheim on Morality and Society* (translated by Bellah, R. N.) (Chicago: The University of Chicago Press, 1973).

Durlauf, S. N. and Blume, L. E. (eds), *The New Palgrave Dictionary of Economics* (Basingstoke: Palgrave Macmillan, 2008).

Eagleton-Pierce, M., 'The Internet and the Seattle WTO Protests', *Peace Review*, 13 (2001), 3, 331–7.

Eagleton-Pierce, M., *Symbolic Power in the World Trade Organization* (Oxford: Oxford University Press, 2013).

Eagleton-Pierce, M., 'The Concept of Governance in the Spirit of Capitalism', *Critical Policy Studies*, 8 (2014), 1, 5–21.

Easterly, W., *The Elusive Quest for Growth: Economists' Adventures and Misadventures in the Tropics* (Cambridge, MA: MIT Press, 2001).

Easterly, W., 'What Did Structural Adjustment Adjust? The Association of Policies and Growth With Repeated IMF and World Bank Adjustment Loans', *Journal of Development Economics*, 76 (2005), 1, 1–22.

Edgeworth, F. Y., *Mathematical Psychics* (London: E. Kegan Paul, 1881).

Eichengreen, B., *Capital Flows and Crises* (Cambridge, MA: MIT Press, 2004).

Eichengreen, B., *Globalizing Capital: A History of the International Monetary System* (Princeton: Princeton University Press, 2008).

El-Erian, M., 'How to Handle the Sovereign Debt Explosion', *Financial Times*, March 10, 2010.

Eliot, G., *Middlemarch* (London: Penguin Books, 2003[1871]).

Elklit, J. and Svensson, P., 'What Makes Elections Free and Fair?', *Journal of Democracy*, 8 (1997), 3, 32–46.

Elliott, J., 'How We Launched Thatcher's "Privatisation" Word in the *FT* in 1979', *The Independent*, April 11, 2013.

Elms, D. K. and Low, P. (eds), *Global Value Chains in a Changing World* (Geneva: World Trade Organization, 2013).

Emery, L., 'Occupy London Heads to Canary Wharf', *The Wharf*, December 13, 2011.

Engelen, E., Ertürk, I., Froud, J., Johal, S., Leaver, A., Moran, M. and Williams, K., 'Misrule of Experts? The Financial Crisis as Elite Debacle', *Economy and Society*, 41 (2012), 3, 360–82.

Engelen, E., Ertürk, I., Froud, J., Leaver, A. and Williams, K., 'Reconceptualizing Financial Innovation: Frame, Conjuncture and Bricolage', *Economy and Society*, 39 (2010), 1, 33–63.

Erickson, J., *The Middle-Class Squeeze: A Picture of Stagnant Incomes, Rising Costs, and What We Can Do to Strengthen America's Middle Class* (Washington D.C.: Center for American Progress, 2014).

Eriksen, T. H., Laidlaw, J., Mair, J., Martin, K., and Venkatesan, S., 'The Concept of Neoliberalism Has Become an Obstacle to the Anthropological Understanding of the Twenty-first Century', *Journal of the Royal Anthropological Institute*, 21 (2015), 4, 911–23.

Erlanger, S., 'Sarkozy Stresses Global Financial Overhaul', *New York Times*, September 25, 2008.

Errunza, V. R. and Padmanabhan, P., 'Further Evidence on the Benefits of Portfolio Investments in Emerging Markets', *Financial Analysts Journal*, 44 (1988), 4, 76–8.

Errunza, V. R., 'Emerging Markets: A New Opportunity for Improving Global Portfolio Performance', *Financial Analysts Journal*, 39 (1983), 5, 51–8.

Escobar, A., *Encountering Development: The Making and Unmaking of the Third World* (Princeton: Princeton University Press, 1995).

Esping-Andersen, G., *The Three Worlds of Welfare Capitalism* (Princeton: Princeton University Press, 1990).

Esteva, G., 'Development', in Sachs, W. (ed.), *The Development Dictionary: A Guide to Knowledge as Power* (London: Zed Books, 1992).

Evans, G. (ed.), *The End of Class Politics?: Class Voting in Comparative Context* (Oxford: Oxford University Press, 1999).

Evans, P., Rueschemeyer, D. and Huber Stephens, E. (eds), *States Versus Markets in the World System* (London: Sage, 1985).

Ewald, F., 'Insurance and Risk', in Burchell, G., Gordon, C. and Miller, P. (eds), *The Foucault Effect: Studies in Governmentality* (Chicago: Chicago University Press, 1991).

Executive Office of the President, National Performance Review, *From Red Tape to Results: Creating a Government That Works Better and Costs Less* (Washington D.C.: US Government Printing Office, 1993).

Fagerberg, J., 'Innovation: A Guide to the Literature', in Fagerberg, J. and Mowery, D. C. (eds), *The Oxford Handbook of Innovation* (Oxford: Oxford University Press, 2006).

Fagerberg, J. and Verspagen, B., `Innovation Studies – The Emerging Structure of a New Scientific Field', *Research Policy*, 38 (2009), 2, 218–33.

Faiola, A., 'The End Of American Capitalism?', *Washington Post*, October 10, 2008.

Fairclough, N. L., *New Labour, New Language?* (London: Routledge, 2000).

Fairclough, N. L., 'Blair's Contribution to Elaborating a New Doctrine of "International Community"', *Journal of Language and Politics*, 4 (2005), 1, 41–63.

Fairclough, N. L., *Language and Globalization* (Abingdon: Routledge, 2006).

Fairtrade International, *Annual Report 2012–13: Unlocking the Power* (Bonn: Fairtrade International, 2013).

Falkner, R., *Business Power and Conflict in International Environmental Politics* (Basingstoke: Palgrave Macmillan, 2007).

Fanon, F., *The Wretched of the Earth* (London: Penguin, 2001[1961]).

Farah, N., *Egypt's Political Economy: Power Relations in Development* (Cairo: The American University in Cairo Press, 2009).

Farnsworth, C. H., 'Agency Proposes Fund of Stocks in 3d World', *New York Times*, December 20, 1985.

Farnsworth, K., *Social Versus Corporate Welfare: Competing Needs and Interests within the Welfare State* (Basingstoke: Palgrave Macmillan, 2012).

Fayol, H., *General and Industrial Management* (translated by C. Storrs) (London: Pitman, 1949[1916]).

Fellenz, M., 'Flexibility in Management Theory: Towards Clarification of an Elusive Concept', *Journal of Strategic Management Education*, 4 (2008), 1, 65–89.

Ferguson, C., *Inside Job: The Financiers Who Pulled Off the Heist of the Century* (London: Oneworld Publications, 2014).

Ferguson, J., 'Anthropology and its Evil Twin: "Development" in the Constitution of a Discipline', in Cooper, F. and Packard, R. (eds), *International Development and the Social Sciences* (Berkeley: University of California Press, 1997).

Ferguson, J. and Gupta, A., 'Spatializing States: Toward an Ethnography of Neoliberal Governmentality', *American Ethnologist*, 29 (2002), 4, 981–1002.

Fernandez, J. P. with Barr, M., *The Diversity Advantage* (New York: Lexington Books, 1993).

Ferrara, P. J., 'The Rationale for Enterprise Zones', *Cato Journal*, 2 (1982), 2, 361–71.

Financial Crisis Inquiry Commission, *The Financial Crisis Inquiry Report*, National Commission on the Causes of the Financial and Economic Crisis in the United States (Washington D.C.: US Government Printing Office, 2011).

Fine, B., *The World of Consumption: The Material and Cultural Revisited* (London: Routledge, 2002).

Fine, B., *Theories of Social Capital: Researchers Behaving Badly* (London: Pluto Press, 2010).

Fine, B. and Jomo, K. S. (eds), *The New Development Economics: After the Washington Consensus* (London: Zed Books, 2006).

Fine, B. and Saad-Filho, A., *Marx's 'Capital'* (London: Pluto Press, 2010).

Flaubert, G., *Dictionary of Accepted Ideas* (translated by Barzun, J.) (New York: New Directions, 1968).

Flew, T., *The Creative Industries: Culture and Policy* (London: Sage, 2012).

Fogel, R. W., Fogel, E. M., Guglielmo, M. and Grotte, N., *Political Arithmetic: Simon Kuznets and the Empirical Tradition in Economics* (Chicago: University of Chicago Press, 2013).

Follesdal, A. and Hix, S., 'Why There is a Democratic Deficit in the EU: A Response to Majone and Moravcsik', *Journal of Common Market Studies*, 44 (2006), 3, 533–62.

Forman, V., 'Transformations of Value and the Production of "Investment" in the Early History of the East India Company', *Journal of Medieval and Early Modern Studies*, 34 (2004), 3, 611–41.

Fornell, C., Mithas, S., Morgeson III, F. V., Krishnan, M. S., 'Customer Satisfaction and Stock Prices: High Returns, Low Risk', *Journal of Marketing*, 70 (2006), 1, 3–14.

Fortune, 'Global 500' (2014). Available at: http://fortune.com/global500/.

Foster, J. B., 'The Financialization of Capitalism', *Monthly Review*, 58 (2007), 11, 1–12.

Foucault, M., *Power/Knowledge: Selected Interviews and Other Writings 1972–1977* (London: Harvester Press, 1980).

Foucault, M., *The Birth of Biopolitics: Lectures at the Collège de France, 1978–1979* (Houndmills: Palgrave Macmillan, 2008).

Fougner, T., 'The State, International Competitiveness and Neoliberal Globalisation: Is There a Future Beyond "the Competition State"?', *Review of International Studies*, 32 (2006), 1, 165–85.

Fougner, T., 'Neoliberal Governance of States: The Role of Competitiveness Indexing and Country Benchmarking', *Millennium: Journal of International Studies*, 37 (2008), 2, 303–26.

Frank, A. G., *The Development of Underdevelopment* (New York: Monthly Review Press, 1966).

Frank, A. G., *Capitalism and Underdevelopment in Latin America* (New York: Monthly Review Press, 1967).

Frank, T., *One Market Under God: Extreme Capitalism, Market Populism, and the End of Economic Democracy* (New York: Anchor Books, 2001).

Fraser, N., *The Fortunes of Feminism: From Women's Liberation to Identity Politics to Anti-Capitalism* (London: Verso, 2013).

Fraser, N. and Gordon, L., '"Dependency" Demystified: Inscriptions of Power in a Keyword of the Welfare State', *Social Politics*, 1 (1994), 1, 4–31.

Freeden, M., *The Political Theory of Political Thinking: The Anatomy of a Practice* (Oxford: Oxford University Press, 2013).

Freedman, L., *Strategy: A History* (Oxford: Oxford University Press, 2013).

Freedom House, *Freedom in the World 2014* (Washington D.C.: Freedom House, 2014).

Freeland, C., *Plutocrats: The Rise of the New Global Super-Rich and the Fall of Everyone Else* (London: Penguin Books, 2012).

Freeman, R. E., *Strategic Management: A Stakeholder Approach* (Boston: Pitman, 1984).

French, W. L. and Bell, C. H., *Organization Development: Behavioral Science Interventions for Organizational Improvement* (Englewood Cliffs, NJ: Prentice-Hall, 1972).

Friedman, A. L. and Miles, S., *Stakeholders: Theory and Practice* (Oxford: Oxford University Press, 2006).

Friedman, M., *Capitalism and Freedom* (Chicago: University of Chicago Press, 2002[1962]).

Friedman, M. and Friedman, R., *Free to Choose: A Personal Statement* (Orlando, FL: Harcourt, 1979).

Friedman, T. L., *The Lexus and the Olive Tree* (New York: Anchor Books, 1999).

Friman, E., *No Limits: The 20th Century Discourse of Economic Growth*, PhD thesis, Department of Historical Studies, Umeå University, Sweden, submitted 2002.

Froud, J., Johal, S., Leaver, A. and Williams, K., *Financialization and Strategy: Narrative and Numbers* (Abingdon: Routledge, 2006).

Fuchs, D., *Business Power in Global Governance* (Boulder, CO: Lynne Rienner, 2007).

Fukuyama, F., *The End of History and the Last Man* (New York: Free Press, 1992).

Gaddis, P. O., 'The Project Manager', *Harvard Business Review*, 39 (1959), 3, 89–97.

Gaillard, N., 'How and Why Credit Rating Agencies Missed the Eurozone Debt Crisis', *Capital Markets Law Journal*, 9 (2014), 2, 121–36.

Galbraith, J. K., *The New Industrial State* (Princeton: Princeton University Press, 1972).

Galbraith, J. K., *The Economics of Innocent Fraud: Truth For Our Time* (Boston, MA: Houghton Mifflin Harcourt, 2004).

Gall, G., Wilkinson, A. and Hurd, R. (eds), *The International Handbook of Labour Unions: Responses to Neo-liberalism* (Cheltenham: Edward Elgar, 2011).

Gamble, A., *The Free Economy and the Strong State: The Politics of Thatcherism* (Houndmills: Palgrave, 1994).

Gamble, A. and Kelly, G., 'The Politics of the Company', in Parkinson, J. E., Gamble, A. and Kelly, G. (eds), *The Political Economy of the Company* (Oxford: Hart Publishing, 2000).

Gane, N., 'The Governmentalities of Neoliberalism: Panopticism, Post-panopticism and Beyond', *The Sociological Review*, 60 (2012), 4, 611–34.

Gans-Morse, J., 'Searching for Transitologists: Contemporary Theories of Post-Communist Transitions and the Myth of a Dominant Paradigm', *Post-Soviet Affairs*, 20 (2004), 4, 320–49.

Gantt, H. L., *Organizing for Work* (New York: Harcourt, Brace and Howe, 1919).

García-Herrero, A. and del Río, P., 'Central Banks as Monetary Authorities and Financial Stability', in Masciandaro, D. (ed.), *Handbook of Central Banking and Financial Authorities in Europe: New Architectures in the Supervision of Financial Markets* (Cheltenham: Edward Elgar, 2005).

Garnham, N., 'From Cultural to Creative Industries', *International Journal of Cultural Policy*, 11 (2005), 1, 15–29.

Gathii, J. T., 'Retelling Good Governance Narratives on Africa's Economic and Political Predicaments: Continuities and Discontinuities in Legal Outcomes Between Markets and States', *Villanova Law Review*, 45 (2000), 971–1035.

GATT, 'Marrakesh Agreement Establishing the World Trade Organization' (1994). Available at: http://www.wto.org/english/docs_e/legal_e/04-wto_e.htm.

Gerber, D. J., 'Competition', in Tushnet, M. and Cane, P. (eds), *The Oxford Handbook of Legal Studies* (Oxford: Oxford University Press, 2005).

Gerber, D. J., *Global Competition: Law, Markets, and Globalization* (Oxford: Oxford University Press, 2010).

Gershon, D. and Straub, G., *Empowerment: The Art of Creating Your Life as You Want It* (New York: Sterling Ethos, 2011).

Gerstner, L. V., *Who Says Elephants Can't Dance?: Leading a Great Enterprise through Dramatic Change* (New York: Harper Collins, 2002).

Getting By Project, *Getting By? A Year in the Life of 30 Working Families in Liverpool* (2015). Available at: http://gettingby.org.uk/.

Ghosh, B. N., *Dependency Theory Revisited* (Farnham: Ashgate, 2001).

Giannone, D., 'Political and Ideological Aspects in the Measurement of Democracy: The Freedom House Case', *Democratization*, 17 (2010), 1, 68–97.

Giddens, A., *Runaway World* (London: Profile Books, 1999a).

Giddens, A., 'Risk and Responsibility', *Modern Law Review*, 62 (1999b), 1, 1–10.

Giddens, A., *The Third Way and Its Critics* (Cambridge: Polity Press, 2000).

Gilbert, D., *The American Class Structure in an Age of Growing Inequality* (London: Sage, 2014).

Gill, S., *American Hegemony and the Trilateral Commission* (Cambridge: Cambridge University Press, 1991).

Gill, S., 'Globalisation, Market Civilisation, and Disciplinary Neoliberalism', *Millennium: Journal of International Studies*, 24 (1995), 3, 399–423.

Gill, S., 'New Constitutionalism, Democratisation and Global Political Economy', *Pacifica Review: Peace, Security & Global Change*, 10 (1998), 1, 23–38.

Glasberg, D. and Skidmore, D., *Corporate Welfare Policy and the Welfare State: Bank Deregulation and the Savings and Loan Bailout* (New York: Aldine Transaction, 1997).

Glennerster, H., 'The Sustainability of Western Welfare States', in Castles, F. G., Leibfried, S., Lewis, J., Obinger, H. and Pierson, C. (eds), *The Oxford Handbook of the Welfare State* (Oxford: Oxford University Press, 2010).

Goldberg, V. P., 'Relational Exchange: Economics and Complex Contracts', *American Behavioral Scientist*, 23 (1980), 3, 337–52.

Goldstein, D. M., 'Decolonialising "Actually Existing Neoliberalism"', *Social Anthropology*, 20 (2012), 3, 304–9.

Goodman, M. K., 'Reading Fair Trade: Political Ecological Imaginary and the Moral Economy of Fair Trade Foods', *Political Geography*, 23 (2004), 7, 891–915.

Goodwin-Gill, G. S., *Free and Fair Elections* (Geneva: Inter-Parliamentary Union, 2006).

Google, www.google.co.uk/about/careers/lifeatgoogle/creating-an-office-for-work-and-play.html (n.d.).

Gooptu, N., 'Introduction', in Gooptu, N. (ed.), *Enterprise Culture in Neoliberal India: Studies in Youth, Class, Work and Media* (Abingdon: Routledge, 2013).

Gordon, A., 'The Work of Corporate Culture: Diversity Management', *Social Text*, 44 (1995), 3, 3–30.

Gourville, J. T. and Soman, D., 'Overchoice and Assortment Type: When and Why Variety Backfires', *Marketing Science*, 24 (2005), 3, 382–95.

Grabher, G., 'Cool Projects, Boring Institutions: Temporary Collaboration in Social Context', *Regional Studies*, 36 (2002), 3, 205–14.

Graeber, D., *Debt: The First 5000 Years* (New York: Melville House Publishing, 2011).

Gramsci, A., *Selections from the Prison Notebooks* (London: Lawrence and Wishart, 1971).

Granovetter, M., 'The Strength of Weak Ties', *American Journal of Sociology*, 78 (1973), 6, 1360–80.

Granovetter, M., 'Economic Action and Social Structure: The Problem of Embeddedness', *American Journal of Sociology*, 91 (1985), 3, 481–510.

Gray, J., *Liberalism* (Minneapolis: University of Minnesota Press, 1995).

Greenpeace, *Carbon Scam: Noel Kempff Climate Action Project and the Push for Sub-national Forest Offsets* (Amsterdam: Greenpeace International, 2009).

Greenspan, A., 'Consumer Finance', Remarks at Federal Reserve System's Fourth Annual Community Affairs Research Conference, Washington D.C., April 8, 2005. Available at: http://www.federalreserve.gov/BOARDDOCS/Speeches/2005/20050408/default.htm.

Gregory, C. A., *Gifts and Commodities* (London: Academic Press, 1982).

Greve, C., 'Public-Private Partnerships in Business and Government', in Coen, D., Grant, W. and Wilson, G. (eds), *The Oxford Handbook of Business and Government* (Oxford: Oxford University Press, 2010).

Grey, T. C., 'The Disintegration of Property', *Nomos*, 22 (1980), 69–85.

Grind, K., *The Lost Bank: The Story of Washington Mutual – The Biggest Bank Failure in American History* (New York: Simon & Schuster, 2012).

Guerrera, F. and Pimlott, D., 'Pandit and King Clash over Basel III', *Financial Times*, October 25, 2010.

Gumbrell-McCormick, R. and Hyman, R., *Trade Unions in Western Europe: Hard Times, Hard Choices* (Oxford: Oxford University Press, 2013).

Gungwu, W., 'To Reform a Revolution: Under the Righteous Mandate', *Daedalus*, 122 (1993), 2, 71–94.

Haass, R. N., 'The Bush Administration's Response to Globalization', Remarks to the National Defense University, Washington D.C., September 21, 2001. Available at: http://2001–2009.state.gov/s/p/rem/5508.htm.

Habermas, J., *Between Facts and Norms: Contributions to a Discourse Theory of Law and Democracy* (Cambridge, MA: MIT Press, 1996).

Hale, S., *Blair's Community: Communitarian Thought and New Labour* (Manchester: Manchester University Press, 2006).

Hall, P. A. and Soskice, D. (eds), *Varieties of Capitalism: The Institutional Foundations of Comparative Advantage* (Oxford: Oxford University Press, 2001).

Hall, R. B., *Central Banking as Global Governance: Constructing Financial Credibility* (Cambridge: Cambridge University Press, 2008).

Hall, S., *The Hard Road to Renewal: Thatcherism and the Crisis of the Left* (London: Verso, 1988).

Hall, S. and O'Shea, A., 'Common-sense Neoliberalism', *Soundings: A Journal of Politics and Culture*, 55 (2013), 8–24.

Hall, S., Critcher, C., Jefferson, T., Clarke, J. N., Roberts, B., *Policing the Crisis: Mugging, the State and Law and Order* (London: Macmillan, 1978).

Hamilton, C., *Growth Fetish* (London: Pluto Press, 2003).

Hanawalt, B. A., '"Good Governance" in the Medieval and Early Modern Context', *The Journal of British Studies*, 37 (1998), 3, 246–57.

Hancké, B. (ed.), *Debating Varieties of Capitalism: A Reader* (Oxford: Oxford University Press, 2009).

Hancock, A-M., *The Politics of Disgust: The Public Identity of the Welfare Queen* (New York: New York University Press, 2004).

Haq, M. U., *Reflections on Human Development* (Oxford: Oxford University Press, 1995).

Hargadon, A., *How Breakthroughs Happen: The Surprising Truth about How Companies Innovate* (Boston: Harvard Business School Publishing, 2003).

Harmes, A., 'The Rise of Neoliberal Nationalism', *Review of International Political Economy*, 19 (2012), 1, 59–86.

Harris, R., 'Conservatism: Ralph Harris Record of Conversation (Visit from Keith Joseph)', March 14, 1974 (IEA Archive, Box 295).

Harrison, G., *The World Bank and Africa: The Construction of Governance States* (London: Routledge, 2004).

Harrison, G., *Neoliberal Africa: The Impact of Global Social Engineering* (London: Zed Books, 2010).

Harvard Business Review, HBR Guide to Networking (Boston, MA: Harvard Business Press Books, 2012).

Harvard Business Review, HBR's 10 Must Reads on Change (Boston, MA: Harvard Business School Press, 2011).

Harvey, D., *The Condition of Postmodernity: An Enquiry into the Origins of Cultural Change* (Oxford: Blackwell Publishing, 1990).

Harvey, D., *A Brief History of Neoliberalism* (Oxford: Oxford University Press, 2005).

Harvey, D., *The Limits to Capital* (London: Verso, 2006[1982]).

Harvey, D., *A Companion to Marx's Capital* (London: Verso, 2010).

Haslam, J., *The Nixon Administration and the Death of Allende's Chile: A Case of Assisted Suicide* (London: Verso, 2005).

Hatton, E., *The Temp Economy: From Kelly Girls to Permatemps in Postwar America* (Philadelphia: Temple University Press, 2011).

Hausman, D. M. and McPherson, M. S., 'The Philosophical Foundations of Mainstream Normative Economics', in Hausman, D. M. (ed.), *The Philosophy of Economics: An Anthology* (Cambridge: Cambridge University Press, 2008).

Hayek, F. A. von, *Individualism and Economic Order* (Chicago: University of Chicago Press, 1948).

Hayek, F. A. von, *The Constitution of Liberty* (Chicago: University of Chicago Press, 1960).

Hayek, F. A. von, 'Competition as a Discovery Procedure', *Quarterly Journal of Austrian Economics*, 5 (2002), 3, 9–23.

Hayek, F. A. von, *The Road to Serfdom* (Abingdon: Routledge, 2008[1944]).

Hayek, F. A. von, *Law, Legislation and Liberty: A New Statement of the Liberal Principles of Justice and Political Economy* (Abingdon: Routledge, 2013[1973]).

Heckscher, E., *Mercantilism* (London: Allen & Unwin, 1934).

Heffernan, R., '"The Possible as the Art of Politics": Understanding Consensus Politics', *Political Studies*, 50 (2002), 4, 742–60.

Hegel, G. W. F., *Outlines of the Philosophy of Right* (Oxford: Oxford University Press, 2008[1821]).

Heilbroner, R. L., 'Capitalism', in Durlauf, S. N. and Blume, L. E. (eds), *The New Palgrave Dictionary of Economics* (Basingstoke: Palgrave Macmillan, 2008).

Held, D. and McGrew, A. (eds), *The Global Transformations Reader* (Cambridge: Polity Press, 2000a).

Held, D. and McGrew, A., 'The Great Globalization Debate: An Introduction', in Held, D. and McGrew, A. (eds), *The Global Transformations Reader* (Cambridge: Polity Press, 2000b).

Held, D. and McGrew, A., *Globalization / Anti-Globalization* (Cambridge: Polity Press, 2007).

Held, D., McGrew, A., Goldblatt, D. and Perraton, J., *Global Transformations: Politics, Economics, Culture* (Cambridge: Polity Press, 1999).

Helleiner, E., *States and the Reemergence of Global Finance: From Bretton Woods to the 1990s* (Ithaca: Cornell University Press, 1994).

Helleiner, E., 'Economic Nationalism as a Challenge to Economic Liberalism? Lessons from the 19th Century', *International Studies Quarterly*, 46 (2002), 3, 307–29.

Helleiner, E., *The Status Quo Crisis: Global Financial Governance After the 2008 Meltdown* (Oxford: Oxford University Press, 2014).

Heller, M. A., 'Property', in Tushnet, M. and Cane, P. (eds), *The Oxford Handbook of Legal Studies* (Oxford: Oxford University Press, 2005).

Hennock, E. P., *The Origin of the Welfare State in England and Germany, 1850–1914: Social Policies Compared* (Cambridge: Cambridge University Press, 2007).

Hermann, C. and Flecker, J. (eds), *Privatization of Public Services: Impacts for Employment, Working Conditions, and Service Quality in Europe* (Abingdon: Routledge, 2012).

Herring, C., 'Does Diversity Pay?: Race, Gender, and the Business Case for Diversity', *American Sociological Review*, 74 (2009), 2, 208–24.

Herzstein, R. E. and Esty, D. C., 'Competitiveness – Not Just a Buzzword', *New York Times*, January 21, 1987.

Hewlett, S. A. and Luce, C. B., 'Extreme Jobs: The Dangerous Allure of the 70-Hour Workweek', *Harvard Business Review*, December 2006, 49–59.

Hewlett, S. A. and Rashid, R., *Winning the War for Talent in Emerging Markets: Why Women Are the Solution* (Boston, MA: Harvard Business Press, 2013).

Heynen, N., McCarthy, J., Prudham, S. and Robbins, P. (eds), *Neoliberal Environments: False Promises and Unnatural Consequences* (Abingdon: Routledge, 2007).

Hickey, S. and Mohan, G. (eds), *Participation: From Tyranny to Transformation* (London: Zed Books, 2004).

Hicks, J., *Value and Capital: An Inquiry into Some Fundamental Principles of Economic Theory* (Oxford: Clarendon Press, 1939).

High, S. and Lewis, D. W., *Corporate Wasteland: The Landscape and Memory of Deindustrialization* (Ithaca: ILR Press Books, 2007).

Hilferding, R., *Finance Capital: A Study in the Latest Phase of Capitalist Development* (London: Routledge, 2007[1919]).

Himley, M., 'Geographies of Environmental Governance: The Nexus of Nature and Neoliberalism', *Geography Compass*, 2 (2008), 2, 433–51.

Hobsbawm, E., 'Socialism Has Failed. Now Capitalism is Bankrupt. So What Comes Next?', *The Guardian*, April 10, 2009.

Hobson, J. M. and Seabrooke, L. (eds), *Everyday Politics of the World Economy* (Cambridge: Cambridge University Press, 2007).

Hodgson, G. M., 'Markets', in Durlauf, S. N. and Blume, L. E. (eds), *The New Palgrave Dictionary of Economics* (Basingstoke: Palgrave Macmillan, 2008).

Hoggett, P. (ed.), *Contested Communities: Experiences, Struggles, Policies* (Bristol: Policy Press, 1997).

Holborow, M., *Language and Neoliberalism* (Abingdon: Routledge, 2015).

Holbrook, M. B. and Hirschman, E. C., 'The Experiential Aspects of Consumption: Consumer Fantasies, Feelings, and Fun', *The Journal of Consumer Research*, 9 (1982), 2, 132–40.

Holland, R. C., 'The New Era of Public-Private Partnerships', in Porter, P. R. and Sweet, D. C. (eds), *Rebuilding America's Cities: Roads to Recovery* (Piscataway, NJ: Rutgers University, 1984).

Holweg, M., 'The Genealogy of Lean Production', *Journal of Operations Management*, 25 (2007), 420–437.

Hood, C., 'Gaming in Targetworld: The Targets Approach to Managing British Public Services', *Public Administration Review*, 66 (2006), 4, 515–21.

Hood, C., 'Public Administration and Public Policy: Intellectual Challenges for the 1990s', *Australian Journal of Public Administration*, 48 (1989), 4, 346–58.

Hood, C., 'A Public Management for All Seasons?', *Public Administration*, 69 (1991), 1, 3–19.

Hood, C., 'Public Management: The Word, the Movement, the Science', in Ferlie, E., Lynn, Jr., L. E. and Pollitt, C. (eds), *The Oxford Handbook of Public Management* (Oxford: Oxford University Press, 2007).

Howe, A., *Free Trade and Liberal England, 1846–1946* (Oxford: Oxford University Press, 1997).

Huanxin, Z., 'Premier Puts the Accent on Reform', *China Daily*, March 6, 2014.

Huber, C. and Scheytt, T., 'The Dispositif of Risk Management: Reconstructing Risk Management after the Financial Crisis', *Management Accounting Research*, 24 (2013), 2, 88–99.

Hughes, J., '"Bric" Creator Adds Newcomers to List', *Financial Times*, January 16th, 2011.

Humphreys, S., *Theatre of the Rule of Law: Transnational Legal Intervention in Theory and Practice* (Cambridge: Cambridge University Press, 2010).

Huntington, S. P., *The Third Wave: Democratization in the Late Twentieth Century* (Norman, OK: University of Oklahoma Press, 1991).

Hurwitz, L., 'Contemporary Approaches to Political Stability', *Comparative Politics*, 5 (1973), 3, 449–63.

Husserl, E., *Experience and Judgment: Investigations in a Genealogy of Logic* (London: Routledge, 1973[1939]).

Hutton, W., 'Time to Sever the Thin Blue Line', *The Guardian*, October 31, 1994.

Hutton, W., *The State We're In: Why Britain is in Crisis and How to Overcome It* (London: Vintage, 1995).

Innes, J., '"Reform" in English Public Life: The Fortunes of a Word', in Burns, A. and Innes, J. (eds), *Rethinking the Age of Reform: Britain 1780–1850* (Cambridge: Cambridge University Press, 2003).

International Labour Organization (ILO), *World Employment and Social Outlook: Trends 2015* (Geneva: International Labour Organization, 2015).

International Monetary Fund (IMF), 'History; Debt and Painful Reforms (1982–89)'. Available at: http://www.imf.org/external/about/histdebt.htm.

International Monetary Fund (IMF), *World Economic Outlook: Crisis and Recovery, April 2009* (Washington D.C.: International Monetary Fund, 2009a).

International Monetary Fund (IMF), *Global Financial Stability Report: Navigating the Financial Challenges Ahead* (Washington D.C.: International Monetary Fund, 2009b).

International Monetary Fund (IMF), www.imf.org/external/about/histdebt.htm (n.d.).

International Union for Conservation of Nature (IUCN), *World Conservation Strategy: Living Resource Conservation for Sustainable Development* (Gland, Switzerland: International Union for Conservation of Nature and Natural Resources, United Nations Environment Program and World Wildlife Fund, 1980).

Irvine, M., 'Rewards and Risks for the Entrepreneur', *Financial Times*, November 27, 1974.

Irwin, D., *Against the Tide: An Intellectual History of Free Trade* (Princeton: Princeton University Press, 1996).

Irwin, D., *Free Trade Under Fire* (Princeton: Princeton University Press, 2009).

Isaacson, W., *Steve Jobs* (New York: Simon & Schuster, 2011).

Iyengar, S., *The Art of Choosing* (New York: Hachette Book Group, 2010).

Jackson, B., 'At the Origins of Neo-liberalism: The Free Economy and the Strong State, 1930–1947', *The Historical Journal*, 53 (2010), 1, 129–51.

Jackson, B. and Saunders, R. (eds), *Making Thatcher's Britain* (Cambridge: Cambridge University Press, 2012).

Jackson, B. B., *Winning and Keeping Industrial Customers: The Dynamics of Customer Relations* (Lexington, MA: D. C. Heath and Company, 1985).

Jacobs, M., 'Green Growth', in Falkner, R. (ed.), *The Handbook of Global Climate and Environment Policy* (Oxford: Wiley-Blackwell, 2013).

Jacoby, N. H., *Corporate Power and Social Responsibility: A Blueprint for the Future* (New York: Macmillan, 1973).

James, P. and Steger, M. B., 'A Genealogy of "Globalization": The Career of a Concept', *Globalizations*, 11 (2014), 4, 417–34.

Jänicke, M., '"Green Growth": From a Growing Eco-Industry to Economic Sustainability', *Energy Policy*, 48 (2012), 13–21.

Jawara, F. and Kwa, A., *Behind the Scenes at the WTO: The Real World of International Trade Negotiations / Lessons of Cancún* (London: Zed Books, 2004).

Jevons, W. S., *The Theory of Political Economy* (London: Macmillan and Co., 1871).

Jevons, W. S., *The State in Relation to Labour* (London: Macmillan and Co., 1882).

Johnson, C., *MITI and the Japanese Miracle* (Stanford: Stanford University Press, 1982).

Johnson, S., *A Dictionary of the English Language* (London: J. & P. Knapton, 1755).

Johnston, W. B. and Packer, A. E., *Workforce 2000: Work and Workers for the Twenty-First Century* (Indianapolis: Hudson Institute, 1987).

Jolly, R., Emmerij, L. and Weiss, T. G., *UN Ideas That Changed the World* (Bloomington, IN: Indiana University Press, 2009).

Jomo, K. S., 'A Critical Review of the Evolving Privatization Debate', in Roland, G. (ed.), *Privatization: Successes and Failures* (New York: Columbia University Press, 2008).

Jones, C. and Murtola, A-M., 'Entrepreneurship, Crisis, Critique', in Hjorth, D. (ed.), *Handbook on Organisational Entrepreneurship* (Cheltenham: Edward Elgar Publishing, 2011).

Jones, C. and Wagstyl, S., 'The Eurozone: A Strained Bond', *Financial Times*, January 18, 2015.

Jones, C. I. and Romer, P. M., 'The New Kaldor Facts: Ideas, Institutions, Population, and Human Capital', *American Economic Journal: Macroeconomics*, 2 (2010), 1, 224–45.

Jones, G., *Beauty Imagined: A History of the Global Beauty Industry* (Oxford: Oxford University Press, 2010).

Jones, O., *Chavs: The Demonization of the Working Class* (London: Verso, 2011).

Jones, S. D., *Masters of the Universe: Hayek, Friedman, and the Birth of Neoliberal Politics* (Princeton: Princeton University Press, 2012).

Joseph, J., 'Resilience as Embedded Neoliberalism: A Governmentality Approach', *Resilience: International Policies, Practices and Discourses*, 1 (2013), 1, 38–52.

Joseph, K., 'Conservatism: Sir Keith Joseph Draft Prospectus ("Centre for Policy Studies Limited")', June 7, 1974(a) (IEA Archive, Box 295).

Joseph, K., 'Speech at Upminster ("This is Not the Time to be Mealy-Mouthed: Intervention is Destroying Us")', June 22, 1974(b).

Joya, A., 'The Egyptian Revolution: The Crisis of Neoliberalism and the Potential for Democratic Politics', *Review of African Political Economy*, 38 (2011), 129, 367–86.

Jung-a, S., 'Workaholic South Koreans to Take More Time Off', *Financial Times*, August 24, 2015.

Kabeer, N., *Reversed Realities: Gender Hierarchies in Development Thought* (London: Verso, 1994).

Kalemli-Özcan, Ş., Sørensen, B. and Yesiltas, S., 'Leverage Across Firms, Banks, and Countries', *Journal of International Economics*, 88 (2012), 2, 284–98.

Kalleberg, A. L., *Good Jobs, Bad Jobs: The Rise of Polarized and Precarious Employment Systems in the United States, 1970s–2000s* (New York: Russell Sage Foundation, 2011).

Kalleberg, A. L., Reskin, B. F. and Hudson, K., 'Bad Jobs in America: Standard and Nonstandard Employment Relations and Job Quality in the United States', *American Sociological Review*, 65 (2000), 2, 256–78.

Kamensky, J. M., 'Role of the "Reinventing Government" Movement in Federal Management Reform', *Public Administration Review*, 56 (1996), 3, 247–55.

Kane, R. (ed.), *The Oxford Handbook of Free Will* (Oxford: Oxford University Press, 2011).

Kantabutra, S., 'What Do We Know About Vision?', *The Journal of Applied Business Research*, 24 (2008), 2, 127–38.

Kanter, R. M., 'Power Failure in Management Circuits', *Harvard Business Review*, 57 (1979), 4, 65–75.

Kanter, R. M., *The Change Masters: Innovation and Entrepreneurship in the American Corporation* (New York: Touchstone, 1983).

Kanter, R. M., *When Giants Learn to Dance: Mastering the Challenge of Strategy, Management, and Careers in the 1990s* (New York: Simon & Schuster, 1989).

Kantorowicz, E., *The King's Two Bodies: A Study in Mediaeval Political Theology* (Princeton: Princeton University Press, 1997[1957]).

Kapur, D., Lewis, J. P. and Webb, R. C., *The World Bank: The First Fifty Years* (Washington D.C.: Brookings Institution Press, 1997).

Kassarjian, H. H. and Goodstein, R. C., 'The Emergence of Consumer Research', in Maclaran, P., Saren, M., Stern, B. and Tadajewski, M. (eds), *The SAGE Handbook of Marketing Theory* (London: Sage Publications, 2010).

Kaufmann, D., Kraay, A. and Mastruzzi, M., *Governance Matters VI: Governance Indicators for 1996–2006* (Washington D.C.: World Bank, July 2007).

Kaufmann, D., Kraay, A. and Mastruzzi, M., *Governance Matters VIII: Aggregate and Individual Governance Indicators 1996–2008* (Washington D.C.: World Bank, 2009).

Kaufmann, D., Kraay, A. and Mastruzzi, M., 'The Worldwide Governance Indicators: Methodology and Analytical Issues', *Hague Journal on the Rule of Law*, 3 (2011), 2, 220–46.

Kaustia, M. and Torstila, S., 'Stock Market Aversion? Political Preferences and Stock Market Participation', *Journal of Financial Economics*, 100 (2011), 1, 98–112.

Kellaway, L., *Sense and Nonsense in the Office* (Harlow: Pearson Education Limited, 2000).

Kenworthy, L., 'Do Social-Welfare Policies Reduce Poverty? A Cross-National Assessment', *Social Forces*, 77 (1999), 3, 1119–39.

Keynes, J. M., *The General Theory of Employment, Interest and Money* (London: Macmillan, 1936).

Keys, B. J., Mukherjee, T., Seru, A. and Vig, V., 'Did Securitization Lead to Lax Screening? Evidence from Subprime Loans', *The Quarterly Journal of Economics*, 125 (2010), 1, 307–62.

Khoja-Moolji, S., 'Producing Neoliberal Citizens: Critical Reflections on Human Rights Education in Pakistan', *Gender and Education*, 26 (2014), 2, 103–18.

Kindleberger, C. P. and Aliber, R. Z., *Manias, Panics and Crashes: A History of Financial Crises* (Basingstoke: Palgrave Macmillan, 2011[1978]).

King, D. and Ross, F., 'Critics and Beyond', in Castles, F. G., Leibfried, S., Lewis, J., Obinger, H. and Pierson, C. (eds), *The Oxford Handbook of the Welfare State* (Oxford: Oxford University Press, 2010).

Kirton, G. and Greene, A., *The Dynamics of Managing Diversity: A Critical Approach* (Oxford: Elsevier, 2005).

Kirzner, I. M., *Competition and Entrepreneurship* (Chicago: University of Chicago Press, 1973).

Kirzner, I. M., *The Driving Force of the Market: Essays in Austrian Economics* (London: Routledge, 2000).

Kjaer, A. M., *Governance* (Cambridge: Polity Press, 2004).

Klarsfeld, A. (ed.), *International Handbook on Diversity Management at Work: Country Perspectives on Diversity and Equal Treatment* (Cheltenham: Edward Elgar Publishing, 2010).

Klein, N., *The Shock Doctrine: The Rise of Disaster Capitalism* (London: Penguin, 2008).

Kleindorfer, P. R., Wind, Y., with Gunther, R. E. (eds), *The Network Challenge: Strategy, Profit, and Risk in an Interlinked World* (Upper Saddle River, NJ: Wharton School Publishing, 2009).

Kohn, M., *Brave New Neighborhoods: The Privatization of Public Space* (London: Routledge, 2004).

Kotler, P., 'From Mass Marketing to Mass Customization', *Planning Review*, 17 (1989), 5, 10–47.

Kotter, J. P., *Leading Change* (Boston, MA: Harvard Business School Press, 1996).

Kotz, D., 'Financialization and Neoliberalism', in Teeple, G. and McBride, S. (eds), *Relations of Global Power: Neoliberal Order and Disorder* (Toronto: University of Toronto Press, 2011).

Kouzes, J. M. and Posner, B. Z., *The Leadership Challenge: How to Make Extraordinary Things Happen in Organizations* (San Francisco: Jossey-Bass, 1989).

Kozinets, R., Sherry, J., DeBerry-Spence, B., Duhachek, A., Nuttavuthisit, K. and Storm, D., 'Themed Flagship Brand Stores in the New Millennium: Theory, Practice and Prospects', *Journal of Retailing*, 78 (2002), 1, 17–29.

Krippner, G. R., 'The Financialization of the American Economy', *Socio-Economic Review*, 3 (2005), 2, 173–208.

Krippner, G. R., *Capitalizing on Crisis: The Political Origins of the Rise of Finance* (Cambridge, MA: Harvard University Press, 2011).

Krueger, A. O., 'The Political Economy of the Rent-Seeking Society', *American Economic Review*, 64 (1974), 3, 291–303.

Krueger, A. O., 'Government Failures in Development', *Journal of Economic Perspectives*, 4 (1990), 3, 9–23.

Krueger, A. O., 'Why Trade Liberalisation is Good for Growth', *The Economic Journal*, 108 (1998), 1513–22.

Krugman, P., 'Dutch Tulips and Emerging Markets: Another Bubble Bursts', *Foreign Affairs*, July–August 1995, 28–44.

Kübler-Ross, E., *On Death and Dying: What the Dying Have to Teach Doctors, Nurses, Clergy and Their Own Families* (London: Tavistock Publications, 1970).

Kuczynski, P. and Williamson, J. (eds), *After the Washington Consensus: Restarting Growth and Reform in Latin America* (Washington D.C.: Institute for International Economics, 2003).

Kunda, G., *Engineering Culture: Control and Commitment in a High-tech Corporation* (Philadelphia: Temple University Press, 2006).

Kuznets, S., with Epstein, L. and Jenks, E., *National Income and its Composition, 1919–1938* (Cambridge, MA: National Bureau of Economic Research, 1941).

Kynge, J. and Wheatley, J., 'Emerging Markets: Redrawing the World Map', *Financial Times*, August 3, 2015.

Laffey, M. and Weldes, J., 'Policing and Global Governance', in Barnett, M. and Duvall, R. (eds), *Power in Global Governance* (Cambridge: Cambridge University Press, 2005).

Lagarde, C., 'The Triple Challenge Facing the Global Economy', *Address to the High-Level Forum on Sustainable Development, United Nations*, New York, September 24, 2013. Available at: http://www.imf.org/external/np/speeches/2013/092413.htm.

Laidlaw, J. 'The Concept of Neoliberalism Has Become an Obstacle to the Anthropological Understanding of the Twenty-First Century', presentation at *Group for Debates in Anthropological Theory (GDAT)*, University of Manchester, December 1, 2012. Available at: http://www.talkinganthropology.com/2013/01/18/ta45-gdat1-neoliberalism/.

Lake, A., 'From Containment to Enlargement', *Remarks of Anthony Lake, Assistant to the President for National Security Affairs*, Johns Hopkins University, September 21, 1993. Available at: http://catalog.hathitrust.org/Record/003792749.

Lal, D., *The Poverty of 'Development Economics'* (London: Institute of Economic Affairs, 1983).

Lanchester, J., *How to Speak Money: What the Money People Say – And What They Really Mean* (New York: W. W. Norton & Company, 2014).

Landefeld, J. S., Seskin, E. P. and Fraumeni, B. M., 'Taking the Pulse of the Economy: Measuring GDP', *Journal of Economic Perspectives*, 22 (2008), 2, 193–216.

Landler, M., 'It's the President's Message, With President Clinton', *New York Times*, August 23, 2012.

Lang, A. T. F., *World Trade Law after Neoliberalism: Re-imagining the Global Economic Order* (Oxford: Oxford University Press, 2011).

Langley, P., *The Everyday Life of Global Finance: Saving and Borrowing in Anglo-America* (Oxford: Oxford University Press, 2008).

Langstraat, F. and Van Melik, R., 'Challenging the "End of Public Space": A Comparative Analysis of Publicness in British and Dutch Urban Spaces', *Journal of Urban Design*, 18 (2013), 3, 429–48.

Lanz, R. and Miroudot, S., 'Intra-Firm Trade: Patterns, Determinants and Policy Implications', *OECD Trade Policy Papers*, 114 (Paris: OECD Publishing, 2011).

Lapavitsas, C., *Profiting Without Producing: How Finance Exploits Us All* (London: Verso, 2013).

Laplume, A. O., Sonpar, K., Litz, R. A., 'Stakeholder Theory: Reviewing a Theory That Moves Us', *Journal of Management*, 34 (2008), 6, 1152–89.

Larsen, C. A. and Andersen, J. G., 'How New Economic Ideas Changed the Danish Welfare State: The Case of Neoliberal Ideas and Highly Organized Social Democratic Interests', *Governance*, 22 (2009), 2, 239–61.

Lawson, N., 'The British Experiment (The Mais Lecture)', City University Business School, London, June 18, 1984.

Lawson, N., *The View from No. 11: Memoirs of a Tory Radical* (Ealing: Bantam, 1992).

Le Grand, J., *The Other Invisible Hand: Delivering Public Services Through Choice and Competition* (Princeton: Princeton University Press, 2007).

Lebowitz, M. A., *The Contradictions of "Real Socialism": The Conductor and the Conducted* (New York: Monthly Review Press, 2012).

Lee, M-D. P., 'A Review of the Theories of Corporate Social Responsibility: Its Evolutionary Path and the Road Ahead', *International Journal of Management Reviews*, 10 (2008), 1, 53–73.

Lefebvre, H., *Le droit à la ville* (Paris: Economica, 1968).

Lerner, J., 'Innovation, Entrepreneurship and Financial Market Cycles', *OECD Science, Technology and Industry Working Papers*, 2010/03 (Paris: OECD Publishing, 2010).

Levi-Faur, D., 'From "Big Government" to "Big Governance"', in Levi-Faur, D. (ed.), *The Oxford Handbook of Governance* (Oxford: Oxford University Press, 2012).

Levi-Faur, D. (ed.), *The Oxford Handbook of Governance* (Oxford: Oxford University Press, 2012).

Levy, J. D., 'Welfare Retrenchment', in Castles, F. G., Leibfried, S., Lewis, J., Obinger, H. and Pierson, C. (eds), *The Oxford Handbook of the Welfare State* (Oxford: Oxford University Press, 2010).

Lewin, K., 'Frontiers in Group Dynamics: Concept, Method and Reality in Social Science, Social Equilibria and Social Change', *Human Relations*, 1 (1947), 1, 5–41.

Lewis, D., *Louder Voices: The Corporate Welfare Bums* (Toronto: Lewis & Samuel, 1972).

Lewis, M., 'Greed Never Left', *Vanity Fair*, April 2010.

Lewis, M., *Flash Boys: Cracking the Money Code* (London: Penguin, 2014).

Lie, J., 'Visualizing the Invisible Hand: The Social Origins of "Market Society" in England', 1550–1750', *Politics & Society*, 21 (1993), 3, 275–305.

Lijphart, A., *Democracy in Plural Societies: A Comparative Exploration* (New Haven: Yale University Press, 1977).

Lindstrom, M., *Buyology: Truth and Lies About Why We Buy* (New York: Broadway Books, 2008).

Lipnack, J. and Stamps, J., *The Age of the Network: Organizing Principles for the 21st Century* (Essex Junction, VT: Oliver Wight Publications, 1994).

Lippmann, W., *The Good Society* (New Brunswick, NJ: Transaction Publishers, 2009[1937]).

Lipton, E. and Hakim, D., 'Lobbying Bonanza as Firms Try to Influence European Union', *New York Times*, October 18, 2013.

London Assembly, *Public Life in Private Hands: Managing London's Public Space* (London: Greater London Authority, May 2011).

Love, P. and Lattimore, R. G., *International Trade: Free, Fair, and Open?* (Paris: Organisation for Economic Co-operation and Development, 2009).

Lovei, M. and Gentry, B. S. (eds), *The Environmental Implications of Privatization: Lessons for Developing Countries* (Washington D.C.: World Bank, 2002).

Lukes, S., 'Durkheim's "Individualism and the Intellectuals"', *Political Studies*, 17 (1969), 1, 14–30.

Lukes, S., *Individualism* (Oxford: Basil Blackwell, 1973).

Lukes, S., *Power: A Radical View* (Houndmills: Palgrave Macmillan, 2005 [1974]).

Lundin, R. A. and Söderholm, A., 'Evolution of Projects as Empirical Trend and Theoretical Focus', in Lundin, R. A. and Midler, C. (eds), *Projects as Arenas for Renewal and Learning Processes* (Dordrecht: Kluwer Academic, 1998).

Luo, T., Mann, A. and Holden, R., 'The Expanding Role of Temporary Help Services from 1990 to 2008', *Monthly Labor Review*, 133 (2010), 8, 3–16.

Luxemburg, R., *The Essential Rosa Luxemburg: Reform or Revolution [1898] and the Mass Strike [1906]* (Chicago: Haymarket Books, 2008).

Lyon, S., 'Evaluating Fair Trade Consumption: Politics, Defetishization and Producer Participation', *International Journal of Consumer Studies*, 30 (2006), 5, 452–64.

Lysandrou, P. and Nesvetailova, A., 'The Role of Shadow Banking Entities in the Financial Crisis: A Disaggregated View', *Review of International Political Economy*, 22 (2014), 2, 257–79.

McBain, S., 'Naomi Klein: "I View Free-Market Ideology as a Cover Story for Greed"', *New Statesman*, October 24, 2014.

McBride, S., McNutt, K. and Williams, R. A., 'Policy Leaning? The OECD and its Jobs Strategy', in Mahon, R. and McBride, S., (eds), *The OECD and Transnational Governance* (Vancouver: University of British Columbia Press, 2008).

MacCallum, G. C., Jr., 'Negative and Positive Freedom', *The Philosophical Review*, 76 (1967), 3, 312–34.

Macartney, H., *Variegated Neoliberalism: Convergent Divergence in EU Varieties of Capitalism* (Abingdon: Routledge, 2010).

McCloskey, D. N., *Knowledge and Persuasion in Economics* (Cambridge: Cambridge University Press, 1994).

Maccoby, M., *The Productive Narcissist: The Promise and Peril of Visionary Leadership* (New York: Broadway Books, 2003).

Maccoby, M., *The Leaders We Need and What Makes Us Follow* (Boston MA: Harvard Business School Publishing, 2007).

McCraw, T. K., *Prophet of Innovation: Joseph Schumpeter and Creative Destruction* (Cambridge, MA: Harvard University Press, 2010).

McDermott, J., 'Zero-hours Work for Britain's Zero-hours Economy', *Financial Times*, August 6, 2013.

McElheny, V. K., 'Technology: U.S. Semiconductor Business and Japan Technology: Semiconductor Fight', *New York Times*, January 18, 1978.

MacEwan, A., 'Globalisation and Stagnation', *Socialist Register 1994: Between Globalism and Nationalism*, 30 (1994), 130–43.

McGregor, D., 'An Uneasy Look at Performance Appraisal', *Harvard Business Review*, May–June 1957, 89–94.

McGulgan, J., 'Neo-liberalism, Culture and Policy', *International Journal of Cultural Policy*, 11 (2005), 3, 229–41.

Machiavelli, N., *The Prince* (Oxford: Oxford University Press, 2008[1532]).

McKenna, C. D., *The World's Newest Profession: Management Consulting in the Twentieth Century* (Cambridge: Cambridge University Press, 2006).

MacKenzie, D. and Millo, Y., 'Constructing a Market, Performing Theory: The Historical Sociology of a Financial Derivatives Exchange', *American Journal of Sociology*, 109 (2003), 1, 107–45.

MacKenzie, D., *An Engine, Not a Camera: How Financial Models Shape Markets* (Cambridge, MA: MIT Press, 2006).

McKinsey & Company, *Women at the Top of Corporations: Making it Happen* (2011). Available at: http://www.mckinsey.com/~/media/mckinsey%20 offices/france/pdfs/women_matter_2010.ashx.

McKinsey & Company, *The Lean Management Enterprise: A System for Daily Progress, Meaningful Purpose, and Lasting Value* (New York: McKinsey & Company, 2014).

McKinsey Global Institute, *Urban World: Cities and the Rise of the Consuming Class* (Washington D.C.: McKinsey Global Institute, 2012).

McKinsey Global Institute, *Financial Globalization: Retreat or Reset?* (Washington D.C.: McKinsey & Company, 2013).

McKinsey Global Institute, *Playing to Win: The New Global Competition for Corporate Profits* (Washington D.C.: McKinsey Global Institute, 2015a).

McKinsey Global Institute, *Debt and (Not Much) Deleveraging* (Washington D.C.: McKinsey & Company, 2015b).

McLuhan, M., *The Gutenberg Galaxy: The Making of Typographic Man* (Toronto: University of Toronto Press, 1962).

McNulty, P. J., 'A Note on the History of Perfect Competition', *Journal of Political Economy*, 75 (1967), 4, Part 1, 395–9.

McRobbie, A., *The Aftermath of Feminism: Gender, Culture and Social Change* (London: Sage, 2009).

Maddison Project Database. Available at: http://www.ggdc.net/maddison/ maddison-project/home.htm.

Magdoff, F. and Tokar, B. (eds), *Agriculture and Food in Crisis: Conflict, Resistance, and Renewal* (New York: Monthly Review Press, 2010).

Magnusson, L., *The Tradition of Free Trade* (Abingdon: Routledge, 2004).

Major, P., *Behind the Berlin Wall: East Germany and the Frontiers of Power* (Oxford: Oxford University Press, 2009).

Malinowski, B., 'The Problem of Meaning in Primitive Languages', in Ogden, C. K. and Richards, I. A. (eds), *The Meaning of Meaning: A Study of the Influence of Language upon Thought and of the Science of Symbolism* (London: Kegan Paul, Trench and Trubner, 1923).

Malthus, T., *An Essay on the Principle of Population* (Oxford: Oxford University Press, 2008[1798]).

Manne, H. G. and Wallich, H. C., *The Modern Corporation and Social Responsibility* (Washington D.C.: American Enterprise Institute Press, 1973).

Mansvelt, J. (ed.), *Green Consumerism: An A-to-Z Guide* (London: Sage, 2011).

Maqsood, A., '"Buying Modern": Muslim Subjectivity, the West and Patterns of Islamic Consumption in Lahore, Pakistan', *Cultural Studies*, 28 (2014), 1, 84–107.

Markowitz, H., 'Portfolio Selection', *Journal of Finance*, 7 (1952), 1, 77–91.

Marquand, D., *The Unprincipled Society: New Demands and Old Politics* (London: Fontana, 1988).

Martin, B. R., 'The Evolution of Science Policy and Innovation Studies', *Research Policy*, 41 (2012), 7, 1219–39.

Martínez Lucio, M., 'Labour Process and Marxist Perspectives on Employee Participation', in Gollan, P. J., Lewin, D., Marchington, M. and Wilkinson, A. (eds), *The Oxford Handbook of Participation in Organizations* (Oxford: Oxford University Press, 2010).

Marx, K., *Capital: Critique of Political Economy, Volume I* (London: Penguin Books, 1990[1867]).

Marx, K., *Capital: Critique of Political Economy, Volume II* (London: Penguin, 1992[1885]).

Marx, K., 'On the Jewish Question' [1844], in McLella, D. (ed.), *Karl Marx: Selected Writings* (Oxford: Oxford University Press, 2000).

Marx, K., *The Eighteenth Brumaire of Louis Napoleon* [1852], in McLellan, D. (ed.), *Karl Marx: Selected Writings* (Oxford: Oxford University Press, 2000).

Marx, K. and Engels, F., *The German Ideology* (London: Lawrence and Wishart, 1970[1932]).

Marx, K. and Engels, F., *The Communist Manifesto: A Modern Edition* (London: Verso, 1998[1848]).

Marx, K. and Engels, F., *Economic and Philosophic Manuscripts of 1844* (Mineola, NY: Dover Publications, 2007[1927]).

Massey, D., 'Vocabularies of the Economy', *Soundings*, 54 (2013), July, 9–22.

Matthews, J., 'The Competitive Advantage of Michael Porter', in Witzel, M. and Warner, M. (eds), *The Oxford Handbook of Management Theorists* (Oxford: Oxford University Press, 2013).

Mauss, M., *The Gift: The Form and Reason for Exchange in Archaic Societies* (London: Routledge, 2002[1950]).

May, C. and Sell, S. K., *Intellectual Property Rights: A Critical History* (Boulder, CO: Lynne Rienner Publishers, 2005).

Mazzucato, M., *The Entrepreneurial State: Debunking Public vs. Private Sector Myths* (London: Anthem Press, 2013).

Mead, L. M., *Beyond Entitlement: The Social Obligations of Citizenship* (New York: Free Press, 1986).

Mead, L. M., *The New Politics Of Poverty: The Nonworking Poor In America* (New York: Basic Books, 1993).

Meadows, D. H., Meadows, D. L., Randers, J. and Behrens III, W. W., *The Limits to Growth: A Report for the Club of Rome's Project on the Predicament of Mankind* (London: Earth Island, 1972).

Megginson, W. L. and Netter, J. M., 'From State to Market: A Survey of Empirical Studies on Privatization', *Journal of Economic Literature*, 39 (2001), 2, 321–89.

Mehr, R. I. and Hedges, B. A., *Risk Management in the Business Enterprise* (Homewood, IL: Richard. D. Irwin, Inc., 1963).

Melville-Ross, T., '"Stakeholder" Plan Must Not Stifle Business', *Financial Times*, January 19, 1996.

Mentzer, J. T., DeWitt, W., Keebler, J. S., Min, S., Nix, N. W., Smith, C. D. and Zacharia, Z. G., 'Defining Supply Chain Management', *Journal of Business Logistics*, 22 (2001), 2, 1–25.

Metcalfe, S., 'Technical Change' in Durlauf, S. N. and Blume, L. E. (eds), *The New Palgrave Dictionary of Economics* (Houndmills: Palgrave Macmillan, 2008).

Meyer, M. W. and Gupta, V., 'The Performance Paradox', *Research in Organizational Behavior*, 16 (1994), 309–69.

Michelman, F. I., 'Ethics, Economics, and the Law of Property', *Nomos*, 24 (1982), 3–40.

Michie, E., *The Global Securities Market: A History* (Oxford: Oxford University Press, 2006).

Michie, E., 'Financial Capitalism', in Neal, L. and Williamson, J. G. (eds), *The Cambridge History of Capitalism Volume II: The Spread of Capitalism: From 1848 to the Present* (Cambridge: Cambridge University Press, 2014).

Migdal, J. S., *State in Society: Studying How States and Societies Transform and Constitute One Another* (Cambridge: Cambridge University Press, 2001).

Mikes, A., 'Risk Management and Calculative Cultures', *Management Accounting Research*, 20 (2009), 1, 18–40.

Mikler, J., 'Global Companies as Actors in Global Policy and Governance', in Mikler, J. (ed.), *The Handbook of Global Companies* (Chichester: Wiley-Blackwell, 2013).

Milanovic, B., *Worlds Apart: Measuring International and Global Inequality* (Princeton: Princeton University Press, 2011).

Miles, S., 'Stakeholders: Essentially Contested or Just Confused?', *Journal of Business Ethics*, 108 (2012), 3, 285–98.

Mill, J., *Elements of Political Economy* (London: Baldwin, Cradock, & Joy, 1821).

Mill, J. S., *Principles of Political Economy* (Fairfield, NJ: Augustus M. Kelley, 1976[1848]).

Mill, J. S., *Considerations on Representative Government* (Buffalo, N.Y.: Prometheus Books, 1991[1861]).

Mill, J. S., *On Liberty and Other Essays* (Oxford: Oxford University Press, 2008[1859]).

Mill, J. S., *Principles of Political Economy and Chapters on Socialism* (Oxford: Oxford University Press, 2008[1864]).

Miller, T., 'From Creative to Cultural Industries: Not All Industries are Cultural, and No Industries are Creative', *Cultural Studies*, 23 (2009), 1, 88–99.

Minsky, H., *Stabilizing an Unstable Economy* (New York: McGraw Hill, 2008[1986]).

Mirowski, P., *More Heat than Light: Economics as Social Physics, Physics as Nature's Economics* (Cambridge: Cambridge University Press, 1989).

Mirowski, P., *Never Let a Serious Crisis Go To Waste: How Neoliberalism Survived the Financial Meltdown* (London: Verso, 2013).

Mirowski, P. and Plehwe, D. (eds), *The Road from Mont Pèlerin: The Making of the Neoliberal Thought Collective* (Cambridge, MA: Harvard University Press, 2009).

Mises, L. von, *Bureaucracy* (New Haven: Yale University Press, 1944).

Mises, L. von, *Human Action: A Treatise on Economics* (London: W. Hodge, 1949).

Mises, L. von, *Liberalism: The Classical Tradition* (Indianapolis, IN: Liberty Fund, Inc., 2005[1927]).

Mises, L. von, *Economic Freedom and Interventionism: An Anthology of Articles and Essays* (Indianapolis, IN: Liberty Fund, 2007).

Mises, L. von, *Socialism: An Economic and Sociological Analysis* (Auburn, AL: Ludwig von Mises Institute, 2009[1922]).

Mishel, L., Bivens, J., Gould, E. and Shierholz, H., *The State of Working America* (Ithaca: Cornell University Press, 2012).

Mitchell, R. K., Agle, B. R. and Wood, D. J., 'Toward a Theory of Stakeholder Identification and Salience: Defining the Principle of Who and What Really Counts', *Academy of Management Review*, 22 (1997), 4, 853–86.

Mitchell, T., 'Fixing the Economy', *Cultural Studies*, 12 (1998), 1, 82–101.

Mitchell, T., 'Rethinking Economy', *Geoforum*, 39 (2008), 3, 1116–21.

Moe, R. C., 'The "Reinventing Government" Exercise: Misinterpreting the Problem, Misjudging the Consequences', *Public Administrative Review*, 54 (1994), 2, 111–22.

Moller, S., Huber, E., Stephens, J. D., Bradley, D. and Nielsen, F., 'Determinants of Relative Poverty in Advanced Capitalist Democracies', *American Sociological Review*, 68 (2003), 1, 22–51.

Mor Barak, M. E., *Managing Diversity: Toward a Globally Inclusive Workplace* (London: Sage, 2014).

Moretti, F., *The Bourgeois: Between History and Literature* (London: Verso, 2013).

Morisawa, T., 'Managing the Unmanageable: Emotional Labour and Creative Hierarchy in the Japanese Animation Industry', *Ethnography*, 16 (2015), 2, 262–84.

Morris, P., 'Freeing the Spirit of Enterprise: The Genesis and Development of the Concept of Enterprise Culture', in Keat, R. and Abercrombie, N. (eds), *Enterprise Culture* (London: Routledge, 1991).

Morris, P. W. G., 'A Brief History of Project Management', in Morris, P. W. G., Pinto, J. and Söderlund, J. (eds), *The Oxford Handbook of Project Management* (Oxford: Oxford University Press, 2011).

Morris, P. W. G., *Reconstructing Project Management* (Oxford: Wiley-Blackwell, 2013).

Morrison, A. D. and Wilhelm, W. J., Jr, *Investment Banking: Institutions, Politics, and Law* (Oxford: Oxford University Press, 2007).

Mosse, D., 'The Making and Marketing of Participatory Development', in Quarles van Ufford, P. and Giri, A. K. (eds), *A Moral Critique of Development: In Search of Global Responsibilities* (London: Routledge, 2003).

Mosse, D., *Cultivating Development: An Ethnography of Aid Policy and Practice* (London: Pluto Press, 2005).

Mouffe, C., *On the Political* (Abingdon: Routledge, 2005).

Mountz, A., Bonds, A., Mansfield, B., Loyd, J., Hyndman, J. and Walton-Roberts, M., 'For Slow Scholarship: A Feminist Politics of Resistance through Collective Action in the Neoliberal University', *ACME, International E-journal for Critical Geographies*, 14 (2015), 4, 1235–59.

Mukunda, G., 'The Price of Wall Street's Power', *Harvard Business Review*, June 2014.

Müller, R. and Turner, R., 'Leadership Competency Profiles of Successful Project Managers', *International Journal of Project Management*, 28 (2010), 5, 437–48.

Murphy, S., Burch, D. and Clapp, J., *Cereal Secrets: The World's Largest Grain Traders and Global Agriculture* (Oxford: Oxfam International, 2012).

Murray, C., *Losing Ground: American Social Policy, 1950–1980* (New York: Basic Books, 1984).

Myrdal, G., *Challenge to Affluence* (New York: Pantheon Books, 1963).

Nader, R., *Cutting Corporate Welfare* (New York: Seven Stories Press, 2000).

Nader, R., Green, M. and Seligman, J., *Taming the Giant Corporation* (New York: W.W. Norton, 1976a).

Nader, R., Green, M. and Seligman, J., *Constitutionalizing the Corporation: The Case for the Federal Chartering of Giant Corporations* (Washington D.C.: Corporate Accountability Research Group, 1976b).

Nadler, R., 'The Rise of Worker Capitalism', *Cato Institute Policy Analysis*, No. 359 (Washington D.C.: Cato Institute, 1999).

Nandy, A. 'State', in Sachs, W. (ed.), *The Development Dictionary: A Guide to Knowledge as Power* (London: Zed Books, 1992).

Naughton, B., *The Chinese Economy: Transitions and Growth* (Cambridge, MA: MIT Press, 2007).

Neal, L., *The Rise of Financial Capitalism: International Capital Markets in the Age of Reason* (Cambridge: Cambridge University Press, 1990).

Nesvetailova, A., 'A Crisis of the Overcrowded Future: Shadow Banking and the Political Economy of Financial Innovation', *New Political Economy*, 20 (2015), 3, 431–53.

Neumann, I. B., *At Home with the Diplomats: Inside a European Foreign Ministry* (Ithaca: Cornell University Press, 2012).

Newell, P., 'The Political Economy of Global Environmental Governance', *Review of International Studies*, 34 (2008), 3, 507–29.

Ngai, P. and Chan, J., 'Global Capital, the State, and Chinese Workers: The Foxconn Experience', *Modern China*, 38 (2012), 4, 383–410.

Nicolaïdis, K., 'European Democracy and Its Crisis', *Journal of Common Market Studies*, 51 (2013), 2, 351–69.

Niman, N. B., 'Biological Analogies in Marshall's Work', *Journal of the History of Economic Thought*, 13 (1991), 1, 19–36.

Nkrumah, K., *Neo-Colonialism: The Last Stage Imperialism* (London: Heinemann, 1965).

Noonan, L., 'Landscape Shifts as the Titans Retreat', *Financial Times*, August 26, 2015.

North, D., 'Markets and Other Allocation Systems in History: The Challenge of Karl Polanyi', *Journal of European Economic History*, 6 (1977), 3, 703–16.

O'Donnell, G. and Schmitter, P. C., *Transitions from Authoritarian Rule: Tentative Conclusions About Uncertain Democracies* (Baltimore, MD: Johns Hopkins University Press, 1986).

O'Malley, P., *Risk, Uncertainty and Government* (London: The Glasshouse Press, 2004).

O'Neill, J., 'Building Better Global Economic BRICs', Goldman Sachs Global Economic Paper No. 66, November 30, 2001.

O'Neill, J., *The Growth Map: Economic Opportunity in the BRICs and Beyond* (London: Penguin, 2011).

Oakeshott, M., 'The Vocabulary of a Modern European State', *Political Studies*, 23 (1975), 2–3, 319–41.

Obama, B., 'Address Before a Joint Session of the Congress', United States House of Representatives, Washington D. C., February 24, 2009. Available at: http://www.whitehouse.gov/the_press_office/Remarks-of-President-Barack-Obama-Address-to-Joint-Session-of-Congress.

Obi, C. and Rustad, S. A. (eds), *Oil and Insurgency in the Niger Delta: Managing the Complex Politics of Petro-violence* (London: Zed Books, 2011).

Ocasio, W. and Joseph, J., 'Cultural Adaptation and Institutional Change: The Evolution of Vocabularies of Corporate Governance, 1972–2003', *Poetics*, 33 (2005), 3–4, 163–78.

Offe, C., *Contradictions of the Welfare State* (ed. Keane, J. B.) (Cambridge, MA: MIT Press, 1984).

Offe, C., 'Governance: An "Empty Signifier"?', *Constellations: An International Journal of Critical and Democratic Theory*, 16 (2009), 4, 550–62.

Ohmae, K., *Triad Power: The Coming Shape of Global Competition* (New York: The Free Press, 1985).

Ohmae, K., *The Borderless World: Power and Strategy in the Interlinked Economy* (New York: Harper Business, 1990).

Ohno, T., *Toyota Production System: Beyond Large-Scale Production* (Portland, OR: Productivity Press, 1988).

Okereke, C., *Global Justice and Neoliberal Environmental Governance: Ethics, Sustainable Development and International Co-Operation* (Abingdon: Routledge, 2008).

Oliver, R. L., *Satisfaction: A Behavioral Perspective on the Consumer* (Armonk, NY: M. E. Sharpe, 2010).

Olivera, O., with Lewis, T., *¡Cochabamba! Water War in Bolivia* (New York: South End Press, 2004).

Ong, A., *Neoliberalism as Exception: Mutations in Citizenship and Sovereignty* (Durham, NC: Duke University Press, 2006).

Open Source Initiative, 'History of the OSI'. Available at: http://opensource.org/history.

Organisation for Economic Co-operation and Development (OECD), *The OECD Jobs Strategy: Pushing Ahead with the Strategy* (Paris: Organisation for Economic Co-operation and Development, 1996).

Organisation for Economic Co-operation and Development (OECD), *Viet Nam: Policy Framework for Investment Assessment* (Paris: Organisation for Economic Co-operation and Development, 2010).

Organisation for Economic Co-operation and Development (OECD), *Towards Green Growth: A Summary for Policymakers* (Paris: Organisation for Economic Co-operation and Development, May 2011).

Organisation for Economic Co-operation and Development (OECD), *Agricultural Policy Monitoring and Evaluation 2013: OECD Countries and Emerging Economies* (Paris: Organisation for Economic Co-operation and Development, 2013).

Organisation for Economic Co-operation and Development (OECD), 'Social Expenditure Update – Social Spending is Falling in Some Countries, But in Many Others it Remains at Historically High Levels', (Paris: Organisation for Economic Co-operation and Development, 2014).

Organisation for Economic Co-operation and Development (OECD), *OECD Health Statistics 2014*. Available at: http://www.oecd.org/els/health-systems/health-data.htm.

Organisation for Economic Co-operation and Development (OECD), *In It Together: Why Less Inequality Benefits All* (Paris: Organisation for Economic Co-operation and Development, 2015a).

Organisation for Economic Co-operation and Development (OECD), 'Hours Worked: Average Annual Hours Actually Worked', OECD Employment and Labour Market Statistics (Paris: Organisation for Economic Co-operation and Development, 2015b). Available at: http://dx.doi.org/10.1787/data-00303-en.

Organisation for Economic Co-operation and Development (OECD)-Public Management Committee (PUMA), *In Search of Results: Performance Management Practices* (Paris: Organisation for Economic Co-operation and Development, 1997).

Orwell, G., *Shooting an Elephant and Other Essays* (London: Penguin, 2009[1950]).

Osborne, D. and Gaebler, T., *Reinventing Government: How the Entrepreneurial Spirit is Transforming the Public Sector from Schoolhouse to State House, City Hall to Pentagon* (Reading, MA: Addison-Wesley, 1992).

Ostry, J. D., Berg, A. and Tsangarides, C. G., 'Redistribution, Inequality, and Growth', IMF Staff Discussion Note SDN/14/02 (Washington D.C.: International Monetary Fund, 2014).

Owen, P. and Malik, S., 'Canary Wharf Takes Legal Action to Keep out Potential Occupy London Protesters', *The Guardian*, November 3, 2011.

Oxfam International, *Rigged Rules and Double Standards* (Oxford: Oxfam International, 2002).

Oxfam International, *Even It Up: Time to End Extreme Inequality* (Oxford: Oxfam International, 2014).

Oxford International, *Dumping on the World: How EU Sugar Policies Hurt Poor Countries* (Oxford: Oxfam International, 2004).

Packard, V., *The Hidden Persuaders* (New York: Pocket Books, 1957).

Page, S. E., *The Difference: How the Power of Diversity Creates Better Groups, Firms, Schools, and Societies* (Princeton: Princeton University Press, 2007).

Pak, J. A. and Solo, S., 'Introducing a New Fortune List', *Fortune*, July 30, 1990.

Park, J., 'Are Entrepreneurs Really the Happiest People on Earth?', *Forbes*, May 16, 2014. Available at: http://www.forbes.com/sites/janepark/2014/05/16/are-entrepreneurs-happier/.

Parker, D., *The Official History of Privatisation: Volume I: The Formative Years 1970–1987* (Abingdon: Routledge, 2009).

Parker, D., *The Official History of Privatisation: Volume II: Popular Capitalism 1987–1997* (Abingdon: Routledge, 2012).

Parry, G., 'The Idea of Political Participation', in Parry, G. (ed.), *Participation in Politics* (Manchester: Manchester University Press, 1972).

Parry, J., 'The Gift, the Indian Gift and the "Indian Gift"', *Man*, 21 (1986), 3, 453–73.

Partington, D., 'Leadership', in Turner, R. J. (ed.), *Gower Handbook of Project Management* (Aldershot: Gower Publishing, 2007).

Pateman, C., *Participation and Democratic Theory* (Cambridge: Cambridge University Press, 1970).

Paterson, M., *Consumption and Everyday Life* (Abingdon: Routledge, 2005).

Paton, R. A. and McCalman, J., *Change Management: A Guide to Effective Implementation* (London: Sage, 2008).

Patton, A., 'Does Performance Appraisal Work?', *Business Horizons*, 16 (1973), 1, 83–91.

Peck, J., 'Workfare: A Geopolitical Etymology', *Environment and Planning D: Society and Space*, 16 (1998), 2, 133–61.

Peck, J., *Workfare States* (London: Guilford Press, 2001).

Peck, J., 'Struggling with the Creative Class', *International Journal of Urban and Regional Research*, 29 (2005), 4, 740–70.

Peck, J., *Constructions of Neoliberal Reason* (Oxford: Oxford University Press, 2010).

Peck, J., Theodore, N. and Brenner, N., 'Neoliberalism Resurgent? Market Rule After the Great Recession', *The South Atlantic Quarterly*, 111 (2012), 2, 265–88.

Peck, J., 'Explaining (With) Neoliberalism', *Territory, Politics, Governance*, 1 (2013), 2, 132–57.

Peck, J. and Tickell, A., 'Neoliberalizing Space', *Antipode*, 34 (2002), 3 , 380–404.

Peñaloza, L., 'Just Doing It: A Visual Ethnographic Study of Spectacular Consumption Behavior at Nike Town', *Consumption, Markets & Culture*, 2 (1998), 4, 337–400.

Pennington, R., *Make Change Work: Staying Nimble, Relevant, and Engaged in a World of Constant Change* (Hoboken, NJ: Wiley & Sons Inc., 2013).

Pennycook, M., Cory, G., Alakeson, V., *A Matter of Time: The Rise of Zero-hours Contracts* (London: Resolution Foundation, 2013).

Pereboom, D. (ed.), *Free Will* (Indianapolis: Hackett Publishing, 2009).

Peston, R., 'Brown Defends "Stakeholder" Plan', *Financial Times*, January 16, 1996.

Peters, G. 'Globalization, Institutions, and Governance', in Peters, G. and Savoie, D. J. (eds), *Governance in the Twenty-first Century: Revitalizing the Public Service* (Buffalo: McGill–Queen's University Press, 2000).

Peters, T., *Thriving on Chaos: Handbook for a Management Revolution* (New York: Harper & Row, 1987).

Peters, T., *The Pursuit of Wow! Every Person's Guide to Topsy-Turvy Times* (New York: Random House, 1994).

Peters, T. and Waterman, R. H., *In Search of Excellence* (New York: HarperCollins, 1982).

Pew Research Center, 'Despite Recovery, Fewer Americans Identify as Middle Class', January 27, 2014.

Pierson, P., *Dismantling the Welfare State? Reagan, Thatcher and the Politics of Retrenchment* (Cambridge: Cambridge University Press, 1995).

Pigman, G. A., *The World Economic Forum: A Multi-Stakeholder Approach to Global Governance* (Abingdon: Routledge, 2007).

Piketty, T., *Capital in the Twenty-First Century* (Cambridge, MA: Harvard University Press, 2014).

Pilling, D. and Zhu, J., 'Hong Kong Tussles Over "Rule of Law"', *Financial Times*, January 14, 2015.

Pine, J. B. and Gilmore, J. H., *The Experience Economy: Work Is Theater & Every Business a Stage* (Boston, MA: Harvard Business School Press, 1999).

Pisani-Ferry, J., *The Euro Crisis and Its Aftermath* (Oxford: Oxford University Press, 2014).

Piven, F. and Cloward, R., *Regulating the Poor: The Functions of Public Welfare* (New York: Vintage Books, 1993).

Piven, F. F., *The Breaking of the American Social Compact* (New York: New Press, 1998).

Plachy, R. J. and Plachy, S., *Performance Management: Getting Results from Your Performance Planning and Appraisal System* (New York: American Management Association, 1988).

Plant, R., 'Community: Concept, Conception, and Ideology', *Politics & Society*, 8 (1978), 1, 79–107.

Plant, R., *The Neo-liberal State* (Oxford: Oxford University Press, 2012).

Plehwe, D., 'Introduction', in Mirowski, P. and Plehwe, D. (eds), *The Road from Mont Pèlerin: The Making of the Neoliberal Thought Collective* (Cambridge, MA: Harvard University Press, 2009).

Poerksen, U., *Plastic Words: The Tyranny of a Modular Language* (University Park, PA: Pennsylvania State University Press, 1995).

Polanyi, K., *The Great Transformation: The Political and Economic Origins of Our Time* (Boston: Beacon Press, 2001[1944]).

Pollitt, C., *Managerialism and the Public Services* (Oxford: Blackwell, 1993).

Pollitt, C. and Bouckaert, G. (eds), *Public Management Reform: A Comparative Analysis – New Public Management, Governance, and the Neo-Weberian State* (Oxford: Oxford University Press, 2011).

Poole, S., *Who Touched Base in My Thought Shower?: A Treasury of Unbearable Office Jargon* (London: Sceptre, 2014).

Popper, K., *The Open Society and its Enemies* (Abingdon: Routledge, 2002[1945]).

Porter, M., 'How Competitive Forces Shape Strategy', *Harvard Business Review*, 57 (1979), 2, 137–45.

Porter, M., *Competitive Strategy: Techniques for Analyzing Industries and Competitors* (New York: Free Press, 1980).

Porter, M., *Competitive Advantage: Creating and Sustaining Superior Performance* (New York: Free Press, 1985).

Porter, M., *The Competitive Advantage of Nations* (New York: Free Press, 1990).

Porter, T., *Trust in Numbers: The Pursuit of Objectivity in Science and Public Life* (Princeton: Princeton University Press, 1996).

Poulsen, L. N. S. and Aisbett, E., 'When the Claim Hits: Bilateral Investment Treaties and Bounded Rational Learning', *World Politics*, 65 (2013), 2, 273–313.

Poulsen, L. N. S., *Bounded Rationality and Economic Diplomacy: The Politics of Investment Treaties in Developing Countries* (Cambridge: Cambridge University Press, 2015).

Powell, W. W., 'Neither Market Nor Hierarchy: Network Forms of Organization', in Cummings, L. L. and Shaw, B. (eds), *Research in Organizational Behaviour* (Greenwich, CT: JAI Press, 1990).

Powell, W. W. and Grodal, S., 'Networks of Innovators', in Fagerberg, J., Mowery, D. C. and Nelson, R. R. (eds), *The Oxford Handbook of Innovation* (Oxford: Oxford University Press, 2006).

Power, M., *The Audit Society: Rituals of Verification* (Oxford: Oxford University Press, 1997).

Power, M., *Organized Uncertainty: Designing a World of Risk Management* (Oxford: Oxford University Press, 2007).

Power, M., 'The Risk Management of Nothing', *Accounting, Organizations and Society*, 34 (2009), 6–7, 849–55.

Prahalad, C. K. and Ramaswamy, V., *The Future of Competition: Co-Creating Unique Value With Customers* (Boston, MA: Harvard Business School Press, 2004).

Prasad, M., *The Politics of Free Markets: The Rise of Neoliberal Economic Policies in Britain, France, Germany, and the United States* (Chicago: Chicago University Press, 2006).

Privatization Barometer, *The PB Report 2013/2014* (Milan: Fondazione Eni Enrico Mattei, 2014).

Proudhon, P-J., *What Is Property? An Inquiry Into the Principle of Right and of Government* (New York: Dover Publications, 1970[1840]).

Prügl, E., 'Neoliberalising Feminism', *New Political Economy*, 20 (2015), 4, 614–31.

Ptak, R., 'Neoliberalism in Germany: Revisiting the Ordoliberal Foundations of the Social Market Economy', in Mirowski, P. and Plehwe, D. (eds), *The Road from Mont Pèlerin: The Making of the Neoliberal Thought Collective* (Cambridge, MA: Harvard University Press, 2009).

PwC, *Global Top 100 Companies by Market Capitalisation*, March 31 2014 update (London: PwC, 2014).

Quigley, J.V., *Vision: How Leaders Develop It, Share It, and Sustain It* (New York: McGraw-Hill, 1993).

Quigley, J. V., 'Vision: How Leaders Develop It, Share It, and Sustain It', *Business Horizons*, 37 (1994), 5, 37–41.

Ramsay, H., 'Cycles of Control: Worker Participation in Sociological and Historical Perspective', *Sociology*, 11 (1977), 3, 481–506.

Ramskogler, P., *Origins of the Crisis: Drawing the Big Picture* (Paris: Organisation for Economic Co-operation and Development, 2014).

Rao, R., *Third World Protest: Between Home and Abroad* (Oxford: Oxford University Press, 2010).

Raymond, E. S., 'Goodbye, "Free Software"; Hello, "Open Source"', (originally published February 8, 1998). Available at: http://www.catb.org/~esr/open-source.html.

Raymond, E. S., *The Cathedral and the Bazaar: Musings on Linux and Open Source by an Accidental Revolutionary* (Sebastopol, CA: O'Reilly Media, 1999).

Raynolds, L.T. and Long, M.A., 'Fair/Alternative Trade: Historical and Empirical Dimensions', in Raynolds, L.T., Murray, D. L. and Wilkinson, J. (eds), *Fair Trade: The Challenges of Transforming Globalization* (Abingdon: Routledge, 2007).

Reagan, R., 'Ronald Reagan's Announcement for Presidential Candidacy', November 13, 1979. Available at: http://www.reagan.utexas.edu/archives/reference/11.13.79.html.

Reagan, R., 'Inaugural Address', January 20, 1981. Available at: http://www.reaganfoundation.org/pdf/Inaugural_Address_012081.pdf.

Reinhart, C. M. and Rogoff, K., *This Time Is Different: Eight Centuries of Financial Folly* (Princeton: Princeton University Press, 2009).

Rhenman, E., *Foeretagsdemokrati och foeretagsorganisation* (Stockholm: Thul, 1964).

Rhodes, R., *Understanding Governance: Policy Networks, Governance, Reflexivity, and Accountability* (Buckingham: Open University Press, 1997).

Ricardo, D., *On the Principles of Political Economy and Taxation* (New York: Dover Publications, 2004[1817]).

Richardson, G. B., 'The Organisation of Industry', *The Economic Journal*, 82 (1972), 327, 883–96.

Ricoeur, P., *The Just* (Chicago: Chicago University Press, 2000).

Ridley-Duff, R. and Bull, M., *Understanding Social Enterprise: Theory and Practice* (London: Sage, 2011).

Rigby, M., Smith, R. and Lawlor, T. (eds), *European Trade Unions: Change and Response* (London: Routledge, 2005).

Rist, G., *The History of Development: From Western Origins to Global Faith* (London: Zed Books, 2008).

Robbins, L., *An Essay on the Nature and Significance of Economic Science* (London: Macmillan, 1932).

Robertson, R., *Globalization: Social Theory and Global Culture* (London: Sage, 1992).

Robinson, E. H., 'The Distinction Between State and Government', *Geography Compass*, 7 (2013), 8, 556–66.

Roccu, R., *The Political Economy of the Egyptian Revolution: Mubarak, Economic Reforms and Failed Hegemony* (Basingstoke: Palgrave Pivot, 2013a).

Roccu, R., 'David Harvey in Tahrir Square: The Dispossessed, the Discontented and the Egyptian Revolution', *Third World Quarterly*, 34 (2013b), 3, 423–40.

Rodríguez, F. and Rodrik, D., 'Trade Policy and Economic Growth: A Skeptic's Guide to the Cross-National Evidence', *NBER Macroeconomics Annual*, 15 (2000), 261–325.

Rodrik, D., 'The Rush to Free Trade in the Developing World: Why So Late? Why Now? Will It Last?', in Haggard, S. and Webb, S. B. (eds), *Voting for Reform: Democracy, Political Liberalization, and Economic Adjustment* (Oxford: Oxford University Press, 1994).

Rodrik, D., 'After Neoliberalism, What?', Remarks at the BNDES Seminar on 'New Paths of Development', Rio de Janeiro, September 12–13, 2002.

Rodrik, D., 'Goodbye Washington Consensus, Hello Washington Confusion? A Review of the World Bank's *Economic Growth in the 1990s: Learning from a Decade of Reform*', *Journal of Economic Literature*, 44 (2006), 4, 973–87.

Rodrik, D., *One Economics, Many Recipes: Globalization, Institutions, and Economic Growth* (Princeton: Princeton University Press, 2007).

Roose, K., *Young Money: Inside the Hidden World of Wall Street's Post-Crash Recruits* (New York: Grand Central Publishing, 2014).

Rose, N., 'Governing the Enterprising Self', in Heelas, P. and Morris, P. (eds), *The Values of the Enterprise Culture: The Moral Debate* (London: Routledge, 1992).

Rose, N., *Powers of Freedom: Reframing Political Thought* (Cambridge: Cambridge University Press, 1999).

Rosenau, J. N., 'Governance, Order, and Change in World Politics', in Rosenau, J. N. and Czempiel, E-O. (eds), *Governance Without Government: Order and Change in World Politics* (Cambridge: Cambridge University Press, 1992).

Rosenau, J. N., *Along the Domestic–Foreign Frontier: Exploring Governance in a Turbulent World* (Cambridge: Cambridge University Press, 1997).

Rosenbaum, E. F., 'What is a Market? On the Methodology of a Contested Concept', *Review of Social Economy*, 58 (2000), 4, 455–82.

Rosenberg, E. S., 'Consumer Capitalism and the End of the Cold War', in Leffler, M. P. and Westad, O. A. (eds), *The Cambridge History of the Cold War Volume 3: Endings* (Cambridge: Cambridge University Press, 2010).

Rosenberg, J., 'Globalization Theory: A Post Mortem', *International Politics*, 42 (2005): 2–74.

Rostow, W. W., *The Stages of Economic Growth: A Non-Communist Manifesto* (Cambridge: Cambridge University Press, 1960).

Rottenberg, C., 'The Rise of Neoliberal Feminism', *Cultural Studies*, 28 (2014), 3, 418–37.

Rousseau, J-J., *The Social Contract* (Oxford: Oxford University Press, 2008[1762]).

Rubin, P. H. and Klumpp, T., 'Property Rights and Capitalism', in Mueller, D. C. (ed.), *The Oxford Handbook of Capitalism* (Oxford: Oxford University Press, 2012).

Runciman, D., 'The Concept of the State: The Sovereignty of a Fiction', in Skinner, Q. and Stråth, B. (eds), *States and Citizens: History, Theory, Prospects* (Cambridge: Cambridge University Press, 2003).

Russell, G. 'The American Underclass', *Time*, August 29, 1977, 14–27.

Rustow, D. A., 'Transitions to Democracy: Toward a Dynamic Model', *Comparative Politics*, 2 (1970), 3, 337–63.

Saad-Filho, A. and Johnston, D. (eds), *Neoliberalism: A Critical Reader* (London: Pluto Press, 2005).

Sachs, J. D. and Warner, A. M., 'Economic Reform and the Process of Global Integration', *Brookings Papers on Economic Activity*, (1995), 1, 1–118.

Sachs, W. (ed.), *The Development Dictionary: A Guide to Knowledge as Power* (London: Zed Books, 1992).

Sachs, W., 'Environment', in Sachs, W. (ed.), *The Development Dictionary: A Guide to Knowledge as Power* (London: Zed Books, 2008[1992]).

Saez, E., 'Wealth Inequality in the United States Since 1913: Evidence from Capitalized Income Tax Data', NBER Working Paper, Working Paper 20625, October 2014.

Safire, W., 'Stakeholders Naff? I'm Chuffed', *New York Times*, May 5, 1996.

Said, E. W., *Orientalism* (London: Penguin, 1978).

Salecl, R., *The Tyranny of Choice* (London: Profile Books, 2010).

Salter, A. and Alexy, O., 'The Nature of Innovation', in Dodgson, M., Gann, D. M., and Phillips, N. (eds), *The Oxford Handbook of Innovation Management* (Oxford: Oxford University Press, 2014).

Samuelson, P., 'The Way of An Economist', in Samuelson, P. (ed.), International Economic Relations: Proceedings of the Third Congress of the International Economic Association (London: Macmillan, 1969).

Sandberg, S., *Lean In: Women, Work, and the Will to Lead* (New York: Alfred A. Knopf, 2013).

Santos, A., 'The World Bank's Uses of the "Rule of Law" Promise in Economic Development', in Trubek, D. M. and Santos, A. (eds), *The New Law and*

Economic Development: A Critical Appraisal (Cambridge: Cambridge University Press, 2006).

Sass, S. A., *The Pragmatic Imagination: A History of the Wharton School, 1881–1981* (Philadelphia: University of Pennsylvania Press, 1982).

Say, J-B., *A Treatise on Political Economy or the Production, Distribution and Consumption of Wealth* (New York: Augustus M. Kelley, 1971[1821]).

Sayer, A., *Radical Political Economy: A Critique* (Oxford: Blackwell, 1995).

Schmalensee, R., 'From "Green Growth" to Sound Policies: An Overview', *Energy Economics*, 34 (2012), S1, 2–6.

Schmidt, V. A. and Thatcher, M. (eds), *Resilient Liberalism in Europe's Political Economy* (Cambridge: Cambridge University Press, 2013).

Schmidt, V. A. and Woll, C., 'The State: The *Bête Noire* of Neo-liberalism or its Greatest Conquest?', in Schmidt, V. A. and Thatcher, M. (eds), *Resilient Liberalism in Europe's Political Economy* (Cambridge: Cambridge University Press, 2013).

Scholte, J. A., *Globalization: A Critical Introduction* (Houndmills: Palgrave Macmillan, 2005).

Schrecker, T. and Bambra, C., *How Politics Makes Us Sick: Neoliberal Epidemics* (Basingstoke: Palgrave Macmillan, 2015).

Schumpeter, J., *The Theory of Economic Development: An Inquiry Into Profits, Capital, Credit, Interest, and the Business Cycle* (Cambridge, MA: Harvard University Press, 1983[1934]).

Schumpeter, J. A., *Capitalism, Socialism and Democracy* (Abingdon: Routledge, 2003[1942]).

Schwab, K., 'Innovation, Collaboration and New Forms of Global Governance', Speech at the Foreign Affairs University Beijing, Beijing, September 22, 2008.

Schwartz, A. J., 'Why Financial Stability Depends on Price Stability', *Economic Affairs*, 15 (1995), 4, 21–5.

Schwartz, B., *The Paradox of Choice: Why More is Less* (New York: HarperCollins, 2004).

Schwartz, D. E. (ed.), *Commentaries on Corporate Structure and Governance* (Philadelphia: ALI–ABI, 1979).

Scott, W. D., *Increasing Human Efficiency in Business: A Contribution to the Psychology of Business* (New York: Macmillan, 1911).

Seabrooke, L., *The Social Sources of Financial Power: Domestic Legitimacy and International Financial Orders* (Ithaca: Cornell University Press, 2006).

Selchow, S., 'Language and "Global" Politics: De-Naturalising the "Global"', in Albrow, M., Anheier, H., Glasius, M., Price, M. and Kaldor, M. (eds), *Global Civil Society 2007/8: Communicative Power and Democracy* (London: Sage, 2008).

Seligman, J., *The Transformation of Wall Street: A History of the Securities and Exchange Commission and Modern Corporate Finance* (Boston: Houghton Mifflin, 1982).

Sell, S. K., *Private Power, Public Law: The Globalization of Intellectual Property Rights* (Cambridge: Cambridge University Press, 2003).

Sen, A. 'The Moral Standing of the Market', *Social Philosophy and Policy*, 2 (1985), 2, 1–19.

Sen, A., *Development as Freedom* (Oxford: Oxford University Press, 1999).

Sen, G. and Grown, C., *Development, Crises and Alternative Visions: Third World Women's Perspectives* (New York: Monthly Review Press, 1987).

Serra, N. and Stiglitz, J. E. (eds), *The Washington Consensus Reconsidered: Towards a New Global Governance* (Oxford: Oxford University Press, 2008).

Shakespeare, W., *Richard II* (Oxford: Oxford University Press, 2011[1597]).

Sharma, A., *Logics of Empowerment: Development, Gender, and Governance in Neoliberal India* (Minneapolis: University of Minnesota Press, 2008).

Sharma, R. R., *Change Management: Concepts and Applications* (New Delhi: Tata McGraw-Hill Education, 2007).

Sharpe, W. F., 'A Simplified Model for Portfolio Analysis', *Management Science*, 9 (1963), 2, 277–93.

Shields, S., *The International Political Economy of Transition: Neoliberal Hegemony and Eastern Central Europe* (Abingdon: Routledge, 2012).

Shihata, I., *The World Bank Legal Papers* (The Hague: Martinus Nijhoff, 2000).

Shore, C. N., 'Audit Culture and Illiberal Governance: Universities and the Politics of Accountability', *Anthropological Theory*, 8 (2008), 3, 278–99.

Sidaway, J. D., 'Geographies of Development: New Maps, New Visions?', *The Professional Geographer*, 64 (2012), 1, 49–62.

Sills, W. C., *Sales Talks: Being a Series of Man-to-man Articles, Instructive and Inspirational, and Written for the Purpose of Increasing and Helping in the Development of Personal and Business Efficiency* (Chevrolet Motor Company, 1920).

Sinclair, T. J., *The New Masters of Capital: American Bond Rating Agencies and the Politics of Creditworthiness* (Ithaca: Cornell University Press, 2005).

Skeat, W. W., *A Concise Etymological Dictionary of the English Language* (Oxford: Clarendon Press, 1901).

Skinner, Q., *The Foundations of Modern Political Thought, Volumes 1 and 2* (Cambridge: Cambridge University Press, 1979).

Skinner, Q., 'The State', in Ball, T., Farr, J. and Hanson, R. L. (eds), *Political Innovation and Conceptual Change* (Cambridge: Cambridge University Press, 1989).

Sklair, L., *The Transnational Capitalist Class* (Oxford: Blackwell, 2001).

Sklair, L., 'The Transnational Capitalist Class and Contemporary Architecture in Globalizing Cities', *The International Journal of Urban and Regional Research*, 29 (2005), 3, 485–500.

Smith, A., *An Inquiry into the Nature and Causes of the Wealth of Nations* (Oxford: Oxford University Press, 1993[1776]).

Smith, J., *Social Movements for Global Democracy* (Baltimore: Johns Hopkins University Press, 2008).

Smith-Doerr, L. and Powell, W. W., 'Networks and Economic Life', in Smelser, N. and Swedberg, R. (eds), *The Handbook of Economic Sociology* (Princeton: Princeton University Press, 2005).

Soederberg, S., *Corporate Power and Ownership in Contemporary Capitalism: The Politics of Resistance and Domination* (Abingdon: Routledge, 2010).

Solarz, M. W., *The Language of Global Development: A Misleading Geography* (Abingdon: Routledge, 2014).

Soliman, S., *The Autumn of Dictatorship: Fiscal Crisis and Political Change in Egypt under Mubarak* (Stanford: Stanford University Press, 2011).

Solomon, B., *Black Empowerment: Social Work in Oppressed Communities* (New York: Columbia University Press, 1976).

Sombart, W., *Der Moderne Kapitalismus* (Leipzig: Duncker & Humblot, 1902).

Sorkin, A. R., *Too Big to Fail: Inside the Battle to Save Wall Street* (London: Penguin, 2009).

Sornarajah, M., *The International Law on Foreign Investment* (Cambridge: Cambridge University Press, 2010).

Soros, G., *Open Society: Reforming Global Capitalism* (London: Little, Brown and Company, 2000).

Sottilotta, C. E., 'Political Risk Assessment and the Arab Spring: What Can We Learn?', *Thunderbird International Business Review*, first available online April 2, 2015.

Spencer, H., *Social Statics* (London: Routledge, 1996[1851]).

Spencer, H., *The Principles of Psychology* (London: Longmans, 1855).

Springer, S., 'Neoliberalism as Discourse: Between Foucauldian Political Economy and Marxian Poststructuralism', *Critical Discourse Studies*, 9 (2012), 2, 133–47.

Spruyt, H., *The Sovereign State and Its Competitors: An Analysis of Systems Change* (Princeton: Princeton University Press, 1994).

Starr, P., 'The Meaning of Privatization', *Yale Law and Policy Review*, 6 (1988), 6–41.

Steadman, M. E., Zimmerer, T. W. and Green, R. F., 'Pressures From Stakeholders Hit Japanese Companies', *Long Range Planning*, 28 (1995), 6, 29–37.

Stearns, F. P., *The Life of Prince Otto von Bismarck* (Philadelphia: J. B. Lippincott Company, 1899).

Stewart, J. B., 'Looking for a Lesson in Google's Perks', *New York Times*, March 13, 2013.

Stiglitz, J. E., 'Reflections on the Theory and Practice of Reform', in Krueger, A. O. (ed.), *Economic Policy Reform: The Second Stage* (Chicago: Chicago University Press, 2000).

Stiglitz, J. E., *Globalization and Its Discontents* (New York: W. W. Norton, 2002).

Stiglitz, J. E., 'Is There a Post-Washington Consensus Consensus?', in Serra, N. and Stiglitz, J. E. (eds), *The Washington Consensus Reconsidered: Towards a New Global Governance* (Oxford: Oxford University Press, 2008).

Stiglitz, J. E., 'The End of Neo-liberalism?', *Project Syndicate*, July 7, 2008.

Stiglitz, J. E., *The Price of Inequality: How Today's Divided Society Endangers Our Future* (New York: W. W. Norton & Company, 2012).

Stoker, G., 'Governance as Theory: Five Propositions', *International Social Science Journal*, 50 (1998), 155, 17–28.

Strahan, P. E., 'Too Big to Fail: Causes, Consequences, and Policy Responses', *Annual Review of Financial Economics*, 5 (2013), 43–61.

Strange, J. M. and Mumford, M. D., 'The Origins of Vision: Charismatic Versus Ideological Leadership', *Leadership Quarterly*, 13 (2002), 343–77.

Strange, S., *States and Markets: An Introduction to International Political Economy* (London: Pinter, 1988).

Strange, S., *The Retreat of the State: The Diffusion of Power in the World Economy* (Cambridge: Cambridge University Press, 1996).

Streeck, W., *Buying Time: The Delayed Crisis of Democratic Capitalism* (London: Verso, 2014).

Structural Adjustment Participatory Review International Network (SAPRIN), *Structural Adjustment: The SAPRI Report: The Policy Roots of Economic Crisis, Poverty and Inequality* (London: Zed Books, 2004).

Stuart, M. and Martínez Lucio, M. (eds), *Partnership and the Modernisation of Employment Relations* (London: Routledge, 2005).

Sturdy, A. and Grey, C., 'Beneath and Beyond Organizational Change Management: Exploring Alternatives', *Organization*, 10 (2003), 4, 651–62.

Sum, N-L., 'Wal-Martization and CSR-ization in Developing Countries', in Utting, P. and Marques, J. C. (eds), *Corporate Social Responsibility and Regulatory Governance: Towards Inclusive Development?* (Basingstoke: Palgrave, 2010).

Sutcliffe-Braithwaite, F., 'Neo-Liberalism and Morality in the Making of Thatcherite Social Policy', *The Historical Journal*, 55 (2012), 2, 497–520.

Swan, E., 'Commodity Diversity: Smiling Faces as a Strategy of Containment', *Organization*, 17 (2010), 1, 77–100.

Swank, D., 'Globalization', in Castles, F. G., Leibfried, S., Lewis, J., Obinger, H. and Pierson, C. (eds), *The Oxford Handbook of the Welfare State* (Oxford: Oxford University Press, 2010).

Swyngedouw, E., 'Dispossessing H$_2$O: The Contested Terrain of Water Privatization', *Capitalism Nature Socialism*, 16 (2005), 1, 81–98.

Tabb, W. K., 'Globalization Today: At the Borders of Class and State Theory', *Science & Society*, 73 (2009), 1, 34–53.

Taylor, C., *Sources of the Self: The Making of the Modern Identity* (Cambridge: Cambridge University Press, 1989).

Taylor, F. W., *The Principles of Scientific Management* (New York: Harper, 1911).

Taylor, F. W., *Shop Management* (New York: Harper, 1919).

Tett, G., *Fool's Gold: How Unrestrained Greed Corrupted a Dream, Shattered Global Markets and Unleashed a Catastrophe* (New York: Little, Brown and Company, 2009).

Thatcher, M., 'Speech to Conservative Party Conference', October 10, 1986. Available at: http://www.margaretthatcher.org/speeches/displaydocument.asp?docid=106498.

Thatcher, M., 'The New Renaissance', Speech to the Zurich Economic Society, University of Zurich, Switzerland, March 14, 1977. Available at: http://www.margaretthatcher.org/document/103336.

Thatcher, M., *The Autobiography* (London: HarperCollins, 2013).

Thatcher, M., *The Downing Street Years* (London: HarperCollins, 1993).

The Economist, 'A Blind Eye to Invisible Trade', July 11, 1981.

The Economist, 'GDP Apostasy', January 31, 2015.

The Economist, 'Ins and Outs', September 18, 2008.

The Economist, 'Reviews; Explaining Pakistan', May 6, 1950.

The Economist, 'Wealthy Politicians', September 28, 2013.

Theodore, N., 'Urban Underclass: The Wayward Travels of a Chaotic Concept', *Urban Geography*, 31 (2010), 2, 169–74.

Thomas, R. R., 'From Affirmative Action to Affirming Diversity', *Harvard Business Review*, 2 (1990), 107–17.

Thomas, R. R., *Beyond Race and Gender: Unleashing the Power of Your Total Work Force by Managing Diversity* (New York: AMACOM, 1991).

Thompson, D. W., *On Growth and Form* (Cambridge: Cambridge University Press, 2014[1917]).

Thompson, E. P., *The Making of the English Working Class* (London: Penguin, 1963).

Tilly, C., *Coercion, Capital and European States, A.D. 990–1992* (Oxford: Blackwell, 1992).

Tilly, C., *The Formation of National States in Western Europe* (Princeton: Princeton University Press, 1975).

Tkacz, N., 'From Open Source to Open Government: A Critique of Open Politics', *Ephemera: Theory & Politics in Organization*, 12 (2012), 4, 386–405.

Tobin, J., 'Money', in Durlauf, S. N. and Blume, L. E. (eds), *The New Palgrave Dictionary of Economics* (Basingstoke: Palgrave, 2008).

Tocqueville, A., *Democracy in America and Two Essays on America* (London: Penguin, 2003[1835, 1840]).

Toffler, A., *Future Shock* (New York: Bantam Books, 1970).

Tolbert, R. C., 'Needed: A Compatible Ideology', *Negro Digest*, 17 (1968), 10, 4–12.

Tönnies, F., *Community and Civil Society* (Cambridge: Cambridge University Press, 2001[1887]).

Towne, H. R., 'The Engineer as an Economist', *Transactions of the American Society of Mechanical Engineers*, 7 (1886), 428–32.

Townsend, H., *FT Guide to Business Networking: How to Use the Power of Online and Offline Networking for Business Success* (Harlow: Pearson Education, 2011).

Townsend, R., *Up the Organization: How to Stop the Corporation from Stifling People and Strangling Profits* (San Francisco: Jossey-Bass, 2007[1970]).

Toye, J., *Dilemmas of Development: Reflections on the Counter-Revolution in Development Theory and Policy* (Oxford: Blackwell, 1987).

Toye, R., 'From "Consensus" to "Common Ground": The Rhetoric of the Postwar Settlement and its Collapse', *Journal of Contemporary History*, 48 (2013), 1, 3–23.

Trentmann, F., 'Beyond Consumerism: New Historical Perspectives on Consumption', *Journal of Contemporary History*, 39 (2004), 3, 373–401.

Trentmann, F. (ed.), *The Making of the Consumer: Knowledge, Power and Identity in the Modern World* (Oxford: Berg Publishers, 2005).

Trentmann, F., *Free Trade Nation: Commerce, Consumption, and Civil Society in Modern Britain* (Oxford: Oxford University Press, 2008).

Trentmann, F., 'Introduction', in Trentmann, F. (ed.), *The Oxford Handbook of Consumption* (Oxford: Oxford University Press, 2012).

Trentmann, F. (ed.), *The Oxford Handbook of the History of Consumption* (Oxford: Oxford University Press, 2012).

Trentmann, F., *Empire of Things: How We Became a World of Consumers, from the Fifteenth Century to the Twenty-First* (London: Allen Lane, 2016).

Trilateral Commission, *The Crisis of Democracy: Report on the Governability of Democracies to the Trilateral Commission* (New York: New York University, 1975).

Trnka, S. and Trundle, C., 'Competing Responsibilities: Moving Beyond Neoliberal Responsibilisation', *Anthropological Forum: A Journal of Social Anthropology and Comparative Sociology*, 24 (2014), 2, 136–53.

Trotsky, L., *The Permanent Revolution & Results and Prospects* (Seattle: Red Letter Press, 2010[1906]).

Trubek, D. M., 'The "Rule of Law" in Development Assistance: Past, Present, and Future', in Trubek, D. M. and Santos, A. (eds), *The New Law and Economic Development: A Critical Appraisal* (Cambridge: Cambridge University Press, 2006).

Tsai, K. S., *Capitalism Without Democracy: The Private Sector in Contemporary China* (Ithaca: Cornell University Press, 2007).

Tsutsui, W. M., *Manufacturing Ideology: Scientific Management in Twentieth-Century Japan* (Princeton: Princeton University Press, 2001).

Turner, L., Nguyen, N. and Bird, K., 'An Overview of Ex Ante Tools for Assessing the Impact of Trade Liberalisation on the Poor', report prepared for BMZ/GTZ, Overseas Development Institute, London, 2008.

Turner, R. S., *Neo-Liberal Ideology: History, Concepts and Policies* (Edinburgh: Edinburgh University Press, 2008).

Turner, T., *A Beginner's Guide to Day Trading Online* (Avon, MA: Adams Media, 2000).

Turner, V. and Bruner, E. M., *The Anthropology of Experience* (Champaign, IL: University of Illinois Press, 1986).

Tylor, E. B., *Primitive Culture: Researches Into the Development of Mythology, Philosophy, Religion, Art, and Custom, Volumes 1 and 2* (London: John Murray, 1871).

Ueköttter, F., *The Greenest Nation? A New History of German Environmentalism* (Cambridge, MA: MIT Press, 2014).

United Nations Conference on Trade and Development (UNCTAD), *Towards a Global Strategy of Development* (Geneva: United Nations Conference on Trade and Development, 1968).

United Nations Conference on Trade and Development (UNCTAD), *World Investment Report: Transnational Corporations and the Infrastructure Challenge* (Geneva: United Nations Conference on Trade and Development, 2008).

United Nations Conference on Trade and Development (UNCTAD), *World Investment Report 2014 – Investing in the SDGs: An Action Plan* (Geneva: United Nations Conference on Trade and Development, 2014).

United Nations Development Programme (UNDP), *Human Development Report 1990* (New York: Oxford University Press, 1990).

United States Government Accountability Office (GAO), *Financial Regulatory Reform: Financial Crisis Losses and Potential Impacts of the Dodd-Frank Act* (Washington D.C.: Government Accountability Office, 2013).

United States Senate Permanent Subcommittee on Investigations, *Wall Street And The Financial Crisis: Anatomy Of A Financial Collapse*, Majority and Minority Staff Report, Permanent Subcommittee on Investigations, United States Senate, April 13, 2011.

Valéry, N., 'Industry Gets Religion', *The Economist*, February 18, 1999.

Van Agtmael, A., *The Emerging Markets Century: How a New Breed of World-Class Companies is Overtaking the World* (New York: Free Press, 2007).

Van der Pijl, K., *Transnational Classes and International Relations* (London: Routledge, 1998).

Van der Zwan, N., 'Making Sense of Financialisation', *Socio-Economic Review*, 12 (2014), 1, 99–129.

Van Harten, G., 'Five Justifications for Investment Treaties: A Critical Discussion', *Trade, Law and Development*, 19 (2010), 2, 19–58.

Van Horn, R., Mirowski, P. and Stapleford, T. A. (eds), *Building Chicago Economics: New Perspectives on the History of America's Most Powerful Economics Program* (Cambridge: Cambridge University Press, 2013).

Van Kersbergen, K. and Van Waarden, F., '"Governance" as a Bridge Between Disciplines: Cross-disciplinary Inspiration Regarding Shifts in Governance and Problems of Governability, Accountability and Legitimacy', *European Journal of Political Research*, 43 (2004), 2, 143–71.

Van Thiel, S. and Leeuw, F. L., 'The Performance Paradox in the Public Sector', *Public Performance & Management Review*, 25 (2002), 3, 267–81.

Varma, A., Budhwar, P. S. and DeNisi, A. (eds), *Performance Management Systems: A Global Perspective* (Abingdon: Routledge, 2008).

Varoufakis, Y., 'Greece's Proposals to End the Crisis: My Intervention at the Eurogroup', *openDemocracy*, June 19, 2015.

Veblen, T., *The Theory of the Leisure Class* (Oxford: Oxford University Press, 2007[1899]).

Venugopal, R., 'Neoliberalism as Concept', *Economy and Society*, 44 (2015), 2, 165–87.

Vickers, J., 'Concepts of Competition', *Oxford Economic Papers*, 47 (1995), 1, 1–23.

Vincent, A., *Theories of the State* (Oxford: Basil Blackwell, 1987).

Vincent, A., 'Conceptions of the State', in Hawkesworth, M. and Kogan, M. (eds), *Encyclopedia of Government and Politics, Volume I* (London: Routledge, 1992).

Visvanathan, N., Duggan, L., Wiegersma, N. and Nisonoff, L. (eds), *The Women, Gender and Development Reader* (London: Zed Books, 2011).

Vogel, E., *Japan as Number One: Lessons for America* (Cambridge MA: Harvard University Press, 1979).

Wacquant, L., *Urban Outcasts: A Comparative Sociology of Advanced Marginality* (Cambridge: Polity Press, 2008).

Wacquant, L., *Punishing the Poor: The Neoliberal Government of Social Insecurity* (Durham, NC: Duke University Press, 2009).

Wacquant, L., 'Three Steps to a Historical Anthropology of Actually Existing Neoliberalism', *Social Anthropology*, 20 (2012), 1, 66–79.

Wacquant, L., 'Symbolic Power and Group-making: On Pierre Bourdieu's Reframing of Class', *Journal of Classical Sociology*, 13 (2013), 2, 274–91.

Wade, R. H., *Governing the Market: Economic Theory and the Role of Government in East Asian Industrialization* (Princeton: Princeton University Press, 2004).

Waldron, J., 'What is Private Property?', *Oxford Journal of Legal Studies*, 5 (1985), 3, 313–49.

Walras, L., *Elements of Theoretical Economics: Or, The Theory of Social Wealth* (Cambridge: Cambridge University Press, 2014[1900]).

Walter, A. and Sen, G., *Analyzing the Global Political Economy* (Princeton: Princeton University Press, 2009).

Walter, A. and Zhang, X. (eds), *East Asian Capitalism: Diversity, Continuity, and Change* (Oxford: Oxford University Press, 2012).

Walter, A., *World Power and World Money: The Role of Hegemony and International Monetary Order* (Hemel Hempstead and New York: Harvester-Wheatsheaf/ St. Martin's Press, 1993).

Walton, J. K. and Seddon, D., *Free Markets and Food Riots: The Politics of Global Adjustment* (Oxford: Blackwell, 1994).

Wapner, P., *Environmental Activism and World Civic Politics* (Albany: State University of New York, 1996).

Warner, M., *Publics and Counterpublics* (New York: Zone Books, 2005).

Warren, M., 'Performance Management: A Substitute for Supervision', *Management Review*, October 1972, 28–42.

Watkins, K., *The Oxfam Poverty Report* (Oxford: Oxfam International, 1995).

Watkins, K. and Fowler, P., *Rigged Rules and Double Standards: Trade, Globalisation, and the Fight Against Poverty* (Oxford: Oxfam International, 2002).

Watson, G. (ed.), *Free Will* (Oxford: Oxford University Press, 2003).

Watson, M., *Political Economy of International Capital Mobility* (Basingstoke: Palgrave Macmillan, 2007).

Weaver, C., *Hypocrisy Trap: The World Bank and the Poverty of Reform* (Princeton: Princeton University Press, 2008).

Webb, S. and Webb, B., *Industrial Democracy* (London: Longmans, Green and Co., 1897).

Weber, M., *The Protestant Ethic and the Spirit of Capitalism* (London: Penguin, 2002[1905]).

Weber, M., *The Vocation Lectures: 'Science as a Vocation'; 'Politics as a Vocation'* (Cambridge, MA: Hackett Publishing Co., 2004[1919]).

Weber, M., *Economy and Society* (Berkeley: University of California Press, 2013[1922]).

Weeden, K. A., 'Is There a Flexiglass Ceiling? Flexible Work Arrangements and Wages in the United States', *Social Science Research*, 34 (2005), 2, 454–82.

Weil, D. N., *Economic Growth* (Harlow: Pearson Education, 2013).

Weintraub, J., 'The Theory and Politics of the Public/Private Distinction', in Weintraub, J. and Kumar, K. (eds), *Public and Private in Thought and Practice: Perspectives on a Grand Dichotomy* (Chicago: University of Chicago Press, 1997).

Weis, A., *The Global Food Economy: The Battle for the Future of Farming* (London: Zed Books, 2007).

Weiss, T. G., 'Governance, Good Governance and Global Governance: Conceptual and Actual Challenges', *Third World Quarterly*, 21 (2000), 5, 795–814.

Weiss, T. G., *Global Governance: Why? What? Whither?* (Cambridge: Polity Press, 2013).

Weiss, T. G. and Wilkinson, R. (eds), *International Organization and Global Governance* (Abingdon: Routledge, 2013).

Wellman, B., 'Structural Analysis: From Method and Metaphor to Theory and Substance', in Wellman, B. and Berkowitz, S. D. (eds), *Social Structures: A Network Approach* (Cambridge: Cambridge University Press, 1988).

Werner, W., 'Corporation Law in Search of Its Future', *Columbia Law Review*, 81 (1981), 8, 1611–66.

Whaley, R. E., 'Derivatives on Market Volatility: Hedging Tools Long Overdue', *Journal of Derivatives*, 1 (1993), 1, 71–84.

Whaley, R. E., 'Understanding VIX' (November 6, 2008). Available at SSRN: http://ssrn.com/abstract=1296743.

White, L. J., 'Credit Rating Agencies: An Overview', *The Annual Review of Financial Economics*, 5 (2013), 93–122.

Whitehead, L., *Democratization: Theory and Experience* (Oxford: Oxford University Press, 2002).

Whitley, R., *Divergent Capitalisms: The Social Structuring and Change of Business Systems* (Oxford: Oxford University Press, 1999).

Wierzbicka, A., *Experience, Evidence, and Sense: The Hidden Cultural Legacy of English* (Oxford: Oxford University Press, 2010).

Wilkins, M., 'Multinational Enterprises to 1930: Discontinuities and Continuities', in Chandler, A. D. and Mazlish, B. (eds), *Leviathans: Multinational Corporations and the New Global History* (Cambridge: Cambridge University Press, 2005).

Wilkinson, R., *The WTO: Crisis and the Governance of Global Trade* (Abingdon: Routledge, 2006).

Wilkinson, R. and Pickett, K., *The Spirit Level: Why Equality is Better for Everyone* (London: Penguin, 2010).

Wilks, S., *The Political Power of the Business Corporation* (Cheltenham: Edward Elgar, 2013).

Williams, C. A. and Heins, R. M., *Risk Management and Insurance* (New York: McGraw-Hill, 1964).

Williams, J. C., Blair-Loy, M. and Berdahl, J. L., 'Cultural Schemas, Social Class, and the Flexibility Stigma', *Journal of Social Issues*, 69 (2013), 2, 209–34.

Williams, R., *Keywords: A Vocabulary of Culture and Society* (London: Fontana Books, 1983[1976]).

Williams, R., *Marxism and Literature* (Oxford: Oxford University Press, 1977).

Williamson, J., 'What Washington Means by Policy Reform', in Williamson, J. (ed.), *Latin American Adjustment: How Much Has Happened?* (Washington D.C.: Institute for International Economics, 1990).

Williamson, J. (ed.), *The Political Economy of Policy Reform* (Washington D.C.: Institute for International Economics, 1994).

Williamson, J., 'Economic Reform: Content, Progress, Proposals', paper presented at the University of Baroda, India, November 23, 1999. Available at: http://www.icrier.org/pdf/John.PDF

Williamson, J., 'What Should the World Bank Think About the Washington Consensus?', *The World Bank Research Observer*, 15 (2000), 2, 251–64.

Williamson, J., 'Appendix: Our Agenda and the Washington Consensus', in Kuczynski, P. and Williamson, J. (eds), *After the Washington Consensus: Restarting Growth and Reform in Latin America* (Washington D.C.: Institute for International Economics, 2003).

Williamson, O. E., *Markets and Hierarchies: Analysis and Antitrust Implications* (New York: Macmillan, 1983).

Willman, P., *Understanding Management: The Social Science Foundations* (Oxford: Oxford University Press, 2014).

Wilson, J. M., 'Gantt Charts: A Centenary Appreciation', *European Journal of Operational Research*, 149 (2003), 430–7.

Wilson, J., *Jeffrey Sachs: The Strange Case of Dr. Shock and Mr. Aid* (London: Verso, 2014).

Winn, P. (ed.), *Victims of the Chilean Miracle: Workers and Neoliberalism in the Pinochet Era, 1973–2002* (Durham, NC: Duke University Press, 2004).

Winters, A., 'Trade Liberalisation and Economic Performance: An Overview', *The Economic Journal*, 114 (2004), 493, F4–F21.

Winters, J. A. and Page, B. I., 'Oligarchy in the United States?', *Perspectives on Politics*, 7 (2009), 4, 731–51.

Wolf-Phillips, L., 'Why "Third World"?: Origin, Definition and Usage', *Third World Quarterly*, 9 (1987), 4, 1311–27.

Wolf, M., *Why Globalization Works* (New Haven: Yale University Press, 2004).

Wolf, M., *The Shifts and the Shocks: What We've Learned – And Have Still to Learn – From the Financial Crisis* (London: Penguin Books, 2014).

Wollstonecraft, M., *A Vindication of the Rights of Women With Strictures on Political and Moral Subjects* (London: J. Johnson, 1792).

Womack, J. P., Jones, D. T. and Roos, D., *The Machine That Changed the World: How Lean Production Revolutionized the Global Car Wars* (London: Simon & Schuster, 2007[1990]).

Woo-Cumings, M. (ed.), *The Developmental State* (Ithaca: Cornell University Press, 1999).

Wood, J. C. and Wood, M. C. (eds), *Henri Fayol: Critical Evaluations in Business and Management* (London: Routledge, 2002).

Woods, N., *The Globalizers: The IMF, the World Bank, and Their Borrowers* (Ithaca: Cornell University Press, 2006).

Woodside, A. G., Sood, S. and Miller, K. E., 'When Consumers and Brands Talk: Storytelling Theory and Research in Psychology and Marketing', *Psychology & Marketing*, 25 (2008), 2, 97–145.

Woodward, D., '*Incrementum ad Absurdum*: Global Growth, Inequality and Poverty Eradication in a Carbon-Constrained World', *World Economic Review*, 4 (2015), 43–62.

World Bank, *World Development Report 1981* (Washington D.C.: World Bank, 1981).

World Bank, *Sub-Saharan Africa: From Crisis to Sustainable Development* (Washington D.C.: World Bank, 1989).

World Bank, *Adjustment Lending and Mobilization of Private and Public Resources for Growth* (Washington D.C.: World Bank, 1992).

World Bank, *Governance and Development* (Washington D.C.: World Bank, 1992).

World Bank, *World Development Report 2000/2001: Attacking Poverty* (Washington D.C.: World Bank, 2000).

World Bank, *A Decade of Measuring the Quality of Governance: Governance Matters 2007* (Washington D.C.: World Bank, 2007).

World Bank, *Localizing Development: Does Participation Work?* (Washington D.C.: World Bank, 2012).

World Commission on Environment and Development ('Brundtland Commission'), *Our Common Future* (Oxford: Oxford University Press, 1987).

World Economic Forum (WEF), *The Global Competitiveness Report 2014–2015* (Geneva: World Economic Forum, 2014).

Wright, E. O., *Class Counts: Comparative Studies in Class Analysis* (Cambridge: Cambridge University Press, 1997).

Wright, E. O., 'Understanding Class', *New Left Review*, November–December 2009, 101–16.

Xing, Y. and Detert, N., 'How the iPhone Widens the United States Trade Deficit with the People's Republic of China', ADBI Working Paper Series, 257 (Toyko: Asian Development Bank Institute, 2010).

Zack-Williams, A. B., 'The Social Consequences of Structural Adjustment', in Brown, E., Milward, B., Mohan, G., Zack-Williams, A. B. (eds), *Structural Adjustment: Theory, Practice and Impacts* (London: Routledge, 2000).

Zhang, L. and Ong, A. (eds), *Privatizing China: Socialism from Afar* (Ithaca: Cornell University Press, 2008).

Žižek, S., *First As Tragedy, Then As Farce* (London: Verso, 2009).

Žižek, S., 'Shoplifters of the World Unite', *London Review of Books*, August 19, 2011.

Zook, C. and Allen, J., *Repeatability: Build Enduring Businesses for a World of Constant Change* (Boston, MA: Harvard Business Review Press, 2012).

INDEX